THE ARCHITECTURE OF MIGRATION

Meigs County, Bedford Township (?). One and a half story log house. Photo: *ca.* 1900. This is the only photograph of a "raising" known to this writer. The house had been moved and was being re-erected, but the raising technique was traditional. The picture was posed, for the men are raising one of their skid-poles. (Compare this photograph to the woodcut from the *Western Miscellany*, Figure 124.)

THE ARCHITECTURE OF MIGRATION

Log Construction in the Ohio Country, 1750–1850

Donald A. Hutslar

OHIO UNIVERSITY PRESS, Athens Ohio

Library of Congress Cataloging in Publication Data

Hutslar, Donald A.
The architecture of migration.

Bibliography: p.
1. Log buildings—Ohio. I. Title.
NA730.03H88 1986 720'.9771 85-2981
ISBN 0-8214-0733-3

. . . No man can so well remember the particulars of history as he who acted in them. . . . What we have to say are all small things, the smallest of the small, and will help to make up the beauty of variety, and serve, . . . as sand and lime in a wall composed of stone or brick. History would be a very unconnected, unintelligible affair without the small matters.

John S. Williams
American Pioneer
October 1843

CONTENTS

INTRODUCTION

The material presented in this text is a resume of many years of accumulating data on log architecture in Ohio and the Upper Ohio Valley. The study began in 1966 as a photographic record of extant structures, with no particular end in mind. While working on various research and restoration projects for the Ohio Historical Society, the author and his wife found contemporary comments on log construction. As the quantity of photographs and notes grew, it became obvious that enough material was available for a monograph on Ohio log architecture. As a consequence, "The Log Architecture of Ohio" was published in *Ohio History* in 1972 (dated 1971), vol. 80, nos. 3 and 4 combined; this monograph was reprinted in May 1977, under its own title.

Perhaps few typological, ethnological, or architectural problems will be solved in the succeeding pages, but the reader should learn to judge the log buildings that remain, and should recognize the vast amounts of fiction written and stories told about the construction and use of such structures. The author does not pretend to be able to recognize all specific details of construction or design as indicative of certain cultural or national typologies. However, it is doubtful any remaining log houses or barns exhibit significant features an architectural historian would be surprised to see. It is likely that there is an "Ohio Style," just as there is an Indiana, Michigan, or Kentucky style. This could be proved only by surveying log architecture and immigration patterns in adjacent states. Yet only a small amount of serious survey work has been accomplished: Montell and Morse in Kentucky, Elbert and Sculle in Illinois, Wilson in Alabama, Jordan in Texas, and Kaups in Minnesota are good examples dealing specifically with log structures; there are also general works touching on log construction.

In order to relate Ohio log architecture to log construction elsewhere in the world, a background chapter is included. Much of this information comes from Clinton A. Weslager's *The Log Cabin in America*, which is an extension of Harold R. Shurtleff's *The Log Cabin Myth*. That both this work and Weslager's book contain similar references is due to the simple fact that there are limited sources from which to draw. One common reference was the compendium of eighteenth- and nineteenth-century travel narratives entitled *Early Western Travels*. Several other narratives, particularly of Indian captivity, are extremely rare and can be found only in major libraries.

The county histories of Ohio contain hundreds of references to log cabins and houses. Unfortunately, many authors and editors copied the same sources without giving credit. Such excerpts imply that the events described took place within the given county, and could be completely erroneous. For example, if one compares pages 212–14 of George F. Robinson's *History of Greene County, Ohio* (Chicago, 1902) with the chapter entitled "The House Warming" in Joseph Doddridge's *Notes, on the Settlement and Indian Wars, of the Western Parts of Virginia & Pennsylvania from 1763 to 1783* (Wellsburgh, Va., 1824), one would find that Robinson copied Doddridge's account (probably from the 1876 edition) word for word without giving credit. This leaves an unfortunate impression, for Greene County, Ohio, in 1800 was not necessarily like western Pennsylvania some thirty-five years earlier. Also, Robinson (or the printer) misspells two words relating to construction, using "bunting poles" for "butting poles" and "hard wood" for "heart wood" (see full quotation, page 228 & 229). Even without knowing the context, the reader can imagine the confusion such mistakes cause.

Although county histories are of secondary importance to the critical historian, they are one of the few sources for the oral traditions surrounding the ephemeral "frontier" and the "cabin in the clearing." Because commonplace events made dull subject matter, unusual occurrences received more than their share of attention. Such inversion has colored the popular view of Ohio history to such an extent that singular events have been accepted as common to the life of each settler. However, following the Treaty of Greene Ville in 1795, the majority of settlers, rather than living under constant threat of attack from Indians or animals, had an everyday routine that was simply dull and monotonous.

I hope this book will bridge the gap between factual historic references to log buildings and practical knowledge on the construction and repair of such structures. Authentic restoration of a log house or barn is certainly possible. The reader should be forewarned, however, that the cost of materials can be staggering—let alone labor.

The author made an attempt to survey log buildings on as wide a scale as possible within the state, but distance and time were unavoidable considerations. A round trip of two hundred fifty miles to examine one building can be tedious, no matter how excellent the structure. Also, time simply was not available to measure, draw, and analyze all the buildings. It was soon apparent that the counties bordering the Old National Road (U.S. Route 40) and south to the Ohio River contained the majority of extant specimens. Consequently, the illustrations come largely from this half of the state. Since most log buildings throughout the state exhibit similar structural characteristics, the best photographs were chosen regardless of the geographic location of the examples. (Weather conditions and time of day were often critical in obtaining good photographs.) That the majority of counties in Ohio are not represented in this work does not mean that log buildings are nonexistent in these counties; however, they are rare in northeastern Ohio and in specific ethnic settlements.

DATING BUILDINGS

The problem of dating log buildings is universal. The very few ca. 1800 buildings in Ohio do bear some characteristics that would indicate their age if literary evidence were not available, but the majority of buildings are not distinctive insofar as constructional details are concerned. Adding to the difficulty of dating is the fact that most extant houses have been remodeled one or more times, if not completely enclosed with later additions. Postconstructional work is usually evident, unless it was done soon after the original building was completed. It requires time to evaluate all details, and, unless the structure is disused and already falling apart, it often takes as long to find the owner and obtain permission to investigate a building as to actually do the work. In the field of antiques, it is an axiom that nothing is valuable until an interest has been expressed, and permission for an investigation is often slow in coming—if at all.

A stylistic dating guide to log buildings in Ohio could probably be established, if a county-by-county survey were undertaken. Much of the effort would be literary, although a major factor would be measuring and drawing the extant structures (not to mention finding them). The actual dating of the buildings would be dependent on the county documents available. A date and style correlation could then be compiled from the data. Whether there is any value in such a study is open to question, since most log houses and barns can be dated, *de facto*, 1815 to 1860 without the necessity of close examination. Perhaps more interesting would be a cultural typology in which certain elements of construction are traced to European precedents. There are slight, but definite differences in construction and spatial utilization between houses built by (or for) immigrants from the Germanic states and the British Isles. For example, the English preferred open fireplaces, while the Germans preferred iron stoves. English houses are usually of pronounced rectangular form, whereas German houses are often square or nearly so. French immigrants seem to have liked interior log crosswalls and double front doors, the latter also a late Federal design trait. No doubt much earlier Saxon cultural characteristics could be recognized among all three nationalities, as has been distinguished in northern Europe. Such details are often mundane, but in future years they could help solve ethnologic if not architectural problems.

Dating log buildings by literary evidence is a tedious task at best. If no private records exist, the only public records that might give a clue are the tax duplicates, and they seldom yield much information. One of the old methods of dating a structure, particularly of log, is to give the building the same date as the original land grant or purchase. This method gives problematical results at best. A few changes took place in log construction in Ohio between the War of 1812 and the Civil War which are helpful in dating an undocumented structure. Until approximately 1825 (there is no method of establishing a precise date), the steeple notch was used almost exclusively on all buildings regardless of function. During the second quarter of the century, the steeple notch was rarely used for a house unless the house was to be sided. The steeple notch remained predominant for barns and outbuildings throughout the rest of the century. Beginning about 1825, the half-dovetail became the common notch for houses, and remained so into the twentieth century.[1]

Another good indication of building age, for at least the first third of the nineteenth century, is the pitch of the roof. The most common pitch was a 9-inch rise in a 12-inch run, or approximately 37 degrees angle. The popularity of the various "revival" schools of architecture, beginning with Greek Revival in Ohio, ended the seemingly consistent use of the 12-9 roof.

A more subtle age indicator lies in the proportions of the building's exterior features. This may seem a moot point since the builder was dependent on the size of trees available, but some guide to proportion seems to have been used (see chapter 11 for a discussion of proportionment systems). Once the eye has become accustomed to the relationships between the length, width, height, and roof pitch of these early buildings, they are surprisingly easy to identify.

One easily recognizable clue to an early house is the presence of one or more large red cedar trees (*Juniperus virginiana*), because the red cedar was a popular early nineteenth-century ornamental. These trees often reveal the site of a forgotten structure.

There is a method, which probably could be used in Ohio, to precisely date the year in which a log was cut. The science of dendrochronology is based on the study of growth rings of a single variety of tree in a specific geographic location. The rate of growth of a tree depends on many factors such as the site, the soil, the amount of rainfall, and seasonal temperature variances. The amount of growth season to season is shown by the width of the annual rings. Trees of the same variety and in essentially the same climatic and site conditions show similar annular patterns. If a chart of this growth pattern is available, an undated specimen can be compared until its annular pattern agrees with the appropriate section in the master chronology. The exact date of cutting can be established if the last growth ring (the "bark ring") is present on the specimen.

A tree ring chronology has been established in the southwestern United States for the *Pinus aristata* spanning more than seven thousand years. A German chronology based on oak now spans one thousand years, and there are hopes of extending it to five thousand years. In England and France, dendrochronology has been used to date various structural timbers in medieval barns and dwellings. Repairs and alterations have been found or disproven, in some instances.

Dendrochronology is presently being used to discover anomalies in radiocarbon dating, beginning about two thousand years ago. It also works at much closer points in time which carbon-14 dating cannot do because of its margin of error; radiocarbon dating for Ohio building materials would be futile. Since two hundred years would be more than ample to cover the history of architecture in Ohio, it is entirely possible that a tree ring chronology could be established for each of the several woods most commonly found in log buildings. Fortunately, the logs usually retain their bark or wane, so the necessary qualification for precise dating is present.[2]

ERRORS

In this work, quotations were checked in their original editions whenever possible. Positive statements and conclusions were based on literary or physical evidence. Yet errors slip into every undertaking.

It is also easy to create myths with a mixture of facts and conjecture. Historical novels, motion pictures and television, and the bicentennial years all have created or reinforced frontier myths. H. L. Mencken's newspaper article, "A Neglected Anniversary," is a classic example. Published in the *New York Evening Mail* on 28 December 1917, the article purportively gave the history of the bathtub. According to Mencken, the first American bathtub was installed on 20 December 1842, by Adam Thompson of Cincinnati. Intended as a joke, the "bathtub hoax" was accepted as literal, sober history. Mencken attempted several refutations, notably "Melancholy Reflections" published 23 May 1926, and "Hymn to the Truth" published about two months later on July 25.[3] He finally gave up in disgust, for the tale was firmly entrenched in the public's mind—it had been published in a newspaper, so it must be true. (A fine illustration of Adam Thompson's bathtub, curiously misdated "1840," may be seen in Eric Sloane's *A B C Book of Early Americana*; Mr. Sloane commented on his mistake in a later book.) Mencken thought his story was so obviously a hoax that nobody would be misled. Think what has happened to historical fact when the intent was to deceive! A famous example is the three volumes of *The Horn Papers: Early Westward Movement on the Monongahela and Upper Ohio, 1765–1795*, published by the Greene County, Pennsylvania, Historical Society, 1945. This work may be found in many local libraries.

RANDOM NOTES ON SETTLEMENT

The settlement of Ohio was well controlled by a regulated system of land survey, and patterns and dates of immigration can be isolated and examined for most areas of the state. For years, this writer has kept a copy of John F. Mansfield's 1806 map of Ohio hanging in his office, the first map of the state authorized by the surveyor general of the United States. The basic surveys are clearly delineated; the boundaries are still evident today, both topographically and ethnologically. The random surveys of the Virginia Military District contrast strongly with the rectilinear grid system along the Scioto and Little Miami river valleys, although architectural styles are reasonably consistent in southwestern Ohio. There is a hard architectural boundary separating the Connecticut Western Reserve from the Congress Lands, particularly noticeable between the counties of Huron, Medina, Summit, and Portage, on the one hand, and Richland, Ashland, Wayne, and Stark, on the other. North of the line, the architecture is strongly Greek Revival; south of the line, a mixture of Federal, Greek Revival, and immigrant German. The uniformity of architecture north of the line is striking, as is the scarcity of log buildings; braced-frame buildings abound, however. The New England background of the Marietta, Campus Martius settlers is obvious from their scant architectural remains. Symmes' Purchase was advertised in the New Jersey, New York, eastern Pennsylvania area, so some odd, early buildings show up which contrast in detail to the Virginia Military District. This latter area displays strong affinity, in its early architecture, to old Virginia, Maryland, southwestern Pennsylvania, and Kentucky. Much of the Congress Land was also settled by emigrants from these older colonies and states, and consequently the extant early architecture remains fairly consistent in style throughout the state.

The northwestern quarter of the state, opened to settlement between 1818 and 1842, is more difficult to define. There is still a strong rural German Catholic section in central western Ohio, descendants of second-quarter, nineteenth-century immigrants, and their braced-frame and brick architecture is quite consistent in style over a wide area—and is amost identical to the architecture of the German Protestant sects (Amish, Mennonite, Separatist) in northeastern Ohio. There are a few first-generation log buildings in both areas. Although the French were in northwestern Ohio by the end of the seventeenth century, no known structures remain. The same is true of the Moravians in northeastern Ohio during the 1770s.

Overall, the survival rate of log buildings, while surprisingly high, still does not fairly represent the diversity of typologies once present in the state. There is no question what the average structures were like, only the extent of variations possible.

The willingness of the nineteenth-century builder to experiment is easily demonstrated even today. Consider the cast-concrete houses of the 1850s, examples of which are known in Troy and Piqua, Miami County, and Spring Valley, Greene County; the vertical, plank-walled houses such as the excellent example in Northfield Center, Summit County, dating to the 1840s; and the horizontal, solid 2x4 exterior and interior walls as found in a house in Brecksville, Cuyahoga County, also dating to the 1840s.

Cast-concrete remains a standard construction procedure today, yet is about 130 years old in practice in the United States. Solid walls of wood have been touted off and on for several years, but are ancient in principle. The sheet-iron "Quonset" hut was in practical use almost 150 years ago, with the principle of the reinforcing corrugations clearly understood. Structural iron and steel were in use in the eighteenth century, and had become so refined in application by mid-nineteenth century that entire store "fronts" (facades) were cast. All these experiments, successes, and failures, in the field of architecture, novel as they might sound coming from a past century, only point up the fact that log construction did not exist because knowledge had not progressed, but because the technique was desirable in a particular geographical area at a particular point in time. It was, in fact, a distinct form of architecture that answered a specific need, and once that need was gone, so were the skills and knowledge of the construction technique. Simple as it might seem, this could be the major reason for the apparent lack of a technical language, or jargon, intimately connected with the craft.

PICTURE CAPTIONS

Most of the captions follow the same sequence of information: (1) county; (2) township, village, or city; (3) type of structure; (4) date, if known; (5) builder or original owner, if known; (6) size; (7) other illustrations of same building; (8) date of photograph; (9) compass direction of photograph; and (10) description. If there is more than one illustration of a given building, the captions will not bear all of the above information. The present condition of many of the structures is not known; at least one-half are no longer in existence. Because many property owners did not wish to have their names mentioned, in an understandable effort to avoid visitors, all names and exact addresses are deleted. Structures on the National Register of Historic Places are another matter, since pertinent information is published by the U.S. Government as part of the conditions of registration. Some photographs include comparison scales: One foot long with one-inch divisions, and six feet long with one-foot divisions; these scales are obvious, when used.

Log houses are described as being one, one and a half, and two story in height. If one story, an adult cannot stand erect in the loft. If one and a half story, the rafters break into the ceiling line on the second floor; it is possible to stand erect in the center of the room, perhaps not at the sides. A two-story house is just that, the second floor ceiling is full height and level; there is always a low loft above the ceiling, whether functional or not. This terminology may not be uniform among current reference sources, but it does agree with the three basic log house styles commonly found today.

No doubt many of the houses and barns could be dated, and the original owners' names found. For this writer, time was not available. However, local historical societies could do this research in their own counties. It remains this writer's contention that few, if any, of the log buildings pictured were constructed by the first owners. The old story that such and such a house was built by the original settler could be correct in the sense that they supplied the funds and ordered the work done—just as today.

More effort should be made to find nineteenth-century photographs of log buildings. The further back in time these structures can be viewed, the better; perhaps nuances of typology could be identified before extensive remodeling removed all traces. Each generation impresses its taste on new and old buildings alike, and it is very difficult to be specific in describing the visual impressions of any one period of time. In Ohio, daguerreotypes could have been taken as early as 1840 (the first such image was made in November 1839, by Alexander C. Ross of Zanesville). Because of the tediousness of the daguerrean sensitizing process, outdoor images were not commonly available until the early 1850s when a variety of simpler photographic techniques were perfected. Artists' renditions are to be distrusted to some extent because, then as now, not all artists were familiar with their subject matter and improvised or obscured details they did not understand or which were not critical to their interpretations. Minute detail was possible for even amateurs, when photomechanical aids such as the camera lucida or camera obscura were used.

Most of the photographs in this book are by the author; the exceptions are noted. A log building can be a particularly difficult subject to photograph due to its monochromatic coloring, its lack of reflectance, and the often harsh contrasts of light and shade. An exterior view of a log building surrounded by snow, or an interior view of the dark chasm of a log barn, become major photographic problems when a minimum of equipment and speed of execution are desired. The flat lighting characteristics of a camera-mounted flash unit often gave mediocre results, but carrying and using such a unit was easier than making a time exposure with a tripod. The old-fashioned flashbulb was preferable to an electronic flash unit for recording the dusty, drab interiors of log buildings probably because of the better reflectance of light in the red band of the spectrum. Because some of the interior views were made with an ultra-wide-angle lens, spatial relationships are exaggerated in reference to normal reading distance, and the rooms appear larger than they really were.

Notes

1. If the logs in a house are found to be lapped or half-lapped over one another, there is little doubt that the house was sided at the time it was built. A mixture of corner notching styles probably also indicates siding was present. Just because a house was built of logs does not mean that the builder or owner preferred logs for aesthetic reasons and wanted to expose them to view. The logs formed the structural support of the building, just as wood studding, bricks, and concrete blocks do today. Few buildings are built with concrete blocks exposed on both inner and outer walls for purely aesthetic purposes. The log walls of 1800 and the concrete block walls of today are identical in function, although different in visual and tactile qualities.
2. The center for dendrochronology in the United States is the Laboratory of Tree-Ring Research, University of Arizona, Tucson. The laboratory offers many publications, most dealing with the Southwest. Persons interested in dendrochronological dating should read chapters 7 and 8 in Berger's *Scientific Methods in Medieval Archaeology*. These chapters can be obtained as an offprint from the University, as well as Ferguson's interesting article "Bristlecone Pine," and Fritts's "Dendroclimatology and Dendroecology."
3. Mencken, *The Bathtub Hoax*, pp. 4–19, all three articles.

I
THE ANTECEDENTS

The oldest known reference to log houses occurs in Vitruvius's *Ten Books on Architecture*, written during the reign of Augustus, 27 B.C. to A.D. 14:

> Among the Colchians in Pontus, where there are forests in plenty, they lay down entire trees flat on the ground to the right and the left, leaving between them a space to suit the length of the trees, and then place above these another pair of trees, resting on the ends of the former and at right angles with them. These four trees enclose the space for the dwelling. Then upon these they place sticks of timber, one after the other on the four sides, crossing each other at the angles, and so, proceeding with their walls of trees laid perpendicularly above the lowest, they build up high towers. The interstices, which are left on account of the thickness of the building material, are stopped up with chips and mud. As for the roofs, by cutting away the ends of the crossbeams and making them converge gradually as they lay them across, they bring them up to the top from the four sides in the shape of a pyramid. They cover it with leaves and mud, and thus construct the roofs of their towers in a rude form of the "tortoise" style.[1]

Colchis was east of the Black Sea and south of the Caucasus region; the district, which had been under Greek and Roman rule, was annexed by Russia in 1866 and today forms the western part of Georgia.

Another early comment on log buildings, made some seven hundred years ago, can be found in Marco Polo's narrative. Polo described the "stove-houses" which were common in Russia and northern Europe:

> They are square buildings made of large beams laid one on top of another and so close-fitting that nothing can be seen through the chinks. The chinks are then well stopped up with lime and other materials, so that neither wind nor cold can penetrate from outside. At the top of the building in the roof is a vent-hole from which the smoke issues when a fire is lit to heat it.[2]

The stove-house had a doorway and window opening as well as a vent hole. These openings were provided with thick felt "shutters."

Neither the geographic location nor the date of origin of log construction is known. Obviously metal axes were all but a necessity—not to mention suitable trees—and the climate moderate to cold, thus requiring a substantial house. Cutting wood with bronze axes was probably a frustrating job, so one is inclined to look to the Iron Age for the real birth of log architecture. The Bronze Age ended in the Near East about 1200 B.C. Although a few wrought iron implements had been used in the third millennium, it wasn't until the end of the second that production of iron in quantity was invented by some barbarian tribe in the Armenian mountains.[3] The use of iron spread rapidly in Asia Minor and Greece and traveled westward with the Phoenicians and Etruscans. Because of the widespread distribution and use of iron tools, it is possible the type of house described by Vitruvius originated much further to the north; several prominent rivers, such as the Volga, the Dnieper (which leads to the Vistula), and the Danube empty into the Black and Caspian seas. Time is of little consideration, for iron had been in use well over one thousand years by the time of Vitruvius.

It is logical that log architecture did originate in northeastern Europe, given the forests and the climate, and was spread by the movement of barbarian tribes displaced to the west and south by the migrations of more eastern tribes. The Ostrogoths and

Vandals could have brought log construction to western Europe. The early Iron Age was a period of great complexity, particularly in matters of trade and territory, and new ideas traveled quickly throughout the European and Asian continents. Log architecture could have arisen as a temporary but secure form of housing for the migrating tribes. Today, log buildings are still prominent in Russia, Poland,[4] Czechoslovakia, and the Scandinavian countries, with some examples in eastern and southern Germany and Austria (no doubt examples can be found throughout the Carpathian, Balkan, and Caucasus mountains).

During the seventeenth century, as the North American continent was being settled, the only nationalities who were familiar with log construction were the Swedes, Finns, Germans, and the French with their allied forms of plank construction. The Russians built a few log structures on the northwest coast which apparently had no influence elsewhere.

In order to simplify the subject, log architecture has been divided into two facets in this study: the historical background of log buildings, and the technical knowledge necessary for their construction. Although to a large extent history and technique are mutually dependent, it does not necessarily follow that a culture lacking the knowledge of log building does not have the tools and technical ability required for such a construction method. Given proper impetus, such a culture could quickly change its mode of building from, say, framed houses to log houses. This was the course of events for most immigrants to the North American colonies in the seventeenth and eighteenth centuries—particularly for the Scotch-Irish and English. Naturally, the history of log building in Ohio falls at the culmination of this structural epoch rather than at its inception.

Although the literature on log building is not extensive, historians such as Shurtleff and Weslager have compiled sufficient evidence from contemporary sources to prove that the practice, at least for domestic purposes, was brought to the continent by immigrants of Scandinavian origin who had a tradition of log construction in their heavily forested countries.[5] Swedes and

Finns apparently first introduced log construction in the area known as New Sweden at the upper end of Delaware Bay, about the middle of the seventeenth century. From this small settlement, the log house spread up the Delaware River into country now embraced by the states of Pennsylvania and New Jersey.

Following closely on the heels of the New Sweden immigrants were those from the Germanic states who brought their own cultural traditions of log construction. This influx late in the seventeenth century initially centered in the Delaware Valley of Pennsylvania. The typology of log building was as diverse as the cultural groups from Germany.

By the end of the seventeenth century, therefore, when the basic precepts of log building on the European continent had been transferred to North America, it would have been possible in most cases to identify the national origin of the occupant of a log house by its method of construction. The next group of immigrants was, in large part, responsible for the diffusion of log building in the colonies and the subsequent loss of nationalistic typology. These people were the Scotch-Irish—Protestant Lowland Scots who had largely resided in stone cottages in northern Ireland a few generations before emigrating to the colonies in several waves beginning early in the eighteenth century. Although there were settlements of Scotch-Irish scattered throughout the colonies, the majority landed in the Delaware Bay area. Naturally the immigrants near the Swedish-Finnish settlements learned that style of log building, while those in the Philadelphia area learned the Germanic style(s).

Because of the great numbers of Scotch-Irish, a migration wave was generated in the colonies, particularly to the west and south into south-central Pennsylvania, Maryland, Virginia, the Carolinas, and Georgia. Thus, by the third quarter of the eighteenth century, due to the movement of the Scotch-Irish as well as the Germans, log building had become the common constructional mode on the boundaries of colonial settlement. As a consequence, the cultural typology of log construction became greatly diluted. The Scotch-Irish, who had no tradition of log building, had no qualms about borrowing elements of any style of construction which they encountered. The majority of log buildings found in Ohio today are of this eclectic "nonstyle."

Log building had not been confined to the Delaware Bay area before the Scotch-Irish arrived; however, most—of the few—contemporary references to log buildings in the New England area prior to 1700 are to buildings for defense, that is, blockhouses or garrison houses. The Dutch immigrants to New Netherland certainly had no tradition of log building and probably possessed scant knowledge of wood construction of any kind for Holland had no large public forests. The same was practically true for the English immigrants because the great forests of England were either denuded or under the control of the Crown by the end of the sixteenth century. The development of England's great naval power during the century had so depleted the timber resources of the island that wood was to become an important item of trade between the American colonies and the parent country in the seventeenth century. Log buildings had apparently been known in early medieval England, no doubt introduced by the Norse invaders, but many generations had passed—and with them the knowledge of log construction—before migration began to the New World.[6] The image of the Pilgrims celebrating the first Thanksgiving Day outside their log cabins is one of fiction, unfortunately still perpetuated through popular literature and art. In reality, they lived first in dug cellars, and when they built houses, they cut timber to make clapboarded, braced-frame structures. Perhaps if the Pilgrims had sought refuge in some state east of Holland, they might have gained knowledge of log construction for domestic purposes.[7]

Log building was known in France, although the horizontal notched log style was far less common than walls composed of vertical logs set in the ground. This style, termed *poteaux-en-terre*, existed in France as late as the nineteenth century, and was used in French settlements in the New World well into the twentieth century.[8] The Russians built numerous log structures in Alaska in the latter eighteenth and early nineteenth centuries, some of which still stand. However, direct Russian influence apparently did not extend beyond the northwest coast of the present United States.

As to the North American Indians of pre-Columbian days, there is no evidence that they ever used *notched* horizontal logs, though they did use log pens, and there is circumstantial evidence that they knew the use of vertically placed logs for defense. It would have been a most difficult task to fell, hew, and notch timber using only stone tools and fire. Several of the prehistoric Indian mounds of the Upper Ohio Valley contained log pen burial vaults. Examples were found in the Mound City Group north of Chillicothe. One mound contained the remains of a vertical post hut over which a crossed log hut, 10 by 12 feet, had been constructed of 6-to-11-inch timbers. Archaeologists found evidence of poles and logs cut with (what they presumed to be) stone axes. The remains of a large log pen were found in a mound southeast of Logan in Hocking County. The structure was compared to a child's "cob house" or a rail corncrib. A mound, near Charleston, West Virginia, held the remains of a vault about 12 feet square and 7- or 8-feet high, made of walnut logs up to 12 inches in diameter. In the same group, a mound contained a polygonal vault 12 feet across and 8- or 10-feet high including its pole roof. The timbers were crossed at the corners.[9]

Several sixteenth-century illustrations portray Indian towns fortified with palisades. For example, Jacques le Moyne de Morgues, a member of the French expedition to Florida in 1564, did several paintings showing palisaded villages. These paintings were engraved by Theodore de Bry and published in Europe in 1591; engraving no. 30, entitled "A Fortified Village," shows a number of Indian huts or wigwams surrounded by a vertical log wall.[10] An Englishman, John White, did several watercolor sketches of Indians while at the Roanoke Colony in Virginia in 1585–86. Several of his watercolors were also engraved by De Bry and published in 1590. "The Town of Pomeiock" (Hyde County, North Carolina) and "The Town of Secota" (Beaufort County, North Carolina) are shown with palisades.[11]

Of the tens of thousands of log buildings that formerly existed in Ohio, several thousand still dot the landscape. Many more are enclosed in other structures, notably houses, still awaiting discovery. As far as the mode of construction is concerned, the log building has proved to be as durable a structure of any other material. This is particularly evident considering the small amount of maintenance most of the log buildings have had in the twentieth century. Aside from the problem of finding logs of a suitable size (and paying for them), a log house would still be a good residence to construct—it would certainly be a great deal sounder than most development houses today. Contemporary houses are "cabins," structurally, compared to mid- and late-Victorian construction.

One of the great motivating forces behind the migration of settlers in the nineteenth century was the desire to establish a permanent home, the "homestead," which would serve generations of the family to come. Consequently, the buildings they constructed were for long-term use. The migration is still present today, and perhaps so is the desire for permanency, but the possibility of finding the homestead, in nineteenth-century terms, is growing more and more remote due to basic social and economic changes. In an agrarian economy, the self-sufficient family was a reality; in an urban-industrial economy, with today's laws and taxes, self-sufficiency even on the farm has become a rarity, if not an absolute impossibility.

There was nothing mysterious or difficult about building with logs. It was the easiest solution at the time to solve the problem of shelter in an undeveloped area. That it survived this temporary phase to become an alternate, permanent mode of construction testifies to its practicality. In another hundred years it may seem strange to historians that our generation would meticulously saw the logs apart and then tediously reassemble them to form a structure.

Notes

1. Vitruvius, *Ten Books on Architecture,* bk. 2, chap. 1, par. 4, p. 39.
2. Latham, *Travels of Marco Polo,* p. 308. Polo's travels were between 1260 and 1295.
3. Childe, *What Happened in History,* p. 182. However, recent research has indicated that the discovery of iron may have occurred more or less simultaneously in many areas in northern Europe as well as the Near East.
4. Momatiuk and Eastcott's "Poland's Mountain People," contains some interesting photographs of log houses including one under construction (p. 110).
5. Today, the showplace of Swedish log architecture is the 75-acre open-air museum in Stockholm known as Skansen. Founded in 1891 by Artus Hazelius, an effort has been made to collect original houses and outbuildings, furniture and implements, throughout the country. The log buildings span four centuries.
6. Dr. R. W. Brunskill, senior lecturer in the School of Architecture, University of Manchester, England, relates that no present evidence of horizontal log construction is known in the British Isles. The oldest examples are on the Faeroes, the Danish Islands 200 miles northwest of the Shetlands. (Letter to the author, 19 October 1973.)
7. For an exhaustive discussion of this topic, two books are authoritative: Shurtleff's *Log Cabin Myth* and Weslager's *Log Cabin in America.*
8. See Peterson's "Houses of French St. Louis," pp. 17–40.
9. References are from quoted sources in chap. 10, "Structure and Contents of Mounds," Fowke's *Archaeological History of Ohio,* pp. 328, 329, 339, 355, 356, and 357.
10. Lorant, *New World,* p. 95.
11. Ibid., pp. 190–91.

II
GENERAL HISTORY

Most early log buildings were erected as temporary structures because they provided the best solution to the immediate need for shelter in an area where processed building material could not be obtained quickly. Other types of temporary shelters—tents, wigwams, lean-tos, dug cellars, wagons—were also used throughout the settlement period, which actually spanned the seventeenth, eighteenth, and nineteenth centuries, depending on locality. The kind of shelter chosen varied with the needs of the residents, who, according to early observers, fell into one of several distinct categories on the frontier.[1]

The first arrivals, the *backwoodsmen* (as they were known by their contemporaries), were sustained by living from the land and trading with both Indians and colonists. They required only the rudest shelters, perhaps wigwams or lean-tos of branches. The *squatters*, who were often in family units, needed more stable housing on the land they didn't own—perhaps roughly finished cabins. The third group, the *pioneers*, wrested homesteads from the wilderness for their families, but moved west with the frontier. Appearing in Ohio by the late 1780s, the pioneers left a legacy of cleared land to their successors, the *settlers*, who improved the land and built permanent structures. For the squatters, the pioneers, and the settlers, the log cabin or house quickly and simply filled an immediate need for a secure home.

Since for the most part the trans—Appalachian area, including the Ohio Country, was heavily timbered, building material was readily available for constructing a house, barn, and outbuildings. On the other hand, the forest was considered the pioneers' greatest enemy for it sheltered the Indian and predatory animal and prevented sunlight from reaching agricultural crops. The removal of as many trees as possible was a necessity for the pioneer farmer. Consequently, the oft heard phrase, "the cabin in the clearing," which evoked a certain romanticism even by mid-nineteenth century, was based on a less poetic reality. Here is a comment by Colonel Keys, an early settler of Highland County, writing about the period between the Indian Wars and the War of 1812:

> The days of Indian fighting were happily just past, and the energy and courage of true manhood were directed to the next great work of civilization—the battle with the stern but relenting forests. This fight was kept up for many years. The stately oak, ash, hickory, sugartree, maple, gum and walnut . . . were of necessity regarded as enemies to the advancement of man and his plans. Extermination was therefore the word. Next to the Indian, these beautiful forests were regarded the worst enemy of man. The settlers made common cause in these attacks on the forests, and the way our noble young men, who made and carried on the warfare upon them, opening up and clearing our farms, in many instances "smack smooth," as the phrase is, was in truth no child's play.[2]

"Who built the first log structure in Ohio?" is just one of many unanswerable questions. Perhaps it was the French fur traders who were engaged with the "western" Indians on the shores of Lake Erie in the seventeenth century. According to *The Jesuit Relations*,[3] the network of Indian missions had been extended to the territorial boundaries of the Erie Nation, the "Nation of the Cat," by 1642. The missionaries had known something of the nation previously through information provided by fur traders. The French began to trade with the Miami Indians at their main village, Teewightewee Town (the same site as Fort Pickawillany, near Piqua, Miami County), about the year 1690. If the French were not the first to build log structures in Ohio, it was probably the English fur traders at Fort Pickawillany, who erected log huts between 1749 and 1752. It is known through contemporary documents that they built a vertical log stockade and a blockhouse.[4] This fur trading post was attacked by Ottawa Indians, led by Charles Langlade and a few fellow French fur traders, in the spring of 1752. Captain William Trent described in his *Journal* the smoke rising from the burning traders' "houses."[5] These "houses" were probably very similar to structures erected by the English traders at Fort Michilimackinac (Michigan)—low cabins, of small round logs set over shallow cellars, in which the furs and trade goods were stored. Perhaps the earliest specific description of a log building in Ohio is from James Smith's narrative of his captivity during the French and Indian War, quoted in chapter 4. As with the traders' huts, the Indian wigwam which he described in 1755 was certainly atypical of the log structures being erected in the eastern colonies.

The period between the French and Indian War and the advent of the Moravian missions is somewhat of a "dark age" in contemporary literature relative to the Ohio Country. There is no doubt that squatters did settle within the present boundaries of Ohio during this period, particularly in the major river valleys. An itinerant preacher and gunsmith by name of Moses Henry supposedly settled in "Chillicaathee," a Shawanese Indian village (now Frankfort, Ross County), in 1769. It is possible he built a log house; at least as an easterner he should have had the knowledge to do so. We know the Shawanee were living in log huts in Chillicaathee by 1772.[6]

During the Revolutionary War, meat hunters for the Continental Army came into present northeastern Ohio from Pennsylvania, and many squatters entered the territory to escape the conflict. It is unlikely that the hunters built permanent shelters, but the squatters certainly did. Their settling on Indian land disturbed the natives so greatly that Continental troops were sent to dislodge the squatters by burning their cabins and cultivated fields—the continued neutrality of the Indians was highly important to the colonial cause. The first such expedition took place in the fall of 1779, when sixty troops of the Eighth Pennsylvania Regiment under Captain John Clarke crossed the Ohio River at Wheeling. Several expeditions followed, without great success, prior to the spring of 1785, when Ensign John Armstrong and twenty men toured part of eastern Ohio expressly to warn off the squatters. They encountered and were told of hundreds of families, not only in the eastern part of the territory, but also throughout what is now Ohio. The population was greater than six years previously, and was so well settled that the squatters had organized their own government in the spring of 1785; "governor William Hogland, west of the Ohio" is mentioned in the Pittsburgh *Gazette*, 29 September 1787.[7]

There are many references, particularly in military correspondence, to squatters' "huts," "cabins," and "houses." Undoubtedly most of these shelters were made of either round or hewed logs. It is possible that a few still exist in eastern Ohio, although proof would be hard to find.

The Great and Little Miami River valleys, in the southwestern corner of Ohio, saw the passage of thousands of militia, camp followers, land speculators, and squatters during the latter part of the Revolutionary War; this area was the "Western Front" of the war. Abraham Thomas was on two of the militia raids against the Ohio Indians. Crossing the Ohio River, near present Cincinnati, in 1782 with George Rogers Clarke's force, Thomas noted that "our last year's stockade had been kept up, and a few people then resided in log cabins."[8] In March 1785, a group of settlers from Washington County, Pennsylvania, went down the Ohio River to Maysville (Limestone), Kentucky, then across the river to the mouth of the Great Miami. After being delayed by a flood, the group explored as far north as the present city of Hamilton during the months of May and June. Their purpose was to establish preemption rights to the choice bottom lands. The group consisted of John Hindman, William West, John Simons, John Seft, and "old Mr. Carlin," plus their families. Hindman later worked as a surveyor for John Cleves

Symmes.[9] They no doubt left log structures as permanent proof of their passage.

The federal troops at Fort Harmar (Marietta) kept note of the river traffic during this period because all the migrants were supposed to go to Kentucky—thus the appellation "Kentucky Boats" for flatboats. Between November 13 and December 22 of 1785, 39 boats averaging 10 persons passed the fort on their way to the "Falls of the Ohio" (Louisville). Some boats stopped before reaching Harmar. During the latter half of 1787, 146 boats passed containing 3,196 migrants, 1,371 horses, 165 wagons, 191 cattle, 245 sheep, and 24 hogs. The following year, ending in November 1788, there were 967 boats carrying 18,370 "souls," 7,986 horses, 2,372 cows, 1,110 sheep, and 646 wagons.[10] Add about one-half the total for overland migration, the numbers of pioneers already in Kentucky, federal troops, fur traders, spies, land speculators, the British, the French, and, of course, the Indians, and one can readily see that the frontier was a busy place during the 1780s. In 1790, a "rough census" indicated a total population of 73,677 in Kentucky, a great number of whom migrated into Ohio.[11]

The oldest known, datable building in Ohio (with the possible exception of the Ohio Company Land Office) was erected shortly after part of present Ohio was officially opened to settlement by the Ordinance of 1787. This extant structure is the Rufus Putnam house in Marietta, which originally was a section of the curtain-walled fortification known as Campus Martius, built by the Ohio Company of Associates beginning in the spring of 1788. Campus Martius was not a military establishment though it was designed as a fortification and administered in a similar fashion (most Ohio Company members had served in the Revolutionary War).

Though commonly referred to as "log," Campus Martius was more specifically "plank wall" in construction: four-inch poplar planks were mortised and pinned into vertical posts placed at varying intervals.[12] Most of the planks were pit-sawed rather than hewed to dimension. Plank construction was used in many late eighteenth-century military forts in Ohio and elsewhere, and also in some domestic building—especially in New England, the former home of many members of the Ohio Company. The Putnam house contains one of the few documented examples of pit-sawed timber in Ohio of which this writer has knowledge.

Campus Martius was a 180-foot square, double-walled stockade, where members of the company and their families lived in apartments between the plank curtain walls. Rufus Putnam occupied a section approximately 36 feet long and 18 feet wide which was two stories high. He had a cellar and a finished garret by late 1790. When the company sold Campus Martius, section by section, beginning in the winter of 1795–96, Putnam bought the blockhouse adjacent to his section and used that timber to almost double the size of his house. The building is now enclosed in a wing of the Campus Martius Museum in Marietta.

Soon after numerous outposts had been established in and around Marietta, another large settlement, Gallipolis, was begun 110 miles down the Ohio River by the Scioto Company to house about five hundred French immigrants of middle-class, urban background. Before the arrival of the immigrants in 1790, more than sixty log houses were erected, under contract between the Scioto Company and Rufus Putnam, who hired Major John Burnham of Essex, Massachusetts, to do the actual construction. Soon after Burnham and about forty men arrived in Marietta, Putnam gave Burnham a letter of instruction, dated 4 June 1790, which offers some interesting details of log construction.

> The object is to erect four block [houses] and a number of low huts, agreeably to the plan which you will have with you, and clear the lands. Your own knowledge of hut building, the block house of round logs which you will have an opportunity to observe at Belleprie, together with the plan so clearly explained, renders it unnecessary to be very particular; however, you will remember that I don't expect you will lay any floors except for your own convenience, nor put in any sleeper or joyce [*sic*] for the lower floors; plank for the

> doors must be split and hewed and the doors hung with wooden hinges; as I don't expect you will obtain any stone for the backs of your chimneys, they must be made of clay first, moulded into tile and dried in manner you will be shown an example at Belleprie.[13]

Putnam obviously was using the term "blockhouse" in a military sense. His "huts" were very primitive log cabins without floors. Apparently the firebox was wood faced with thin clay tiles, since Putnam surely would not have used the term "tile" for "brick."

The French botanist Andre Michaux, who visited Gallipolis in 1793, later wrote that "the houses are all built of squared logs merely notched at the ends instead of being Mortised."[14] This is an interesting statement for it shows that Michaux was familiar with a mortised style of construction—probably not unlike that used at Campus Martius—and, in fact, he may previously have visited Campus Martius. Also, this method of corner framing was in use in French military construction, with which he was no doubt familiar. It is surprising that he had not seen more examples of the notched corner; at least he implies that such a method was unusual to him. Assuming that Michaux's "houses" were the same as Putnam's "huts," it is puzzling to note that they were constructed of hewed logs. Putnam's outline of spartan finishing details indicates the use of round logs.

Michaux could have been mistaken, but C. F. Volney's visit to Gallipolis during the second week of July 1796, seems to bear out his statement. Volney reached Gallipolis at nightfall on July 9: "I could only distinguish two rows of little white houses, built on the flat summit of the bank of the Ohio. . . .[15] On July 10: "Their houses, though whitewashed, were nothing but huts made of trunks of trees, plastered [daubed] with clay, and covered [roofed] with shingles, consequently damp, and badly sheltered from the weather. The village forms a long square, composed of two rows of houses, built contiguous. . . .[16] It is doubtful, though certainly not impossible, that round log cabins would have been whitewashed on the exterior; Volney implies that they were roughly made, but standard pattern hewed log houses. This is further borne out by the shingle roofs, which would have required rafters and sheathing, rather than the typical clapboard roofs of cabin construction.

By 1802, when Michaux's son visited Gallipolis, most of the French settlers had moved away, leaving "about sixty log-houses, most of which being uninhabited, are falling into ruins.[17]

From the formal settlement of Marietta in the spring of 1788 to the outbreak of the Indian Wars during the winter of 1790–91, several settlements were attempted along the Ohio River—some successful, some not. Columbia (1788), North Bend (1789), and Manchester (1790) were soon overshadowed by Losantiville cum Cincinnati (1789) due to its better geographic location. Numerous, small "Kentucky Stations" were dotted all along the river course, a few well into the state along interior rivers.

Even though the first half of the 1790s was a period of Indian warfare in Ohio, some settlers continued to enter the territory. Many of these people were probably drawn to the area because of the conflict, knowing there was always a market for goods and produce where military operations were being conducted. Once the Treaty of Greene Ville was concluded in 1795, the Great Miami River Valley was settled with amazing speed.[18] Many soldiers and militia who had been with Clark and Wayne in the campaigns stayed to take up residence.

A group of land speculators, mainly from New Jersey and headed by John Cleves Symmes, purchased 248,000 acres between the Big and Little Miami Rivers northward from the Ohio River. Symmes moved to Ohio to handle the sale of the land, consequently, he carried on an extensive correspondence with his eastern proprietors. In a letter written on New Year's Day, 1790, he described his log buildings in the village of North Bend (Hamilton County) for the benefit of several gentlemen in Elizabethtown, New Jersey. This is an exceptional description for this period:

> The first or most easterly one is a good cabin, 16 feet wide & 22 feet long, with a handsome stone chimney in it; the roof is com-

posed of boat-plank set endways obliquely, and answers a triple purpose of rafters, lath, and undercourse of shingle, on which lay double rows of claboards which makes an exceeding tight and good roof. The next is a Cottage 16 feet by 18, & two and a half stories high; the roof is well shingled with nails. The third is a cabin 15 feet wide and 16 feet long, one story high with a good stone chimney in it; the roof shingled with nails. The 4th is a very handsome log house 18 feet by 26 and two stories high, with two good cellars under the same, the second cellar being sunk directly under the first in order to guard more effectually against heat and cold. This large cabin is shingled with nails; has a very large and good stone chimney which extends from side to side of the house for the more convenient accommodation of strangers, who are constantly coming and going; and never fail to make my house their home while they stay in the village. In this chimney is a large oven built of stone. Adjoining to this house, I have built me a well finished smoke-house 14 feet square; which brings you to a fortified gate of 8 feet for communication back. All the buildings east of this gate are set as close to each other as was possible. Adjoining to and west of the gate is a double cabin of 48 feet in length and 16 feet wide, with a well built stone chimney of two fire places, one facing each room. This roof is covered with boat plank throughout and double rows of claboards in the same manner with the first described cabin. In these several cabins I have fourteen sash windows of glass. My barn or fodder-house comes next with a stable on one side for my horses, and on the other, one for my cows. These entirely fill up the space of twelve poles. This string of cabins stands [blank] feet from the bank of the river and quite free from and to the south of the front or Jersey Street of the city.

Now gentlemen I beg of the proprietors this small piece of land at some price which they may set, that I may have the fee thereof vested in me. These buildings have cost me more than two hundred pounds specie, and I cannot afford to let them go to strangers for nothing; the mason work alone come to more than one hundred dollars. There is not another house on the ground that has either cellar, stone chimney or glass window in it; nor of any value compared with mine. . . .[19]

Symmes's impressive row of buildings along the Ohio River were no doubt necessary to his business of selling land.[20] His concern over his property was due to a realignment of the "city" of North Bend by the eastern proprietors, placing him on land reserved for their use. Symmes may have been exaggerating the value of his property on purpose, but there is every reason to believe his physical descriptions are correct. The two log cabins with "boat-plank" roof framing are fascinating structures. The planking was apparently angled 45 degrees to the length of the building, from the plate to the ridge, and formed a solid, self-supported underroof. His 48- by-16-foot "double cabin" with a central chimney was the form known today as "saddle-bag"; two such houses, and a painting of a third, have been found in the Little Miami River Valley. Perhaps other contemporary comments about double cabins may refer to this configuration rather than the double-pen, or breezeway, form; in any case, few examples remain. Symmes's letter makes it clear that it was possible to construct any type of structure on the frontier of 1789.

Symmes could afford the cost of construction, however, where the average settler could not. It was also more difficult the further inland the settler traveled from the Ohio River. When Felix Renick reached the village of Franklinton (west-central Columbus) on 22 October 1798, he found "a considerable number of log cabins, most of which had recently been put up, and were without chinking, daubing or doors. Doorways were however cut out, and blankets hung up in them . . . ."[21] By this time North Bend had all but disappeared; Cincinnati was well on its way to becoming the "Queen City of the West"; and Nathaniel Massie's braced-frame house in Adams County, which is still standing, was one year old. The settlement of Ohio was literally on a day-by-day, mile-by-mile basis during the 1790s, and wholesale immigration didn't really occur until after the War of 1812.

Documenting extant buildings of the 1790s is an extremely difficult task (in fact, documenting any building for about the first half of the nineteenth century is difficult). In the case of log structures there are a few typological clues, but years of use, disuse, and remodeling often make it impossible to interpret physical features. Literary evidence is usually nil, with exceptions like the Putnam or Massie houses which did not lose their identities through the years. It is possible that the oldest building in Ohio is the Ohio Company Land Office, Campus Martius Museum, Marietta. It has been declared so many times. The company records mention the construction of an "office" in 1788, certainly months before Putnam's house was completed within the curtain walls of the stockade. However, what was done with the "office" during the Indian Wars? Certainly with Campus Martius completed the records would have been kept within the stockade. A more logical date for the office would be after the sale of Campus Martius, which began late in 1795, following the Treaty of Greene Ville.

The land office has been heavily remodeled through the years, the interior woodwork and doors certainly coming from the stockade or one of the late 1790 houses constructed from stockade salvage material. The walls are made of plank, approximately four and a half inches wide, apparently dovetailed at the corners though this writer has never been able to examine the exterior because of the siding; it appears, from the interior, to be full-dovetailed. There are several alterations to wall openings. The wall planks could also have come from the stockade after its sale. It is strange to think that if the company needed a quick shelter to preserve their records they would go to the effort of hewing and sawing tree trunks down to planks: Why not a round log cabin?

No doubt the oldest log house in Ohio, of which there is an accurate visual record, was one from Fort Harmar which was exhibited at the centennial of the founding of Marietta (see fig. 28). This house was definitely standing in 1788, and could have been built as early as 1785. The oldest extant log house may be the one Neil Washburn supposedly built in southern Brown County in 1793. The evidence is traditional and circumstantial, but the house stood in the right location before it was removed to the county fairgrounds. Its typology is correct for the period—asymmetrical door and window placement, tall in proportion to its breadth. The ceiling joists could have been flatboat salvage.

The next oldest possibility is a log house that stood in Elizabethtown, Hamilton County; it is now located in Shawnee Lookout Park just south of Elizabethtown, where it was restored by the Hamilton County Park District. A family history of the early twentieth century identified the house as one of three built jointly by three men in 1795 prior to bringing their families into the territory. No unusual claims were made for either the men or the house, and the structure does indeed look early with its few asymmetrical openings, tall profile, and narrow 180-degree turn corner stairway (see fig. 29).

In Anderson Township, Hamilton County (the Mt. Washington area on the east of Cincinnati), there is a small log house that has been reliably dated to 1796 by the local historical society and is being preserved by them. It, too, displays the few, asymmetrical openings of the 1790s plus a large stone chimney that appears original (see fig. 35).

Half of Newcom Tavern, in Deeds Park, Dayton, was constructed in 1796; it was enlarged in 1798. The building served many purposes in the nineteenth century, was remodeled and "restored," and moved; no doubt its configuration is close to its original appearance, but there is much new wood and log gables that certainly didn't exist in 1798 (see fig. 37).

There is a log house at the south edge of Waynesville, Warren County, that could predate the 1797 founding of the village, though the evidence is, again, circumstantial; the house was still inhabited in 1972, but has since been badly damaged by fire.[22]

The part log, part stone Treber Tavern still standing in Tiffin Township, Adams County, was built on Zane's Trace in 1798. John Treber was a gunsmith who, in a way, was forced into the tavern business because so many travelers stopped at his house.

The James Galloway "cabin" at Xenia, Greene County, is often dated in the late 1790s (this writer made the same mistake in his earlier monograph). It is, in fact, Galloway's second log home and was constructed in 1803 on the site of his earlier cabin. Six years later he built a stone house a short distance north; all three houses were located about three miles north of Xenia along present U.S. Route 68 which follows an old Indian trail and military road.

Which Galloway house did Tecumseh visit? Probably all three.[23] (See figs. 39 and 40.)

Extant log buildings of the period between 1800 and the War of 1812 are certainly not rare; many excellent examples exist over the state, mostly in the southern half and the southwest quarter in particular. Many are illustrated in this book.

Notes

1. Early writers who perceived that a unique pattern of civilization had developed on the frontier included Baily, *Journal of a Tour in Unsettled Parts of North America*, and Blane, *Excursion through the United States and Canada.*
2. Scott, *History of the Early Settlement of Highland County*, p. 148. Similar statements are frequently found in county histories. (William Keys or Keyes, 1778–1864.)
3. Thwaites, *Jesuit Relations* 21:191.
4. Trent, *Journal*, pp. 43–44, 91.
5. Ibid., p. 85.
6. Jones, *Journal*, p. 56.
7. Downes, "Ohio's Squatter Governor," p. 273.
8. Howe, *Historical Collections of Ohio*, p. 357.
9. Cist, *Cincinnati Miscellany* 2:357.
10. Information from the *Massachusetts Gazette*, 13 March 1786; Harmar Papers, 9 December 1787; and the *Columbian Magazine*, January 1789. Quoted in Roosevelt, *Winning of the West* 3:97–98.
11. Greene and Harrington, *Census*, p. 192.
12. Plank wall construction was common in Canada where it was known as "Manitoba Frame." An interesting, twentieth-century eyewitness account of Canadian frame and log construction practices, including pitsawing, may be found in Sherwood, "Building in the North." Also, see Richardson, "Voyageur Construction Methods," who quotes an 1832 description of plank wall construction at Lac du Flambeau in western Wisconsin. Richardson also wrote the very informative "Comparative Historical Study of Timber Building in Canada." John Cleves Symmes, writing to Robert Morris from Post Vincennes, Northwest Territory, 22 June 1790, commented:

    > The buildings are low, Old, and ugly, mostly log-houses (tho hewed) but the logs do not lay horizontal as the Americans build, but stand erect with one end set well in the ground, & and upper end spiked to or framed into a plate which runs horizontally round the house; few houses are more than one story. . . . (Bond, *Correspondence of John Cleves Symmes*, p. 288.)

13. Dawes, "Major John Burnham," p. 43.
14. Michaux, "Travels into Kentucky," p. 34.
15. Volney, *View of the Climate and Soil of the United States of America*, p. 358.
16. Ibid., p. 359.
17. Michaux, *Travels to the West*, p. 100.
18. Comment from a letter by John Cleves Symmes to Jonathan Dayton, Cincinnati, August 6, 1795:

> If the Indian treaty should turn out favorable to the frontiers, I think it will be practicable to push the settlements up to my rear line, in which case our country will become somewhat respectable. But all Kentucky and the back parts of Virginia and Pennsylvania are running mad with expectations of the land office opening in this country—hundreds are running into the wilderness west of the Great Miami, locating and making elections of land. (Bond, *Correspondence of John Cleves Symmes*, p. 174.)

The Greene Ville Treaty, so important to the settlement of Ohio, was signed by the various Indian nations on 3 August 1795; it was ratified by the U.S. Senate on 22 December.

19. Symmes to Jonathan Dayton, Daniel Marsh, and Matthias Ogden; Northbend [Ohio], 1 January 1790; Bond, *Correspondence of John Cleves Symmes*, pp. 111–12.
20. Symmes's main house was destroyed by fire in March 1811. The chimney and fireplace ruins were still visible in 1860 according to Lossing, *Pictorial Field-Book of the War of 1812*, p. 572. Lossing also provided an illustration of the "First House" in North Bend on page 571, which was still standing in 1867. The illustration shows a tall one- and one-half story structure with an asymmetrical door and window—just what one would expect based on surviving 1790s log houses.
21. Felix Renick, "A Trip to the West," *American Pioneer*, 5 February (1842) vol. I, p. 80.
22. Log buildings are highly resistant to fire; the wood will char to a certain depth depending on its condition and variety, but as the charred surface grows deeper it also becomes more effective in insulating the timber. Heavy timber framing has long been considered a preferred risk by fire insurance rating bureaus, and a superior type of construction by fire protection groups. Extensive testing has proven the superiority of wood over steel in sustaining dead weight during a fire; see National Lumber Manufacturers Association, *Comparative Fire Test of Timber and Steel Beams*.
23. Galloway, *Old Chillicothe*, pp. 121–22 (also illustration and caption following p. 280). Photograph of 1809 stone house is in the W. A. Galloway Papers, Greene County Public Library, Xenia.

III
THE CABIN IN THE CLEARING

"Log Cabin Song"

I love the rough log cabin,
It tells of the olden time,
When a hardy and an honest class
Of Freemen in their prime,
First left their fathers' peaceful home,
Where all was joy and rest,
With their axes on their shoulders
And sallied for the West,

With a fal, lal, la,
With a fal, lal, la,
With a fal, lal, la, fal, la.

Of logs they build a sturdy pile,
With slabs they roof'd it o'er.
With wooden latch and hinges rude,
They hung the clumsy door,
And for the little window lights,
In size two feet by two,
They used such sash as could be got,
In regions that were new;

With a fal, lal, la, etc.

The chimney was compos'd of slats,
Well interlaid with clay,
Forming a sight we seldom see,
In this a later day;
And here on stones for fire dogs,
A rousing fire was made,
While 'round it sat a hardy crew
With none to make afraid;

With a fal, lal, la, etc.

I love the old log cabin,
For here in early days,
Long dwelt the honest Harrison,
As evry Loco says;
And when he is our President,
Which one year more will see,
In good hard cider we will toast,
And cheer him three times three;

With a fal, lal, la, etc.

In a comparatively short span of time the log cabin in Ohio ceased to be regarded as a functional necessity and assumed a certain "romantic" aura, in the dictionary sense of "the imaginative or emotional appeal of the heroic, adventurous, remote, mysterious, or idealized," that is, "having no basis in fact." A more cogent example of this romanticism could not be found than in the Harrison presidential campaign of 1840.

General William Henry Harrison of North Bend, Hamilton County, Ohio, was almost sixty-seven years old, when, in 1839 as the Whig party presidential candidate, he became identified with log cabins, even though he had been born in a James River, Virginia, mansion, and had never lived in a log building as such. On 11 December 1839, the Baltimore *Republican*, a newspaper opposed to the Whigs, printed a column by John de Ziska, who derisively said of Harrison the westerner: "Give him a barrel of hard cider, and settle a pension of $2000 a year on him, and our word for it, he will sit the remainder of his days in his log cabin by the side of the 'sea-coal fire' and study moral philosophy!"[1]

De Ziska knew not what he wrought; the "log cabin and hard cider" allusion became the catchphrase that bound together the most divergent political factions in the western states and elected Harrison to the presidency. In actuality, Harrison's only connection with a log cabin was that a one-room log house had been incorporated at the western end of his North Bend home when it was enlarged. Although Harrison never claimed to have been born in a log cabin, he did nothing to dispel the image created in the campaign—the first truly professional political campaign in the history of the United States.

Not only did the 1840 campaign set a pattern for several generations of politicians—for to have been born in a log cabin became tantamount to success in politics—it began the mystique of the log cabin. Real log cabins were placed on running gear and paraded in many towns.[2] An amazing number of objects, from handkerchiefs to Staffordshire tea services, were decorated with a log cabin and a cider barrel. The log cabin became a symbol of "the good life," real or imaginary, to tens of thousands of persons in the United States of 1840. To aging pioneers it represented their youth, hope, ambition: It was their "Republican Palace."[3] To the young, it was a symbol of the accomplishments of their parents and grandparents, often made in the face of great odds, and was a spur to their own achievements.

By 1840, the rigors of frontier life, at least for the eastern half of the country, had been sufficiently overcome to allow such a romanticized view of pioneering and log cabin life to develop. The War of 1812 was the beginning of the end of the "frontier" period in Ohio. After 1815 the rise of urban centers, growth of industry, and development of agriculture progressed at an amazing speed. The traditional basis of pioneering—agriculture—first felt the effects of mechanization in the late 1830s and ten years later, agricultural periodicals were implying that a farmer was backward if he were not making use of the various machines available. Ceding of the last Indian reservation in Ohio in 1842 really marked the end of the state's frontier. No wonder, then, that the older generation felt a certain longing for the less complex days of the "log cabin in the clearing."

That the end of the frontier period in Ohio did indeed arrive about 1840 is no better evidenced than in the following excerpt from the *Western Courier and Piqua Enquirer*:

> HUSKING PARTY. . . . We like to recur occasionally to the customs and pastimes of our ancestors. . . . We know that these may, at first view, appear rude and forbidding—that the sensibilities of the fashionables of the present generation would be shocked at the bare idea of a Quilting Frolic—an Appleparing, or a Husking Party. . . .

This sounds like current rhetoric, but it was published 18 November 1837. Although the original article may have been reprinted from another newspaper, probably eastern, the fact that the description could be applied to western Ohio in 1837 reinforces the conclusion that the end of an epoch had been reached.

Although log building continued throughout the century in

Ohio, the reasons for its continuance were relative to each specific site. By mid-nineteenth century, the log house had become confined to the rapidly disappearing, unsettled areas and to the less economically successful sections of the state. By then sawed timber could be obtained throughout Ohio, and the balloon-frame house had become the standard, reasonably priced housing. It had been easy to construct a log building in the midst of a forest; the logs did not have to be moved far to the building site. However, once the overall forest covering Ohio had been broken into small units by settlement, it was easier to saw the timber into usable sizes to be transported over a wide area.

The greatest number of log houses built after 1850 were in the southeastern quarter of the state, where iron furnaces, charcoal and later coke, were well established by midcentury. (This region was photographed early in the twentieth century by Professor Wilbur Stout of Ohio State University.) There are many log houses still standing, and occupied, in the countryside of the "Hanging Rock" iron furnace region. A number of these houses were built by workers who operated small farms following the decline of the charcoal furnaces, because of a lack of wood for charcoal, shortly after the Civil War. A few of the furnaces converted to coke and managed to operate until recently. This writer has heard that at least as late as 1937, a log house was built in the traditional style in southeastern Ohio. Log barns and farm outbuildings were built into the twentieth century; the log corncrib and tobacco shed were ideally suited for the small harvests and the drying conditions needed for those crops.

A few statistics are available that give an indication of the number of log houses extant in Ohio in the twentieth century. In March 1939, the U.S. Department of Agriculture published the results of a farm-housing survey conducted in the winter of 1934.[4] In the nine Ohio counties surveyed, there were 794 log houses being used as residences (4.3 percent of 18,464 houses surveyed). These counties were: Adams, Ashland, Ashtabula, Darke, Madison, Monroe, Muskingum, Paulding, and Sandusky. No log houses were located in Ashtabula County, and less than one percent of the houses were log in each of the counties of Ashland, Paulding, and Sandusky. In Monroe County, 15.8 percent of 2,029 houses were log; in Adams County, 11.3 percent of 2,269 houses.

One can take the average of houses per county, roughly 88, times the number of counties in Ohio, also 88, to obtain a vague idea of the number of log houses in use in the state in 1934: 7,744. This is as good a generalization as any obtainable. What the total would be now is equally as vague, though probably it would be lower even if all log structures were counted. However, a recent survey of Athens County turned up over 100 log buildings. A similar survey in Butler County found at least 65 structures, with some expectation that the total would reach a hundred.

As a comparison, in the fall of 1790 Cincinnati contained about 40 "framed and hewed-log two-story houses."[5] In 1795, Cincinnati had 94 cabins and 10 frame houses for about 500 inhabitants.[6] The next ten years saw the population double and construction techniques change. In 1805, there were 53 log cabins, 109 frame, 6 brick, and 4 stone houses.[7] An 1810 census of Cincinnati listed 232 frame houses, 55 log houses, 37 brick houses, and 14 stone houses; of the total, approximately 13 percent were log.[8] This proportion was probably true for most urban areas in early nineteenth-century Ohio. Of course, the presence of sawmills and artisans in such areas affected the type of housing erected. In 1803, Marietta had about 550 residents and 91 dwellings, 65 of which were frame or plank (Campus Martius houses, no doubt), 11 of brick, and 3 of stone.[9] This count presumably indicates there were only 12 log houses within Marietta. Chillicothe contained 202 stone, brick, and "timber clapboarded" dwellings in 1807. Most of the houses were supposedly "well painted."[10]

Today, the remaining log structures are primarily in the southern half of the state. The southeastern quarter has more buildings than the southwestern, but older buildings are more frequent in the latter area. Some very fine log barns are to be found in the east-central region, in and around Guernsey County. The principal routes of migration into and through

Ohio should indicate where to look for early buildings—and such, indeed, seems to be the case, for the most consistent distribution of buildings lies along the old routes, such as Zane's Trace and the National Road, and in the various river valleys which terminate at the Ohio. Possibly many of the main Indian trails, such as the Grand Council Trail through central Ohio, would show a similar pattern of settlement if the routes could be accurately determined.

It is difficult today to imagine how quickly the frontier did retreat, not only from Ohio but from the entire eastern half of the country. There were pockets of unsettled, uncleared land in Ohio until the last quarter of the nineteenth century (wet, rocky, or hilly), and some bounty land for Civil War enlistees was awarded in southeastern Ohio, but there was certainly no danger attached to settlement save ignorance. An entire generation, at the most two generations, witnessed the progress from wilderness to urbanization. A fascinating glimpse of the romance attached to frontier life, and the log cabin, by this generation was revealed by the actor Edwin Booth when he was invited to a Philadelphia mansion:

> When dining with owners . . . my hostess, on rising from the table, without giving a hint of the unusual in her manner, said: "We'll have our coffee in the back woods!" She guided me through the stately hall to a door that looked like a rough cabin of the far west mountains! There was a fireplace—just the sort a man might jumble up for himself! Unsorted sticks—not evenly cut city cordwood—were burning in it. A black kettle was hanging on a crane steamed [*sic*] away; a bearskin was underfoot. Oh, everything that should have been there was. And the roof had a hole in it. I was so taken aback that I gazed at the leaky roof and asked like a fool, "What do you do when it rains?" There was a triumphant laugh. That was the line I should have spoken on the cue they gave me. That was what they were hoping I might ask. Every newcomer asked about the rain. There was no need for explanation. The leaky roof was sheltered from the elements, for it was underneath an upper story of the house proper. I congratulated my hosts upon their achievement of a "real thing." It was adventure. Even the citi-

fied coffee could not destroy my illusion. Days came galloping back, that were quite as rough, with the coffee not so civilized and—when I had to wash the dishes.[11]

A similar fascination for the past produced what was probably the first romantic novel of frontier Ohio, *Philip Seymour*, in 1858.[12] The novel was based on an actual incident of the War of 1812—the murder of a pioneer family—and proved to be highly popular; today, it is hard to believe the work could have been taken seriously.

Notes

The words to "Log Cabin Song" are from the *Washington* (Pa.) *Reporter*; the music is by Alexander Kyle. The song was published by C. E. Horn, New York, 1840. Harrison's only association with a log cabin is described in Howe, *Historical Collections of Ohio*, pp. 230–31.

1. Weslager, *Log Cabin in America*, p. 262.
2. On 4 July 1840, a "great Whig barbecue" was held in Zanesville. An eyewitness account of the event was written the following day by F. W. Howard, of Roseville, and sent to his brother in Boston. There were log cabins of all shapes and sizes as well as other campaign gimmicks such as a giant ball: "Keep the ball rolling!" Extracts of this letter were published in *Biographical and Historical Memoirs of Muskingum County, Ohio* (Chicago, 1892), pp. 205–206. On pp. 206–207 there is a rare, detailed description of the raising of a "Liberty Pole" during the campaign of 1844. These accounts are excellent for the political aura of the period.
3. A phrase common in the early nineteenth century. For example, a letter from Benjamin Thurston (Lawrence County) to Daniel Plumer (Newbury, Mass.), 15 May 1819: ". . . done at my Republican Palace (Log Cabin) this day and date above written." Manuscript Collection, Ohio Historical Society Library.
4. U.S. Department of Agriculture, *The Farm-Housing Survey*.
5. Symmes to Jonathan Dayton, Cincinnati, 4 November, 1790; Bond, *Correspondence of John Cleves Symmes*, p. 135. However, the Robinson and Fairbank *Cincinnati Directory*, 1829, p. 150, says there were only two frame houses in 1790.
6. *Cincinnati Directory*, 1819, p. 29.
7. Ibid., p. 29.

8. *Liberty Hall* (Cincinnati), 13 November 1810.
9. Harris, *Journal*, p. 122.
10. Cutler, *Topographical Description*, p. 35.
11. Goodale, *Behind the Scenes*, pp. 88–89. Booth (1833–93) spent his boyhood in California. This episode occurred about 1880.
12. See *Philip Seymour; or, Pioneer Life in Richland County, Ohio. Founded on Facts*, by James F. M'Gaw. (Mansfield: R. Brickerhoff, 1858 and 1883, 1902, 1908).

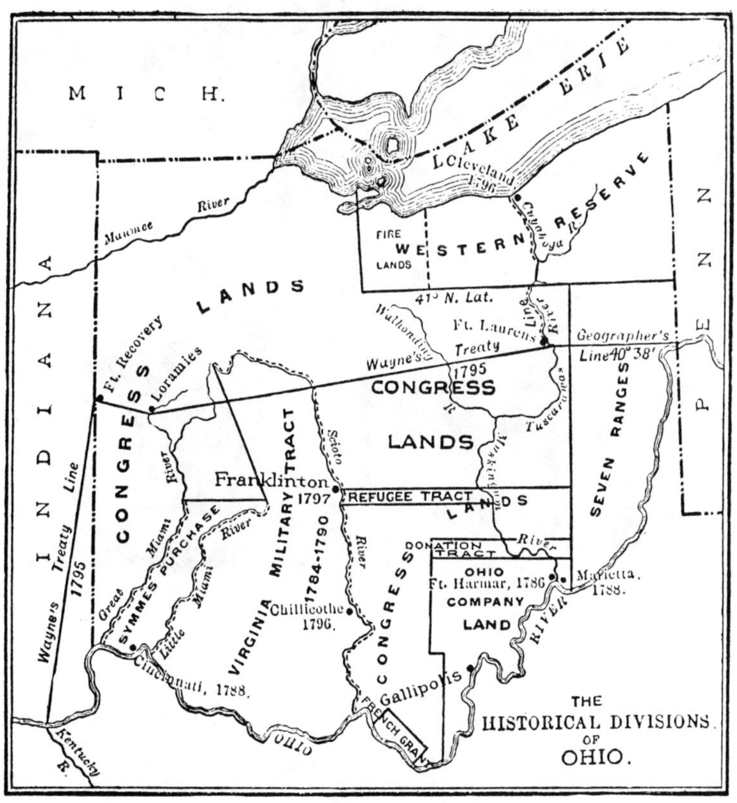

1. Historical divisions of Ohio.

2. Sheet music cover: "THE LOG HOUSE. A Song. presented to the Western Minstrel. by John Mills Brown. No. 19, Of the Sylviad. A. P. Heinrich To His Log House. Boston, March 14, 1826." According to the handwriting on the chimney, Heinrich was writing poetry in Bardstown, Kentucky, in 1818.

LOG CABIN SONG

Respectfully dedicated to the Citizens of the

FIRST WARD, NEW YORK.

The words taken from the

WASHINGTON REPORTER P^A^

THE MUSIC COMPOSED BY

NEW YORK, *Published by* C.E.HORN, *367 Brodway*.

3. Sheet music cover: "LOG CABIN SONG," music composed by Alexander Kyle to a political poem from a newspaper; published in New York, 1840. Intended for the William Henry Harrison presidential campaign. The log house as a Greek Revival Temple or an Alpine retreat, certainly an Upper New York State interpretation.

FOR TIPPECANOE,

AND TYLER, TOO.

Let fame to the world
Sound America's voice;
Our pride is our Country,
Just Laws are our choice.

4. Harrison presidential campaign ephemera: Harrison and Tyler silk campaign ribbon with an excellent cartoon of a log cabin with a weighted roof and stick chimney. The artist knew his subject well. There were dozens of similar ribbons issued during the presidential race of 1840, the first modern political campaign.

5. Harrison presidential campaign ephemera, "Log Cabin and Hard Cider" theme depicted on Staffordshire (England) teapot, 1840. There is a decided Sino-European quality about the scene, a mysterious Arcadia which the artist could only imagine.

6. Harrison presidential campaign ephemera, wounded veteran being led to log cabin—and barrel of hard cider—while new day dawns (which certainly looks like the seal of the State of Ohio). Woodblock print, hatbox cover, 1840.

7. Harrison presidential campaign ephemera (?), slip-cast stoneware log cabin, salt-glazed, with blue and green decoration. Possibly made in Ohio, 1840.

8. A "corncob pen," frequently mentioned as a child's toy in 19th century literature. See Figure 9.

VARIETY COB HOUSE BUILDING BLOCKS.

These Blocks, for beauty, perfection and variety, surpass anything of the kind yet designed for our little friends. They will prove a treasure to the whole household. The little baby on the carpet will never weary of the endless ways of building with them. Boys and girls will find continual delight in the puzzles and houses they present, and adults can join with equal pleasure in playing their pretty and instructive games.

Each set contains an assortment of 176 Letters.

Each set will make six different Picture Puzzles, and a row of modern House Puzzles.

Each set will build a Cob Honse or Log Cabin, and Houses, Towers, Fences, and other structures in great variety.

Each set can be used to play a superior Letter Game, and to form words and sentences.

Each Puzzle House, Game, or use that these Blocks are intended for, is as perfect as though it were made for that special purpose alone. Complete set in box by express, **$2 00**

9. "Cob house" building blocks. Illustration from the 1886 *Price List of Out & Indoor Sports & Pastimes* of Peck and Snyder, n.p.

Log Cabin Building Blocks.

Hardwood, finely finished, 10 inches long, 10 inches wide, 13 inches high, packed in a Wood Box..................per doz., **$9.00**

10. A log cabin "Mansard Palace". Illustration from the 1883 *Wholesale Catalogue* of L. H. Mace and Company, p. 47.

11. "Western Clearing," by William Henry Bartlett, engraved and printed in Cincinnati. Illustration from *The Ladies' Repository*, vol. XV (March, 1855), p. 123 *ff*. The same image was used by Currier and Ives as "Among the Pines. A First Settlement." Bartlett (1809–1854) was an English artist who made four trips to the United States between 1836 and 1852. The representation seems accurate; many settlers erected temporary huts before constructing their cabins.

12. Hamilton County, Miami Township. Blockhouse in the "Sugar Camp Settlement," built in 1789, standing in 1846. Illustration from Howe, *Historical Collections of Ohio* (1847), p. 236. This traditional form blockhouse was located three miles below North Bend, two miles from the Indiana line. The use of the word "blockhouse" in the 18th century often denoted a hewed, rather than a round, log structure; therefore, many "blockhouses" were simply hewed log houses of standard pattern.

13. Miami County. "Davis' Clearing 1½ Mile South West of Piqua, Ohio." This 1831 sketch by Thomas Kelah Wharton (1814–1862) shows several rough, round-log structures of the type traditionally associated with the "Frontier." (See Figure 14.) Illustration courtesy of the Prints Division, The New York Public Library; Astor, Lenox, and Tilden Foundation.

14. Miami County. "Dalzell's Clearing 1 Mile South West of Piqua, Ohio." This excellent sketch, made in 1831 by Thomas Kelah Wharton, shows several trees girdled and burned during clearing. Wharton, born in England, lived in several states including Ohio. (See Figure 13.) Illustration courtesy of the Prints Division, The New York Public Library; Astor, Lenox, and Tilden Foundations.

15. "House in the Clearing," from *Diary of a Trip to Niagara*, p. 29 (unpublished manuscript). An unfinished log house with a temporary shed roof. This was probably a familiar scene on the frontier. Reproduction courtesy of the Manuscript Division, New York Public Library.

16. "American Log-House, Snake-Fence, etc." Watercolor by John Halkett, *ca.* 1822. Notice the balance-gate and girdled trees. Reproduction courtesy of the Library of the Hudson's Bay Company, Winnipeg, Manitoba, Canada.

17. Greene County, Beavercreek Township. Log Cabin built by Benjamin Whiteman, *ca.* 1798. Stereotyped woodblock from Howe, *Historical Collections of Ohio*, 1847, p. 193. The cabin was still occupied when Howe wrote his history. In 1803, the first Greene County court session was held in this cabin; the small "pole hut" to the right served as a jury room.

18. Licking County, Village of Granville. Braced-frame residence and shop of Benjamin B. Loar. Daguerreotype captioned "Before December 1849." Loar was a well-known Licking County gunsmith. The large, 12 over 12 window sashes suggest the building was constructed for a workshop. Two front doors are often found on houses of the 1820s, including log houses, kitchen and/or parlor or hallway, so their presence does not necessarily indicate a commerical structure. Note the almost barren hill where Denison College now stands.

19. "Log House in the Forests of Georgia," 1828 *camera lucida* drawing by Captain Basil Hall, *Travels in North America*, plate XXII, London, 1829. This is an optically accurate, pre-photographic image of a traditional log cabin with weighted roof.

20. This woodcut illustrated an article entitled "Our Cabin; or, Life in the Woods," a lengthy, comprehensive, and often humorous description of building and living in a log cabin, written by John S. Williams for the *American Pioneer*, October, 1843 (see Appendix E). The cabin was built during the winter of 1800–01 in Colerain Township, Belmont County, for the Williams family, newly arrived from North Carolina. This illustration was plagarized by many authors; for example, Baughman's *History of Richland County, Ohio*, vol. 1, p. 30 *ff*., where the caption reads "The Baughman Cabin," and the *New Historical Atlas of Allen Co., Ohio*, pp. 86 and 89, in which the same cabin served both Indian and pioneer (see Figures 24 and 25).

21. "Creek House in 1791," Georgia. The weighted roof and stick chimney were typical for Ohio log cabins during the settlement period. Illustration from Schoolcraft, *The Indian Tribes of the United States*, vol. I, 1884.

22. "Council House of the Hog Creek Shawanees." This is the photograph from which the lithograph, Figure 23, was copied. After the Indians ceded their reservation, this council house (which apparently was not completed) was used as a residence. Note the roof ribs and the long clapboard roofing. Illustration courtesy of the Allen County Historical Society.

23. "Old Council House of the Shawnees," from the *New Historical Atlas of Allen Co., Ohio*, 1880, p. 86. See Figure 22. This lithograph was copied directly from a photograph. The council house was very much like any log house, though it had a rib and clapboard roof. The Shawanees of Wapakonetta, who held about 66,000 acres in Allen County, were removed to a reservation on the Kansas River in 1832.

24. "P. H. Ts Cabin," from the *New Historical Atlas of Allen Co., Ohio*, 1880, p. 86. See Figures 20 and 25. Williams' cabin, which first appeared in the *American Pioneer* in 1843, has been endlessly copied.

25. "A Pioneer Home," from the *New Historical Atlas of Allen Co., Ohio*, 1880, p. 89. See Figures 20 and 24. It is amusing that the same woodcut was copied by different artists for the same atlas. The Williams' cabin has also been used to illustrate the first settlement at Cincinnati.

26. Greene County, Village of Clifton. Slab hut with pole shed. Photo: *ca.* 1890. The man was a wood cutter, according to the 1880 census. The hut to the left was constructed of "off-falls" from one of the Clifton sawmills. The shed, which appears to have been freshly daubed with mud, was built of small tree trunks. Except for the metal roofing, such an abode could have been found in Ohio a hundred years earlier.

27. Location unknown, possibly southeastern Ohio near Ohio River. Photographs *ca.* 1913. A) Painted log houses with additions. Settlement suggestive of "company town," iron or coal region. B) Log cabin with trapped gable and roof ribs, nailed clapboard roof. C) Log cabin with trapped gable and roof ribs, addition constructed of mud-plastered poles in tradition of wattle and daub.

28. Washington County, City of Marietta. One and a half story log house dated 1788. Photo: 1888. The sign on the house reads: "The Log House In Which Gov. St. Clair Signed Treaty With Indians In 1788." The signboard(?) leaning against the house appears to be covering a fireplace opening. If this was the front of the house, it had a porch; if the rear, a shed addition: Note the untrimmed logs projecting from the corners above the whitewash line. The date on the sign is slightly wrong, for St. Clair signed the treaty with the Ohio Country Indians at Fort Harmar on January 9, 1789. Fort Harmar was located on the south bank of the Muskingum River, across from Campus Martius and Marietta. Presumably the house was on its original site; it could date as early as 1785 when the fort was constructed.

29. Hamilton County, Village of Elizabethtown. Original location, Whitewater Township near the Ohio River. Two story log house, built in 1795 by Jeremiah Chandler, Charles Barthow, and John Bonham for the Chandler family. (See Figures 30, 31, 32, 33, 182.) Photo: 19 August 1973. One of three log houses constructed in 1795 by the above men in partnership, according to Chandler family tradition. The evidence is circumstantial, but, in this writer's opinion, sound. Typologically, the house is correct.

30. Hamilton County, Village of Elizabethtown. Two story log house. (See Figures 29, 31, 32, 33, 182.) Photo: Spring, 1973, courtesy of the Hamilton County Park District. The braced-frame addition on the left (south) was probably added after the house was moved from near the Ohio River. When an early building aligns to a surveyed street or road, it is good reason to suspect the structure was moved.

31. Hamilton County, Village of Elizabethtown. Two story log house. (See Figures 29, 30, 32, 33, 182.) Photo: 19 August 1973. North end and west side. The chimney may always have been on the interior for there are no stains on the gable logs, and the corner stairwell looks original beside the chimney. Often one can do no more than guess on these early, remodeled structures.

32. Hamilton County, Village of Elizabethtown. Two story log house. (See Figures 29, 30, 31, 33, 182.) Photo: 19 August 1973. South end and west side. Two doors were needed for the south addition. With one door in the back wall and no windows, the rear shed addition could have been constructed with the house, else at a very early date.

33. Hamilton County, Miami Township. Two story log house. (See Figures 29, 30, 31, 32, 182.) Photo: 15 August 1975. The Hamilton County Park District moved this house two miles south from Elizabethtown to their "Shawnee Lookout Park." Considering the condition of many of the wall logs and the difficulties of moving, the restoration work was well handled (the gables were probably clapboarded, however).

34. Brown County, City of Georgetown. One and a half story log house, *ca.* 1793. Photo: April, 1977. Rear view of Dixon—Washburn house. Door and window on end of house are additions. Some logs replaced. Originally, the house had only front and back doors and a single front window. The fenestration would be in keeping with other extant 1790 houses.

35. Hamilton County, Anderson Township. One and a half story log house built *ca.* 1796 by Ichabod Miller. Size, 21 by 18 feet; 14 foot eave. Photo: 20 February 1972. South front, east end. This house is located in the Mount Washington area of Cincinnati, and is maintained by the local historical society. This was near the site of Columbia in the 1790s, one of the earliest settlements in Ohio. (National Register of Historic Places.)

36. Montgomery County, City of Dayton. Two story log house and tavern. (See Figure 37.) Photo: February, 1969. Present west side, rear. "Newcom Tavern" is now located in Carillon Park, where it was moved in 1964. Previously, it had stood on Monument Avenue east of Main Street, where it had been moved in 1892. Its original site was near the southwest corner of Main and Monument. Buildings such as this, which have been remodeled and repaired as well as moved, are difficult, if not impossible, to evaluate; one can only rely on the basic configuration, not the details of construction, as being close to "original."

37. Montgomery County, City of Dayton. Two story log house built *ca.* 1798 for Colonel George Newcom. Moved in 1892 and 1964. (See Figure 36.) Photo: February, 1969. Present east side, front. "Newcom Tavern" has been through numerous remodelings and restorations. On arriving at the site of Dayton in 1796, Newcom built a small log cabin, then hired one Robert Edgar to build a hewed log house; Edgar's 22 by 18 foot house is probably the left side of the tavern in this view. Apparently the house had been altered to its present configuration by 1798. The enlarged structure was completely whitewashed on the exterior. It has served as a house, school, church, courthouse, tavern (until 1836), and store.

38. Greene County, City of Xenia. Two story log house built in 1803 by or for James Galloway. This photograph was taken by the author about 1945. The pictures of the Galloway house in this book, see Figures 39, 40, 41, 42, document the wanderings and fate of a single structure, a history that can be quickly forgotten.

39. Greene County, City of Xenia. Two story log house, 1803. (See Figures 38, 40, 41, 42.) Photo: 8 July 1967. Front, originally faced west. This house was built on the site of Galloway's 1797 cabin, approximately four miles north of Xenia. It was moved to Xenia in 1937, then to this site in 1965. Tecumseh, the famous Shawanee chief, visited this house on occasion.

40. Greene County, City of Xenia. Two story log house, 1803. (See Figures 38, 39, 41, 42.) Photo: 8 July 1967. Rear, originally faced east. The lack of second story windows implies the double porch was original to the house; double porches were used on log houses at Fort Wayne prior to 1806, and John Johnston had a double porch on his log house north of Piqua in 1808.

41. Greene County, City of Xenia. Two story log house, 1803. (See Figures 38, 39, 40, 42.) Photo: 6 April 1974. Present south side, front. The tornado of April third passed over the Galloway house. The roof structure remained partially intact when it fell behind the house; however, the wall logs of the second floor must have been scattered some distance, for only a few were recovered. The Galloway house was damaged in much the same manner as nearby brick and frame houses.

42. Greene County, City of Xenia. Two story log house, 1803. (See Figures 38, 39, 40, 41.) Photo: September, 1976. (The sign bears the date of Galloway's first structure.) The Galloway house rebuilt. The house used for replacement logs is shown in Figures 162, 178, 198, 204. Galloway built a third house, of stone, about a quarter of a mile north of this structure in 1809.

IV
INDIAN HOUSING

There are many descriptions of Indian housing in Ohio in the eighteenth century, although references to log buildings are scarce. One of the earliest and best reports is given by Col. James Smith in his *An Account of the Remarkable Occurrences in the Life and Travels of Colonel James Smith, During his Captivity with the Indians in the Years 1755, '56, '57, '58, & '59*. The log "cabin" which he described was built west of Cleveland, near the mouth of Black River, in the winter of 1755–56. Smith lived in this structure while he was held captive by a mixed group of Indians, primarily Caughnewagas but including Delawares and Wyandots. This rudimentary log building could have had Indian rather than European antecedents, although it is unlikely it was entirely of Indian origin because the eastern Indians had been in contact with whites some 140 years by the time of Smith's description.

> They made their winter cabin in the following form: they cut logs about fifteen feet long, and laid these logs upon each other, and drove posts in the ground at each end to keep them together; the posts they tied together at the top with bark, and by this means raised a wall fifteen feet long, and about four feet high, and in the same manner they raised another wall opposite to this, at about twelve feet distance; then they drove forks in the ground in the

> centre of each end, and laid a strong pole from end to end on these forks; and from these walls to the poles, they set up poles instead of rafters, and on these they tied small poles in place of laths; and a cover was made of lynn bark, which will run even in the winter season.
>
> At the end of these walls they set up split timber, so that they had timber all round, excepting a door at each end. At the top, in place of a chimney, they left an open place, and for bedding they laid down the aforesaid kind of bark, on which they spread bear skins. From end to end of this hut along the middle there were fires, which the squaws made of dry split wood, and the holes or open places that appeared, the squaws stopped with moss, which they collected from old logs; and at the door they hung bear skin, and notwithstanding the winters are hard here, our lodging was much better than what I expected.[1]

John Heckewelder, a Moravian missionary, describes a similar structure in his *Narrative.*[2] The Delawares, at Captives' Town (Antrim Township, Wyandot County), also built a similar structure in December 1781. David Zeisberger, the famous Moravian missionary, described it as "a structure of poles laid horizontally between upright stakes, the crevices being filled with moss."[3] This structure, intended as a church, was built "in less than a fortnight." Since the details of the winter cabin and the church are essentially the same, it is possible that the cabin was the product of the few Delawares among the Caughnewagas. By conjecture, this style of log building, based on the traditional bark "long house," was probably a version of the white settler's log house constructed in a fashion commensurate with the tools the migratory Indians wished to carry. Smith refers to the Indians using their "tomahawks" to cut the logs and peel the bark. These tomahawks were probably what are referred to today as "squaw axes," smaller versions of the poll-less European ax. The upright stakes used to support the walls could easily have been driven with a large stone. Actually, there is nothing about these structures that would require the use of iron tools, but it is debatable whether such cabins were known by Indians before the onset of Western civilization.

Zeisberger wrote a history of the North American Indians while he was living at the Moravian missions in present Tuscarawas County, Ohio, in 1779–80. He commented on Indian housing:

> Houses of the Indians were formerly only huts and for the most part remain such humble structures, particularly in regions far removed from the habitation of whites. These huts are built either of bast (tree-bark peeled off in the summer) or the walls are made of boards covered with bast. They are low structures. Fire is made in the middle of the hut under an opening whence the smoke escapes. Among the Mingoes and the Six Nations (western Iroquois and New York State Iroquois) one rarely sees houses other than such huts built entirely of bast, which, however, are frequently very long, having at least from two to four fire-places; . . . . Among the Delawares each family prefers to have its own house, hence they are small. The Mingoes make a rounded, arched roof, the Delawares on the contrary, a high pitched, peaked roof. The latter, coming much in contact with the whites, as they do not live more than a hundred miles from Pittsburg, have learned to build block houses or have hired whites to build them. Christian Indians generally build proper and comfortable houses and the savages who seek to follow their example in work and household arrangement learn much from them.[4]

What Zeisberger meant by "the walls are made of boards" is hard to fathom; the Shawanese houses at Little Chillicothe (now Oldtown, Greene County) in 1779 were also made of "board."[5] As early as 1666 the Mohawks along the Mohawk River in the village of Tenontogare (west of Schenectady, New York) lived in braced-frame buildings with plank walls. The buildings followed the plan of the traditional bark long houses, some being over 100 feet long and housing eight families.[6] No doubt the technique came directly from the French; it is remarkable how quickly the Indians adopted this relatively complex—when compared to log—method of construction.

The term "blockhouse" was in use in the eighteenth and nineteenth centuries to differentiate between a hewed log and a round log structure; the hewed log house was called a blockhouse. Of course, blockhouse was also a military term having a different connotation. Since a squared log house generally had smaller gaps between the logs, it was safer to defend than a round log cabin. Thus the term blockhouse was applied to a very strong military fortification, a soundly constructed house for personal defense, or a house built of hewed logs rather than round logs. The semantics of "blockhouse" has caused a great deal of confusion among historians, amateur and professional, and has led to much misinterpretation. Unfortunately, it is often impossible, when reading old documents, to decide which meaning was intended.[7]

If any Indian nation was in a position to use and spread log building, it was the Delaware. They were descendants of the Lenape Nation, probably western Indians who had moved to the Susquehanna and Delaware rivers and the Delaware Bay area well before whites arrived in North America. The Delawares on the Schuylkill River moved to the Susquehanna in 1709 because of pressure from the Five Nations to join in warfare, first against the French, then against the English. (Thomas Dongan, former governor of New York, had sold the lands of the Susquehanna River valley to William Penn in January 1696.) By 1728 the Delawares were complaining about a colony of Palatine Mennonites settling on Indian land in Montgomery County, Pennsylvania.[8] The Delawares subsequently moved slowly to the west, many in close alliance with the Moravian missions in Pennsylvania and then in Ohio in the 1770s and 1780s. Some of the Ohio Delawares went on to Canada, where their descendants are still living. Throughout these moves, the Delawares were in the precise geographic locations to learn log building techniques from the Swedes and Finns in the seventeenth century, and from the Germans in the eighteenth century. Most of the Nation, but not all tribes, were known to be "peacemakers," who seemingly stayed near the European settlements by choice. Consequently, their nomadic habits and Indian customs were subjected to enormous pressures of change.

The comments by Smith on Indian log building in Ohio

could refer to the Delawares; certainly the group at Captives' Town were Delawares. At Easton, Pennsylvania, in July of 1757, Delaware Chief Teedyuscung made the following request of the governor of Pennsylvania: "And as we intend to make a Settlement at *Wyomen*, and to build different Houses from what we have done heretofore, such as may last not only for a little Time, but for our Children after us; we desire you will assist us in making our Settlements, and send us Persons to instruct us in building Houses. . . ."[9] The village of Wyomen was near present Wilkes-Barre. The request was granted; ten "cabins," 10 by 14 feet, and one cabin, 16 by 24 feet, were constructed of hewed, dovetailed logs. In September 1768, according to Zeisberger, the village of "Garochati on the Pemidhannek" [River] in western Pennsylvania had "houses built in various styles. . . ." The account continues: "Some are weather boarded block-houses and have chimneys. Some are two story houses, having a staircase on the outside. These houses have a tower-like appearance, because they are not more than fourteen feet in length and in breadth. All the work on them was done by Indians and, considering that they have very crude tools, the structures are very creditable to the builders."[10] The previous year, September 1767, Zeisberger had visited Friedenshuetten, Pennsylvania: "From the 26th to the 29th I found much pleasure in visiting the Indians in their dwellings. Many were engaged in building log houses. They build very neat houses of hewn timber, with chimneys and glass windows, and fit them up very tastefully."[11] Friedenshuetten was indeed an elaborate Indian mission. John Heckewelder also visited the village in 1767; in his *Narrative* he comments:

> Their meeting-house was much too small to contain their number—wherefore they built a large and spacious church, of squared white pine timber, shingle roofed, with a neat cupola and bell on the top. . . . They did all their work in the best manner possible, both in building and fencing, so that at this time there were forty well built houses of squared timber, and shingle roofed, in the village; and the gardens back of them were all in good clapboard fence.[12]

The three Moravian missions in Ohio—Schoenbrunn, Gnaddenhuetten, and Lichtenau—located along the Tuscarawas River in Tuscarawas County, were begun some five years later than Friedenshuetten. The layout of these villages, which were devoted primarily to the Delawares, was very similar to that of the missions in Pennsylvania. The Ohio missions, established just before the Revolutionary War, lasted only a short time because the Christian Delawares were subjected to much harassment by Indian allies of the British. Nicholas Cresswell, the redoubtable English diarist, visited Schoenbrunn, arriving at the village on Sunday afternoon, 27 August 1775. He wrote:

> It is a pretty town consisting of about sixty houses, and is built of logs and covered with Clapboards. It is regularly laid out in three spacious streets which meet in the centre, where there is a large meeting house built of logs sixty foot square covered with Shingles. Glass in the windows and a Bell, a good plank floor with two rows of forms. Adorned with some few pieces of Scripture painting, but very indifferently executed. All about the meeting house is kept very clean.[13]

Both Zeisberger and John Ettwein described the house of Chief Netawatwes at Gekelemukpechunk (present Newcomerstown, Tuscarawas County), the capital of the Delawares. Zeisberger states that, in 1770, Gekelemukpechunk "was a large and flourishing town of about one hundred houses, mostly built of logs."[14] He was the guest of Netawatwes, whose house had a shingle roof, board floors, a staircase, and a stone chimney. When Ettwein was at the village in 1772, Netawatwes still had his "well built house of nicely squared logs, with a shingle roof."[15]

The Reverend David McClure also visited Newcomerstown. He described the village, "Kekalemahpehoong," in his *Diary* under the date 21 September, 1772: "Some of the houses are well built, with hewed logs, with stone chimnies, chambers & sellers. These I was told were built by the english captives, in the time of the French wars."[16] McClure described Netawatwes' house as "the largest, & built of small square logs." Planks around the walls, covered with the skins of buffalo and bears, served for beds and seats.[17] In the entry for Friday, 25 September, 1772, McClure described the "Conjuror's" house:

> I was in the Conjuror's house, it was the best built in town except the king's. A cellar with stone wall—a stare case, a convenient stone chimney & fire place & closets & apartments, gave it the appearance of an english dwelling. Between the house & the bank of the River was a regular & thrifty peach orchard. The house was for sale, but no one would purchase it. The price was fixed as low as one dollar. Such dread have they of the secret & invisible power of the Conjurors.[18]

It is somewhat difficult to resolve the anomaly suggested by McClure—that of an Indian shaman attempting to sell his house! One can only wonder why he was selling; presumably he would be selling to any buyer, yet a fur trader shouldn't have been afraid of the Conjuror's "secret & invisible power." Life in colonial Ohio was certainly anything but simple, at times.

By the third quarter of the eighteenth century, Indians other than the Delawares were building log structures within the state. The Shawanese village of Little Chillicothe (present Oldtown, Greene County) was attacked by a company of militia under Col. John Bowman in May 1779. A white prisoner of the Shawanese described the village at the time of the attack:

> Northeast of the center of the town stood the council house—a large building, said to have been sixty feet square, built of round hickory logs, one story high, with gable ends open and upright posts supporting the roof. . . . There were several board houses or huts in the south part of the village—some ten or twelve.
>
> [During the attack] the men reached the board shanties on the south; and at once began the work of plundering, giving the savages ample time to fortify themselves by fastening securely the door of the huge building they had congregated in.[19]

Since Bowman did not risk an attack on the council house, one must assume that it was well constructed and easily defended. The remains of this building supposedly were still visible in 1840.

In 1772, the Reverend David Jones described the Indian village of "Chillicaathee," which stood on the present site of Frankfort, Ross County. In this Shawanese village the houses were made of logs, but apparently in a haphazard fashion: "Nor is there any more regularity observed in this particular than in their morals, for any man erects his house as fancy directs."[20] In the Reverend Oliver M. Spencer's narrative, *Indian Captivity*, there is a description of the English fur traders' village known as "The Glaize," which stood at the junction of the Auglaize and Maumee rivers at the present site of the city of Defiance, Defiance County. In 1792 this post consisted of "five or six cabins and log houses." The residence of one George Ironside was "a large hewed log house, divided below into three apartments."[21] These "apartments" were used, respectively, as a warehouse, store, and dwelling. There was also a small stockade enclosing two log houses—one a storehouse and the other a residence.

Spencer provides an excellent description of an Indian bark cabin belonging to an Iroquois "priestess," Cooh-coo-cheeh, living with the Shawnee in northern Ohio.

> Covering an area of fourteen by twenty-eight feet, its frame was constructed of small poles, of which some, planted upright in the ground, served as posts and studs, supporting the ridge poles and eve [*sic*] bearers, while others, firmly tied to these by thongs of hickory bark, formed girders, braces, laths, and rafters. This frame was covered with large pieces of elm bark, seven or eight feet long, and three or four feet wide; which being pressed flat, and well dried to prevent their curling, fastened to the poles by thongs of bark, formed the weather boarding, and roof of the cabin. At its western end was a narrow doorway, about six feet high, closed, when necessary, by a single piece of bark placed beside it, and fastened by a brace, set either within, or on the outside, as occasion required. Within, separated by a bark partition, were two apartments, of which the inner one . . . was occupied as a pantry, a spare bed

> room, and at times as a sanctuary . . .; the other . . . was in common use by the family, both as a lodging, sitting, cooking, and eating room. On the ground, in the centre of this apartment, was placed the fire; and over it, suspended from the ridge pole in the middle of an aperture left for the passage of the smoke, was a wooden trammel. . . .[22]

Certainly bark had been a traditional building material among the Indians before they became familiar with whites, although the use of roofing shakes by the latter might have altered the Indian method of overlapping or sizing roofing material. Bark roofing on an Indian log cabin is mentioned by John Brickell in his "Narrative of John Brickell's Captivity among the Delaware Indians." Brickell, who was captured in 1791, spent that summer with one "Whingwy Pooshies" and his wife somewhere on the Auglaize River near the Maumee towns. (Brickell and Spencer were quite close, geographically, at about the same time.) Brickell made the following comments: "Our cabin was of round logs, like those of the first settlers, except the roof was of bark and it had no floor. It consisted of a single room with a French made chimney of cat-and-clay. The door was made of hewed puncheons. . . .[23] It is most enlightening that Brickell related the round log cabin to "first settlers"; he certainly implies that two styles of construction were recognized, round and hewed log. His reference to a cat-and-clay chimney as being "French" in style is the only such comment found by this writer. There is no reason to think the English settlers in New England in the seventeenth century learned such a style from the French. Perhaps the continuity of such a building practice was stronger among the French traders and settlers than the English, et al., by the end of the eighteenth century. However, in William Nowlin's 1876 book, *The Bark Covered House*, the cat-and-clay chimney is called "Dutch."[24] Since the Nowlin family was from eastern New York State before settling in Wayne County, Michigan, in the mid-1830s, the designation "Dutch Chimney" was probably of New York origin. Inasmuch as Brickell felt the cat-and-clay chimney was French and Nowlin thought it was

Dutch (German, one presumes), there is every reason to suspect that this method of construction was so established in the United States that its true origin had been forgotten—if ever known. Some ethnic groups, and certain small isolated communities, continued the use of the stick chimney well into the nineteenth century, particularly in the antebellum South.

It is obvious that Indians in direct contact with Western civilization quickly adapted log construction to their own needs. The Delawares, long under the influence of the Moravian Christian Indian missions in both Pennsylvania and Ohio, could build very elaborate log houses when the need arose. An old story, occasionally encountered in a county history, credits the Indians with having known log construction before whites arrived. It is easy to see how such an assumption was made, considering that most immigrants were ignorant of any aspect of the Indians' way of life. To stumble on an Indian village of log houses in the wilds of Ohio in the eighteenth century must have confused many a pioneer. It is entirely feasible that the Delawares and/or the Moravians were responsible for the surprisingly widespread use of the log house by various Indian tribes in Ohio. However, it is certain that the Indians contributed nothing to Western knowledge of log building in the seventeenth century, and probably knew nothing of log structures prior to this time with the possible exception of using logs for stockade walls.

If any forms of shelters could be said to be "typical" of the Indians of any tribe resident in eighteenth-century Ohio, they would be the bark-covered wigwam and multi-family "long house." Both were constructed of poles which were stuck into the ground, bent in arches and fastened at the top, and covered with bark (usually slippery elm) or occasionally skins or woven mats. In 1790 the common dwellings at Upper Sandusky "were all constructed of bark supported by corner posts and cross timbers, to which the bark was secured by strings made of its inner fibres."[25] During the latter half of the century, however, the Indians utilized a wide variety of shelters, and were building their traditional wigwams of "board" or "plank" and their long houses, or council houses, of log. As might be expected, the council house, which served religious, governmental, and social needs, remained fairly consistent in form and construction to the end of the reservation period in Ohio (1842), the greatest changes being in methods of construction as new generations of Indians, without the strong traditions of their eighteenth-century ancestors, came along.

Of course, the cultures of all the Indian tribes resident in Ohio suffered declines based on the Indians' reliance on trade goods and the establishment of trade and agricultural centers in reservation districts. This cultural breakdown was under way by at least mid-eighteenth century among the tribes and clans emigrating to Ohio and was very apparent during the Revolutionary War period when so many villages were mixtures of individuals rather than unified families or clans. With increased dependency upon manufactured goods, one would expect more and more Western influence on the traditional Indian cultures, and this is exactly what happened; the preceeding quotations demonstrate the presence of the white's tools and dwellings. The council house at Newcomerstown in 1772, a "a long building covered with hemlock bark," had a "swinging door at each end."[26] No doubt a hinged door is meant; here was true eclecticism on the frontier.

About thirty-seven years later, the council house at Greentown, Ashland County, which was 50 feet long by 30 feet wide, was constructed of the age-old pole substructure, but covered with clapboards.[27] It is conceivable that small strips of bark were mistaken for clapboards, but it is equally as possible the clapboards came from a sawmill. By the fall of 1809 there were many vertical mills at work in Ohio, and the Indians were probably as quick to adopt the use of sawed lumber as they were any of the other products of Western civilization. However, the word "clapboard" was used too frequently in the eighteenth century, and before Ohio sawmills, to describe the covering of roofs and walls of Indian dwellings to doubt the veracity of the observers, so it must be assumed the Indians were well-versed in riving timber. The old Wyandot council house at Crane Town (the first Upper Sandusky was renamed Crane Town after

Tarhe's death in 1818) reinforces this contention, for its appearance, ca. 1824, was described by the Reverend James Finley as "an open building, made of split slabs, laid between two posts stuck in the ground, and covered with bark peeled from the trees."[28] Henry Howe notes that the old council house was built "principally" of bark, and was about 100 feet long by 15 feet wide.[29] The method of construction goes directly back to the mid-eighteenth century—the use of posts to support the side walls, in this case of "split slabs" instead of logs, and bark roofing probably laid on a framework such as described by James Smith.

If the dwelling Smith described could be accepted as an Indian version of log cabin construction, could not the Upper Sandusky council house be a version of French "Manitoba Frame" construction? It is possible—each could even be a version of the other. But another possibility presents itself—that the use of posts supporting walls of logs or split timber, as well as a ridge-poll form of roof framing, may have had a long tradition among various Indian tribes and date to the first contacts with whites on the eastern seaboard. As stated earlier, it is doubtful the technique could be older because of the difficulty of working timber without metal tools, but the possibility does exist.

Upper Sandusky was extremely important during the last quarter of the eighteenth century for it served as a rendezvous for the Ohio Indians allied to the British headquartered at Detroit—military strategy, political intrigue, and fur trade economics centered around the village during the Revolutionary and Indian War period. During the nineteenth century, the village was part of the Wyandot reservation which was ceded to the United States in 1842. As part of the reimbursement procedure under the treaty, a careful survey was made of the reservation in 1844 which included details of the Indians' dwellings, outbuildings, and land improvements. Sheet 7 of the survey covers the township containing Upper Sandusky and portions of the eight surrounding townships. There were a total of 77 log cabins and 64 log houses on this one section of the reservation.

No doubt some of the structures dated to the eighteenth century. The descriptions are given as written by the surveyor: Cabin, 16. Old Cabin, 14. Log Cabin, 36. Round Log Cabin, 7. Hewed Log Cabin, 12. Log House, 5. Hewed Log House, 28. Hewed Log House, Shingle Roof, 4. Good Hewed Log House, 13. Round Log House, 4. Double Hewed Log House, 2. Hewed Log Barn, 2. Hewed Log Stable and Cribs, 1. Plank House, Weatherboarded, Shingle Roof, 1. Double Hewed Log House, Shingle Roof, Porch, 1. Good Hewed Log House, Two Rooms, Porch, 1.[30]

Notes

1. Smith, *An Account of the Remarkable Occurrences*, pp. 37–38.
2. Heckewelder, *Narrative*, p. 298.
3. De Schweinitz, *Life and Times of David Zeisberger*, p. 529.
4. Zeisberger, "David Zeisberger's History," pp. 17–18.
5. Randall, "Bowman's Expedition," p. 454.
6. Edmonds, *Musket and the Cross*, p. 410.
7. For several hundred years the German word *Blockhaus* or *Blochhaus* meant a strong, defensible structure which obstructed a passage, such as a road, valley, or river. By the eighteenth century the word had acquired a new meaning, a primary meaning to many non-Germanic immigrants, which indicated a timber structure.
8. These early movements of the Delawares can be traced in Eshleman's *Lancaster County Indians*, which is a compilation of various colonial documents.
9. Thomson, *An Enquiry*, pp. 115–16.
10. Hulbert and Schwarze, "Morvavian Records," p. 82.
11. Ibid., p. 9.
12. Heckewelder, *Narrative*, p. 97.
13. Cresswell, *Journal*, p. 106. A copy of a "Gnaddenhuetten Diary" in the collections of the Ohio Historical Society comments that "Mr. Anderson came with a gentleman from Pittsburgh" on August 28. This is circumstantial evidence, but presumably refers to Cresswell; much in Cresswell's narrative seems overly fortuitous, and needs supporting evidence. There is no comment on his visit in the society's copy of a "Schoenbrunn Diary." In Heckewelder's *Narrative*, p. 128, the dimensions of the Schoenbrunn "chapel" are given as 40 by 36 feet, certainly quite a bit

different from Cresswell's 60-foot walls. The church at Gnaddenhuetten was smaller; both were built of hewed logs, had shingle roofs, and cupolas and bells in a manner similar to the Friedenshuetten church. The Jones's *Journal* entry for Sunday, 14 February 1773 gives the size of the Gnad-denguetten church as about 22 by 18 feet and comments there was a good floor and chimney.

14. De Schweinitz, *Life and Times of David Zeisberger*, p. 366.
15. Hamilton, *John Ettwein*, pp. 261–62.
16. McClure, *Diary*, p. 61.
17. Ibid., p. 62.
18. Ibid., p. 68.
19. See "Bowman's Expedition," pp. 454–55. This same information, with more detail, is quoted in Galloway's *Old Chillicothe*, p. 13; he credits the Draper manuscripts. Galloway says the Indians had early learned the use of the ax, saw, and auger from white prisoners, and had purchased the tools from French and English traders for more than fifty years. He had many friends among the "Absentee Shawnees," descendants of over 1,000 members of the tribe who had emigrated to Missouri before the first attack on Chillicothe in 1779, so the oral tradition was probably sound.
20. Jones, *Journal*, p. 56.
21. Spencer, *Indian Captivity*, pp. 90–91.
22. Ibid., pp. 78–81.
23. Brickell, "Narrative of John Brickwell's Captivity," p. 47.
24. Nowlin, *Bark Covered House*, p. 90.
25. Johnston, *Narrative*, p. 92. See also McClure, *Diary*, p. 61.
26. McClure, *Diary*, pp. 62–63.
27. Hill, *History of Ashland County*, p. 51.
28. Finley, *Life Among the Indians*, p. 422. After the death of Tarhe, The Crane, in 1818, the Indians moved their council house about four miles southwest and named the new site "Upper Sandusky." The old village by that name was renamed Crane Town. The "old council house" stood about one and a half miles north of Crane Town.
29. Howe, *Historical Collections*, p. 552. The Seneca council house, in Green Creek Township, Seneca County, was about sixty by twenty-five feet; see Butterfield, *History of Seneca County*, p. 162.
30. "Map of the Surveys in the Wyandot Cession at U. Sandusky," Sheet 7. 9 March 1844. Attested by William Johnston, surveyor general, Cincinnati. Townships 1, 2, and 3 South, Ranges 13, 14, and 15 East.

V
THE PIONEERS AND SETTLERS

> While pioneer life had its rough sides, and its deprivations, it must not be supposed, for a moment, that it was a dark and gloomy life, and destitute of joys and pleasures. There is a certain peculiar pleasure attached to it that is almost indescribable. Chopping in the woods, burning brush and log heaps, wife and children joining in the work; the quiet and solitude of the forest, fishing and hunting; the relief from the restraints and conventionalities of refined society; the hope for future prosperity; of nearer neighbors; of better roads and markets; of bridges, stock-growing, fields enlarging, sons and daughters growing into usefulness—these and a thousand and one other incidents made "the life in the woods" wonderfully fascinating, and created around it a halo of most peculiar happiness and loveliness. Any survivor of that generation of men, will now exclaim, when recurring to those days: "The life in the woods for me!"[1]

The greatest difficulty encountered in dealing with contemporary literature on log building is not the scarcity of references, but their abundance. Although only a sampling can be included here, most references are of a similar nature, for variants of construction were of little interest to the pioneers and settlers of the Ohio Country. What was important was that buildings of any kind could be erected in a frontier area. That thousands of log buildings went up at the turn of the nineteenth century proves that our ancestors were able to meet wilderness conditions and prosper—and that the log structure was not nearly as difficult to build as is commonly imagined today.

"Log cabin life" is a subject dealt with to the point of tedium in many Ohio county histories, but finding technical descriptions of log construction in any source is another matter. It was probably such a mundane occupation that details interesting to our generation were seldom noted. Because many references include construction as part of log cabin life, some structural details appear in this chapter. More specific details of construction from contemporary sources are included in chapter 12.

Thomas Worthington, an Ohio governor and United States senator, built a double-pen log house on his estate at Chillicothe in 1801–02. This "Belleview" grew to be more than 80 feet long before the family moved into the extant stone mansion known as "Adena."[2] An excellent description of Worthington's log home is given by his daughter, Sarah, in *Private Memoir of Thomas Worthington, Esq.*:

> Our first habitation there [our temporary dwelling at Adena, to which my parents had removed in 1802] was very comfortable, and in several of the rooms there was even an air of elegance apparent. It was built of hewed logs, filled between the timbers with stones and plaster, whitened with lime within and without. Two large pens, as they were termed, in the interior about eighteen feet square, a story and a half high, were first raised at about twenty feet from each other. The space between was weather-boarded and plastered within. This was the drawing-room, duly adorned by pier-glasses . . . and the old mahogany and cherry tables and chairs brought from Virginia. The old fashioned brass andirons brightened the fire-place. The room was well carpeted, and the windows were hung with the prettiest of white curtains, trimmed with fine netting, the work of my mother and other relatives. On one side of the parlor was my father's library, which was furnished with a bed, for hospitality. On the other side was my mother's room. Then followed a range of inferior construction, for the dining-room,

> kitchen, and rooms for the servants—all with half stories above, which served as bed rooms for the family, store rooms, etc.[3]
>
> This house . . . extended, in its length of seven or eight rooms, in nearly a direct line on the lawn some thirty yards below the steps leading to the hall door of the present residence, the library being the southernmost and nearest the steps.[4]

This was undoubtedly the best finished and furnished double-pen log house in Ohio in 1802. It provides contrast to the usual descriptions of the rough accommodations found in most log cabins.

The fact that a building was made of logs did not mean that it had to be crude in construction or in furnishings. Most permanent log houses and barns were, in reality, well made and finished. Whereas the log cabin was a part of the wilderness epic in Ohio, the log house represented established settlement. There is truly a difference between living in a house built of logs—and a log house. The first implies necessity, primitiveness; the second, a conscious choice. A sophisticated family from the East might well build a log house simply because they expected to begin a brick or stone house as soon as help and material were available. Conversely, another family might be content to exist in a log cabin due to indolence or the expectation of moving with the frontier. This "indolence" was noted by the eastern traveler, Cyrus P. Bradley, in his "Journal" in June 1835, when he wrote of the log cabins in Pickaway Township, Pickaway County. "Many wealthy farmers, who are worth fifty thousand dollars and who both occupy and rent vast tracts of rich and profitable territory, are content to live and die without comfort and without self-respect in these wretched hovels."[5]

There is no doubt that most settlers expected to improve their homesteads and were content with a log cabin only until they were able to provide a larger, more formal home. In Ohio it is still common to see a combination of a small house, usually frame or sided-log, attached to a large brick or frame Victorian house. The original structure was retained as a summer kitchen or work area when the new house was built. Thomas Hulme described the underlying attitude well in this paragraph from his journal:

> At present his [Mr. Birkbeck's] habitation is a cabin, the building of which cost only 20 dollars; this little hutch is near the spot where he is about to build his house, which he intends to have in the most eligible situation in the prairie for convenience to fuel and for shelter in winter, as well as for breezes in summer, and will, when that is completed, make one of its appurtenances. I like this plan of keeping the old loghouse; it reminds the grand children and their children's children of what their ancestor has done for their sake.[6]

Hulme was writing of a homestead in Illinois. In reference to Ohio, and in a sarcastic vein, is the comment from the "Journal" of Cyrus P. Bradley, a native of New Hampshire who spent two years at Dartmouth College, then took a trip west for his health. Filled with pessimism by much that he observed in Ohio, he wished he had the skill of a Mrs. Trollope in his writing. However, there is no doubt his descriptions are accurate, for his critical eye was not tempered by romanticism. The following description of log houses found between Marion and Sandusky was made about 13 June 1835:

> There are occasional huts located in these unhealthy situations [wet prairies], and here and there an open log-shed adjoins one of these cabins, in which is kept a fresh team of horses for "the stage." We entered one house—'twas a new one—properly a log-house—the logs being roughly hewn and notched at the ends and a place being left for a window sash. It was all in one room, about two-thirds of which has a raised floor, of timber chopped down to about three inches in thickness. At one end, was a large fireplace, on the bare ground and the kitchen utensils were hung around it. The chimney, as is invariably the case, was outside of the building, of sticks of wood built cob-house fashion and plastered with clay—the oven of clay and brick is a separate structure, out doors, and erected upon wooden blocks. . . . We took the liberty to peep into the first structure, the "old house," for this which I have been describing is the second step towards grandeur, and one more than most of these

> settlers make, which looked rather forlorn in its dismantled, inglorious condition. . . . This structure is called the cabin and is the settlers' primitive residence—composed of rough, unbarked logs, heaped up as we build log fence, with a hole to crawl in, and perhaps another for a window. First in the scale, is the cabin, then the log-house, then the frame building, and then brick. . . . Specimens of all these, as they have been in turn occupied and deserted, may be occasionally seen on the farms of some industrious and enterprising farmer.[7]

It might be added that Bradley saw little to admire in Ohio, probably because of the enormous contrast between the New England he knew and the emerging settlements. In admiring Mrs. Trollope, Bradley reveals himself as a pretentious and subjective interpreter of a new world which he did not understand.

The double-pen log building, as described by Worthington's daughter, was a standard solution to the problem of achieving a maximum of space with a minimum of material and effort. The references to such houses in Ohio are common, but no examples have yet been located (1984). The double-pen barn can still be found, however, throughout the southern half of the state. This design was ideally suited to the functions of a barn in the nineteenth century (see chapter 8). Fortescue Cuming wrote of two double-pen buildings, a house and a tavern, in his *Sketches of a Tour to the Western Country* (1807–09). The double-pen structure was admirably suited to a tavern, and many have been described in Ohio.

> Four miles from hence [Cambridge, Guernsey County] through a hilly country, brought me to Beymer's tavern, passing a drove of one hundred and thirty cows and oxen, which one Johnston was driving from the neighbourhood of Lexington in Kentucky, to Baltimore. . . .
>
> The drover with six assistants, two horsemen, two family wagons, and the stage wagon, put up at Beymer's for the night, so that the house which was only a double cabin, was well filled. . . .
>
> I had a good supper and bed, and found Beymer's double cabin a most excellent house of accommodation. . . .[8]

43. Brown County, Perry Township. Two story log tavern and house. (See Figures 44, 211.) Photo: Late summer, 1969, by Susannah Lane. Though no doubt displaying some alteration and repair, this view of the house is probably much as it appeared after being converted from a tavern. The date of remodeling is unknown, but, stylistically, it must have occurred about 1840.

44. Brown County, Perry Township. Two story L-shaped log tavern/house dating about 1810. Size, 48 by 18 feet, with 18 foot "L". (See Figures 43, 211.) Photo: August, 1972. South, front. This large structure was apparently built as a tavern, remodeled into a house about 1840, returned to a tavern during the latter part of the century, then back again to a house. The original fenestration is apparent in this photo, single windows between the present double windows (compare to the Ft. Whistler building, Figure 45). The lower right window was cut out for a doorway to a tap room during the building's second use as a tavern. Originally, there was a large chimney on the west end (left); it was moved to the interior during the first remodeling. The chimney on the right terminates on the second floor. The former log "L" on the northwest corner (left, rear) was probably used as a kitchen; two walls are missing, no doubt due to a fire, leaving one log wall to the rear of the central hall and two replacement frame walls. This structure cannot be considered a true double-pen house because it was planned and constructed with a unified fabric. (National Register of Historic Places.)

45. Daguerreotype made in 1852 of the demolition of the last building of "Ft. Whistler," in Ft. Wayne, Indiana. Ft. Whistler was constructed in 1815. Compare this building with the tavern/house in Brown County, Figure 44.

46. Putnam County, Perry Township. Double-pen log tavern built *ca.* 1821 by Sebastian Shroufe. Illustration from Howe, *Historical Collections of Ohio* (1847), p. 428 *ff*. Henry Howe sketched this tavern in 1846 while working on his history of Ohio. According to a letter by Samuel S. Holden, son of Pierson B. Holden whose name is on the signboard, the tavern was constructed by "two men and a woman," one of the men being Shroufe (or Sroufe, Srouff, Srofe). Shroufe apparently settled in Section 21 of Perry Township in 1821; the tavern was up by 1828 when an election was held in it. The Holden family acquired the property from Shroufe. A similar tavern, "M'Intire's," was described and drawn from memory for Howe's chapter on Muskingum County.

47. "Dwelling of a Settler in Indiana," 1833 watercolor by Karl Bodmer (1809–1893). This double-pen log house was not finished. The pen to the right has its fireplace opening, but it is being used as a barn; the roof was not completed, for the roof-jack is still in place. Reproduction courtesy of the Joslyn Art Museum, Omaha, Nebraska; the Northern Gas Company Collection.

48. Half of stereo photograph entitled [Rutherford B.] "Hayes' Army Headquarters" (probably West Virginia). Photograph by George W. Kirk, Huntington, *ca.* 1864. Double-pen log house. Right pen converted to barn, or to military use, by elongation of original window opening. A classic form of frontier structure.

49. Belmont County, Mead Township. One and a half story double-pen log house. Photo: *ca.* 1915. Half the house was still standing in 1977. Family tradition holds that the house was doubled to allow a husband and wife separate quarters. The story could be true, but the house is simply another variant of the double-pen configuration; see Figure 51, a similar house in Adams County.

50. Ross County, Huntington Township (?). Double-pen log house. Photo: Date unknown, probably mid-1930s. By all appearances, this was a double-pen structure; the space between the pens, however, was not a third of the length of the house. The house probably dated to the second quarter of the 19th century, and originally had been sided. (This structure burned many years ago and is known only through this one photograph.)

51. Adams County, Tiffin Township. One and a half story double-pen log house. Photo: Spring, 1977, courtesy of Stephen Kelley. Front faces west. The stairway is at the southeast corner of the breezeway (right, rear). Both exterior chimneys were built of stone. The narrow "breezeway" was probably always enclosed.

52. Clermont County, Miami Township. Two story saddle-bag house. Each pen 15 feet square; chimney space, 5 feet wide, stone chimney. (See Figure 53.) Photo: 15 May 1976. West, front. This is the only complete saddle-bag house known to this writer. It has been moved to "Caesar's Creek Pioneer Village" in Warren County. This side was framed-in, with doors at both levels to connect the pens.

53. Clermont County, Miami Township. Two story saddle-bag house. (See Figure 52.) Photo: 15 May 1976. East, back. There were no doors into the pens in this chimney space, which may have been enclosed for a storage area. The central walls of the second floor are crudely constructed, several round logs were used, and the room to the north does not appear to have been finished. This building could be as early as the 1790s, on the basis of design and construction techniques.

54. Warren County, Turtle Creek Township. Saddle-bag log house built *ca.* 1816 by or for Samuel Steddon (?). Overpainted oil sketch by Marcus Mote, 1847; Ohio Historical Society Collections. This house was the birthplace of Mrs. Mote. The saddle-bag log house is a descendant of the central chimney, half-timber houses of the Middle Ages. The design was still utilized to some extent in braced-frame construction in 19th century Ohio, mostly among New England immigrants. This sketch should be compared to Figure 55, an almost identical structure also in Warren County. (Mote advertised himself as a daguerreotypist in the late 1840s, and this sketch leaves the impression it was composed by optical means, perhaps a *camera obscura.*)

55. Warren County, Massie Township. Saddle-bag log house. (See Figures 54, 56, 128, 165, 196.) This watercolor shows the one and a half story log kitchen which had been east of the central chimney. The picture is signed and dated, but the first letter of the artist's name is illegible: "_eubrecht '20." The letter appears to be K, N, or H.

56. Warren County, Massie Township. Saddle-bag house built *ca.* 1819 by or for Amos Hawkins (?). (See Figures 54, 55, 128, 165, 196.) Photo: 19 February 1972. Front, north. A one and a half story kitchen, which stood at the east end (left), and was removed within recent years. The house served as a granary for many years. There were three rooms on the first floor, two small ones on the west side of the door. The stairwell was central, also to the west, or right, of the door. This house was moved to the "Caesar's Creek Pioneer Village" near Wellman, Warren County. (Compare this photograph to the Mote painting, Figure 54; the two houses were about eight miles apart.)

57. Greene County, City of Fairborn (old Fairfield). Two story log house, built *ca.* 1805. Photo: September, 1976. South gable, front to east. Originally, it was a small but well-built house with single rooms on each floor and a kitchen addition to the rear. A double-porch was added fairly early, probably with the kitchen.

58. Seneca County, Venice Township. One and a half story log house. Size, 24 by 18 feet. Photo: June, 1969. Front, south. A plain, well-built house which was probably sided because the corner joints vary between steeple-notches and half-laps. The window to the right was placed against the door jamb so that small sections of logs would not have to be supported. The stairwell was probably in the right corner.

59. Greene County, Beavercreek Township. One and a half story log house built in 1803 for William Maxwell. (See Figure 205.) Photo: *ca.* 1903. Maxwell was the first publisher in the Northwest Territory, printing *The Centinel of the North-Western Territory* in Cincinnati between 1793–96. There is nothing remarkable about his house, but it is datable and therefore typologically important.

60. Franklin County, Mifflin Township. One and a half story log house. Size, 24 by 16 feet; eave, 12 feet. Photo: 24 October 1968. This is a good example of a plain log house of the Greek Revival period, with undereave windows and an interior chimney with stove. It was probably constructed between 1840–45.

61. Greene County, Caesar Creek Township. One and a half story log house built in 1833. Size, 24 by 15 feet. (See Figures 179, 187, 191, 215.) Photo: May, 1971. Front, north side. This log house was finished in the Greek Revival style, and is interesting for its details. There was a log wall between the front doors which did not extend to the second floor where the large window is located. (Such windows have been found on several log houses.) The porch roof at left covered grain or flour bins (?) on either side of the chimney, possibly indicating a missing room.

62. Tuscarawas County, Village of Zoar. One and a half story round log house, built (by tradition) in 1817. Photo: *ca.* 1890. (See Figure 63.) This is apparently one of the original houses erected by the Zoarites, and was used as the first Meeting House.

63. Tuscarawas County, Village of Zoar. One and a half story round log house constructed during winter of 1817–18 for Joseph Bimeler. Photo: Fall, 1967. Though typologically not a cabin, this house was of primitive and hasty construction; note the widely spaced round logs and the large floor joists. It survived because the Separatist Community was frugal of their possessions. The ends of the steeple-notched logs have the customary tear-drop appearance.

64. Franklin County, Village of Groveport. Two story log house with a one and a half story log addition. (See Figures 125, 140, 155, 189, 212.) Photo: 11 November 1974. Front, north, view to south. This is a large, substantial house with many interesting details. The original chimney/fireplace was on the east side. The central chimney, for a stove, might be original because of the off-center front door. There is a vertical board partition wall to the right of the door. In 1975 this house was moved by the local historical society to a new location.

65. Miami County, City of Troy. Two story log tavern built in 1808, and a one and a half story log house (at rear) built in 1803 by or for Benjamin Overfield. Photo: Fall, 1969, by Susannah Lane. This is a good example, though remodeled, of the large, well-proportioned log buildings erected in Ohio before the War of 1812. The word "tavern" is often misleading, for the majority of early taverns were simply houses with minor interior alterations to handle guests. The closest to true log, commerical structures would be the tavern in Brown County, Figure 44, and the taverns in Montgomery County, Figures 37 and 142.

66. Franklin County, Perry Township (City of Columbus). Two story log house with one story vertical log addition. (See Figures 67, 146, 147.) Photo: *ca.* 1894. View to the northwest. Compare this photograph to Figure 67.

67. Franklin County, Perry Township (City of Columbus). Two story log house with vertical log addition. (See Figures 66, 146, 147.) Photo: June, 1971. Compare this photograph to Figure 66; it is as close to the same camera angle as possible. The corner of the log house begins at the left of the French doors. This house is now surrounded by streets and apartment buildings.

68. Butler County, Oxford Township. Two story log house. (See Figures 69, 129, 157, 160, 161, 169, 180, 195, 201.) Photo: 1 June 1971. West end. The lower window appears to be original, though enlarged. The addition at the rear (north) was an early self-supported, braced-frame kitchen.

69. Butler County, Oxford Township. Two story log house. (See Figures 68, 129, 157, 160, 161, 169, 180, 195, 201.) Photo: July, 1973. Rear of house, north, and west end. The rear windows and lower door appear original to the house; the upper door was cut to reach the loft of the braced-frame kitchen addition. No windows could be cut to the right of the door because the corner stairwells extended to the center of the house.

70. Warren County, Village of Franklin. Two story log house which served as a post office in 1805. Second site, 1975. (See Figures 199, 228, 229.) Photo: 15 August 1975. Front, originally faced west. This house had additions at either end and the back. A large, well proportioned and constructed log house. Windows enlarged. Chimney not original to exterior.

71. Morgan County, Deerfield Township. One and a half story log house on a stone basement. Photo: Fall, 1972, by Donald R. Smith. Colonel John Morgan, of "Morgan's Raid" fame, stopped at this house in July, 1863. It was then the residence of the John Weaver family. The house had a basement kitchen and a large porch. The logs under the porch roof were whitewashed. The cornice molding to the back of the house stylistically appears to date before 1850.

72. "Flailing," woodcut from a "Specimen Book" of printer U. P. James, Cincinnati, *ca.* 1831. Similar cuts, depicting seasonal activities, were used as almanac calendar headings in Great Britain and Europe as well as the United States.

73. "Flax Scutching Bee." A log double-pen barn, house, and corncrib are shown in this oil painting by Linton Park (1826–1906). Reproduction courtesy of the National Gallery of Art, Washington, D.C.; Gift of Edgar William and Bernice Chrysler Garbisch.

74. Madison County, Deer Creek Township. Double-pen log barn. Pens, 18 by 21 feet. (See Figures 75, 84.) Photo: 13 April 1975. West side and south end. Barn pens are usually square, but it is no rarity if they are not. This was a tall double-pen structure, with three or four "extra" upper wall logs. Sheds had been added to all sides except the north. Note the rafter mortises in the plate. Stalls were originally built into the south pen.

75. Madison County, Deer Creek Township. Double-pen log barn. (See Figures 74, 84.) Photo: 13 April 1975. Puncheons from barn floor: Length, approximately 5 feet; diameter, 15 to 18 inches; thickness, 10 to 12 inches. These puncheons were so large they didn't require pegs to fasten them to the sleepers. The only other true puncheons seen by this writer were in a smokehouse in Greene County, Figure 112.

76. Darke County, Wayne Township. Double-pen log barn. Each pen 21 foot square. (See Figure 77.) Photo: July, 1967. East side. This style of construction was quite common in Ohio, when sheds were planned as part of the barn. Alternate logs on each pen were used as tie-beams for the shed framing. Note the hewed butts of the logs in the mow areas. The stalls appeared to be original. A two story log house stood a short distance south of this barn.

77. Darke County, Wayne Township. Double-pen log barn. (See Figure 76.) Photo: July, 1967. South pen, view to south. Ohio double-pen log barns were consistent in the utilization of the pens: one was used for stalls, and one, as in this photograph, served as a mow. The opening at the upper left gave access to the shed mow.

78. Franklin County, Franklin Township. Double-pen log barn. (See Figures 101, 109.) Photo: 27 January 1968. Overmow, central breezeway, view to north. The overmow was used to store sheaves of grain, which was threshed as needed on the floor immediately below. After mid-19th century, most overmow logs were removed from barns to allow the use of mechanical hayforks.

79. Guernsey County, Millwood Township. Double-pen log barn. (See Figure 164.) Photo: 10 October 1966. End of 18 foot hewn feed trough. Holes for these troughs are often found in log barns. In this barn, the trough and the vertical supports for the stall partitions were mortised and had to be installed during construction.

80. Warren County, Clear Creek Township. Double-pen log barn with sheds. Each pen, 28 feet 6 inches square. (See Figures 81, 82, 83.) Photo: June, 1969. Front, north. This particular barn had an amazing roof line. The sheds projecting on each side of the main doorway were a common alteration when the entry height to the central floor had to be maintained.

81. Warren County, Clear Creek Township. Double-pen log barn. (See Figures 80, 82, 83.) Photo: June, 1969. Threshing floor. Though this floor was nailed instead of pegged, it was of the same pattern as the 1826 floor in the Johnston barn, Figure 95. The pattern was common early in the 19th century. What distinguished a threshing floor from other floors was the sub-flooring which prevented the grain from falling between and through the joints.

82. Warren County, Clear Creek Township. Double-pen log barn. (See Figures 80, 81, 83.) Photo: June, 1969. Small doorway to stalls. Of particular note are the wooden pintles set into the door jamb. This form of hinge is mentioned in literature, but is rarely found today (one other example was seen in a small house *cum* barn in Greene County). The door battens were extended and drilled with holes corresponding to the pintles. Two short pegs (or a single long rod) were used as hinge pins, the battens resting on top the pintles.

83. Warren County, Clear Creek Township. Double-pen log barn. (See Figures 80, 81, 82.) Photo: June, 1969. North entrance. These were large, hinge-post doors. The vertical board on the left edge of the door was the latch. It pivoted at the apex of the diagonal brace. A small access door in one of the main doors, such as the small door to the lower left, was typical to all barns.

84. Madison County, Deer Creek Township. Double-pen log barn. (See Figures 74, 75.) Photo: 13 April 1975. Hinge-post and upper bracket, main barn door. The double entrance doors on the east side of the barn were hinged in this manner. Surprisingly, a fairly common method in Ohio. The lower ends of the hinge-posts fit into sockets in the sill. The use of wood hinges was probably by choice rather than necessity.

Cuming's other stop at a double-pen house was not as successful as at Beymer's. "Indeed we were not permitted to enter the eating room, but with a sort of sullen civility, were desired to sit down in an open space which divides two enclosed ends from each other, but all covered with the same roof, and which is the usual style of the cottages in this part of the country. The space in the middle is probably left unenclosed, for the more agreeable occupancy of the family during the violent heats of summer."[9] This double-pen log house, belonging to the Crumps family, was located at the present site of South Point, Lawrence County. It is doubtful that the Crumpses were running a tavern, so their attitude to Cuming was perhaps justified.

Since formal houses of accommodation were scarce in a frontier area, most travelers depended on the settlers for food and shelter. Naturally some settlers were happy for the opportunity to visit with these travelers and hear the news from other parts of the country—and receive a little hard cash for the food and shelter provided, because money was always scarce on the frontier. Others simply could not provide enough food for their own families, let alone for travelers, yet felt compelled to do so because of an unwritten law of the frontier that a traveler should always find accommodation where he or she asked. These latter citizens of the wilderness were often described as "sullen." On the other hand, they usually charged exorbitant amounts for services rendered. One misconception common today is that travelers in the wilderness were fed and sheltered free, depending upon the ability of the settler. This is not true; the traveler was expected to pay something. Francis Baily, who had heard the same tale in the eighteenth century, quickly discovered he was always charged at a settler's house. Since the settler had few crops and an uncertain market, he was usually quite willing, for cash, to provide bacon, milksops, and a portion of his floor to the—often unwary—traveler.

Beymer's tavern was no doubt very similar to McIntire's Hotel, Zanesville, a woodcut of which was reproduced in Henry Howe's *Historical Collections of Ohio.* McIntire's was the first hotel in Zanesville, dating 1800. The illustration is probably reasonably accurate, considering that it was done forty-seven years later from memory. As good as these two taverns *cum* hotels were reputed to be, the average tavern of the time before the War of 1812 era necessitated a strong constitution or a state of near exhaustion for the average traveler to enjoy its hospitality. John Bernard left his impression of backwoods Virginia taverns in one succinct sentence:

> "All you could obtain at these places were eggs and bacon, hoe-cake, and peach brandy; a bed stuffed with shavings, on a frame that rocked like a cradle, and in a room so well ventilated that a traveller had some difficulty in keeping his umbrella erect, if endeavoring, under this convenience, to find shelter from the rain while in bed."[10]

An Englishman, John Woods, in "Two Years' Residence in the Settlement on the English Prairie, in the Illinois Country," gives an excellent resume of log cabin construction (much of which is quoted in chapter 12) and good descriptions of a pioneer's cabin of the rudest sort and a double-pen house:

> Many cabins, belonging to the Americans, have no ceiling nor windows, and some of them have no floor, nothing but the bare earth, and some are not mudded, but open on all sides. Locks to doors are nearly unknown, but wooden bolts are common with the English: many of the American houses have only a latch, and some have not even that.
>
> The cabin I inhabit first consisted of a double one, with a porch 20 feet wide between them: this I have since converted into two rooms; the end rooms are of logs, the centre ones of frame and board, with a brick chimney. At the back of the cabin I have added a cellar, &c.[11]

Woods and Thomas Hulme were writing about the same area in Edwards County, Illinois, known variously as the "English Prairie," "Birkbeck's Settlement," and "Wanborough."[12]

As the log house was unknown in England, some of the best descriptions of log building are found in the writings of English travelers curious about such structures. An "English Gentleman," one William Blane, was aware of the peculiar aura surrounding the "log cabin in the clearing": "The environs of the cabin appear very extraordinary to an European; for it is generally built in a small clear spot in the midst of a forest, and surrounded with large trees which have been *girdled*, and blackened with fire, till they resemble huge pillars of charcoal."[13]

This method of clearing, standard to the frontier, had been practiced by the Indians before Western civilization arrived in North America. Although an ax was indispensable to the pioneers, they balked at having to clear acres of forest with an ax alone. Girdling, or the cutting away of the sap-bearing wood in a circle around a tree trunk, quickly killed a tree. When the tree had dried sufficiently, it was burned while still standing (see fig. 15). Blane described the process well. "Among the most laborious occupations of the settler is the cutting down the trees. Some of these are so gigantic, that the labour of chopping them down would be immense. He therefore cuts off the bark in a belt about four or five inches wide, and this is called *girdling*. The tree dies, and the year after, when it is dry, it is set on fire, and continues to burn slowly until gradually consumed."[14] Some stumps were dug out later, though most settlers simply planted around them, allowing them to rot.

The clearing surrounding a cabin was almost a requirement in the old forestation of Ohio, even presuming a cabin could be built without cutting the immediate trees. William Lang explains. "There was no terror in the howling of the wintry blast when the little clearing had grown large enough to prevent the trees from falling on the cabin. The family, snugly tucked away in their warm beds, in the little cabin, lit up from the big fireplace, were not annoyed by the howling, whistling and whining of the winds in the tree-tops, nor by the crashing of breaking limbs, and the thundering of a big, falling tree."[15] This fear of falling trees (note Williams's comment, appendix E) seems to have been very common among the first settlers, so there must have been a basis in fact.

Contrary to popular opinion, Ohio was more barren of trees

in the latter nineteenth century than today. Wood was a free or very inexpensive fuel, and the continual demand for steam power in industry, steamboats and railway trains, domestic heating, the charcoal industry, timber for frame building and fencing, and the burning of trees to clear land—plus dozens of other uses—practically cleared the virgin forestation. The charcoal industry died for want of timber, which in turn closed the charcoal iron furnaces. By midcentury coal was becoming the primary fuel for commercial use. According to contemporary accounts, settlers hated the forest and did their best to eradicate it. The horse-drawn grain reaper and mowing machine allowed the farmers to cultivate many times the acreage they were accustomed to harvesting by hand. As a consequence, most large timber in farming areas disappeared. It is easy to see how, as the nineteenth century progressed, log building retreated to the areas of the state unsuited to mechanized farming or industry—areas still forested. Economically, the argricultural and industrial areas of the state could afford more regal architecture than that of log. Practically, the large timber remaining was more valuable for commercial mill work than for log structures.

Although photography was being practiced in Ohio in the 1840s—Alexander C. Ross of Zanesville is credited with the first efforts in 1839—it is unfortunate that only a few photographs showing the landscape of this period are known to exist. The camera would have pictured the landscape as it was, not as an artist wished it to be. Since there is much literature in the 1830s and 40s devoted to advice on landscaping and home decoration, we must conclude that the villages and countryside had a very unkempt, barren appearance. One daguerreotype, taken in Granville late in 1849, shows the hill on which Denison University now stands as completely barren; a daguerrean panorama of the Cincinnati waterfront in 1848 shows few trees on the surrounding hills. The perspicacious Blane had a comment on this aspect of the American Scene.

> An American has no idea that any one can admire trees or wooded ground. To him a country well cleared, that is where every stick is

cut down, seems the only one that is beautiful or worthy of admiration.

All the land in the immediate neighbourhood of Cincinnati is without a tree upon it. This is the case with all American towns; . . . . When the Americans improve in taste, this indiscriminate destruction of the fine trees will be regretted.[16]

Foreign travelers were particularly aware of the desolate quality of the American landscape in comparison to England and Europe generally. In *American Notes for General Circulation* (London, 1842), Charles Dickens described his trip through Ohio, offering many comments on the barrenness of the countryside. Captain Basil Hall, who wrote of log houses in his *Travels in North America, in the Years 1827 and 1828*, implied the same desolation as noted by Dickens. "The houses are generally left unpainted, and being scattered about without order, look more like a collection of great packing boxes, than the human residences which the eye is accustomed to see in old countries."[17]

Because many of the English travelers carried certain prejudices against the former colonies, their writings often stirred up storms of protest in the United States. Dickens's serialized book, *The Life and Adventures of Martin Chuzzlewit* (London, 1844) presented a whimsical view of an Englishman trying to settle in an uninhabitable frontier "Eden." The area described could well have been the "English Prairie" in Illinois, for the author must have been aware of the writings of Woods, Hulme, Blane, and other English travelers. Dickens denied any malicious intent, which is undoubtedly true. However, it is interesting to speculate that if we present citizens of the United States were transported back in time to the first half of the nineteenth century, would our reactions be similar? A person is conditioned by his or her environment—social, political, economic, and, one might add, aesthetic. No doubt we would be very aware of environmental waste in nineteenth-century Ohio, if we could return.

Notes

1. Lang, *History of Seneca County*, pp. 192–93.
2. The name "Adena" was later applied to a certain prehistoric Indian culture, the remains of which were found on the estate. If Worthington had continued to live in the log house on that site, we might now have the "Belleview Indians" instead.
3. Peter, *Worthington*, pp. 34–35.
4. Ibid., p. 50.
5. Bradley, "Journal," p. 236.
6. Hulme, "Journal," p. 281.
7. Bradley, "Journal," pp. 246–47.
8. Cuming, *Sketches of a Tour*, pp. 206–8.
9. Ibid., pp. 134–35.
10. Bernard, *Retrospections of America*, p. 153. A fine compilation of references on traveling and tavern life can be found in Yoder, *Taverns and Travelers*.
11. Woods, "Two Years' Residence," p. 278.
12. The English settlements were in and around present Albion, Illinois; Wanborough no longer exists. (Letter from Roger D. Bridges, 17 August 1973, Illinois State Historical Library.)
13. Blane, *Excursion through the United States*, p. 181.
14. Ibid.
15. Lang, *History of Seneca County*, p. 193.
16. Blane, *Excursion through the United States*, p. 125.
17. Hall, *Travels in North America* 1: 130.

VI
PUBLIC BUILDINGS

Any building could serve a "public" function, whether to afford protection as a blockhouse or to house a large number of persons as a school or church or to be part of social organization as a courthouse or jail. In the settlement and governmental development of Ohio, beginning with small, local concentrations of population, the requirements for public buildings would have been minimal. Needed space was rented; then, as the village, township, or county grew, standing property was purchased or small buildings constructed. Public officials often had their offices in their own homes. The local tavern might serve for school, church, post office, and court in any given community. Such was the case with the Newcom Tavern in Dayton. County "seats," that is, "seats of justice," did present certain requirements, in particular courthouses and jails, while Ohio was still a territory. It is incorrect to think that public buildings always had certain architectural or structural features that set them apart; until after the War of 1812, one might be hard-pressed to tell the difference between standard log houses and many county courthouses.

BLOCKHOUSES AND KENTUCKY STATIONS

Although the various forts erected within the boundaries of the state were certainly "public buildings," it is not the purpose of this work to deal with military installations for they are a separate study with their own peculiar history. It suffices to say that horizontal and vertical plank walls were common to the more ambitious Ohio forts, such as Harmar, Washington, Jefferson, Hamilton, and Meigs, and that plank construction did not seem to influence general house-building techniques—at least, conclusive evidence is lacking, written or physical (such as the Putnam House, Campus Martius, Marietta). The laborious task of hewing or sawing planks, then mortising them into posts, was probably more work than most settlers wished to undertake; military structures were another matter, for the men were normally available for such time-consuming tasks.

The frontier "blockhouse" was derived from ancient military tradition, and by the time Ohio was being settled the design and construction of a blockhouse, for private or community use, had become rather simple and standardized. Perhaps the only true distinguishing feature of a blockhouse was the overhang to protect the first floor exterior perimeter. In theory, blockhouse logs were placed tightly together to prevent bullets and arrows from entering, and there was a minimum of openings for the same reason. In practice, however, most blockhouses were rough affairs unless they also served as residences.

In the autumn of 1790 about twenty men constructed a blockhouse of beech logs at "Big Bottom" near the Muskingum River in present Windsor Township, Morgan County. The logs were laid far apart, and were not chinked even though the weather was cold. The blockhouse was two stories high, had puncheon floors, a fireplace, and stairs.[1] Surprised by an Indian raiding party, twelve persons were killed in and near the blockhouse, which the Indians tried to burn by pulling up the floor and starting a fire with the puncheons; the interior and roof burned, but the green wall logs remained standing.[2] This attack heralded the so-called Indian Wars of the 1790s which were terminated with the Treaty of Greene Ville in 1795.

The Indian Wars naturally caused more blockhouses and stockaded compounds to be built throughout the state, particularly the Kentucky Stations north of Cincinnati. Settlers further north near the 1795 Greene Ville Treaty line never felt safe until the end of the War of 1812. Dunlap's Station, in present Colerain Township, Hamilton County, was attacked in January 1791. One man was killed and another wounded in the first volley by the Indians, who simply shot between the logs of the building containing the hand gristmill. The houses, which had shed roofs and formed part of the stockade wall (the so-called Kentucky Station configuration), had their lowest sides to the exterior; one inhabitant had seen a dog jump from a stump to the roof of a house.[3] Miraculously, the station managed to survive the wars.

During the War of 1812, the settlers of the southern third of Ohio did not feel overly compelled to protect themselves, but such was not the case near the 1795 treaty line. Fortunately, a few of the original settlers of this area were alive when a widespread interest in local history developed during the 1876 centennial celebration; some good firsthand accounts of the frontier, and architecture, were recorded. In the spring of 1812, the settlers of present Lake Township, Ashland County, fortified the cabin of James L. Priest. The cabin was changed to a double-pen house, each pen being about 40 by 20 feet. This structure was surrounded by a picket of split timber about 12 feet high; an entrance gate was hung on wooden hinges. Seven families lived in or near this small, quarter-acre fort for most of the war.[4]

As noted earlier, the term "blockhouse" has come to mean a certain style of defensive structure, whereas during the eighteenth century (particularly in Germanic settlements) blockhouse might mean a hewed log house as opposed to an unhewed log cabin. A well-constructed log house, with a minimum of openings provided with heavy shutters and doors, was almost as sound a refuge as the traditional blockhouse with overhang, certainly much better than a cabin. The Kentucky Station took advantage of a series of rough cabins, or sheds, placed so their back walls formed a quadrangular stockade. Of significant value was the fact that the station could shelter a large number of settlers as well as their livestock. There is no doubt there was safety in numbers, real as well as psychological. Where few settlers were congregated, the fortified house or blockhouse had to serve, and the settlers' livestock and personal belongings were possible sacrifices to safety. A small stockade, such as that built around Priest's house in Ashland County, was the only alternative.

Descriptions of blockhouses are fairly common in Ohio county histories. The following is typical:

> They were generally constructed of hewn logs, closely jointed or fitted together, two stories high; the length and width of the building being about twenty by thirty feet. The logs resting on each other, prevented the balls from entering the cracks or crevices. The corners were carefully notched and fitted, so that the building was really quite strong. There was but one door, or entrance, made of thick planks or puncheons, hung on strong wooden or iron hinges, and bolted or fastened on the inside, so as to prevent ingress unless much force should be used,—the door being thick enough to prevent ordinary musket or rifle balls from passing through it. The first story was generally about eight or nine feet high. Sometimes the floor consisted of well packed earth. The second story generally projected over the lower one, about three feet, on the sides and ends. This over-jut rested upon logs or joists, which were allowed to project over the first story. The second story was about seven or eight feet high, and was perforated with numerous port-holes, pointing in every direction, so as to guard against the approach of an enemy. The floor of this story was thick and strong, and had port-holes pointing downward, so that if an enemy came under the projection, to set fire to the building, he could be shot from above. There were also port-holes in the lower story. . . . The roof was of clapboards, supported by logs. These little forts, or block-houses, were generally placed in an open space, upon some slight elevation of ground. . . . they were always placed near a pure, sparkling spring. In such a fort, or block-house, twenty-five or thirty families could be accommodated with tolerable quarters. . . . We do not learn that more than two block-houses of this county [Ashland], were surrounded by stockades.
>
> Life in the block-houses was exceedingly irksome and monotonous; and the inmates were always pleased when assured they could safely return to their deserted cabins and stock. Of course, hours and weeks were spent in reciting and reiterating stories of revolu-

tionary adventure, and pioneer hardships, until all could repeat them.[5]

This description brings up the question whether the blockhouse at Big Bottom was not, in fact, a standard hewed dwelling because of the gaps between the logs and the lack of an overhang. Of course, individual skill in hewing timber, particularly in cutting corner notches, varied tremendously; experience was certainly required to fit the logs closely together.

The "irksome and monotonous" life in the blockhouses and stockades is exemplified in the marvelous story of Griffin Greene's perpetual motion machine. A stockade, known as "Farmers' Castle," was built near present Belpre (Belle Prairie), Washington County, during the Indian Wars. In the fall of 1792, Greene, one of the directors of the Ohio Company, for lack of anything to do within the confines of the stockade, conceived and constructed a perpetual motion machine of considerable size and expense. It had three arms, about 12 feet long and weighted with lead, connected to a large wheel. Although the specifications are somewhat hazy, it appears that the arms were mounted vertically either on the wheel or an axle, and two descending arms were supposed to give sufficient force and momentum to raise the third, ad infinitum. The machine did not function, of course, but Greene was as shrewd as he was ingenious, and converted the parts into a floating gristmill based on his memory of a tide mill he had seen in Holland. The floating mill proved to be highly successful, serving the settlements near Belpre, and, moved downriver, Gallipolis.[6]

The log blockhouse survived through the nineteenth century as the frontier pushed steadily westward. It became a standardized fixture in military literature, such as Dennis Mahan's *Complete Treatise on Field Fortification*,[7] and was used during the Civil War to guard strategic points and prison encampments.

JAILS AND COURTHOUSES

Portage County can boast, on the score of public buildings, nothing but a shell, which is alternately occupied by bipeds and quad-

> rupeds, and which, from its dilapidated state, is equally easy of access to both—and in which, we may, at different times, hear the preachers of the Gospel, the expounders of the law, and the birch of the schoolmaster, and consequently the squalls of the children, the squealing of the pigs, and the bleating of sheep. 'Tis, in fact, occupied as a Court House and meeting-house, and we all know it has become proverbial as the county sheep-pen.[8]

The above structure was completed in the summer of 1810 and sold in 1829 because a new courthouse was nearing completion. (Unfortunately, the old courthouse was a frame rather than a log building, but the quote was too good to be ignored.)

With rare exceptions, the first county public buildings were of rough construction and served a multitude of purposes. This was particularly true of courthouses, though even jails were adaptable as meeting places. County commissioners' records are excellent sources of information on these public buildings and are the only reliable, though at times hopelessly incoherent, contemporary specifications for log buildings known to this writer. Jails were always carefully specified, probably due to their specialized function. Many structures were adaptable as jails, however.

Because of their durable construction, the early blockhouses often served other purposes when their primary function was no longer needed. During the War of 1812, two blockhouses, one of round and one of hewed logs, were erected on the public square in Mansfield, Richland County. By September 1813, the hewed-log blockhouse had been altered to serve as a county jail and courthouse, lower and upper floors, respectively. The carpenter work for the alteration was advertised for bids on July 24, and the advertisement is interesting because it mentions an exterior stairway, a feature occasionally seen in illustrations.

> Ordered, that the said work be done in the following manner, to wit.: Two floors of solid hewn timber, of the thickness of at least six inches, to be squared and jointed in a workmanlike manner; and on the outside, a stairway, with a platform at the head thereof of suitable size, and a door to enter the upper story therefrom, with a

suitable casings and hinges for the same; and a glass window, containing twelve lights of glass, cased in like manner as the door; and suitable seats for the court; and a latch for the upper door, and lock and chain for the lower door, and iron hinges for the same, all of which work and preparations must be done in a workmanlike manner."[9]

The successful bidder was one Luther Coe: $46.00 plus $2.00 for a handrail to the stairway. Aside from the strength of the flooring, the original blockhouse must have been considered adequate for a jail; apparently it had only one door, and small portholes instead of windows. A new combined jail and courthouse was built late in 1816. The lower floor, the jail, was made of one-foot square logs laid as a double wall with an intervening one-foot space filled with stone.[10] This was the only public building in Mansfield until 1827, when a brick courthouse was constructed, and it served many public functions. Both the original blockhouses were auctioned off in December 1816, the round log structure bringing $20.00 and the remodeled hewed-log blockhouse $56.40.[11]

Albert Graham's *History of Richland County* contains more detailed accounts of the 1813 jail and courthouse, but he and his informants seem to have confused details of this structure with the similar building constructed in 1816. A few of the comments are worth quoting, despite the confusion, for interior descriptions are rare for early nineteenth-century public buildings; first, James Rowland:

> In 1820, about the center of the public square, . . . there was an edifice about 30x20 feet, and two stories in height. The lower story was constructed of hewed logs, that had been originally used in another part of the town for a block-house. The second, or upper story, was frame work, and the house was weather-boarded on all sides, both above and below. The stairway leading to the entrance of the second story, was outside the building, on the north side, and the building was not painted either inside or out. This edifice served for various purposes. . . . People of all denominations . . . worshiped in the upper story. There, too, the county courts were held, and public meetings generally. On the east and west sides

of this room were fireplaces, and a stove right in the center, and often in the coldest weather, by reason of the flues drawing downward instead of upward, the fuel had to be carried out or the fire quenched, or the inmates suffered by smoke. In that room, I preached every alternate Sabbath for two or three years. The Judge's bench was on a slight elevation above the floor, and the fixtures in front of it, and the appearance around the bar, were in perfect harmony with the appearance of the room and house. The lower story was divided into three apartments; the west half being used as a jailer's residence, and the south apartment of the east half as a cell—a close, tight place—where criminals were confined, and were said to suffer considerably sometimes by the rats; the north part of the east half was a place of confinement for persecuted debtors.[12]

Rowland must have been describing the jail and courthouse of 1816, yet he states that the first story was made of reclaimed logs, and that the design was similar—if not the same—as the 1813 structure. A second informant, one Henry Newman, seems to bear out the contention that an older first story was reused in 1816:

The hewed-log block-house was built in the fall of 1813. . . . The logs that formed the under story were dovetailed; the under and upper floor laid with hewed logs. The under story, after the war, composed the first jail; the upper story projected eight inches on every side, and was large enough for a court house for the court. It had one twelve-light window, 8x10 glass, on the gable end (north wall), and port-holes above and below."[13]

David McCullough (born in Pennsylvania, 1810), who came to Mansfield in 1822, said that "the logs were nicely hewn, and laid very closely together, but the wall was not double."[14] McCullough seems to be contradicting Graham's description of the stone-filled, double-walled jail of 1816; it is possible the county commissioners did specify such construction, which Graham found in their minutes, but that the jail was not built in that fashion, or else the later informants were simply mistaken in looking back sixty years—this being the more likely answer.

The first Clark County jail was a rough log structure, so insecure, as tradition relates, that it was necessary to tie a bear outside the door to prevent escapes. The second jail was a two-story building with a cell on the first floor, a debtor's cell immediately above, and quarters for the jailer on both floors. The cell was surrounded by layers of walls, beginning on the outside with brick, then timber, stone, timber, and finished with plank for a total thickness of 46 inches at the front and back and 43 inches at the gable; the brick wall was omitted through the center of the building. The jail was contracted on 23 July 1823, to one Elijah Ferguson under a $3,000 bond. Corner notching is mentioned in the specifications:

> The wooden part of the Cell . . . is to be put up in the form of 2 log-houses of Squared Whiteoak timber not less than 10 inches Square laid down and fitted Close on each other and each piece dovetail*d* at the Ends to unite the Corners firmly together and so as to lay Close on Each other the 1st two of timber in these walls are to be Sound Burroak Squared of the Size and laid and dovetail*d* in the manner before mentioned. The Space between these 2 walls is to be 12 inches which Said Space of 12 inches is to be laid with Stone hammered to the width So as to fill Said Space close at each Side—[15]

Courthouses and jails were the major visible, tangible proof of civil government on the frontier, and as a consequence are often mentioned in period literature. The first jail in Cincinnati was built early in 1793, a plain log cabin, one and a half stories and about 16 feet square. It was primarily for debtors, common on the early frontier, who were allowed to wander freely (hopefully to work) during the day, but were required to spend their nights in confinement. Less than two years passed before a larger jail was necessary. The new jail was a two-story log building, about 15 by 20 feet in size, with a shingle roof. Late in 1795 this building was moved to a new location, with the aid of eight yoke of oxen, and in 1845 was being used as a tailor shop.[16]

Another early jail was still in existence in the 1840s, surviving as a section of the Washington County courthouse. Samuel

Hildreth described it as the oldest combined structure still standing in Ohio:

> This court house was built in the year 1798, but was not completed until the following year. . . . It is remarkable only from the fact of its being the oldest structure of the kind in the state of Ohio. The jail portion of this edifice [occupies] the back part of the building, and has no windows in sight. It is constructed of hewed yellow poplar logs, eighteen inches square, laid double, so that the walls are three feet thick. They are placed so as to break joints, like stone work or masonry, and fastened together with iron bolts. The floors, sides, and ceiling over head, in the jail rooms, are all built in this substantial manner, with doors and iron gratings of proportionate thickness. . . . The main building is a frame, of two stories; being forty-five feet in length, and thirty-nine feet in breadth. The lower story, in front, is divided into two rooms, with a passage between them, leading to the jail in the back of the building. These rooms are occupied by the jailor and his family. The upper story, in front, was the court room, and is forty feet long by twenty broad, and thirteen feet in height. It is lighted by seven windows, and warmed by two fire-places. A flight of steps leads from the court room to two jury rooms, over the jail, raised about four feet above the main hall.[17]

A peculiarity noted in several descriptions of these early Ohio jails is the (seemingly) enormous thickness of the walls. The reason for a three-foot wall is obscure, unless the backwoodsman was a breed apart as romantic literature has pictured him. More than likely an escape was a "break-in" rather than a "break-out"; the thick walls would slow the efforts of axmen attacking an exterior wall, and the noise should alert some interested party. No doubt the thick walls also discouraged spoken messages. In none of the descriptions is there any mention of how the cells were heated. Fire, carefully applied and controlled, could have been used to weaken the logs sufficiently to allow escape, so it is probable that prisoners, if any heat was provided, were given coals in a sealed container.

The most interesting jail specifications found were those of

Montgomery and Athens counties. In September 1804, one David Squier was the successful bidder for the construction of the Montgomery County jail of Dayton; the jail cost $229.00.

> The building to be executed in the following manner, to wit: The building is to be of good straight round logs thirty feet long and sixteen feet wide—The logs to be at least twelve inches in diameter at the smallest end and the walls of the house to be raised twelve feet in height, with a partition of logs of the above description, so as to leave a vacancy in no place of more than three inches between them; the least room to be ten feet in width, for the safekeeping of persons charged with or convicted of crime, which soon is to be ceiled with inch and half plank and to have a good strong floor of hewed logs, not less than six inches thick, with a loft also of hewed logs of the same; under floor covered with plank of one and a half inch thick. The loft and floor of the large apartment may be laid with two inch planks, well secured with pins, on a sufficient number of sleepers and joists not more than two feet apart—There is to be two good strong doors made of two inch thick planks, and double rivetted or spiked together, and hung with strong hinges. There is to be in the smallest appartment one window of a size sufficient for four lights of glass eight by ten, also two in the large appartment of twelve lights of glass, eight by ten, with shutters made of two inch plank double, the doors and windows to be well secured with iron paid for by the pound at the customary price. There is to be a good cabin roof, and the whole done in a good and workmanlike manner by the thirteenth day of December next, together with a chimney, in one corner of the large appartment, of stone, with one fireplace at least four feet in the back. The payments will be made at the completion of the work and good and sufficient security required of the persons contracting.
>
> The Commissioners will fix on the place for the doors and windows.[18]

This jail is particularly interesting in that is was nothing more than a very large log cabin, having round log walls, a "cabin" or weighted roof, and puncheon floors. However, the iron work, windows, and stone fireplace and chimney were refinements not found in cabin architecture. This jail was presumably replaced by a stone structure late in 1812, the specifications notable in that at least 40,000 nails (minimum) were required to reinforce the floors, doors, and windows.[19]

The specifications for the Athens County jail, written 17 and 18 April 1805, are so interesting (and confusing) that they deserve to be reprinted in full: see appendix A.[20] At least the inmates of this incredibly solid structure were supplied with an indoor toilet if not a fireplace; further comments are included in the appendix. Appendix B gives the specifications for the third jail in Greene County, which were written on 6 December 1808. There is one phrase of great value to the history of log construction in these Greene County specifications; it is the first comment found by this writer in sixteen years of research that unmistakenly names a type of corner notch: ". . . the corners to be raised in half dove tailed order. . . ."[21] The importance is twofold: the half-dovetail was in use in Ohio before the War of 1812; and, by indicating "half" a dovetail, other descriptions using the word "dovetail" could mean full-dovetail. The walls were not doubled on this jail, but each log was pinned at the corner. It has long been the opinion of this writer that the half-dovetail notch was used primarily for blockhouses, or similar strong fortifications, before it found its way into general construction. Examples of the notch are still rare in Ohio for the first quarter of the nineteenth century. The first jail in Zanesville, also constructed in 1808, was a two-story structure of hewed logs lined with three-inch plank.[22]

Whereas jails seemed to be truly specialized structures on the frontier—assuming a jail to be a building strong enough to leave a prisoner unattended—the county courthouses were another matter. Courts could be, and were, held in any type of structure. Often space was rented in a tavern or a private home. As noted earlier, it was as common then as now to combine the courtroom and jail in one structure. Most nineteenth-century Ohio county histories have ample information on the courts and courthouses for the simple reason that lawyers and judges held high positions in local society—and many authored the histories. Henry Howe's *Historical Collections of Ohio* (1847) contains many accounts of the early judicial system as well as several illustrations of county courthouses. The long account of the Greene County court and the description of the log cabin that served as courthouse is typical (see fig. 18).[23]

Nothing unusual has come to light about the construction of the early log courthouses except that they were, like churches, schools, and taverns, simply modified houses—if indeed modified at all. A detailed account of the territorial statehouse in Chillicothe was given by William Creighton, an early settler of Ross County, in the *American Pioneer* in 1842. Chillicothe was made the seat of government for the Northwest Territory in 1800; during that year and the next the legislature met in a large log structure, located on the corner of Second and Walnut streets, while the stone "Old Court House" was being constructed. The first, log statehouse

> extended along the former of those streets thirty-six, and the latter twenty-four feet; was two stories high; built of hewed logs; covered with shingles, and was erected by Mr. Bazil Abrams in 1798. To the main building . . . was attached a hewed log building about twenty-four feet long and eighteen feet wide, of the same height, and covered in like manner with the main building; the wing was weatherboarded; board partitions were put up in the first and second stories of the wing so as to form two rooms of about sixteen feet square, one above and one below, leaving passages between them and the main building about eight feet wide. The door from without leading into the passage opened on Walnut street; at the west end of the passage a narrow flight of winding steps led to the upper story, and on each side of the passages above and below were doors by which an entrance might be had to the wing and main building. To the main building there were two doors exclusive of those named, one of which opened on Second, and the other on Walnut street. In the main building there were ten, and in the wing five windows of twelve lights in each, eight by ten. In the main building the windows were arranged in the lower story, one on the east, and two on the south, and in the second story, one on the north, three on the south, and two on the east; and in the wing in the lower story, one on the west, and one on the east; and in the upper story, one on the west, and two on the east.

> In the lower room of the wing, colonel Thomas Gibson, then auditor of public accounts for the territory, kept his office, and the upper room was tenanted by a small family. The upper story of the main building was a place of resort for gamblers, and more especially those who were fond of playing billiards. . . .
>
> The lower room of the main building was occupied in a manner altogether different from the upper. In it the sages of the territorial legislature assembled for the purpose of enacting such laws as in their judgment were best calculated to promote the interest of the infant republic. . . . In it, the heralds of the cross of different denominations, more especially the Presbyterians and Methodists, from time to time proclaimed the glad tidings of salvation. . . . During the last war [1812], that house was used as a recruiting rendezvous and barracks for the United States' troops, since which period it has been called the "Old Barracks," and in 1840, it was pulled down, the logs were then sound, and the roof on the south side, which was made of blue-ash shingles, and had been on forty-two years, was sound and without a leak.[24]

The "Old Barracks" was in configuration a large two-story log house with a second log house added as a wing. At least the account implies that the larger house was constructed first, then enlarged, rather than both structures having been built at the same time. However, the arrangement of interior space and fenestration suggests that either there was extensive remodeling of the first structure or the wing had been planned. Mr. Abrams may have built the main house for his own use, then found he could make some income by remodeling and renting it to the territorial legislature. The main floors were 36 by 24 feet, which means that the joists were either spanning the entire 24-foot width or were supported by summer beams at midpoint; in either case, such wide spans were not capable of supporting a great deal of weight without bracing (there must have been posts and summers). It would be interesting to know if the billiard table was slate; if so, it would go far in proving that anything, however heavy or exotic, could be transported into frontier Ohio if the need, or desire, existed. So much for the argument that *necessary* goods couldn't be transported at that date!

TAVERNS, SCHOOLS, AND CHURCHES

The tavern was, more often than not, the main public building in a settlement and was utilized seven days a week, day and night. Log taverns normally followed the usual house configurations, perhaps fewer partitions on the first floor, more on the second for sleeping quarters. The double-pen plan was very popular, for the bar and the quarters for travelers could be isolated by log walls from the family area. The majority of the early, so-called taverns were nothing more than private homes with no especial provisions for guests and no architectural features to reveal their actual use. Guests ate with the family and slept on the floor. The first tavern license granted in Xenia, Greene County, was on 15 November 1804. The tavern proper was a two-story, double-pen log house; it was built for the express purpose of being a tavern, and stood across Main Street, south side, from the present courthouse square. The upstairs west room was used by the court. In a corner of the room directly below "there was an old-fashioned bar—the upper part enclosed with upright slats of wood, with a little wicket, through which the grog was handed out. . . ."[25] Howe illustrates similar taverns in Muskingum and Putnam counties.[26] The enclosed bar was common to many of the barrooms, usually a wooden cage above a solid counter, a feature still found in England and Europe. Original American examples are rare today.[27]

Actually, Ohio log taverns are about as rare. One of the best examples known to this writer is in Perry Township in Brown County (see fig. 44). It is also the largest log residence presently known, being 42 feet long and 18½ feet wide. It originally had an 18½ foot "L" extending from the northwest corner, but only the interior wall remains. The "L" was built concurrently with the rest of the structure, an intricate form of construction, and served as a kitchen; the missing log walls, now replaced with frame, were burned away. The central hall, formed by interior log walls, has a ladder stairs to the second floor hall; this would be in keeping with the use of the structure as a tavern. The lower eastern room was the bar or taproom. It had a separate exterior door as well as a door to the hall, and was obviously designed to be isolated from the rest of the building. The date of the tavern is unknown, but since it lies on an early stage route northeastward from Cincinnati to Chillicothe, there is every reason to believe it was built before the War of 1812, perhaps as early as the date of statehood (1803).

Another interesting, original tavern was uncovered in Miamisburg, Montgomery County (see fig. 140). No absolute date is known for this structure either, but it must be as early as the previous example for it faced a ford across the Great Miami River just within Symmes's Purchase. Its construction is presently unique for Ohio, with full-dovetailed corners and joists supported by summer beams. Unfortunately, the building has had considerable remodeling in the past which makes the original interior configuration hard to determine. There are two front doors facing west towards the river, separated by two central windows; these openings are symmetrically repeated by four windows on the second floor. No doubt one door served the taproom, possibly the one to the south. The first and second floors are well structured with joists and summers. A large exterior chimney stood on the south end, with fireplaces on both floors. The interior walls were covered with very long straw plastered with clay. Room partitions were the usual vertical boards. By all evidence, the building was well finished. The Newcom Tavern in Dayton, Montgomery County (see fig. 37), retains some semblance of its exterior design and interior space, as does the Overfield Tavern in Troy, Miami County (see fig. 65).

Of all the log public buildings, the schoolhouse was indisputably the crudest in construction and the least maintained, if contemporary accounts can be believed. The romance of childhood clouded the late Victorians' minds when reflecting on their school days. Not only were the schools poorly heated and lighted, sanitation facilities were rare to nonexistent. This is not sheer speculation, based on a comparison with today's academic palaces; educators were well aware of the problem before mid-nineteenth century. An excellent contemporary resume may be found in Henry Barnard's book, *School Architecture*, although there are few references to Ohio considering the book was published in Cincinnati.[28]

The county histories are filled with descriptions of early schoolhouses, fascinating in one respect because the log cabin style of construction—even the weighted roof—held on until midcentury when it had all but disappeared for other purposes. Here is a typical description, in this case from Whetstone Township, Crawford County: "A school cabin was built just south of the Campbell farm during the spring of 1828. It was a large rough-log structure, with one door hung on wooden hinges, and two windows, each containing two or three panes of glass."[29] A commoner description would have oiled paper instead of glass in the windows, the sign of true primitiveness to the Victorians. These schools existed by the hundreds around the state, though most were being replaced by frame or brick structures before midcentury. One of the best commentaries on a log schoolhouse known to this writer is a letter written about 1910 by Mr. Reuben S. Mason; it is quite lengthy, so it is included as appendix F.

In Ohio, schools and churches were the only log buildings that consistently used gable-end entrances. This is not to say all did, only that the probability, judging from contemporary sources, is high for any given building. A gable entrance was fine for a structure intended for public assembly, usually a large, single room; otherwise, it created some problems of interior space arrangement that were not easily overcome in a log house.

Churches were constructed in a similar fashion as the schools—if anything, perhaps a little rougher. A log church was simply an intermediary step between the private home and the large, permanent meetinghouse. There was little reason to make an elaborate log structure if there was any hope the congregation would expand. Time, energy, and money were best spent making a permanent edifice once the congregation was established. As with schools, many churches were simply remodeled log houses, the only alteration being the removal of the partitions. One such building was the Columbia Baptist Church,

Hamilton County, which was touted as the "First House of Worship in Ohio" in the *American Pioneer.*[30] Howe copied the illustration of the church, but disputed its age, 1790, by quoting Oliver M. Spencer's narrative: "Fresh to my remembrance is the rude log-house, the first humble sanctuary of the first settlers of Columbia, standing amidst the tall forest trees, on the beautiful knoll, where now [1834] is a grave-yard, and the ruins of a Baptist meeting-house of later years."[31] The church was destroyed in 1835 after having been in poor condition for over five years. Whether or not the building was the first church in Ohio is beside the point; the weatherboarded log house shown is interesting because it is early, if not 1790, and the artist clearly pictured the pattern of the short, hand-rived clapboards. The structure was also tall for its perimeter dimensions, another indicator of an early date. As Spencer states, the congregation apparently erected a rough cabin before building this better-finished meetinghouse—but note that that was just what it was, a house.

Log churches, like schools, are mentioned hundreds of times in the county histories; however, such buildings are rare today. This writer knows of two. One still occasionally used is "Old St. Peter's" Roman Catholic Church, Lawrence Township, Tuscarawas County, completed in 1840. It is of standard church configuration with gable entry, bell tower, and nave windows, but is now covered with siding. The other, the Determan Evangelical Church built in 1848, stands as a storage building on a farm in Adams Township, Seneca County. No doubt others exist, but their identity has been lost or they are still hidden under remodeling.

Notes

1. Barker, *Recollections*, pp. 68–69.
2. Howe, *Historical Collections*, p. 378.
3. Cist, *Cincinnati Miscellany*, p. 218.
4. Hill, *History of Ashland County*, p. 60.
5. Ibid.
6. Barker, *Recollections*, pp. 88–89.

7. Mahan, *Complete Treatise on Field Fortification*, pp. 96–101.
8. *Ravenna* (Ohio) *Courier*, 21 October 1826; quoted in Brown and Morris, *History of Portage County*, pp. 317–18.
9. Graham, *History of Richland County*, p. 384.
10. Ibid., p. 385.
11. Ibid.
12. Ibid., pp. 456–57.
13. Ibid., p. 457.
14. Ibid.
15. Manuscript in the collections of the Clark County Historical Society, Springfield, Ohio; courtesy of George Berkhofer.
16. Cist, *Cincinnati Miscellany* 1:51.
17. Hildreth, "Old Court House and Jail," p. 163.
18. Road Commissioners' Record, Montgomery County, Ohio; Book A, p. 8, 28 September 1804. Quote from typed transcription made by the Montgomery County Historical Society. Punctuation supplemented.
19. Ibid., p. 154; 2 July 1811. (See chapter 12.)
20. Athens County Board of Commissioners' Book, entries under 17 and 18 April 1805. Transcription by author from photo-facsimile of original manuscript through courtesy of Ms. Helen Baker, Athens, Ohio.
21. Broadstone, *History of Greene County* 1:143.
22. *Proceedings at the Dedication of the Muskingum County Court House*, Zanesville, Ohio, 1877, p. 23.
23. Howe, *Historical Collections*, pp. 193–97.
24. Creighton, "Chillicothe Court-House," pp. 206–7. Creighton relates (p. 206) that Bazil Abrams was so fond of billiards that he lost all his money and his house in twenty-four hours of continuous play during the summer of 1801. Abrams left for the south "from whence he never returned." The "blue-ash" mentioned is *Fraxinus americans quadrangulata.*
25. Howe, *Historical Collections*, p. 198, quoting Thomas Coke Wright. This was probably Jimmie Collier's tavern. Rhea Mansfield Knittle owned "a half-pint, blown, patterned, expanded wine-cruet, with an applied hollow handle and a circular foot" used by Collier in his tavern. (See Knittle, *Early Ohio Taverns*, p. 21.)
26. Howe, Ibid., p. 385 and opp. 428. See fig. 46.
27. One of these bars may be seen in "Our House" Tavern in Gallipolis, Gallia County. It was originally in a tavern in the village of Venice, west of Sandusky, Erie County; date unknown, but after the War of 1812.
28. Barnard, "School-Houses As They Are," in *School Architecture*, pp. 15–45.
29. Perrin, Battle, and Goodspeed, *History of Crawford County and Ohio*, p. 553.
30. Williams, "First House of Worship," p. 41.
31. Howe, *Historical Collections*, p. 229.

VII
HUTS, CABINS, AND HOUSES

HUTS

There were several recognized forms of shelters in use on the frontier that were cruder than the log cabin. These were the real initial structures, if they can be so distinguished. "Hut," "shed," and "lean-to" are terms frequently encountered in early journals; most of these shelters used some variation of posts and ridgepole to support leafy branches or split timber roofing. The following description is quite typical; a form of shelter which the Indians also used, the "cabin" was built in Mifflin Township, Ashland County, in March 1809:

> The cabin was constructed by planting two forks in the ground about twenty feet apart, and placing a ridge pole on them, and then leaning split timber against the pole, making a sort of shed roof, the base being about twelve feet wide, leaving a small opening at the top for the escape of smoke. The ends were closed by setting poles in the ground, leaving a door at one end. The cracks were carefully closed with moss gathered from old logs. The floor consisted of the smooth, well packed earth.[1]

James Copus and his wife and family of nine children lived in this hut for about eighteen months. It was located three-fourths of a mile northeast of Charles' Mill, on Zimmer's Run, in Ashland County. Who was the innovator and who the borrower, the white settlers or the Indians? In this case, Copus apparently copied the Indians' long house pattern, but the construction technique could have been from either culture.

Such structures were known as "camps" in the eighteenth century, a term denoting rather primitive living conditions that came to be applied to shelters. Here is John Cleves Symmes on the subject, writing from North Bend, Hamilton County, in May 1789:

> We raised what in this country is called a camp, by setting two forks of saplins in the ground, a ridge-pole across, and leaning boat-boards which I had brought from Limestone [Maysville, Ky.], one end on the ground and the other against the ridge-pole; encloseing the end of the camp, and leaving the other open to the weather for a door where our fire was made to fence against the cold which was now very intense. In this hut I lived six weeks before I was able to erect myself a log house & cover it so as to get into the same with my family & property.[2]

Although twenty years apart, the Copus's and Symmes's huts were exactly the same in conception. As quoted in chapter 2, Symmes made extensive use of boat planks in house construction; these were, of course, "Kentucky" or flat boats designed for a one-way trip down the Ohio River. When boat planks or split timber were not readily available, tree branches, brush, or bark could be used.

Howe quotes C. B. Squier of Sandusky, Erie County, on the settlement of the "Fire-Lands" in north-central Ohio:

> These early settlers generally erected the ordinary log cabin, but others of a wandering character built bark huts, which were made by driving a post at each of the four corners and one higher between each of the two end corners, in the middle, to support the roof, which were connected together by a ridge pole. Layers of bark were wound around the side of the posts, each upper layer lapping the one beneath to shed rain. The roof was barked over, strips being

> bent across from one eave over the ridge pole to the other and secured by poles on them. The occupants of these bark huts were squatters, and lived principally by hunting. They were the semi-civilized race that usually precedes the more substantial pioneer in the western wilderness.[3]

Squier was writing of a period just before and during the War of 1812, the first settlers appearing in the spring of 1808. Forty years later, some parts of the Firelands (so-called because the tract, of half a million acres, was set aside by Connecticut to reimburse its citizens who lost property by fire due to Tory raids during the Revolutionary War) were still wild and attracted fur trappers and hunters. The bark hut described sounds much more like an Indian structure than the earlier mentioned examples.

A bark lean-to, or shed, was the home of Benjamin Tappan in Ravenna Township, Portage County, for the last half of 1799. He and his companion, by name of Bixley, "lived in a bark camp, as it was called. It was a place about eight feet square, open towards the East & close on the other three sides & on top, built of Linn bark [basswood or American linden]. At the front side it was high enough for a man to stand up & it sloped back to about 2 feet off the ground. Our fire was in front, in the open air."[4] It is likely that Symmes's and Tappan's use of "camp," a standard frontier term, meant just what it does today—a temporary situation, not descriptive of any specific form of shelter—a definition probably derived from the military. A person can "camp" on the open ground, or in a tent, or a bark lean-to, or in a house for that matter. In fact, as Tappan implies, his was called a "bark camp" simply because bark was the material utilized for a shelter.

In the late fall of 1799, Tappan, Bixley, and two Quakers raised a log "cabbin" 22 by 18 feet in size, a story and a half in height, and shingled it also, in one day. Tappan and his companion then did the chinking and laid puncheon floors. On New Year's Day, 1800, they moved from their bark camp into their new cabin. Tappan commented in his autobiography that "nothing remarkable occurred this first winter. I found use for all my mechanical skill in making furniture for my house & tools for farming. I split puncheons of cherry (which was abundant) &, having hewed them thin enough, made partitions so as to divide my cabbin into three rooms."[5] Assuming Tappan made no unusual division of space, his home would have consisted of one room about 13 by 18 feet (with a fireplace and exterior doors), two rooms about 9 feet square, and a full loft. This was a good size structure, apparently a house because of the shingle roof, rather than a cabin in the classic sense, that is, rafters instead of ribs.

Returning for a moment to the most primitive "camps," the different types were summed up by A. A. Graham in 1880 when writing his history of Richland County:

> The earliest settlers often lived for weeks and months, with their families, in what was called a "pole cabin;" [*sic*] that is, a cabin made of small poles and sticks, and covered with brush and bark. These could be erected by the head of the family, without assistance, in twenty-four or forty-eight hours. . . . Hundreds of these brush cabins were erected. The settlers generally arrived in the spring, and the first consideration was to put in a crop of corn or wheat . . . therefore they put off building their permanent cabins until fall, or until the spring crop was attended to, and in the mean time these temporary brush structures were erected. . . . Sometimes they brought tents . . . at other times they camped out without shelter except such as their covered wagons afforded.[6]

Graham reflects the late development of his part of the state because of the proximity of the Indian lands. The distinction between huts and other such primitive shelters and log cabins is often shadowy, and there is no reason a pole hut could not be as comfortable as a cabin. It should be noted that covered wagons were not common in Ohio until after the War of 1812. The military used freight wagons, usually pulled by oxen, during the Indian Wars of the 1790s and the War of 1812, but the settlers favored two-wheel wagons ("ox-carts") because they were easier to maneuver in the forest. Oxen were preferred over horses because they could endure more hardships—and were, possibly, better tasting if the need arose. The large wagon had no place in Ohio until roads and bridges were numerous; the military roads of the War of 1812 greatly helped the interior development of the state, but it wasn't until the National Road began inching across Ohio in the 1820s that the "covered wagon" traffic could materialize.

Of all the incredible tales of early Ohio, the story of the Perry children of Delaware County ranks near the top, and illustrates the almost total ignorance many immigrants had of frontier conditions. In the fall of 1803, Levi and Reuben Perry, aged eleven and nine years, were left alone in their new cabin near Delhi while their father returned to Philadelphia for Mrs. Perry. Because of illness, neither parent could journey to Ohio until the following June. The boys were left alone, their nearest neighbors being fifteen miles away. The winter was severe. The Perry cabin was unfinished, having neither daubing, fireplace, or chimney. The boys had no gun—they did trap rabbits—and knew nothing of forest life, the family having recently come from Wales. Needless to say, in great romantic tradition, Levi and Reuben survived, and for an amazing eight months.[7] Certainly their cabin was no better, if as good, as the huts and lean-tos mentioned earlier, yet to the modern reader "cabin" certainly implies a reasonably comfortable home. These nebulous distinctions between the various types of frontier shelters, and the endless variations and modifications possible with each form, often make it difficult to know what type of shelter a particular author is discussing. Such should not be the case with log cabins and log houses, however.

CABINS AND HOUSES

Although opinions vary over the meaning of "log cabin" and "log house," and the current tendency is to call all log buildings for human habitation "log cabins," distinctions were made in the eighteenth and nineteenth centuries (just as they were in the use of "blockhouse" referred to earlier). In the 22 October 1814, issue of Lancaster's early newspaper, the *Ohio Eagle*, there is an ad for 160 acres of "good land" and the following buildings: "a good Log House, Cabin, and Stable. . . ."[8] The Reverend James Finley, at old Camp Meigs, one mile south of Upper Sandusky, in the winter of 1819–1820 "built a cabin-house, twenty by twenty-three feet, and without a door, windows, or loft. . . . The winter soon became extremely cold. We made a stable of one of the old block-houses for our cattle; and cut, hauled, and hewed logs to put up a double house, forty-eight feet long by twenty wide, a story and a half high. We hauled timber to the saw-mill, and sawed it ourselves into joists and plank. . . ."[9] These quotes are just two of many that clearly distinguish between cabins and houses, and help to prove that log houses were not log cabins. It remains to define both types of structures.

This writer favors the description written by Thaddeus M. Harris in his *Journal of a Tour into the Territory Northwest of the Alleghany Mountains; Made in the Spring of the Year 1803*.

> The temporary buildings of the first settlers in the wilds are called *Cabins*. They are built with unhewn logs, the interstices between which are stopped with rails, calked with moss or straw, and daubed with mud. The roof is covered with a sort of thin staves split out of oak or ash, about four feet long and five inches wide, fastened on by heavy poles being laid upon them. "If the logs be hewed; if the interstices be stopped with stone, and neatly plastered; and the roof composed of shingles nicely laid on, it is called a *log-house*." A log-house has glass windows and a chimney; a cabin has commonly no window at all, and only a hole at the top for the smoke to escape.[10]

Harris, who was in the Ohio Country at the right time to see log construction near its height, was obviously interested in such buildings and made an effort to be accurate in his description.

On the basis of Harris's semantical distinction, the log cabin has become extinct in Ohio and only the log house remains. This is true because log cabins were expected to serve only a few years. It would be interesting to know if the furor over the log cabin during the Harrison presidential campaign referred to these primitive structures only, not log houses—in which thousands of Ohioans resided in 1840—which were houses coincidentally built of logs. Considered in these terms, the log cabin really *was* the symbol of the frontier to the citizen of 1840 who was recalling an era twenty-five to fifty years before.

The distinction between cabin and house was also indicated in the writings of John Johnston, federal agent at the Fort Wayne Indian Agency in the first decade of the nineteenth century. At that settlement, all the buildings regardless of size and function, were log. The following descriptions are taken from an annual report compiled by Johnston in 1804: The Indian agent's house of hewed logs was 28 feet long, 24 feet wide, two stories high, and had a shingle roof. A large brick chimney stood at the west end. Each story had a fireplace, four windows of twelve lights, and two "apartments." There was a stone-lined cellar under the entire structure. The "Indian House," apparently for overnight visitors, was 25 feet long by 20 feet wide and one story high. It was built of rough logs and had a "clawboard" roof, and a chimney of "cat and clay" on the south end. The public store was built of hewed logs 40 feet long (no width given), was one and a half stories, and had a shingle roof. It had two rooms, sales and storage; the upstairs was for corn and "lumber" (lumber, in this sense, means "surplus or disused articles"). The doors and windows were double-bolted. The agency had many outbuildings which were not detailed; these included a smokehouse, chicken house, and stables. The "skin house," for storing the green hides taken in trade, was 26 by 22 feet, of rough logs, and had a "clawboard" roof; the floor was excavated 2½ feet below the sill to gain some coolness.[11]

The interesting part of Johnston's description is the clear differentiation he draws between the two methods of log construction. The examples are not exactly the same as those described by Harris, but there are points of similarity: "Cabin" style—rough logs, clapboard roof, stick chimney; "house" style—hewed logs, shingle roof, brick chimney, glass windows, cellar.

The distinctions between cabin and house are further delineated in the informative autobiography, *Recollections of Life in Ohio from 1814 to 1848*, by William Cooper Howells, father of the well-known author, William Dean Howells. The Howells family settled in Jefferson County during the War of 1812.

> The farmers lived simply. They were all in about the same social condition, and nearly equal as to wealth. . . . The houses and improvements depended upon the length of time they had been on the place. A man who had just settled was not expected to have much of a house, or other buildings. The first care was to get up what would do, and this was usually a good sized log cabin of round logs, covered with clapboards; that is, split pieces, four feet long and six inches wide, and weighted down on the roof with logs. A barn of the same materials was built. . . . Such barns . . . were mostly made by putting up two log pens—say eighteen feet square, that is all the logs eighteen feet long—at a distance of about eighteen feet apart; the pens were carried up to about twelve feet high, when logs were placed so as to connect the two pens under one roof. . . .
>
> The best farm houses were made of hewn logs, that is, logs flattened to a regular thickness. These were notched together, so that they nearly touched each other in the wall. The interstices were filled with pieces of wood, in a rough way, and then, for a good house, this "chinking" was plastered over with a good mortar of lime and sand, on the inside and outside of the wall. . . . The corners of the house were trimmed down, and doors and windows cut through the logs and cased up. . . . A good house would have a shingled roof, a brick chimney and well laid floor above and below. A very common house floor, as well as barn floor, was made up of what were called puncheons—that is, thick slabs split out of logs, hewn on the face and edges and cut to a level beneath. . . . Our new house had this kind of floor. It was of hewn logs, but had a clap-board roof.[12]

References to puncheon floors are quite common; though many must still exist in Ohio, this writer has seen only two examples. Even as early as 1800 dimensioned lumber for most building purposes was being sawed by the fledgling Ohio milling industry. The gristmill and sawmill proprietors, who were among the first settlers, were apparently dependent only on adequate water sources.[13] General Benjamin Whiteman moved his milling operation from Dayton to the falls of the Little Miami River (Clifton, Greene County) in 1805 because, in his opinion, Dayton was becoming too crowded with mills. Such comments are, of course, relative in time and geographic location. There were in Ohio, in 1805, large, developing urban and agricultural areas, as well as completely unsettled land and the remnants of several Indian tribes. Thus one man could complain of oversettlement while another decried the Indians and the wilderness. This adds confusion to the "temporary" cabin versus the "permanent" house controversy in terms of dating, for obviously they existed simultaneously.

There is considerable contemporary literature on the construction of log buildings describing techniques used. One aspect of construction, however, is usually missing from the accounts: the methods and terminology of corner notching. Because two types of interlocking corners predominated in Ohio, the steeple (or saddle-notch) and the half-dovetail, perhaps this detail was simply taken for granted because it was regarded as commonplace. Corner notching was just one of many tasks connected with the raising of a log building, and, though it seems complicated today, it was probably accomplished as quickly as other aspects of the construction.

NOTCHING

Since the publication of the author's first monograph on log architecture, several contemporary names of corner notches have been found. As will be seen, one name is at great variance with past reference works. Names had to exist for the various forms of notching and be understood by the majority of settlers; it would be illogical to think otherwise. Allowing that such names did exist, then the writers of county histories, personal memoirs, journals, and other eighteenth and nineteenth century popular literature did use them; the fault is our inability to recognize—perhaps accept—the terms used. Since almost all extant examples of Ohio log architecture exhibit only two types of corner notching, what are today called half-dovetail and steeple or inverted-V, then some terms or phrases designative of these notches must be contained in past descriptions of construction practices. Fortunately, a good reference appeared in Michael Broadstone's history of Greene County in a reprint of the specifications for the third county jail, dated 6 December 1808; the logs were to be "half-dovetailed."[14] This was the only original comment found naming half-dovetailing, and it is particularly interesting because of the early date. There is no serious question about half-dovetailing being used in the eighteenth century—no doubt the technique is much older—just that datable Ohio examples seem to cluster in the second quarter of the nineteenth century. Also, only one half-dovetailed double-pen barn has come to light, though one might expect more examples to remain if the technique was widely practiced. Therefore, it must be assumed that the half-dovetail was used primarily for house construction, utilizing moderately sized logs ranging from 10 to 15 inches in diameter. It has been my contention for some time that half-dovetailing was related to blockhouses or simple fortifications. The logs could be closely joined, but without the tedious fitting required with full-dovetailing.

Of the several hundred log buildings seen by this writer, only one was completely full-dovetailed—the Gephart Tavern (ca. 1811) in Miamisburg, Montgomery County. Certainly the indications are that full-dovetailing was not common in Ohio, though it is premature to take too much for granted on the evidence of one example. Solidly joined full-dovetailed walls were desirable, and were used through the central and northern seaboard states. In any case, "full-dovetail" seems to have been a traditional description. What causes difficulty is knowing what plain "dovetail" implies: Full or half? The word is common in Ohio literature. For years, this writer assumed that full-dovetail was meant. The Broadstone reference supports this assumption; however, the use of "dovetail" alone may have been considered ambiguous. If this was the case, then the above reference simply proves the half-dovetail was in use at a point in time. This writer now believes that "dovetail" refers to the prevalent technique of half-dovetailing. More references are needed to settle the matter. Only 1 full-dovetailed house from approximately 400 examined would make the technique seem rarer than it actually was. Because of the closely joined logs, full-dovetailing must have been extensively used on blockhouses and military fortifications.

The "steeple" or "inverted V" is the other common Ohio corner notching technique. It was widely used for house and barn construction until the second quarter of the nineteenth century, then continued for farm outbuildings and houses intended for immediate clapboarding. The steeple-notch allowed logs of widely different diameters to be used together. It was not as well-suited to small diameter logs as was the half-dovetail because the cuts had to be made too shallow to be secure. The author's first clue that there was a definite name for the notch came from William Lang's *History of Seneca County*, in which he comments on the "skill and practice" needed "to make the notches fit the saddles neatly. . . ."[15] It seemed logical that such a common notch must have had a name (no doubt several names), and a name frequently encountered. If the corners were in fact "saddle-notched," then the old definition of saddle-notch in reference to round-log construction, which so many authors have used, must be reinterpreted. ("Steeple-notch" is probably a southern or southeastern term rather than upper midwestern. Apparently "Inverted-V" is a modern definition.) That saddle-notch could be the same as steeple-notch received some support by Angus Sherwood's article "Building in the North." He commented that the "notch and saddle" was used for such structures as piers, dams, and cribbing, the logs of which were firmly locked when loaded; round logs were notched with the "round notch," in which the upper log was fitted over the log below.[16] (Such an arrangement allowed water to drain away from the notch.)

85. Greene County, Spring Valley Township. Double-pen log barn probably built by William McKnight of Virginia about 1807. (See Figures 86, 110, 111, 112, 177.) Photo: 13 January 1973. North front, door to west pen. Pegged doors are occasionally mentioned in literature, but this barn displayed the only two examples yet seen by this writer. Figure is the reverse side.

86. Greene County, Spring Valley Township. Double-pen log barn. (See Figures 85, 110, 111, 112, 177.) Photo: 13 January 1973. Inside view of the door in Figure 85. The boards were pegged to the battens, which in turn were tenoned to the hinge-post. The hinge-post fits in a hole in the sill, but the upper wooden hinge bracket is missing; note the wear on the post where the bracket had been fastened. The main barn doors were reportedly constructed in the same fashion.

87. Greene County, Miami Township. Door of a braced-frame barn (near a brick house in which the plaster is signed and dated, "1828 Stacy Haines"). Photo: July, 1967. All of the small doors on the lower level of this well-constructed bank barn with overbay have wooden hinge-posts. Note that the wooden cleat at the upper end of the hinge-post has pulled down, revealing the fastening pegs. This form of hinge was very common in the Virginia Military District, and in the southwest quarter of Ohio in general.

88. Ross County, Buckskin Township. Double-pen log barn. Pens, 20 feet square; eave, 12 feet. (See Figures 89, 90.) Photo: 27 January 1968. West side. The sheds were apparently original to the barn, for no doors had been affixed to the pens. The breezeway had been stone-flagged; it would be interesting to know if the floor had been used for threshing, for stone does not seem practical.

89. Ross County, Buckskin Township. Double-pen log barn. (See Figures 88, 90.) Photo: 27 January 1968. Southeast corner of south pen. In all probability this barn was intended to have hewed logs, for the sills and lower wall logs were so-shaped (the approach of winter may have been the deciding factor). The round logs were steeple-notched in the usual manner. When viewed from the end, such notches assume a teardrop form.

90. Ross County, Buckskin Township. Double-pen log barn. (See Figures 88, 89.) Photo: 27 January 1968. Southwest corner of north pen. The south pen had been divided into stalls, the north pen left open for a mow. Since log barns were rarely chinked, a good deal of time could have been saved by leaving the logs round, as in the case of this barn.

91. Miami County, Washington Township. Double-pen log barn. (See Figures 92 through 98.) Photo: June, 1971. East side of barn during disassembly. Three men, working with a crane, dismantled the barn in about three days. A new foundation was laid and the barn was rebuilt, repairs being made as needed. Some damaged logs were spliced; several logs had to be replaced, as did almost all mow logs. Over 40 logs, 30 feet long and 18 inches in diameter, were used.

92. Miami County, Washington Township. Double-pen log barn built in 1808 by James Kigans for John Johnston. The original cost was $280. Each pen, 29 feet 8 inches square. (See Figures 91, 93 through 98.) Photo: June, 1971. North end, view to south. This is the largest barn of this type yet found in Ohio, and amazingly enough it is well documented. Its basic size of approximately 90 by 30 feet was enlarged by perimeter sheds to 111 by 54 feet, in 1826; a wooden threshing floor was also installed at that time. In 1851–52 a new, steeply pitched roof was built. (National Register of Historic Places.)

93. Miami County, Washington Township. Double-pen log barn. (See Figures 91, 92, 94 through 98.) Photo: July, 1967. North pen, west entrance. These steeple-notched logs were from 15 to 18 inches in diameter. The upper, overmow logs were half-lapped and notched. The open mortises near the center were for two different sheds, the first dating 1826.

94. Miami County, Washington Township. Double-pen log barn. (See Figures 91, 92, 93, 95, 96, 97, 98.) Photo: June, 1971. Half-lap joint in plate. The white oak plates were composed of two sections, 60 and 30 feet long, 15 by 12 inches perimeter. Two sets of rafter mortises appear because of the altered sheds. The 1851–52 roof rafters butted on top of the plates, and were fastened with large spikes.

95. Miami County, Washington Township. Double-pen log barn. (See Figures 91 through 94, 96, 97, 98.) Photo: 11 April 1967. Section of threshing floor installed in 1826 by John Keyt and John D. Heller. The log sleepers or joists, 12 to 18 inches in diameter, were placed 29 to 42 inches on-center, with 12 inch sections at each side next to the pens. The threshing floor was doubled, the upper boards being 6½ feet long, 13 inches wide, and 2 inches thick. The lower boards sealing the joints of the upper flooring were 6½ feet long, 7 inches wide, and ¾ inches thick. The floor was laid in sections running east and west. At every third sleeper, the boards were butted to a longitudinal strip. Each board of the doubled floor was pegged to two sleepers. A similar threshing floor was found in a barn in Warren County, see Figure 81.

96. Miami County, Washington Township. Double-pen log barn. (See Figures 91 through 95, 97, 98.) Photo: October, 1971. The east shed framing on the restored pens. The correct post spacing was known by in-place foundation stones. The braces were fitted into the original mortises in the logs. (This barn is a functional building today, part of the Johnston Farm restoration, Piqua Historical Area, administered by the Ohio Historical Society. The barn is on the National Register of Historic Places.)

97. Miami County, Washington Township. Double-pen log barn. (See Figures 91 through 96, 98.) Photo: 25 October 1978. Sycamore log grain bins. These traditional bins, with fire-charred interiors to preserve the wood and contents, are a type frequently mentioned in 19th century literature. They are now scarce, though this writer has seen many of them on farms through the years.

98. Miami County, Washington Township. Double-pen log barn. (See Figures 91 through 97.) Photo: June, 1971. Door jamb, north pen. Note the mortise for the pintle hinge, the dada for the original door, and the ends of the pegs holding the logs.

99. Auglaize County, St. Marys Township. Double-pen log barn, each pen 20 by 28 feet. Photo: 21 October 1973. Brace for shed frame. The braces had to be anchored, due to the thrust of the rafters against the shed framing. The tight chinking between the logs below the brace was unusual for a barn, as was the use of half-dovetailing for the logs. West-central Ohio was largely settled in the 1830s by immigrants from the Germanic States, so these details may indicate ethnic preferences. Another half-dovetailed double-pen barn is located near Ottawa, Putnam County.

100. Guernsey County, Londonderry Township. Double-pen log barn. Photo: 10 October 1966. Cross-beam for anchoring shed framing. In this case, the sheds were planned before construction began; commonly, they were added later. There is no evidence that either procedure is indicative of a time period or an ethnic background of a builder.

101. Franklin County, Franklin Township. Double-pen log barn, built *ca.* 1813, by or for William Miller. Each pen, 24½ feet square; height to eaves, 16 feet. (See Figures 78, 109.) Photo: 27 January 1968. Front, south. Logs used as cross-beams to support roof plate. This side may have had sheds, as did the north side, but no evidence of the framing remained.

102. Monroe County, Seneca Township. Single-pen log barn. Size, approximately 18 feet square. Photo: 3 May 1972. North end. This type of barn is common to southeastern Ohio, and appears frequently in marginal agricultural areas of the state.

103. Monroe County, Seneca Township. Small hillside log barn. Photo: 3 May 1972. North side. A form common to the hilly areas of Ohio, particularly in the southeast quarter, these small barns made good use of the natural levels provided by hillside sites. Note the shake roof and the method of capping the ridge. Usually the projecting shakes of the cap were on the side of the roof towards the prevailing wind.

104. Clark County, Greene Township. Double-pen log bank barn, near brick house dated 1827 on facade; barn may be earlier. Pens, 24 feet square; overall length, 66 feet; framed 6 foot forebay. Photo: 30 May 1971. Exhibiting excellent craftsmanship, the ends of each log are chamfered, this is a true bank barn with forebay. The roof trusses, braces, and purlins are common to braced-frame construction. This combination of techniques argues in favor of the 1827 date.

105. A traditional corncrib constructed of poles and split timber, often called "split rail." It was built in the 1920s, and is located near Friendship, Ripley County, Indiana. Photo: August, 1977.

106. Noble County, Beaver Township. Tobacco barn. Photo: 3 May 1972. These tall tobacco barns, or kilns, built for smoke and heat curing, were common throughout eastern Ohio in the 19th and early 20th centuries. This barn displays both hewed and round logs, so it may be an altered or repaired structure. The house to the rear was also log. (For a description of the use of these barns, see Figure 107, Belmont County.)

107. Belmont County, Somerset Township. Tobacco barn or kiln, approximately 15 feet square, 25 feet in height. Photo: 3 May 1972. The tobacco barn was a common structure in eastern Ohio in the 19th century. The tobacco was first tied in hands and placed over poles to wilt, then transferred inside. Curing was effected by both heat and smoke, from a wood fire, which passed through a stone flue laid the length of the building. Later, a furnace was used outside the building, allowing only the heat to reach the interior; a milder tobacco was the result.

108. Jackson County, in the Hanging Rock Iron Region of southeastern Ohio. Photograph by Prof. Wilbur Stout, Ohio State University, *ca.* 1914. One and a half story house with spring house, *ca.* 1850. This view may show back of house which originally had shed addition; window added when addition removed. Exterior chimney also removed and opening covered with vertical clapboarding.

109. Franklin County, Franklin Township. Log smokehouse, inscribed above the door: "Wm. Miller 1813." (See Figures 78, 101.) Photo: 27 January 1968. This small smokehouse is of interest mainly because it is dated. Its form is traditional to the Ohio Country. A two story log house stood nearby, close enough that when it burned the shape of a washtub was charred on the front of the smokehouse.

110. Greene County, Spring Valley Township. Log smokehouse. (See Figures 85, 86, 111, 112, 177.) Photo: 13 January 1973. The writer would have passed by this small structure; fortunately his wife did not. It contained the first example of a puncheon floor either had seen. This smokehouse stood on the Elam farm just north of the William McKnight property. The log construction on the two farms appeared to have been by the same person(s).

111. Greene County, Spring Valley Township. Log smokehouse. (See Figures 85, 86, 110, 112, 177.) Photo: 13 January 1973. The walls of this interesting smokehouse were chinked with carefully shaped blocks of wood anchored with pegs, showing excellent workmanship. The building is now at the "Caesar's Creek Pioneer Village" in Warren County.

112. Greene County, Spring Valley Township. Log smokehouse. (See Figures 85, 86, 110, 111, 177.) Photo: 13 January 1973. Detail of puncheon floor, pegs, and sleepers. The puncheons were random width, but averaged about 12 inches. They were approximately 4 feet in length and 4 inches in thickness in the center. These puncheons were the type used in cabins and houses. (See also Figure 75, Madison County.)

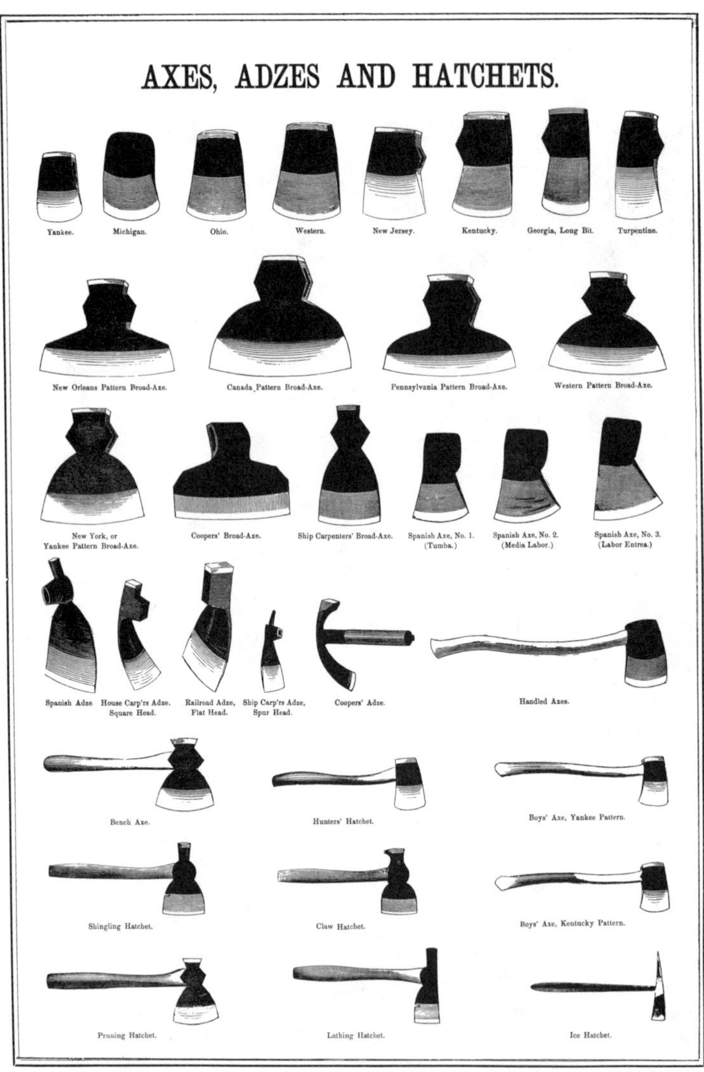

113. "Axes, Adzes and Hatchets," 1865 Russell and Erwin Hardware Company catalog, p. 73. These tools were probably manufactured by the famous Collins Company of Collinsville, Connecticut, which was founded in 1828. Despite the names, most of these patterns originated in the 18th century or earlier. Some are still manufactured.

114. Washington County, City of Marietta. Original exterior wall of the Putnam House, *Campus Martius*, 1788. (See Figures 151, 174, 207.) Photo: February, 1968. Two sawpits were established by the Ohio Company in the summer of 1788 to supply the planks for the stockade. The planks range from 8 to 16 feet long, and are about 4 inches thick by 12 inches wide. Pitsawing left shallow, irregular kerfs that occasionally crossed one another to form X's. In comparison, the vertical, waterpowered sash-saw left a regular succession of evenly spaced kerfs. Sash-sawed wood is very common in Ohio, and is often mistaken for the former. Two sawmills were operating near Marietta in 1789, though their output was small.

115. Section of slippery elm log from Chief Tarhe's cabin at Cranetown, near Upper Sandusky, Wyandot County. The 18 by 14 foot cabin was torn down in 1850, but pieces were saved as souvenirs. This section averages 7 inches in diameter.

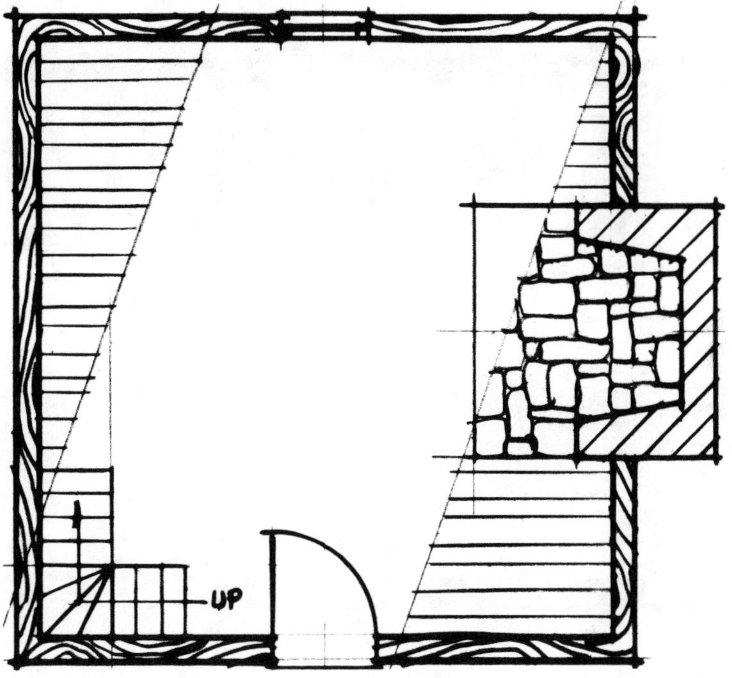

116. 1) Square house. The stairwell was usually on the wall opposite the fireplace. It is possible an extant square house could have been half of an original double-pen structure. Square houses were not common in Ohio. (Average size noted: 18 feet square, one and a half stories.)
Delineated by Dellas H. Harder, Architect

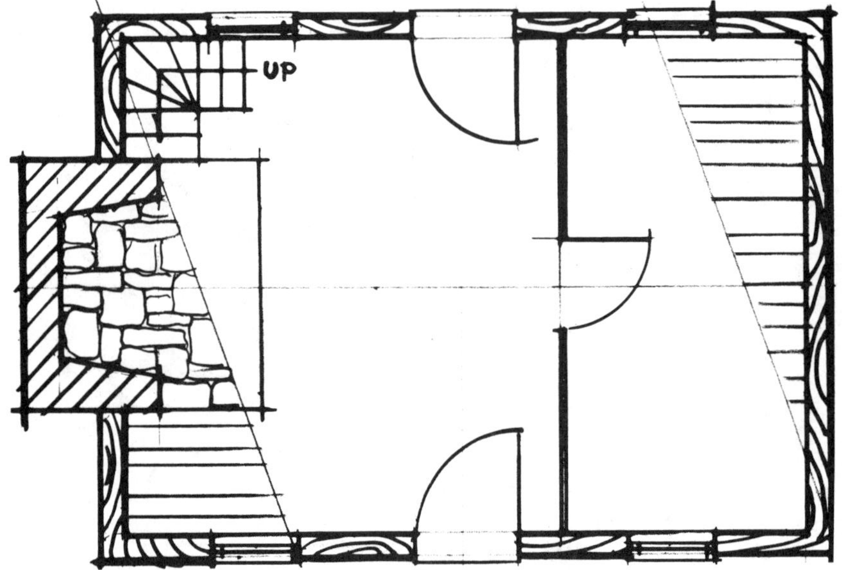

116. 2) Rectangular single or double room house. The stairs were almost always beside the fireplace. The front and back doors usually faced one another, though the window openings might vary from building to building. The interior wall partition was normally of vertical boards. (Average size noted: Length, 21 feet; width, 15 feet; one or one and a half stories; attic open to roof.)

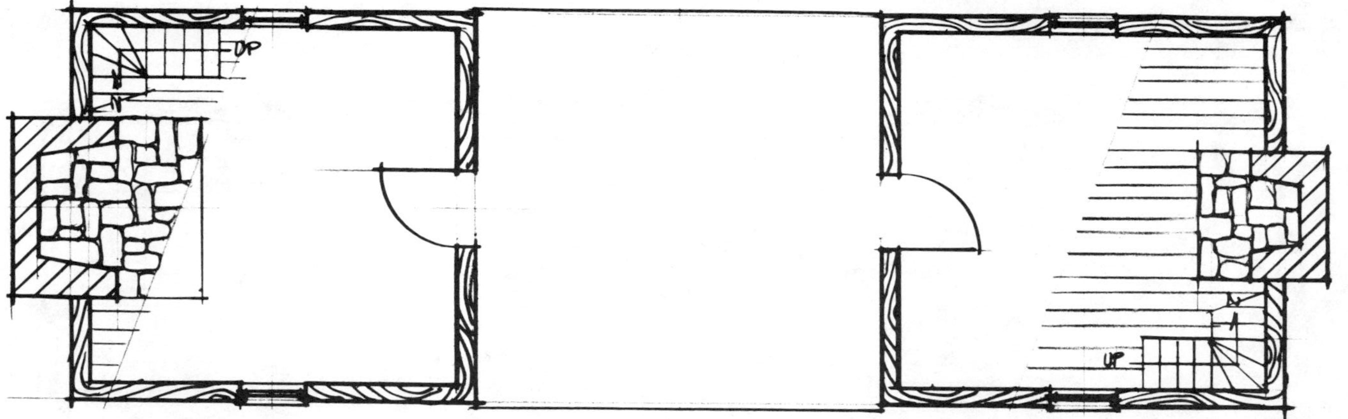

116. 3) Double-pen house with open or closed breezeway. In warm climates the breezeway was customarily left open ("dogtrot"). Both open and closed breezeways were used in Ohio. The placement of the doors and windows as shown was typical for both style structures. (Average size noted: None reported; two 15 foot pens would form a structure 45 feet long, one and a half or two stories.)

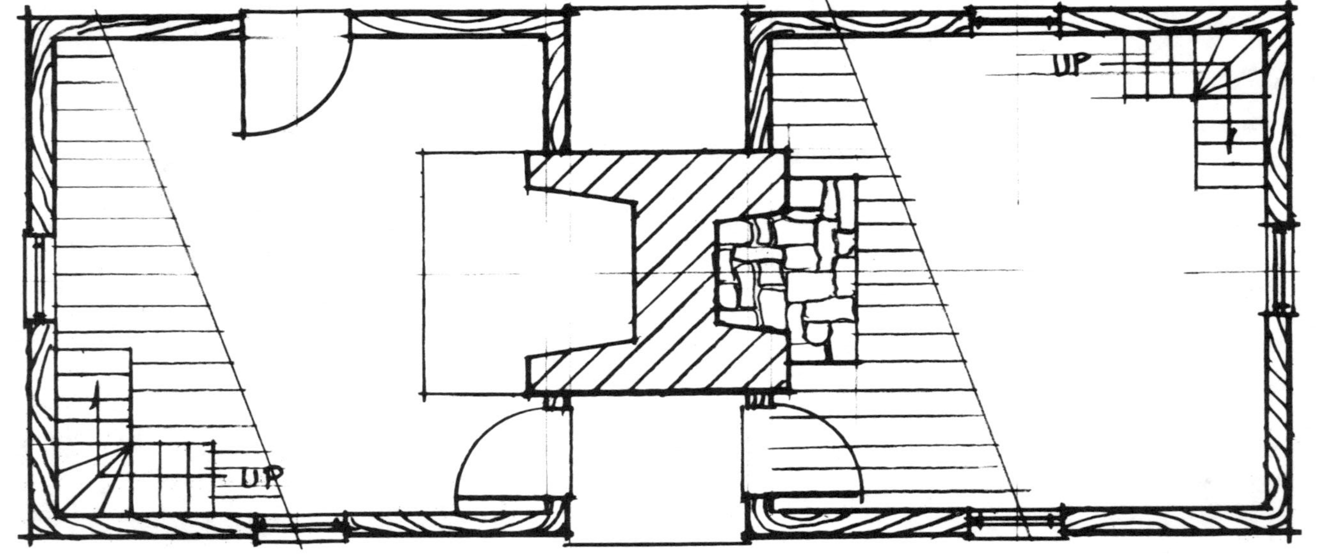

116. 4) Saddle-bag house. Though this style of house required two log pens as did the breezeway structure, the pens were separated only by the depth of the chimney. This style of house was not as common in Ohio as it was in the eastern and southeastern states. (Average size noted: Two few have been reported to establish an average size; the Clermont County example has 15 foot square pens with a 5 foot separation for the chimney. These houses often utilized both a one and a half and a two story section.)

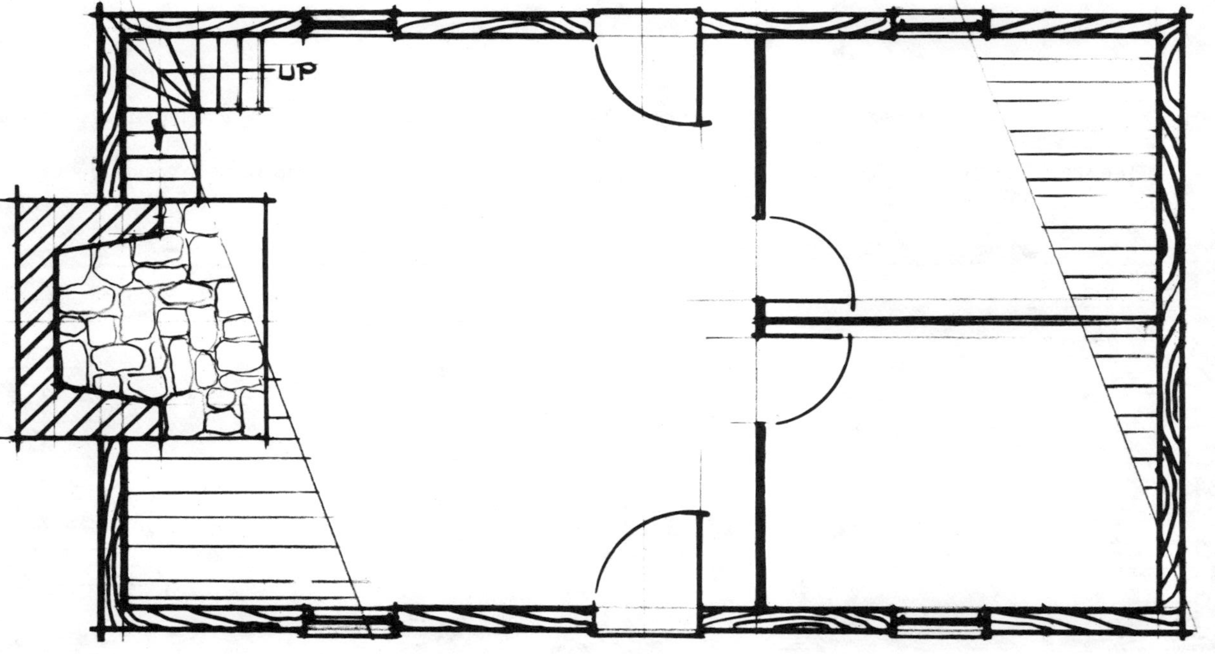

116. 5) Two story house with several rooms. Ceiling heights of the first and second floors were about the same, with a low garret above the second floor. Interior wall partitions were usually of vertical boards. The stairwell could be in a corner or in the center of the house. These large log houses were frequently as well finished as houses of brick or stone. (Average size noted: Length, 30 feet; width, 18 feet.)

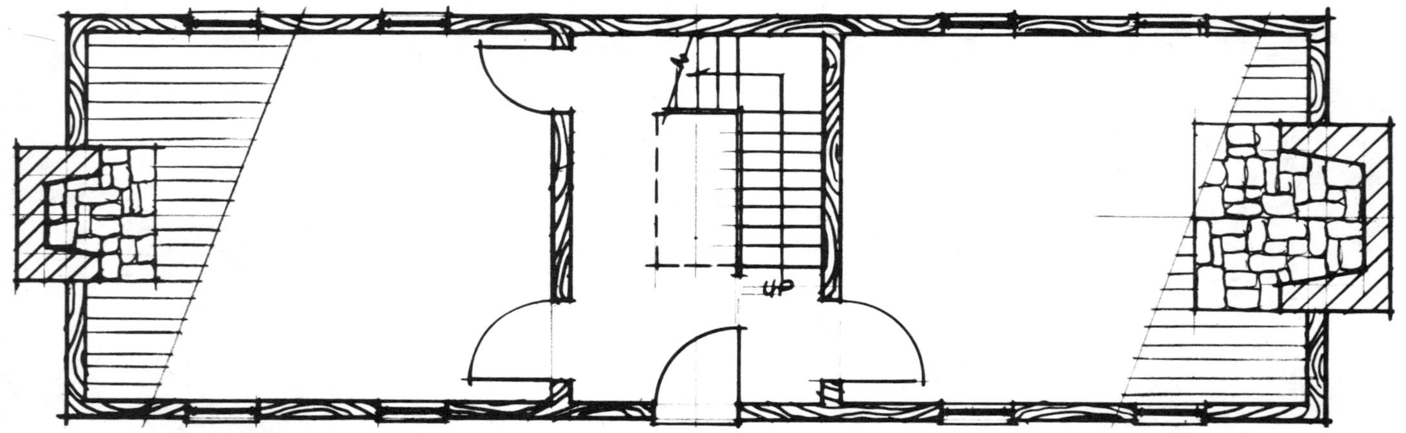

116. 6) Double-house. This could be a true double-pen house, with a narrow separation between the pens forming a hallway with staircase, or a unified structure with central log cross-walls. The latter definition is probably best, for the house had to be considered in its entirety during construction. (Average size noted: Apparently always large. The tavern in Brown County is the largest known in Ohio, and is 48 feet long, $18\frac{1}{2}$ feet wide, and has a 9 foot hall.)

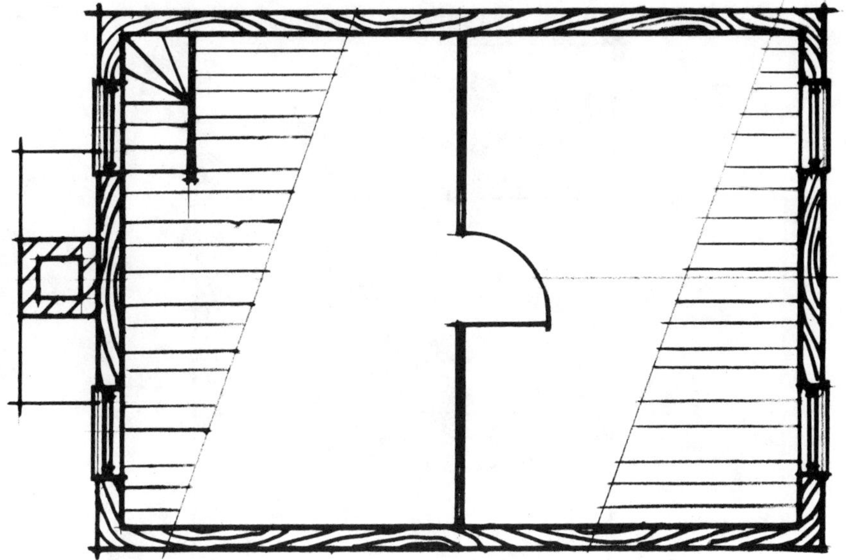

116. 7) Second floor. A common pattern for a one and a half story house, with or without a board partition. Small gable windows. No fireplace. This arrangement, with minor variations for heating or partitions, was used for two story houses as well.

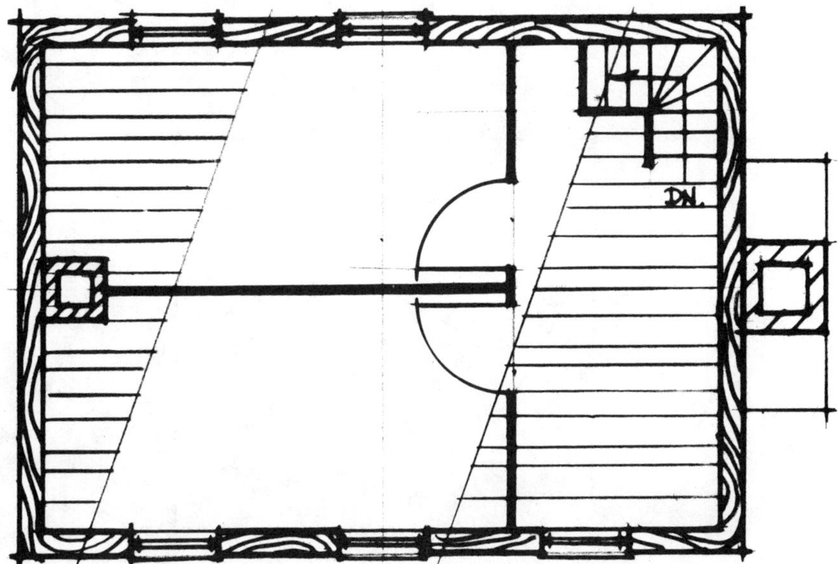

116. 8) Second floor. A variant plan for a two story house in which two longitudinal rooms and an end hall are formed by board partitions. The rooms and hall were usually well illuminated by several windows. A small chimney often served two stoves.

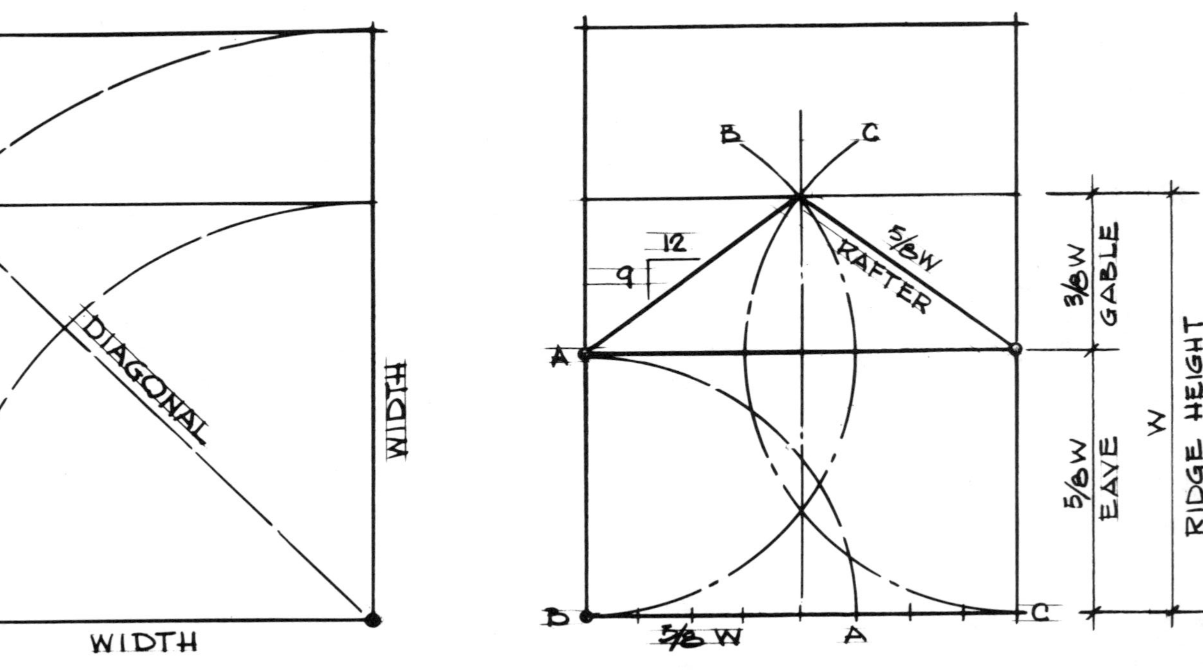

117. (*a*) Simple geometric proportionment of a log house using a straight-edge and compass. (*b*) Proportionment of gable elevation using same instruments.

118. "Design for a Log-House," an architect's conception, from Calvert Vaux, *Villas & Cottages*, 1864 ed., p. 128. From bare necessity to rustic pleasure: The log house in transition.

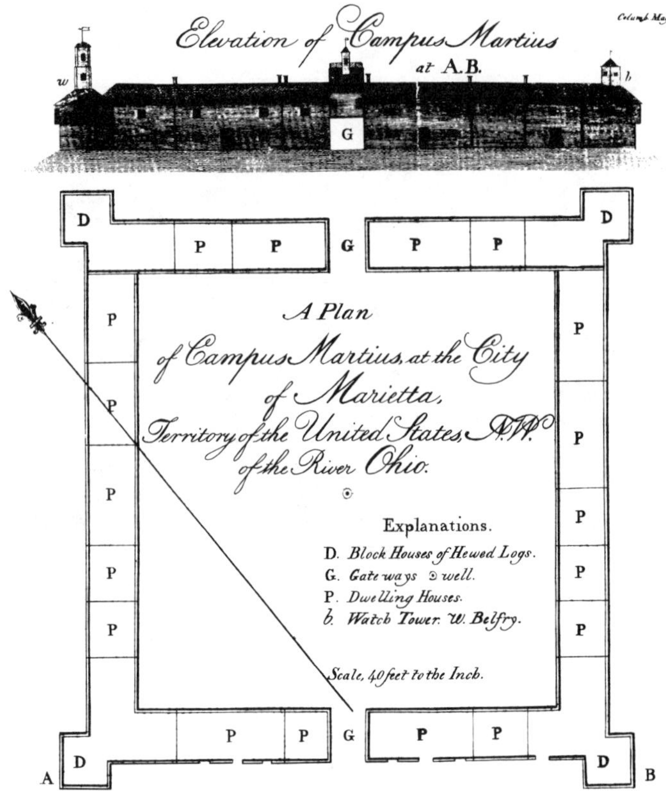

119. An elevation and plan of *Campus Martius* drawn by Winthrop Sargeant for *The Columbian Magazine* (Philadelphia), November, 1788. Sargeant, Secretary for the Territorial Government, lived in a small apartment over the main gate. This southwestern facade and the perimeter walls were completed by late summer, but the interior walls were not completed until the following year, and the stockade really wasn't finished until 1791 under the threat of an Indian attack. The completed partitions within the curtain-walls were not exactly as shown, but the facade is probably accurate.

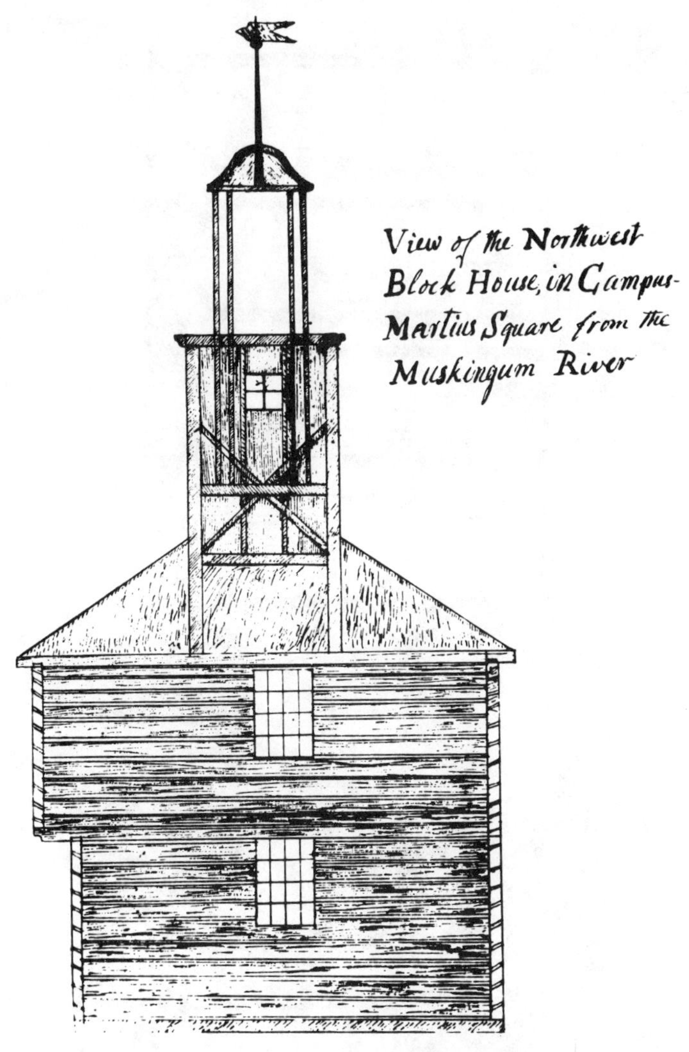

120. "View of the Northwest Block House in Campus Martius Square from the Muskingum River." Copy from Dawes Library, Marietta College. A contemporary drawing, showing half-dovetailed logs and the interior framing of the watch-tower. This blockhouse was the first structure built on the site, 1788, and it was slightly smaller and constructed differently than the three later blockhouses. Note that Sargeant's drawing, Figure 119, shows it correctly; most later illustrations show the blockhouses exactly alike. This, the northwest blockhouse, was used for public meetings, and served as a church and school.

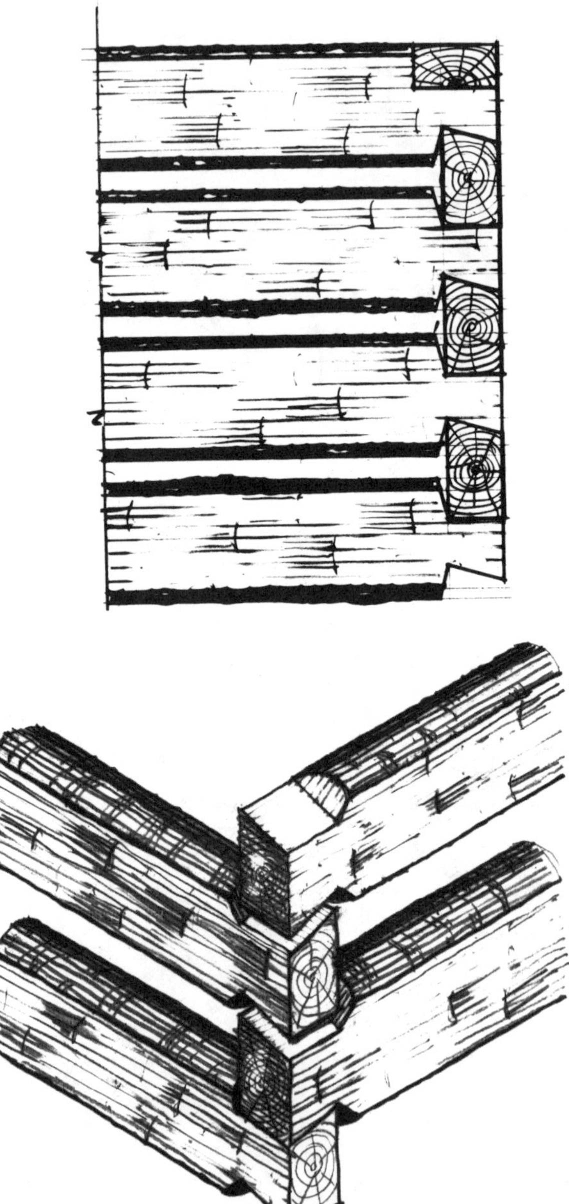

121. (*a*) Half-dovetail notching. This was a common style of notching in Ohio. It was sparingly used during the first quarter of the nineteenth century, and is seldom found on structures other than houses or small outbuildings. Half-dovetailing permitted a close joining of logs. The logs were seldom large; a width of 8 inches and a diameter of 10 to 12 inches was average.

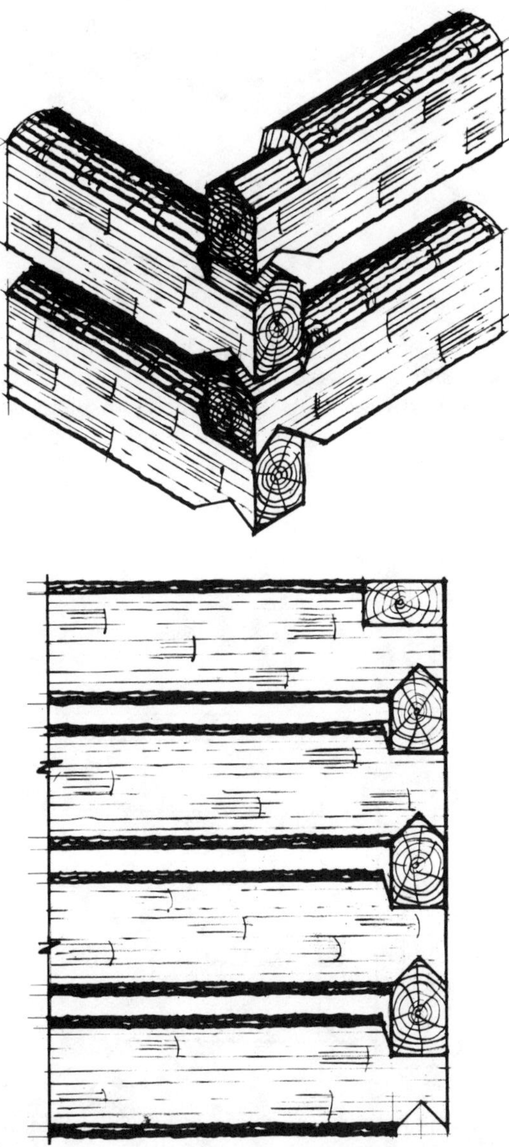

121. (*b*) Steeple, inverted-V, or, correctly, saddle notching. Steeple notching was used on almost all structures in Ohio until the mid-1820s when it gradually disappeared in house building unless the house was to be sided. This style of notching allowed logs of varying diameters to be used together, though 12 to 24 inches are the usual limits. It is the standard log barn notch.

121. (*c*) Round-log saddle notching. This very rudimentary form of notching is usually associated with the log cabin and corncrib. The logs were customarily left round, 6 to 8 inches in diameter being average. In Canada, this notching style was termed "hog pen." The logs were notched over each other, lower side only, to allow water to drain from the joint.

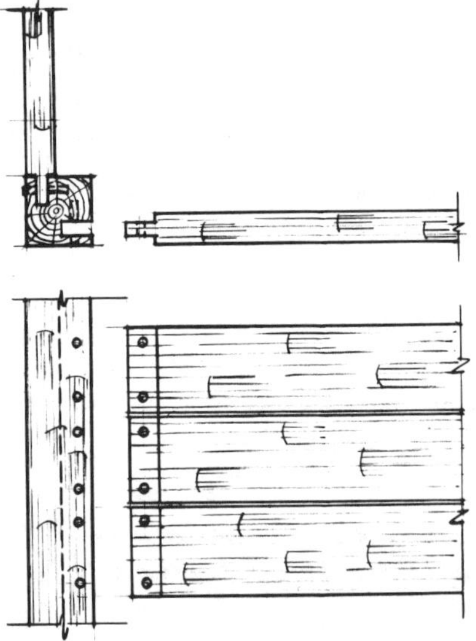

121. (*d*) Running mortise and tenon joint. This style of joint is included in the general category of log construction, though it really belongs to "plank wall" construction, in Canada known as "Manitoba frame." Obviously such fabrication required more time and care than one of the common notching systems. The few buildings found in Ohio using this method of joining have logs, or planks, ranging from 4 to 10 inches in width.

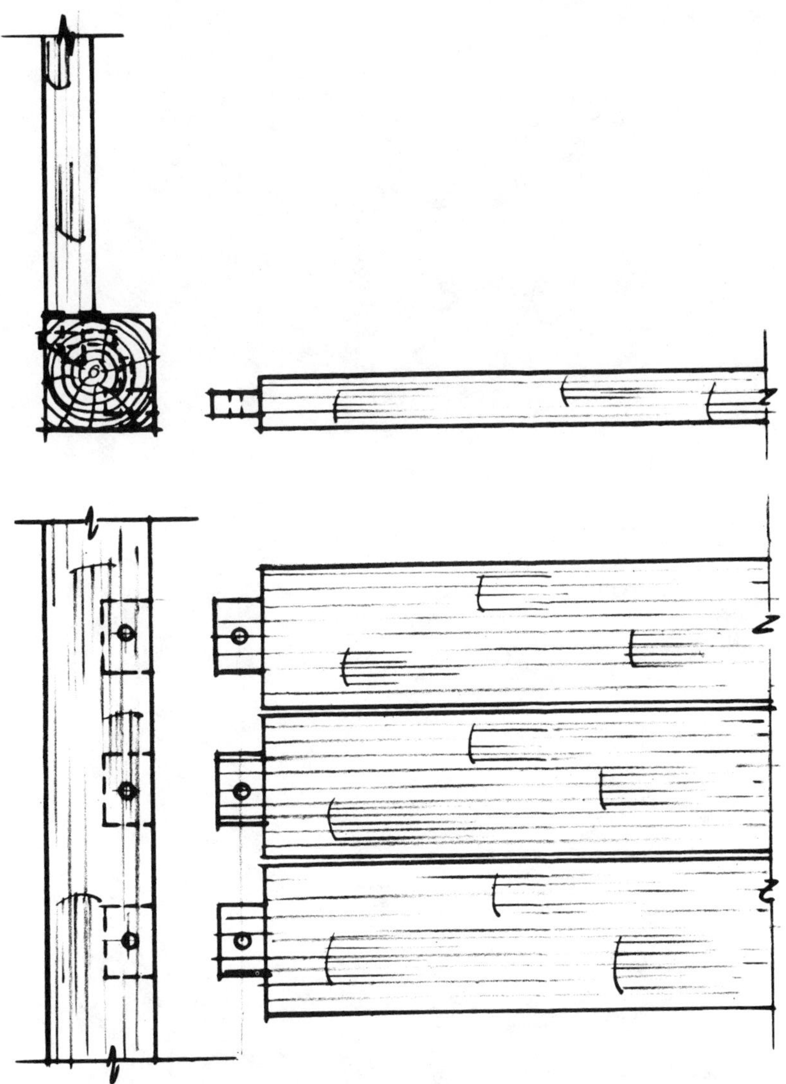

121. (*e*) Single mortise and tenon joint. This joint, which certainly was an adaptation of braced-frame technique, has been found on several houses of direct Germanic ancestry. The "logs" used were of full 8-inch width, usually about 12 inches in diameter. The houses look like standard log construction until one notices the vertical corner posts, then the fact that the logs on opposite sides are parallel, not offset.

121. (*f*) Full-dovetail notching. While scarce in Ohio, this was a fairly common style of notching on the eastern seaboard in the eighteenth century. Walls built in this fashion were often so tightly joined no chinking and daubing were required. It is the most difficult to cut, but the best of the notching techniques.

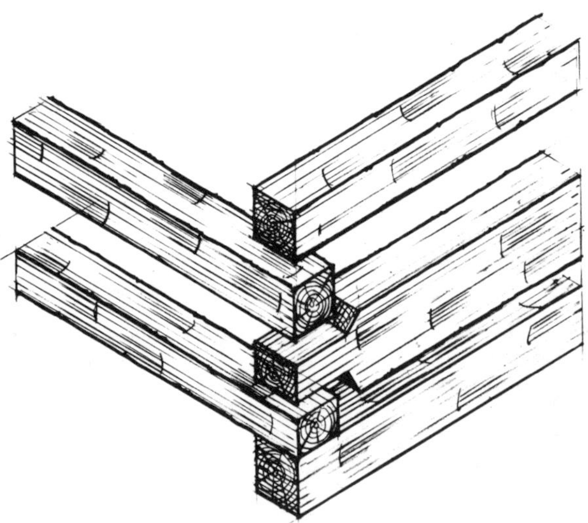

121. (*g*) Full- and half-lap corners. There was no interlock between logs with this building style. Lapped corners are commonly found on houses that were sided when built. There was a great deal of space between full-lapped logs. These corner styles were frequently pegged or nailed because of the lack of an interlock.

122. Parts of a log cabin. This illustration was used for the article "Our Cabin; or, Life in the Woods," by John S. Williams, *American Pioneer*, October, 1843 (Appendix E). The cabin was built during the winter of 1800–01 in Colerain Township, Belmont County.

A) Eave beam	F) Ridgepole	M) Full-dovetailed firebox
B) Butting Pole	G) Clapboards	N) Cat and daub chimney
C) Knee	H) Trapping	O) Chimney prop
D) Weight pole	K) Sill	R) Ceiling joist
E) Rib	L) Saddle-notched corner	S) Floor joist

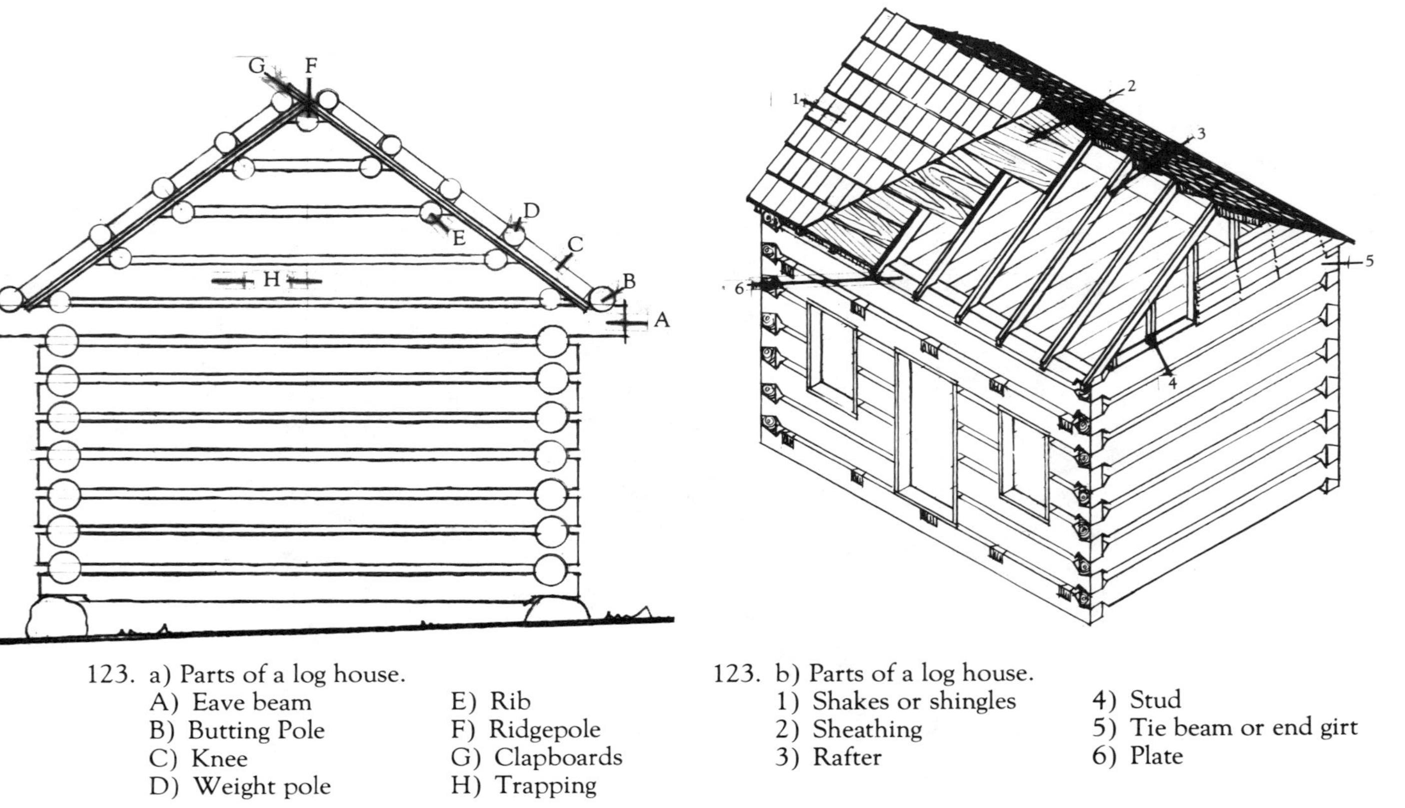

123. a) Parts of a log house.
A) Eave beam
B) Butting Pole
C) Knee
D) Weight pole
E) Rib
F) Ridgepole
G) Clapboards
H) Trapping

123. b) Parts of a log house.
1) Shakes or shingles
2) Sheathing
3) Rafter
4) Stud
5) Tie beam or end girt
6) Plate

The best evidence in favor of "saddle-notch" comes from a chapter written by William Patrick in Joshua Antrim's *History of Champaign and Logan Counties from Their First Settlement.*[17] Patrick's description of log construction is so good—perhaps the best—it has been included as appendix G. On page 16, Patrick clearly describes the steeple-notch and says that it was "familiarly known as the *saddle.*" The cross logs were "notched" to fit the saddles. The cabin he describes has features of both round and hewn log construction.

Here are three authors, widely divided in time, using similar descriptive terms for the steeple-notch. Further, Sherwood adds a needed term for the round log notch, simply "round notch," and, one wonders, if the old statement about "notching logs" might well be semantically correct for the simple operation of fitting round logs together.[18] Consequently, it is entirely possible that "saddle-notch" should replace or at least stand side by side with "steeple-notch," and should be removed from the jargon of round log construction. To complicate matters further, the common corner interlocks can be called, simply, "notches" or "dovetails." In a given area at a given point in time, the use of "notch" could mean only one thing—a steeple-notch. With the passage of time and disuse of the term, "notch" could be equally as descriptive of a half-dovetail. There is no doubt that such semantical shifts did occur during the full course of the nineteenth century. Add other anomalies such as geographic and ethnic isolation, and widely divergent terms could be in use at the same time.

In Ohio, the Scotch-Irish and Germans always seemed more compatible to one another than either were to the English or French; other ethnic cultures were never present in sufficient numbers during the settlement phase to affect local jargon. The words and descriptive terms relative to log construction, then, are probably direct translations of German speech, or are words coined by the Scotch-Irish to describe building techniques foreign to their culture. Because of the possible combinations of words inherent in such a haphazard system of assembling a vocabulary, it is surprising a fairly concise array of terms did arise. Only corner-notching seems to have eluded the commentators. This hints at very simple descriptive words, *vide* the foregoing comments; complex terms would have been remembered because of their very complexity and quaint obsolescence. Finally, the saddle-notch will probably remain the steeple-notch, and the round notch will remain the saddle-notch, just as every log house will remain a log cabin, because the terms have become common knowledge through use in this century. Additional information may be revealed, as more diaries and manuscripts of the eighteenth and nineteenth centuries are discovered.

A very good description of building a log cabin appears in the Reverend Joseph Doddridge's book, *Notes, on the Settlement and Indian Wars, of the Western Parts of Virginia and Pennsylvania from 1763 to 1783*:

> The fatigue party consisted of choppers, whose business it was to fell the trees and cut them off at proper lengths. A man with a team for hauling them to the place, and arranging them, properly assorted, at the sides and ends of the building, a carpenter, if such he might be called, whose business it was to search the woods for a proper tree for making clapboards for the roof. The tree for this purpose must be straight grained and from three to four feet in diameter. The boards were split four feet long, with a large frow, and as wide as the timber would allow. They were used without plaining [*sic*] or shaving. Another division were employed in getting puncheons for the floor of the cabin; this was done by splitting trees, about eighteen inches in diameter, and hewing the faces of them with a broad axe. They were half the length of the floor they were intended to make.
>
> The materials for the cabin were mostly prepared on the first day and sometimes the foundation laid in the evening. The second day was allotted for the raising.
>
> In the morning of the next day the neighbors collected for the raising. The first thing to be done was the election of four corner men, whose business it was to notch and place the logs. The rest of the company furnished them with the timbers. In the meantime the boards and puncheons were collecting for the floor and roof, so that by the time the cabin was a few rounds high the sleepers and floor began to be laid. The door was made by sawing or cutting the

logs in one side so as to make an opening about three feet wide. This opening was secured by upright pieces of timber about three inches thick through which holes were bored into the ends of the logs for the purpose of pinning them fast. A similar opening, but wider, was made at the end for the chimney. This was built of logs and made large to admit of a back and jams [*sic*] of stone. At the square, two end logs projected a foot or eighteen inches beyond the wall to receive the butting poles, as they were called, against which the ends of the first row of clap boards was supported. The roof was formed by making the end logs shorter until a single log formed the comb of the roof, on these logs the clap boards were placed, the ranges of them lapping some distance over those next below them and kept in their places by logs, placed at proper distances upon them.

The roof, and sometimes, the floor were finished on the same day of the raising. A third day was commonly spent by a few carpenters in leveling off the floor, making a clap board door and a table. . . .

In the mean time masons were at work. With the heart pieces of the timber of which the clapboards were made, they made billets for chunking up the cracks between the logs of the cabin and chimney, a large bed of mortar was made for daubing up those cracks; a few stones formed the back and jambs of the chimney.[19]

In one of the earliest Ohio county histories, *History of Athens County, Ohio*, Charles M. Walker gives an excellent description of the construction of a log cabin:

The first business of each settler was to make a little clearing and erect a log cabin, which was built with unhewed logs, poles, clapboards, puncheons, and, in those days, wooden pins instead of nails. In its erection, no tools were necessary except an axe, an auger, and, perhaps, a cross-cut saw. Straight trees of the proper size were cut down, and either drawn by a team, or carried with the assistance of neighbors, to the building spot. The logs being cut of proper lengths were notched and laid up somewhat as children build cob-houses. If a large, or "double" cabin was desired, the logs were laid up to form two square pens, with an open space between, connected by a roof above and a floor below, so as to form a parallelogram, nearly three times as long as wide. In the open space, the family sometimes took their meals in pleasant weather, and it

> served the triple purpose of kitchen, lumber [storage] room, and dining room. The roof was covered with thin splits of oak, something like staves, about four feet long, from four to six inches wide, and about one-third of an inch thick. Instead of being nailed, these staves or clapboards were generally confined in their place by heavy timbers, laid at right angles across them, giving the roof a unique and rough appearance. A door-way and windows were made by chopping out the logs of proper length and hight [*sic*] before laying them up, so as to make suitable apertures. . . . The floors (when any were used) were made of short, thick plank, split from poplar, walnut, or oak. In some cases, the more wealthy settlers had the logs hewed on the inside, and the puncheon floor hewed and planed. . . . Finally, the spaces between the logs were filled with timber, split like fire wood, from some soft tree, and made impervious to wind and rain by daubing the cracks with mud.[20]

The Harris, Doddridge, and Walker descriptions are quite similar considering they were written over a sixty-six-year span (and assuming no borrowing of notes occurred).[21] Walker mentions as tools an ax, auger, and saw, although the building he describes really did not need the latter item; Doddridge adds the frow and broadax. It is worth noting that an ax alone was sufficient to make a rough cabin, though probably most settlers had an auger, and many owned a saw. The broadax and hand adze were also common tools. With the addition of a frow and nails, a well-finished log house could be constructed. The ax and auger were the basic tools for a reasonably well-constructed house (chapter 10 describes tools and their uses in greater detail).

Walker's description of the method used in forming window and door openings was atypical in log construction, though it may reflect a certain ethnic typology. The common method of constructing these openings, after the walls have been raised, is given by John Woods. "A door-place, of the usual size, is cut through the logs, and two pieces of wood are nailed or pegged up to the ends of the sawed logs, to keep them in their places, and to serve for door-posts;. . . . The windows are made in the same manner as the door-places."[22] Woods also describes the doors and windows used in such openings.

> The doors are generally made of cleft-boards, nailed or pegged on some ledges [battens], with wooden hinges, made in the following manner. A piece in the back part of the door is left longer than the door, and enters a hole in the sill; and at the top of the door a piece is also left to rest against the top of the door-place, which is covered with a piece of wood, either nailed or pegged over it. The windows are always sash ones; the usual size of the glass is eight inches by ten; the windows are sometimes made to open with hinges, and others to slide backwards and forwards, while others take out and in. When the doors are made of sawed boards they have eight or ten panes of glass in them, and then it is seldom there is any other window in the cabin.[23]

Woods is describing the common board and batten door, but with a wooden hinge. On one vertical edge of the door a board, heavier than the rest, extended a few inches above the top and bottom edges for a hinge post. The ends of this board were shaped as round as possible. The bottom of the hinge post fit into a hole in the sill or threshold. The top was encircled by a separate piece of wood fastened to the door lintel. The author has seen several examples of this type of door hinge still in use in Ohio, but only on barns.

Woods's comments on windows (in Illinois) apply in Ohio, though glass sizes could vary. The use of door lights in Ohio log cabins and houses may not have been as common as Woods found, however. Certainly examples still exist, but usually on paneled doors. Woods does comment that they were normally found on cabins without other windows. Oiled paper, often referred to as a substitute for glass, was used in Ohio, but not as commonly as popular history might imply. For example, "Windows made of a little twelve-by-twelve piece of oiled paper. . . ."[24] and "There was no glass to be had for the window, and for the want of it a piece of paper pasted over the hole let light enough through to see by, especially when the paper was greased."[25] Window glass was an important item of trade in the Northwest Territory, and Pittsburgh and eastern Ohio were centers of glass production early in the nineteenth century. A wilderness did not remain a wilderness long, particularly in Ohio, for the trader and the merchant were hard on the pioneers' heels—if they had not actually preceded them. There probably never was a time in Ohio, even before the Indian Wars (remember the Indian houses at Newcomerstown), that glass could not be obtained, though the price might be high. This latter consideration, rather than the scarcity of glass, no doubt gave rise to the use of substitutes. Much of the glass used in the United States at the end of the eighteenth century actually came from England as ballast in English merchant vessels. This glass, less expensive than the American product, was generally considered to be of better quality and found its way into the Ohio River trade.

An early comment on the use of glass in Ohio appears in Oliver Spencer's narrative of his Indian captivity. The Spencer family moved into Ohio about 1792 and settled in an area known as Columbia, a tentative village near the mouth of the Little Miami River in Hamilton County. Spencer described the "small log cabin" his father built.

> Its narrow doors of thick oak plank, turning on stout wooden hinges, and secured with strong bars braced with timber from the floor, formed a safe barrier to the entrance below; while above, on every side were port holes, or small embrasures, from which we might see, and fire upon the enemy. Of windows we had but two, containing only four panes of glass each, in openings so small, that any attempt to enter them by force must have proved fatal to an assailant.[26]

By implication, the windows were limited in size for purposes of defense and not for lack of glass.

Francis Baily, an exceptional observer, was at Columbia in the spring of 1797. In his *Journal of a Tour in Unsettled Parts of North America in 1796 and 1797*, he describes the residence of one Dr. Bean.

> His house was built of logs, as all the houses in these new settlements are, and consisted of a ground floor containing two rooms, one of which was appropriated to lumber [storage]: the other served all the purposes of parlour, bedroom, shop, and everything else; (though there was a little outhouse, where they occasionally

> cooked their victuals, and also washed); and it did not appear as if it had been cleaned out this half-year. There were two windows to throw light into the room; but there had been so many of the panes of glass broken, whose places were supplied by old hats and pieces of paper, that it was very little benefited by the kind intention of the architect.
>
> When the time drew nigh for us to retire to rest, we were shown to one corner of the room where there was a ladder, up which we mounted into a dismal kind of a place without a window; but instead thereof, there were a number of crevices between the logs, which had never been filled up. . . . the wind blew so strong, and there were so many holes in the room, that we were incommoded by a continual current of air the whole night. . . .[27]

To Dr. Bean, at least, the presence or absence of a few panes of glass must have been of little consequence. What is interesting is that he did have two glazed sash windows which attracted Baily's attention, not because of their uniqueness for Ohio in 1797, but because numerous panes were broken.

As with the controversy over window glass versus oiled paper, a discussion on the fireplace and chimney and all their variations has generated a great deal of fact and fiction. There are perhaps four variants that could be used in cabin or house: (1) an open fire on a dirt floor with a smoke hole in the roof (see the Houmard description in chapter 11); (2) an enclosed wooden firebox lined with clay, mortar, brick, stone, or some combination thereof; (3) a brick firebox; and (4) a stone firebox. The last three categories might be found with one of three types of chimneys: (1) stick and clay, in common jargon "cat-and-daub" or "wattle-and-daub"; (2) brick; and (3) stone. All these systems were used in Ohio. Obviously the open fire would have been found in only the most primitive of cabins. Lang describes the use of large stones as a rude firebox, or the use of a clay bank if the cabin was next to a hillside; a stick and clay chimney, and a stone or clay hearth, completed the fireplace.[28] The wooden firebox and "catted" chimney are mentioned too often in literature to classify them as rarities in Ohio, although their use was generally confined to the very early settlements or the most temporary of structures. Due to the high fire hazard involved with such fireplaces and chimneys, their replacement was guaranteed as soon as brick could be fired or suitable stone found and laid.

Though backlogs were used with brick and stone fireboxes, and date far back in English and European history, it was the wood firebox that continued the tradition in the United States. Any large firebox required a backlog to fill the depth and reflect heat into the room. Lang writes from experience that

> the back-log, about six feet long, and two or three feet in diameter, if green, lasted longer than a dry stick, of course, but it always disorganized the house to put a back-log to its place. It was handled and rolled over with hand-spikes, and when in its place, it was an easy matter to build a good fire in front of it, thus throwing the heat forward into the room.
>
> For want of help to get the back-log to its place, it often became necessary to hitch a horse or an ox to it, and thus "snake" it into the house lengthwise. The log-chain was then unhitched, and the "critter" led out of the opposite door.[29]

Woods gives a good description of a lined, wooden firebox and a stick chimney, but since his text refers to sketches, it will be paraphrased.[30] Most fireplaces (certainly in Ohio log buildings) were placed at the center of one of the gable ends, with the chimney exterior to the structure. An opening was formed through the wall as described earlier in this chapter. Enclosing the opening on the exterior was a three-sided firebox of round or hewed logs, the ends notched into the wall of the house (see fig. 21, "Our Cabin"). A stone or clay hearth laid inside the firebox extended through the opening into the interior of the house. The inside of the firebox was lined with clay, mortar, stone, or brick. Woods's example was lined with stone set in clay. A chimney was built on the firebox using small sticks laid in the same fashion as the walls of the house—without notching, however. This stick chimney was thoroughly daubed with clay. As long as the daubing remained intact, the fireplace and chimney were reasonably safe. A variant of this style of fireplace used a double-walled firebox of plank, with the interior space filled with clay. Since the inner wall of wood burned away as the fireplace was used, the clay hardened and provided a fire-proofed lining.

Josiah Marshall's emigrants' handbook, which was popular during the 1850s when the Middle West and Far West were being settled, described two methods of constructing wooden chimneys for the log "shanty." One method was the common stick chimney, as described earlier; the second method, however, produced a safer chimney:

> The chimney is built at one end of the shanty, . . . by making, as it were, four ladders, spars of which, ten inches or so apart, and then filling up the spaces with what are sometimes called "cats," being mortar mixed up with hay (wild meadow hay the best,) or straw, and moulded by the hand into lengths, according to the breadth of the spars in the ladders; and these are laid over the spars and joined together, each succeeding course being joined to the one below, and thus form when dry a continued and solid chimney, perfectly free from harm by the fire, which the first described chimney (by split pieces of wood,) is not.[31]

There is a painting by Marcus Mote (1817–98) entitled "Mary Craig Dunlevy" which shows a brick-lined wood firebox. Mote could well have used an extant fireplace for his model. The firebox bricks are not neatly laid, but have fallen away at the sides. A chain and hook for hanging a kettle can be seen in the upper center of the hearth. The brick lining rises only about half the height of the firebox, and logs or plank can be seen above it. (Unfortunately, the painting is in such poor condition that the above details do not show clearly in a photograph. For another Mote photograph/painting, see fig. 54.) Graham described a similar "chain and hook" arrangement: "The lug-pole across the inside of the chimney, about even with the chamber floor [ceiling], answered for a trammel. A chain suspended from it, and hooks were attached, and from this hung the mush-pot or tea-kettle. When a meal was not in preparation, and the hook was endangered by fire, it was shoved aside to one end of the lug-pole for safety."[32] The settlers near Kirkersville in Licking County utilized bog iron ore to line their fireplaces. This ore was found when a swamp was drained. It was cut into bricks 12 to 15 inches long and 6 to 8 inches broad. According to a local historian, "The fire in due time welded those bricks together, making the most satisfactory and durable of all fireplace lining."[33]

The sizes of fireplaces varied considerably, but from a practical viewpoint most were too large and inefficient for heating and too small for cooking. Count Rumford (Benjamin Thompson—actually an American) wrote extensively on the fireplace at the turn of the nineteenth century, particularly on the inefficiency of the large deep firebox, but apparently his comments did not alter traditional practice except in urban areas where architect-builders were at work.[34] Rumford recommended a very shallow fireplace with the sides and back slanting to reflect as much heat as possible into the room. This, of course, was not a cooking fireplace. He devised the "Rumford Roaster," an ovenlike brick stove with built-in kettles, for cooking.[35]

Various devices were both handmade and commercially manufactured for cooking at an open fireplace; the crane is the best known today. A cooking fireplace required a deep hearth for a work area, for the kettles and skillets required varying degrees of heat which could be achieved only by their careful positioning or by manipulation of the fire itself; when needed, a small quantity of coals could be scraped from the fire onto the hearth (a good description can be found in Nowlin, *The Bark Covered House*).[36]

Most of these fireplaces had mantels, either a completely framed unit fastened to the wall or simply a shelf composed of a board resting on pegs. Though cooking fireplace mantels are not common in Ohio today, the author has seen a few dating from the first quarter of the nineteenth century. They are invariably very tall, 6 to 6½ feet, because the shelf had to be above head height. Original mantels are often found to be burned away where the vertical sides meet the hearth.

Between 1855 and 1859 General Roeliff Brinkerhoff (1828–1911) of Mansfield wrote a series of articles on the history of Richland County for his newspaper, the *Mansfield Herald*. Many of these articles were reprinted in another Mansfield newspaper, *The Ohio Liberal*, in the 1870s. The following description of log cabin building was written in February 1858, from material given to Brinkerhoff by one James Sirpliss "and others," and is taken from the 1876 reprint. It is a good account complete with terminology, although the article has a multitude of grammatical and typographical errors with which the reader must contend, such as calling the logs supporting the eaves "cave beams" and "cave bearers." "Cave" is a typographical error, for Spencer, among others, uses the term "eave" bearers. "Chinking" and "chunking," and "clapboard" and "clawboard" are no doubt simple dialectical variants.

> As a general thing log cabin raisings presented a general attendance, the settlers turning out *en masse*, especially when it was understood that there was to be on hands for ready use a *quantum sufficit*," of the extract of corn or rye. This was an important consideration in those days of rustic simplicity. . . . Another important consideration among many of the settlers was the position in which the edifice should stand. This position was due *north and south*, the better to observe the rising and setting of the sun, and for marking the hours in which they were to be called from labor to refreshment.
>
> A primal log cabin is composed of logs, puncheon clap boards, with stone or wooden chimneys, and oiled paper window lights.
>
> After the erection of the cabin, the next operation is the putting on of the roof and the completion of the chimney. Instead of shingles, the roofs were laid with *clap boards* which are that kind of lumber and somewhat resembles staves out of which barrels are made, being split with an instrument called a *frow*.
>
> *Puncheons* are planks made by splitting logs, into several slabs of certain thickness. These answered for flooring boards, tables, benches, &c. The *cave beams* are those ends and logs which project over to receive the *butting poles*, against which the lower row of clap boards rest, in forming the roof.
>
> The *trapping* is the roof timbers composing the gable ends; and the *ribs* are those logs on which the clap boards are placed.
>
> The *trap logs* are those of unequal length lying above the cave bearers, and form the gable ends of the building upon which the ribs rest. The *weight poles* are those small logs laid on the roof, which keep down the clap boards to their proper place.

The *knees* are pieces of heart timber placed above the butting poles, successively to prevent the weight poles from falling off.

The next process after the erection of the cabin, is the chunking and daubing process, and in this operation the chimney is completed.

On entering the cabin, the first, and indeed an important consideration was the construction of bedsteads. . . . Holes were made in the logs, . . . and poles inserted therein; the projecting ends were then fastened to suitable uprights by means of withes made out of bark. Cross poles were then laid across from side to side, and fastened down in the same manner.

In most cabins, ladders, consisting of several rungs, were used instead of stairs and were the means by which the younger members of the family ascended the upper part of the cabin to rest during the night. . . . The second floor . . . was laid with clapboards, without being made fast, so that they were easily displaced, and consequently, those who slept upstairs, were constrained to move over them cautiously, from fear of being precipitated upon the puncheon floor beneath them.[37]

The alignment of a cabin or house "north and south" was a general practice, particularly when there were no roads or topographic features to suggest a different position. The main reason for building a residence to face south was to get as much sunlight as possible into the structure—through the windows, if any, and the door.

An erudite account of a raising was given in an address by Henry B. Curtis in September 1885:

In the first place you must realize, if you can, that the work to be done was usually at the greatest disadvantage, and hence much more difficult than the same work, and in the same primitive style, could now be done. An ax, a saw, and an auger, and the hammer taken from the doubletree of his wagon [linch-pin], usually constituted all the mechanical tools with which the rude architect was to rear and construct the house that probably for the succeeding fifteen or twenty years must be the home for his family. . . . After a few days spent in an improvised shanty, or perhaps the interior of the covered wagon, the pioneer sets himself seriously to work in the construction of his log cabin. Having selected his spot, the tall, straight young trees of the forest are to be felled, measured, cut, and hauled to the place; at the same time properly distributed to form the several prospective sides of the proposed structure. The "skids" are provided upon which to run up the logs. The clap-boards, rived from the cleanest white oak blocks, rough and un-shaved, are made ready for the roof. Whiskey, then about twenty-five cents per gallon, is laid in, and due notice given to such neighbors as can be reached, of the day appointed for the "raising."

When the time comes, and the forces collect together, a caption is appointed, and the men divided into proper sections, and assigned to their several duties. Four men most skillful in the use of the axe, are severally assigned to each corner; these are the "corner men," whose duty it is to "notch" and "saddle"—as it were, like a dovetail—the timbers at their connection, and preserve the plumb, "carrying up" the respective corners. Then there are the "end men," who, with strong arms, and the aid of pikes, force the logs up the "skids" and deliver them to the corner men. In this way the building rises with wonderful rapidity; the bearers for the roof logs are adjusted; the broad clap-boards laid with skill, the "weight-poles" placed upon the successive courses, and the shell of the cabin is completed. The frolic is ended and a good supper crowns the day's work. Then follow the "puncheon" floor, made of heavy planks split from timber and dressed on one side with an axe; the big log fire place; the beaten clay hearth; the stick and clay chimney; the "clinking" [*sic*] and "daubing;" the paper windows, and the door with wooden latch and hinges. . . .

The above is the primitive log cabin; but it was subject to many modifications and degrees of advanced pretensions. The cabin might be single, or double, with a gangway between, covered by a common roof. It was made of hewed logs, or "scutched," which was a superficial hewing made after the building was up. So, too, its elevation was suited to the condition of the family; and sometimes the corners squared or dressed down; and perchance the clap-boards nailed on, when so luxurious an article as nails could be obtained, in lieu of the "weight poles."

These were various forms of the residences of the pioneers. They were all log cabins, but the primitive form first described predominated; the improved form indicating the ambition, prosperity and taste of the proprietor and his family. Such was the beginning of settlements in all this range of beautiful country, embracing the

> central counties of Licking, Knox and Richland, and others adjacent, through which a gentleman may now drive with his carriage and pair as through a park.[38]

Curtis gives an excellent description of the traditional method of raising the log walls. Obviously, raising an extremely high wall required other measures, such as block and tackle or animal power. Although Curtis was certainly aware of various distinctions in the quality of construction of log cabins, he does not apply the term "house" to the better finished structure. He uses, rather, "primitive form" and "improved form." He does imply that the primitive cabin was intended to last fifteen to twenty years, or until the pioneers were permanently established on their land. This estimate fits well with the supposition that such structures were most common between the end of the Indian Wars and the War of 1812. Because of the unsettled conditions on the frontier during this period—the continued threat of Indian warfare and war with Great Britain, the uncertainty of treaty and private property boundaries—there is no doubt many families financially able to erect substantial houses and barns did not do so simply because of fear of losing them. The loss of a few log buildings was negligible in comparison to braced frame, brick, or stone structures.

According to Brinkerhoff and Curtis, whiskey was a prime necessity at a raising. The custom must have been an old one. Doddridge describes an all-night "housewarming" after a raising, which must have included a bit of drinking, and Baily mentions the fact when he was at the site of Waynesville, Warren County, in March of 1797:

> The next morning nothing was to be heard but the noise of the axe resounding through the woods. Every one who was expert at that art was gone out to cut down trees to build our friend [Samuel Heighway] a house, and before night they had got several of the logs laid and the house raised several feet. They all joined cheerfully at this work, but then it was expected that our friend should not deny them the use of the whiskey barrel in the meanwhile, which makes it come as expensive as if you were to hire so many men to do it for you. . . .[39]

The last sentence is revealing, for it implies a considerable quantity of whiskey was consumed; the number of settlers in the community could not have been very large.

The present city of Chillicothe was the site of early settlement in Ohio, where many houses were erected before 1800. On 25 September 1923, the *Daily News-Advertiser* described in some detail a log house that had been torn down to make way for the newspaper's new press building. By reputable evidence, the house was standing in 1800 and had been sided and plastered prior to 1820 when a brick house was built adjoining it. The article states, in part:

> When the workmen began demolishing the one-story frame structure in the rear of the brick portion it was found to be an ancient weatherboarded log cabin. The cabin was built of hand-hewn, squared logs [of beech], as solid as the day they were put in. The interstices between the logs were filled with short blocks of wood and the "chinking" was of clay. The rafters supporting the roof were poles about five or six inches in diameter squared on one side and with the bark left on the rounded side. At one end they were notched to fit together with wooden pins driven through augur [*sic*!] holes. The sheeting of the roof was split boards. There was a brick chimney about ten feet wide in the base, and clay was used instead of mortar. The old open fireplace was over five feet wide.
>
> Later on the structure was weatherboarded on the outside and plastered inside. Hand-split hickory laths were used fastened to the logs with hand-wrought nails. There were no nails used in the original work on the cabin. . . .
>
> Originally there was a rear room to the cabin and a porch on the west side.

The reporter was really describing a well-built log house which had been preserved as an addition to a newer house. If this house was built prior to 1800, the typology of the Ohio log house had been set in the eighteenth century: structural details might have varied around the state, but hewed logs, pole rafters, clapboarded gables, brick or stone fireplaces, glass windows, puncheon or board floors, and shingle or shake roofs were standard features throughout the nineteenth century.

The log cabin remained consistent in style as well. In the spring of 1827, Samuel Williams (who was regarded as an excellent "corner-man") constructed a round-log cabin, for a summer residence, about four miles north of Chillicothe on the west side of the Scioto bottoms. The 22 by 16 foot cabin was traditional in every respect, including a clapboard roof, oak plank floor, and wooden chimney with a stone-lined firebox. A six-foot deep porch was built along one side, and fronting it was a ten-foot square "board" kitchen.[40] The log cabin was well on its way to becoming a rustic summer house, a purpose that was well entrenched in the eastern states by midcentury, *vide* Calvert Vaux's "Design for a Log-House" of 1858 in *Villas and Cottages*.[41]

Perhaps the last vestiges of the primitive log cabin were the hunters' and trappers' cabins built during the nineteenth and early twentieth centuries. Since professional or "market" hunters and trappers usually stayed on their grounds for several months during the winter season, their accommodations, while meager, had to protect them from severe weather. Eldred N. Woodcock, a professional trapper, described a "hut" he and his partner built in Cameron County, Pennsylvania, in 1869:

> We rolled up the usual box log body, about 10 x 14 feet. We put up a bridge roof, putting up about four pairs of rafters and then using three or four small cross poles for roof boards. We then peeled hemlock bark, making the pieces about four feet long, which we used for shingles to cover the roof with. After the roof was completed, we felled a chestnut tree which we split into spaults [spalls] about four feet long. With these we chinked all the cracks between the logs, striking the axe into the logs, close to the edge of the chinking and then driving a small wedge in the slot made by the axe to hold the chinking in place.
>
> Next we gathered moss from old fallen trees and stuffed all the cracks, using a blunt wedge to press the moss good and tight. . . . We found a bank of clay that was rather free of stones and made a mortar by using water. . . . The chinking and mossing had been done from the inside, while we now filled the space between the logs good and full of mortar, or rather mud. . . .
>
> After the [stone] fireplace was completed, we hung a door, using

> hinges made of blocks of wood and boring auger holes through one end. Shaping the other end on two of these eyes to drive in two holes boring into the logs close to the door jams. The other two eyes were flattened off and made long enough for door cleats as well as to form a part of the door hinge. Now a rod was run through these eyes or holes in these pieces. This formed a good solid door hinge.[42]

In the vein of Woodcock was Elmer H. Kreps's *Camp and Trail Methods.* Chapter 9, "Permanent Camps," contains a good description of building a log cabin, including drawings of the gable framing and a wooden-hinged door.[43] This is a traditional cabin, not a twentieth-century summer resort.

Doubtless, there were many families on the frontier who had no desire to live in a log cabin. For them, a well-finished log house was an acceptable substitute until a brick or stone house could be constructed (the Worthingtons, Johnstons, and Galloways, for prominent examples). To other settlers, the log house was a mansion in comparison to a cabin. Because "history" is relative to the attitudes of the individual participants, interpretation of events is often difficult and this leads to generalities. One individual can consider his or her homestead to be on the frontier, while another individual, at the same moment in time and but a few miles away, is worrying about overcrowding. This is why it is so difficult to draw a hard line between a log cabin and a log house, or to place these structures in specific time periods.

Further, common knowledge that we accept as fact may be wrong; new information in neglected archives could reveal truths that might now seem illogical. Only fictionalized history is safe, for it is self-authenticating. "Buffalo Bill" Cody was pressured, by public belief in the romantic literature written about him, to become a fictionalized image of himself. For most people and events, however, this fictionalization occurs after the fact. The facts are embellished, embellishment becomes fiction, fiction becomes tradition, tradition becomes sacrosanctity. To break the chain of tradition is a feat comparable to not just searching for, but finding the Holy Grail.

Notes

1. Hill, *History of Ashland County*, p. 50.
2. Bond, *Correspondence of John Cleves Symmes*, p. 63. Symmes to Jonathan Dayton, 18, 19, and 20 May 1789, Northbend. Obviously, the hut had been built in the winter, much earlier than May. Dayton (1760–1824), a prominent national figure from New Jersey, speculated in western lands; he was the proprietor of Dayton, Ohio. He was arrested as an accomplice of Aaron Burr, but not tried.
3. Howe, *Historical Collections*, p. 151.
4. "Autobiography of Benjamin Tappan," p. 131.
5. Ibid.
6. Graham, *History of Richland County*, p. 235. Graham has many interesting stories to tell, but it is often hard to determine whether his information was firsthand from Richland County, or taken from various older histories such as Doddridge's *Notes on the Settlements and Indian Wars*.
7. Howe, *Historical Collections*, p. 571.
8. *Ohio Eagle*, p. 1.
9. Finley, *Life Among the Indians*, p. 285.
10. Harris, *Journal of a Tour*, p. 15.
11. Johnston, "Annual Report, September 30, 1804."
12. Howells, *Recollections*, pp. 154, 118.
13. Hutslar, "Ohio Waterpowered Sawmills."
14. Broadstone, *History of Greene County*, 1: 143. See appendix B.
15. Lang, *History of Seneca County*, p. 186.
16. Sherwood, "Building in the North," 3, p. 4.
17. William Patrick, "Character and Hardships of the Pioneers in Ohio," in Antrim, *Champaign and Logan Counties*, pp. 12–31.
18. In his original monograph, this writer made an error in accepting several latter-day descriptions of round-log notching as being correct; the total lack of examples can be given as a weak excuse. Correctly executed, round logs were notched as Sherwood describes, the upper over the lower, rather than both sides of each log being notched. This latter technique was used, but only when the pen had to withstand outward pressure—a corn crib or a pig pen, and so forth. Obviously, notching the upper surface of a log would present a pocket in which water could collect and eventually cause rot.
19. Doddridge, *Notes on the Settlement and Indian Wars*, pp. 134–37.
20. Walker, *History of Athens County*, pp. 115–16.
21. As has been mentioned elsewhere in the text, there are many references in county histories on "how to" build log structures. It is difficult to identify initial sources among the authors. Some descriptions are so similar that copying must have occurred. On the other hand, the techniques outlined by all the sources have enough in common that they must, in es-

sence, be true or one would also find contradictions. The following histories have references similar to the ones quoted: Lang, *History of Seneca County*, pp. 185–89; Hill, *History of Ashland County*, p. 69; Thomas, *Nathan M. Thomas*, pp. 12–13; and Graham, *History of Richland County*, pp. 248–49.

22. Woods, "Two Years' Residence," p. 276.
23. Ibid., p. 277.
24. Graham, *History of Richland County*, p. 235.
25. Lang, *History of Seneca County*, p. 187.
26. Spencer, *Indian Captivity*, p. 14.
27. Baily, *Journal of a Tour*, pp. 198–200.
28. Lang, *History of Seneca County*, pp. 185–86.
29. Ibid., p. 193.
30. Woods, "Two Years' Residency," pp. 276–77.
31. Marshall, *Farmers and Immigrants Complete Guide*, p. 53. This writer has seen a *carte de visit* photograph, of about 1865, showing a catted chimney protected by an enormous gable overhang; the cabin was apparently in a southern state.
32. Graham, *History of Richland County*, p. 248. Graham's reasoning is a little hard to follow. The hook was presumably of green wood, though it is conceivable an iron hook could become so hot it would bend.
33. Schaff, *Etna and Kirkersville*, p. 116.
34. Rumford, *Essays, Political, Economical, and Philosophical*, specifically vol. 1, pp. 302–87, and vol. 3, pp. 386–407, both essays entitled "Chimney Fireplaces."
35. A Rumford Roaster many be seen on plate LIX, page 111, of Benjamin's *American Builder's Companion*.
36. Nowlin, *Bark Covered House*, p. 92.
37. Brinkerhoff, "History of Richland County."
38. Curtis, "Pioneer Days in Central Ohio," pp. 242–43.
39. Baily, *Journal of a Tour*, p. 207.
40. Williams Manuscript, Ohio Historical Society.
41. Vaux, *Villas and Cottages*, pp. 123–28.
42. Woodcock, *Fifty Years*, pp. 141–42.
43. Kreps, *Camp and Trail Methods*, pp. 92–109.

VIII BARNS AND OUT-BUILDINGS

Until the general adoption of harvesting equipment in Ohio during the 1850s, the two basic barn designs—English and German—had remained relatively unchanged for at least two hundred years, varying only in exterior surface treatment or size, depending upon the experience of the builder, the laborers and construction materials available, and the amount of arable land and number of animals maintained by the farmer.[1] For all practical purposes, the barn was an implement just as a scythe or pitchfork; an implement of heroic proportions, to be sure, but as carefully designed to complement the labor necessary in harvesting and storage as any hand tool. The interior spatial designs originated in the British Isles and Northern Europe, and were brought to the middle American colonies by the Germans and Scotch-Irish—the pioneers on the frontier. No unusual structural alterations were required during the settlement of Ohio, because crops and farming techniques were essentially the same in the states immediately east and south.

The barns and outbuildings of late eighteenth- and early nineteenth-century Ohio farmsteads were a natural outgrowth of three factors: (1) the specific topography and geology of the individual farms, which could dictate structural configuration; (2) the ethnic or environmental background of the farmers (as reflected through the barn builders); and (3) the type of farming practiced, whether general farms of mixed crops and livestock or specialty farms of a single crop or animal, which determined the interior spatial configuration of the barns and the number of supportive outbuildings.[2]

The majority of initial settlement farms, which could date from 1788 to the mid-1850s depending on the area of the state, had small field sizes because of the difficulties of clearing, tilling, and harvesting with a limited labor force and few implements. On the other hand, Ohio farmers never seriously suffered from a lack of markets or transportation for their surplus. The military campaigns of the Indian Wars of the 1790s; the War of 1812 and the following rush of settlement; the availability of river and lake transport; the rapid emergence of urban and industrial centers; and the development of canals and railroads in the second quarter of the nineteenth century gave most farmers adequate markets. Pork production in southwestern Ohio, with Cincinnati or "Porkapolis" as its center, and the dairy industry in northeastern Ohio, with Cleveland as its terminus, are examples of agricultural specialization made possible by the transportation facilities developed between the War of 1812 and the Mexican War.[3]

The rapid immigration to the Ohio Country following the Ordinance of 1787 indicates that the settlers knew the territory was geographically suited to the same farming operations which they were accustomed to in the eastern states, and, as a corollary, the same type of farm buildings. Specific crop varieties were soon sought to meet local climate and soil conditions; just as today, wheat and corn were the mainstays.

Ohio displays some interesting topographic settlement patterns due to the different methods of survey and sale of the land over an extended period of time.[4] At one extreme is the Virginia Military District with its indiscriminate metes and bounds surveys. This area, located between the Scioto and Little Miami rivers northward from the Ohio River to the Greene Ville Treaty Line, was reserved for Virginia veterans of the Revolutionary War and the French and Indian War. Acreage granted was determined by military rank and length of service, varying from 100 to 15,000 acres. The shapes of the tracts were unrestricted, thus creating many irregularly shaped farms the configurations of which were often determined by topographic features such as hill, stream, and swamp margins. As might be expected, farm buildings were usually sited with regard to the peculiarities of the landscape, taking advantage of streams, springs, and hillsides for water supply, drainage, and protection from winter winds.

The relaxed, meandering nature of the landscape created by the Virginians, however legally confusing, can be contrasted with the formal landscape of the Connecticut Western Reserve. Though there were inaccurate boundary and interior surveys, the New England proprietors laid out the five-mile square townships and roads as geometrically correct as possible. The Greek Revival architecture of the Western Reserve was as formal and inflexible as the "lots" themselves. Farm buildings seldom nestled into the countryside; instead, they bravely faced the elements.

The "Congress Lands," under the jurisdiction of several federal land offices, composed the major portion of the salable land in Ohio. The land was surveyed on a grid system of six mile square townships composed of 36 sections (unless reduced by topographic features). Each one mile square section contained 640 acres; a one-family farm was generally considered to be a quarter-section, or 160 acres, which is little different from today's average farm of about 155 acres.[5]

These various methods of land division were a major factor in determining both the configuration and size of farms in the nineteenth century and the pattern of today's rural landscapes. The difference between the farms of the Virginia District and the Congress Lands is quite apparent in counties divided by the Scioto River, such as Franklin, Pickaway, Ross, Pike, and Scioto, as any outline map will show. If the personal character of the settlers marked the landscapes of the Virginia and New England districts, the same can be said of other areas which were settled by immigrants from eastern states or foreign countries.

The 1970s saw the publication of many books and articles on barns. Romanticism found yet another vanishing landmark to cloud with fact and fiction. Writers have attempted to classify barns into certain styles according to interior arrangements and methods of construction, as well as the ethnic backgrounds of the builders and owners. To do so, meaningfully, is much more difficult than the mere proposition. The best older book of this nature is by Charles H. Dornbusch, entitled *Pennsylvania German Barns*.[6] Several of the types shown in this book can be found in Ohio, such as the double-pen log barn indicated as "Type B"; however, the queen-post roof frame shown is not typical of log barns in Ohio. (The definitive work on Ohio barns remains to be done, a most difficult and tedious undertaking at best.)

The double-pen log barn is also dealt with in a more recent monograph, "The Pennsylvania German Tri-Level Ground Barn," published in the quarterly of the Pennsylvania German Society.[7] The three floor levels are created by the natural incline of the site, although the highest level is the central threshing floor. Several barns are illustrated in the monograph; however, barns are also illustrated that are on such minor contours that one must question exigencies of construction rather than conscious design. Perhaps the tri-level barn is a transverse bank barn? The hillside tri-level barn is attributed to the Palatinate Germans of southeastern Pennsylvania.

The so-called Pennsylvania-Dutch influence, best reflected in large stone-gabled bank barns, is occasionally seen in Ohio, but not as frequently as suggested in popular literature and commercial advertising. The bank barn was best adapted to a hilly or rolling countryside which allowed on-grade access to the first and second floors. The Mennonite/Amish evolved their own style of barn, a large braced-frame structure with an L or T extension at the rear, usually banked, which today is most prevalent in Holmes, Wayne, Stark, and Tuscarawas counties. However, the barns of members of the sects in Union and Madison counties do not display the same idiosyncrasies. The German Roman Catholics of Shelby, Darke, Mercer, and Auglaize counties, many of whom immigrated in the 1830s to work on the

Miami Extension Canal, replaced their own log settlement barns during the fourth quarter of the nineteenth century with large braced-frame barns inspired by the agricultural literature of the period. Neighboring the Germans immediately to the south in Darke and Miami counties are French Roman Catholics, whose ancestors immigrated in the late 1840s and early 1850s. In the present age of agribusiness, these families have retained their relatively small nineteenth-century farms, which range from 80 to 160 acres, and correspondingly small three- and four-bay braced-frame barns.

Southeastern Ohio was never suited for large-scale crop farming because of the hilly terrain, though several river valleys have excellent land, but small general farms were common. Many of the residents worked at subsistence farming and at one of the iron furnaces or coal mines; industrial wages were seldom sufficient to support families. One-room log and braced-frame barns are still in use, as well as some well-constructed double-pen and braced-frame bank barns in the prosperous valleys. In addition, there are many tall tobacco houses, both log and frame, once used for heat-curing tobacco, a method no longer practiced in Ohio. Northwestern Ohio was opened to farming by extensive ditch and tile drainage and the Miami-Erie Canal during the second and third quarters of the nineteenth century. Farms were (and are) devoted to wheat and soybeans and market vegetables. The barns are large multibay braced-frame structures, and they reflect the eclecticism in design brought about by the national agricultural press during the second half of the century.

Southwestern Ohio, comprising most of the Virginia Military District, "Symmes's Purchase" between the Miami rivers, and some Congress Lands, has the greatest variety of barn designs and construction techniques due to the broad ethnic background of those who settled in the region, and a sound economy throughout the nineteenth century which allowed farmers to improve old or construct new buildings as needed. There are many barns dating from the first quarter of the century. Among the various designs that can be found in the region are double-pen log barns and three-bay braced-frame bank barns, stone gabled Pennsylvania-style bank barns, four- and five-bay braced-frame barns, a few octagon barns, and, for the twentieth century, balloon-framed, brick, and tile barns which often look more like industrial buildings than farm structures.

An asymmetrical entrance, four-bay barn is most typical of this section of the state. This design, simply an enlargement of the English-style three-bay barn, allocated an extra bay beside the entrance for an integrated two-bay dairy or stanchion and box-stall area. (Once common in the Western Reserve, some of these barns, featuring the square silos peculiar to this area and dating from the last decade or so of the nineteenth century, are still in existence.)

The ancient Saxon combined barn and house,[8] with the family and livestock housed on the same level, and the Swiss or Southern German form (the so-called Sweitzer barn),[9] with living quarters above the livestock, must be considered so rare in Ohio—as purposefully chosen designs—to be anything but anachronisms. No doubt many settlers shared temporary quarters with their livestock when first moving to the frontier; such arrangements are occasionally mentioned in Ohio county histories. Henry Howe pictures a Swiss house in Columbiana County simply because such architecture was unusual in Ohio.[10] If a few houses were constructed, it is entirely possible that the house/barn design was also utilized. No examples are known.

Whether log or braced-frame, the structural system of a barn creates large interior spaces known as "bays." Therefore, the double-pen log barn would have three closed bays (because of the walls); the framed barn would have any number of open bays depending on size. If the structure is built on a foundation high enough to allow a lower level and require an earthen ramp to reach the main floor, it is known as a "bank barn"; barns built on a hillside are of similar style and are usually called bank barns also. Doubtless, the erection of a log structure on a tall, narrow foundation presented certain difficulties, for the double-pen log bank barn is not common in Ohio, either in literature or extant specimens. The author has seen examples in Fairfield, Mahoning, Guernsey, Warren, and Clark counties. The framed, three-bay bank barn is scarce in the state at present, though not as rare as its counterpart in log.

From pioneer times until at least the 1840s, it was not customary to stable any farm animals except the most valuable, such as the work horses or oxen, though exceptions were made in particularly severe weather. If a farmer could afford the structure, the bank barn was an excellent solution for handling both crops and livestock. By utilizing a hillside or creating an earthen ramp, a barn could have two, occasionally three, distinct work levels. The lower level was customarily divided into loose stalls, box stalls, stanchions, a feeding pen, and often bins for storing vegetable roots for feeding cattle. For added protection and more storage space, the upper structure usually extended over the doors leading into the basement, the extension being known as the "forebay." The connected "barn lot" was also part of the basement complex, where livestock could be fed and watered. The main barn floor was reached from the side opposite the basement doors, one level higher. This created a problem in the lack of a continuous passage for wagons through the barn. On the other hand, the storage of feed and hay immediately above the livestock and the warm shelter provided by the basement presented advantages. In fact, the basement was often excessively warm from the body heat of the animals, and had to be ventilated with ductwork reaching to roof cupolas.

Historically, the three-bay barn is the most interesting configuration found in Ohio. This design dates at least to the seventeenth century, and owes its popularity as much to the requirements of the single-family frontier farmstead of North America as to English or North European farming practices. By the late eighteenth century, the three-bay barn had received an official recommendation from the British Government and had been described in builders' books such as *The Carpenter's Pocket Directory* by William Pain, and, early in the nineteenth century, Abraham Rees' *Cyclopaedia, or Universal Dictionary of Arts, Sciences, and Literature.* [11] Known today as the "English" barn, the design became as standard to the ever-advancing frontier as the log cabin, and was as conveniently constructed of logs as it was of mortised posts and beams—the "braced frame" technique.

An interesting cultural interchange occurred during the expansion of the western frontier in the eighteenth century. The Scotch-Irish, who had no tradition of log construction, learned the technique from colonists of Central European background; the interior arrangement of their houses and the adherence to open fireplaces, however, remained traditional to the British Isles. The northern Germans, on the other hand, rather than adopting the Saxon barn as it evolved in the Netherlands and the Hudson Valley, with its naves and gable entrance, constructed a log version of the English three-bay barn. In practical terms, log construction was the quickest and easiest frontier building technique, and the English-style barn was best suited to the construction methods available as well as the exigencies of frontier farming.[12]

Logs were used to construct about every type of building known to eighteenth- and nineteenth-century Ohioans. The methods of construction varied little, however, whether the building was a springhouse or a barn. The lengths of logs available usually governed the perimeter size of a structure, or at least caused a revision in technique so that shorter logs could be joined to form a longer wall. Also, there was a practical limit to the height of a structure, not only because of the difficulty of raising the logs, but also because of the weight exerted on the notched corners.

Of all log buildings other than houses still in everyday use in Ohio, the log barn leads the list. Log barns came in every size and in a variety of shapes. A log house of fair size, such as 18 by 24 feet and one and a half or two stories, plus sundry outbuildings, was ample accommodation for a settler and his family. However, the size of his barn was another matter, for the duties of farming centered around this building no matter how many outbuildings were erected. Consequently, the barn was as large as possible, depending upon the considerations mentioned earlier. Gigantic timbers were numerous during the initial settlement of Ohio, but the very size of such logs militated against their use (see chapter 10). A barn's structural stability depended upon the logs that spanned corner to corner with a minimum of openings; of course some apertures had to be quite large. The simplest solution to gaining the greatest size and stability was to build the double-pen log barn. In fact, the number of log pens did not need to be limited to two, but could either stretch in a line indefinitely or be arranged in a square; some barns of three or more pens still exist. Fortunately, the plain double-pen log barn has survived in surprising quantity.

As with log houses, the dating of log barns is usually arbitrary because written evidence is hard to find and building techniques changed little over decades. It would be safe to say that most extant double-pen barns in Ohio date from the first third of the nineteenth century. Reference has been made to the John Johnston barn (Piqua) which has proved to be a valuable guide in dating similar barns, for it is well documented in Johnston's papers. It was finished in 1808, sheds and a threshing floor were added in 1826, and a new roof was installed in 1852.

Shortly after the War of 1812 the Howells family built a double-pen barn in Jefferson County, which is described by William C. Howells:

> This summer we also built a barn of logs, and as hickory timber was plenty, we made it of hickory logs peeled of the bark. In this way they were very durable, looked well and were easily hauled, which was done by the process called "snaking" that is, dragged on the ground by a chain tied around one end of them. The logs were cut twenty-four feet square, when raised. There were two pens put up twenty-four feet apart, and raised on one foundation, which was twenty-four by seventy-two. They were in this way carried up to a proper height, when they were connected by logs and a common roof. This made a double barn, with stabling and more room at each end, and a barn floor and wagon-shed in the middle. Such was the universal style of barns in that country, and it was as good as could be made of logs. Many of them are yet to be seen all over that part of Ohio, but they are mostly out of use.

> The settlers were mainly from western Pennsylvania, though many had come in from the western part of Maryland and Virginia, and the prevailing nationality was the Scotch-Irish of the second generation. . . .[13]

It is interesting that Howells mentions the dominant nationality of the settlers in eastern Ohio, for it accords with present thought on how log construction spread on the frontier.

A double-pen barn in Guernsey County is reputed to have originally been a church in which the "Leatherwood God" preached in 1828. This writer, having seen the structure, is doubtful it was ever anything but a barn, but it is entirely possible that it served as a "church" for the redoubtable Joseph C. Dylks. A more reliable date can be placed on a barn standing south of Columbus, one of several log buildings erected about the year 1813; the smokehouse has this date carved in the door lintel. A double-pen log bank barn with overbay in Clark County stands near a brick house bearing the date 1827; the barn was probably built slightly earlier than the house. Consequently, by circumstantial evidence if nothing else, one presumes the double-pen barn to date 1800 to 1830. Obviously many were built later, but the large framed barn was gaining precedence by 1830.

Each area of the log or framed barn had its designated use, a function evolved from generations of practical use by farmers. The following general description was for framed barns in Massachusetts, but could be equally applied to double-pen log barns in Ohio:

> On one side of the threshing floor of the barn were the stables for the horses and cattle and upon the other the great haymow. On the scaffold over the stables the "horse hay" was garnered, and upon the "little scaffold" over the far end of the barn floor were nicely piled the bound sheaves of wheat, rye or barley, the butts all placed outward so as to hinder the entrance of the mice. Over the great beams were scaffolds made of round poles and pieces of waste lumber, generally, in such condition as to make a first-class man trap. On this scaffold was heaped the crop of oats, all awaiting the

> thrashing by the hand flail, the use of which generally began about Thanksgiving time.[14]

The "scaffolds" were simply temporary mow floors and as dangerous as indicated (how many readers have stepped through unseen holes in hay mows?).

The log barns of Highland County, prior to the War of 1812, were recalled by Colonel Keys, writing in the latter part of the nineteenth century; note the similarity of interior functions relative to the preceeding quotation:

> It was not uncommon for a hand to have to attend twelve or fifteen log rollings during a single spring, and try it when you will, it will be found laborious work. Added to this, were cabin raisings for new comers, and house and barn raisings for the old settlers. These barns were almost universally built of hickory logs peeled. These were built double, with a thrashing floor in the center, stables on each end, and mows over all. These barns were covered with clapboards, and generally clapboard doors. They were, however, a very pretty structure but not durable, and it is quite probable that there is not a barn of this kind in the county at this time. The peeling of the bark was a substitute for the hewed logs which succeeded. The logs were . . . at least a foot over, sometimes more. . . . The raising of these barns was heavy work, and the able-bodied men for ten or twelve miles round were called out, and they never failed to attend. The work consumed the entire day, often two, and generally broke up with a frolic at night. . . . The stables were built of small unhewn logs or poles with clapboard roof and door—the whole structure the work of four or five hands for one day. But the peeled hickory log barns were quite a different thing. They were counted the heaviest raisings of the time, and hands were invited for many miles round. Such raisings were not unattended with danger, particularly if the force was light or whisky plenty. It was a post of honor to be one of the "corner men" of such a raising, and none but the most experienced and expert cornermen were permitted to take a position on one of these barns. They were generally able to get one up to the square in a day. After that a few hands could easily finish it at their leisure.[15]

124. "The Raising," woodcut from *The Western Miscellany*, vol. I, July, 1848, p. 342. This woodcut appears to be earlier than its publication date, possibly by 10 or 15 years. Compare to Frontispiece.

125. Franklin County, Village of Groveport. Two story log house with log addition. (See Figures 64, 140, 155, 189, 212, 225.) Photo: 11 November 1974. Northeast corner, front. A typical corner-stone, sill arrangement. The floor joists rest on the sills.

126. Noble County, Beaver Township. Two story log house. (See Figures 203, 222.) Photo: 3 May 1972. Sill, northwest corner. Good, solid construction was evident throughout this house, which was probably sided soon after it was built. The notching for the sill is standard for a steeple-notched structure.

127. Clark County, Greene Township. Two story log house. (See Figures 156, 166, 170, 202, 208, 226.) Photo: 18 August 1972. Sill, northwest corner. The sill is laid horizontally to support the floor joists, a standard method of construction. Good surface drainage prevented this sill from dry-rotting.

128. Warren County, Massie Township. Saddle-bag log house. (See Figures 54, 55, 56, 165, 196.) Photo: 19 February 1972. Sill, southeast corner. This house displayed excellent workmanship throughout. Because there were at least two houses of similar design in Warren County, and one in Clermont County, it is tempting to think professional builders were at work. This was a strong Quaker settlement area, which lends some credence to the idea of reliable, skilled craftsmen, as well as the retention of a somewhat archaic house design. The fitting of the sill and wall logs were remarkably precise. If this house was constructed about 1819, then it is the earliest datable half-dovetailed structure in Ohio.

129. Butler County, Oxford Township. Two story log house. (See Figures 68, 69, 157, 160, 161, 169, 180, 195, 201.) Photo: July, 1973. The first floor log joists rest on the sill log, a common method of construction. If the joists rested directly on the ground, they would be known as "sleepers" (in the old jargon).

130. Meigs County, Columbia Township. One and a half story log house. Size, 18 by 15 feet. Photo: May, 1970. This small, hillside house stood on laid-stone corner foundations. The log floor joists rested on the sills, and the flooring ran to the exterior of the walls. Small blocks were placed on the flooring above each joist, either to support the first wall logs or (more likely) to hold the joists in place.

131. Champaign County, Village of St. Paris. One and a half story log house. Photo: March, 1970. Compare to Figure 132, which was taken three years later. The log sill is standard pattern for a steeple-notched structure. Its width was necessary to support the floor joists.

132. Champaign County, Village of St. Paris. One and a half story log house. Photo: May, 1973. Compare to Figure 131, which was taken three years earlier. The logs were cleaned and bleached by weathering, but show no obvious signs of deterioration; some daubing is missing.

133. Clinton County, Vernon Township. Two story log house. Photo: August, 1969, by Susannah Lane. The lower logs are steeple-notched and the upper logs are half-dovetailed. Usually this combination means a reworked structure. The steeple-notching was awkwardly handled.

134. Highland County, Union Township. One and a half story log house. Photo: Late summer, 1969, by Susannah Lane. A good example of the rigidity of a log structure; the entire pen tipped without dislodging the notched corners. These logs appear to be very large in diameter for half-dovetailing.

135. Franklin County, Plain Township. One and a half story log house. (See Figure 136.) Photo: June, 1975. The shape of a steeple-notch is clearly shown in this photograph. Notice how the corner staircase was constructed. This heavily remodeled house had been soundly assembled. (Reconstructed on new site in 1976.)

136. Franklin County, Plain Township. One and a half story log house. (See Figure 135.) Photo: June, 1975. The plate-logs, which received the outward thrust from the rafters, were half-lapped and pegged to the adjacent logs. This is a detail difficult to see unless a structure is taken apart.

137. Franklin County, Village of Shadeville. One and a half story log house. Photo: 11 September 1975. No doubt this structure was moved, for all the logs were numbered. Similar examples have been seen in and around Columbus, strangely enough. Log buildings were easily, and frequently, moved.

138. Tuscarawas County, Village of Zoar. One and a half story log house built during the winter of 1817–18; known as "Zeeb's Cabin," from a later resident. Photo: Fall, 1967. This is a standard steeple-notched house, though the logs are wider than the usual 8 inches. One peculiarity noted in this area, which had many settlers from southern Germany, was the use of a long, sharply defined upper notch, and a long, rather shallow lower notch. Perhaps this notching technique reflected its parentage in the Swabian alps. It is known through a newspaper account that all Zoar buildings were roofed with tile by 1825 (when a tornado blew them off).

139. Shelby County, Loramie Township, near the Village of Russia. Two story log house with interior log crosswall and framed additions. Photo: 17 October 1978. The log crosswall seems to have been common to French immigrant houses at mid-19th century. This detail was photographed in the attic of a lean-to addition; the house was otherwise completely sided and plastered. The log crosswall was probably conceived as structural bracing to strengthen the long side walls. As a secondary advantage, it would insulate the rooms.

140. Franklin County, Village of Groveport. Two story log house with log addition. (See Figures 64, 125, 155, 189, 212, 225.) Photo: 11 November 1974. The two notching systems most frequently used in Ohio—saddle or steeple on the left (two story), half-dovetail on the right.

141. Madison County, Deer Creek Township. Two story log house. Photo: 22 October 1976. West gable. Lapped corners. This house was moved a short distance north from its original site, so it could have been sided at that (unknown) time. However, because lap joints have little resistance to outward thrust, it is this writer's opinion that lap-jointed houses were always sided during initial construction.

142. Montgomery County, City of Miamisburg. Two story log tavern. Built by or for Daniel Gephart about 1811. (See Figure 217.) Photo: 13 August 1976. Southeast corner. This is an interesting structure, obviously built as a tavern facing a ford across the Great Miami River. The corners are full-dovetailed; the floor joists are supported by summers; there are two front doors on the west side, placed at the ends of the facade. These structural elements do not suggest Ohio typology. The tavern is located just within Symmes' Purchase, which was advertised in the mid-eastern states. Symmes and the land company proprietors were from New Jersey, Gephart was from Pennsylvania.

143. Warren County, Village of Wellman, "Caesar's Creek Pioneer Village." One and a half story log house. Photo: September, 1977. This house was located near the Hawkins house, Figure 56, and was moved to the recreated village to replace the missing kitchen of that saddle-bag structure. The house has full-dovetailed corners.

144. Ottawa County, Catawba Island Township. One and a half story log house built *ca.* 1853 for Henry Luckert (?). Size, 24 by 16 feet. (See Figure 145.) Photo: 23 October 1975. South, front; not on original site. Though this house is of typical mid-19th century configuration, the notching system is rare for Ohio. It is of Swedish/Finnish origin, and is known as the "tooth" (*hammasnurkka*) or "lock" (*lukkonurkka*) notch in the latter country. (Refer to the articles by Dr. Matti Kaups in the Bibliography.)

145. Ottawa County, Catawba Island Township. One and a half story log house. (See Figure 144.) Photo: 23 October 1975. The Finnish *hammas* or *lukko* notch, more common to the Upper Great Lakes than Ohio.

146. Franklin County, Perry Township (City of Columbus). Two story log house with vertical log, three-wall addition. (See Figures 66, 67, 147.) Photo: June, 1971. Added as a kitchen, this structure is so far unique in Ohio. It answers the description of the French *poteaux-sur-sole* style, but it is highly doubtful the builder was French or so-influenced. The eight inch wide logs are 7 feet, 10 inches in height, and are tenoned into mortises in the sills and plates. The logs could have been taken from an older building and adapted in this manner.

147. Franklin County, Perry Township (City of Columbus). Two story log house with vertical log, three-wall addition. (See Figures 66, 67, 146.) Photo: June, 1971. The logs had been chinked, daubed, and whitewashed, leaving clear indications of a 20 inch high chair rail and a baseboard. A plaster wall was installed about 1854, by evidence of 1853–54 newspapers found wadded between the ceiling joists. The foundation of a large cooking fireplace/chimney is in the cellar under the end wall of the kitchen addition.

148. Wayne County, Green Township. Two story log house, built *ca.* 1818, with mortised log addition dating after 1833; first owned by the Barnett family, then enlarged by the Hoover family. (See Figures 149 and 213.) Photo: 6 November 1975. Front, south, and west end. The original house is at the left; the central window was the front door when the house stood alone. A single chimney was located on the exterior of the east end. The house is of interest primarily because of the addition. (National Register of Historic Places.)

149. Wayne County, Green Township. Mortised log addition to a two story log house. (See Figures 148, 213.) Photo: 6 November 1975. This addition is a free-standing, three-walled structure composed of hewed logs mortised into vertical corner posts. Newspapers dated 1854 were found glued to the logs under the plaster; however, the addition was probably added when the Hoover family acquired the property in 1833, so the newspapers indicate a later remodeling. The mortised-log technique seems unique to south German immigrants, with examples in Ohio and Pennsylvania.

150. Holmes County, Berlin Township. One and half story framed log house with basement kitchen. Photo: 12 May 1977. Whether this is a style in itself, an adaptive form of half-timber construction, or an amalgamation of American and German techniques, is not known. The house appears much like the common notched-log house, but the logs are tenoned and pegged into vertical corner posts. A few examples of this technique have been found in northeastern and western Ohio among the German Amish/Mennonite settlements. (See Figure 149, Wayne County.)

151. Washington County, City of Marietta. Plank section of *Campus Martius*, built in 1788–89, occupied by Rufus Putnam. (See Figures 114, 174, 207.) Photo: 26 October 1967. The "Putnam House" was originally a part of the southeast curtain-wall of the *Campus Martius* stockade. Built by the Ohio Company of Associates, construction began in the early summer of 1788, and parts of the stockade, including the horizontal plank exterior wall shown in this photograph, were completed by the end of the year. (The vertical planks cover the original doorway.) Wall planks mortised into vertical posts was common military construction in the 17th and 18th centuries. In Canada this was known as the "Manitoba Frame" style, and continued into the 20th century. The Putnam House is now enclosed within a wing of the *Campus Martius* Museum, administered by the Ohio Historical Society. (National Register of Historic Places.)

152. Adams County, Brush Creek Township. Two story log house with small notched and pegged plank addition. Photo: Spring, 1977, courtesy of Stephen Kelley. This addition was three-walled; the planks of the front and back walls were pegged into small corner posts. The outside corners of the addition were full-dovetailed.

153. Shelby County, Loramie Township. Two story log house, east side, second site. (See Figure 154.) Photo: 17 October 1978. This house was constructed in the 1850s for, and possibly by, French immigrants. Two front doors are a common feature in this area. Though the floor joists are hewed, the finish trim and floorboards are millwork. Note the overhanging plate, which is another feature of these houses. This may have provided a nailing surface for a soffit. (This house has been moved to a new site.)

154. Shelby County, Loramie Township. Two story log house, west side, second site. (See Figure 153.) Photo: 17 October 1978. This house was designed for a lean-to addition, a common configuration in this French settlement area. Also typical of these 1850s houses are the overhanging plates supported at the corners by projecting wall logs. Longer houses of this pattern had central log crosswalls for added wall support (see Figure 139).

155. Franklin County, Village of Groveport. Two story log house with log addition. (See Figures 64, 125, 140, 189, 212, 225.) Photo: 11 November 1974. First floor window, west end of two story section. The original window opening is quite apparent. Windows are commonly found to be altered on log houses.

156. Clark County, Greene Township. Two story log house. (See Figures 127, 166, 170, 202, 208, 226.) Photo: 18 August 1972. Window, first floor front, right side. The original window opening is obvious because of the jamb board. Of interest are the holes in the five logs on each side of the window which were used to peg planks to the logs to hold them in place while the openings were being cut.

157. Butler County, Oxford Township. Two story log house. (See Figures 68, 69, 129, 160, 161, 168, 180, 195, 201.) Photo: July, 1973. Window casing, front left. The molding was planed directly on the casings, and the logs pegged to them. Each casing, installed as a unit, was mortised and tenoned together. In this picture, one of the tenons can be seen at the lower left.

158. Warren County, Village of Franklin. Two story log house. (See Figures 70, 199, 229.) Photo: 15 August 1975. Rear window enclosed with lath and plaster. This was a common method of dealing with unwanted openings during remodeling. Plaster marks on the furring strip at the right edge of the photograph indicate this wall had also been lathed and plastered.

159. Greene County, Miami Township. One and a half story log house moved from the Village of Pitchin, Clark County. Photo: May, 1971. This house has a central undereave window which seems to have been peculiar to this area during the 1830s and 40s. Here is standard window and door framing: half-notched logs above and below openings; jamb boards supporting cut logs; separate window and door frames inside the jamb boards; 6 over 6 sash with cylinder-glass panes; and, less common, a board and batten door with beaded boards and original (?) door light. The cracks between the jambs and frames would have been covered with applied trim.

160. Butler County, Oxford Township. Two story log house. (See Figures 68, 69, 129, 157, 161, 169, 180, 195, 201.) Photo: July, 1973. Door casing with transom, south front. The door and window casings are unusual in two ways: The molding patterns were planed directly on the casings, and the casings were pegged directly to the logs (without jamb boards). Braces for a later, small porch roof were mortised into the log above the door.

161. Butler County, Oxford Township. Two story log house. (See Figures 68, 69, 129, 157, 160, 169, 180, 195, 201.) Photo: 1 June 1971. First floor, rear doorway to kitchen addition. Apparently, a miscalculation was made in the height of the door opening: The cut for the top of the doorway is in the second log; notice the auger holes, at the upper right of the casing, that were required to extend the door to its proper height.

162. Greene County, Miami Township. One and a half story log house. (See Figures 178, 198, 204.) Photo: 12 November 1967. Detail of front, south side. This appeared to be the original board and batten door. Note the two sets of ceiling joist mortises above the door and the furring strips for siding. Traces of daubing was on all walls.

163. Morgan County, Village of Roxbury. One and a half story log house. Photo: *ca.* 1890. (This detail was enlarged from a photograph of the Muskingham River at Roxbury.) This house stood on Ohio Company land, so it is possible it was constructed in the 1790s. It had trap logs and ribs, so the roof may originally have been "weighted." The roofing in this case appears to be clapboards.

164. Guernsey County, Millwood Township. Double-pen log barn. (See Figure 79.) Photo: 10 October 1966. In the foreground, a section of roof plate with well-defined rafter mortises. The rafters were held in place with pegs, a standard technique in Ohio. The lower end (eave overhang) of a shaped rafter is at left center. Such decorative treatment is often found on barns and houses (see Figure 165, Warren County).

165. Warren County, Massie Township. Saddle-bag log house. (See Figures 54, 55, 56, 128, 196.) Photo: 19 February 1972. Eave, northeast corner. As with all other structural details of this house, the eaves were well designed and constructed. The eave beams were projected from the walls, as were the plates. Note that the wall logs below the eave beam are full-dovetailed; this was to tie the upper section of the walls together to support the outward thrust of the rafters. The rafter ends were nicely contoured.

Peeled hickory logs are often mentioned, as in the Howell quote, but the reason for "peeling" is obscure. As a guess, the hickory was peeled because the rough shell or shag bark made handling difficult and made an unpleasant surface to rub against once the barn was finished (see fig. 89).

As farm mechanization increased, the functions of the barn slowly altered, which brought about changes in architectural design and construction. Until the late 1830s farm operations, particularly crop harvesting, were done largely by hand labor.[16] Most Ohio farmers seem to have had a plow and a drag or harrow, if they were not using a hoe to dig hills for planting, but all farmers had to harvest crops with hand tools: the scythe or cradle scythe, the sickle, the rake, the pitchfork, and the corn knife were necessities. But what was to be done with crops after harvesting, particularly when grain and stalk had to be separated for use? How could hay be kept clean and dry between growing seasons? Outdoor methods of storage were used, such as the grain shock and the haystack, but the ideal solution was a large enclosed structure combining both processing and storage facilities which was safe from weather and animals. The barn had long been established in Europe and Britain before its arrival in North America, but nowhere else on the globe had there been such a need for the large privately owned structures that evolved in the fertile New World. (Tithe barns and monastic barns had often been of enormous size in Britain and Europe during the Middle Ages.)

Peter Kalm, the Swedish naturalist who traveled in the American colonies during the years 1748–51, was particularly impressed by the size of the barns between Trenton, New Jersey, and New York City:

> The *barns* had a peculiar kind of construction in this locality, of which I shall give a concise description. The main building was very large almost the size of a small church; the roof was high, covered with wooden shingles, sloping on both sides, but not steep. The walls which supported it were not much higher than a full grown man; but on the other hand the breadth of the building was all the

> greater. In the middle was the threshing floor and above it, or in the loft or garret, they put the unthrashed grain, the straw, or anything else, according to the season. On one side were stables for the horses, and on the other for the cows. The young stock had also their particular stables or stalls, and in both ends of the building were large doors, so that one could drive in with a cart and horses through one of them, and go out at the other. Here under one roof therefore were the thrashing floor, the barn, the stables, the hay loft, the coach house, etc. This kind of building is used chiefly by the Dutch and Germans, for it is to be observed that the country between Trenton and New York is not inhabited by many Englishmen, but mostly by Germans or Dutch, the latter of which are especially numerous.[17]

Kalm describes a Saxon barn, a design rare in Ohio even though many German immigrants in western Ohio were from the Saxon belt in northern Germany (which ranges from Holland to Poland). An example of the Saxon barn can be found at the Maria Stein Convent in Mercer County. Disregarding building techniques and utilization of space, the basic difference between Saxon and English barns is the central passage, which is lengthwise in the Saxon plan. The double-pen log barn presents similar work areas, but in the English plan, with a passage the width of the structure.

Based on investigation of a large number of double-pen log barns throughout Ohio, it is apparent that they generally went through a series of revisions as farm productivity increased. The most significant changes were sheds around the perimeter, wooden threshing floors, and increased height (or pitch) of the roofs.

Original Structure. This three-bay barn, as outlined by Howells, consisted of two square log pens, separated by a distance equal to the length of one pen wall, covered by a single expanse of roof. Hinged doors, usually on both sides, enclosed the central work area; the floor was customarily tamped earth. The lower half of at least one log pen, which had doors and often window openings, was used for stabling animals. Joist logs across the pen provided support for a ceiling for the stalls and a mow floor above. In the majority of barns examined, only one pen had been finished with stalls and a mow; the other pen was left open. The central bay had logs placed across it from pen to pen, forming an "overmow" just under the roof. By custom, it was in this mow that unthreshed grain was placed for storage; after threshing, the straw was forked into the small mow over the stalls. The large mow, or open pen, was usually reserved for hay.

The log pens were never chinked and daubed as were houses. If the stall area needed weatherproofing in a severe winter, straw was stuffed between the logs or long clapboards nailed over the gaps. Mow areas were seldom enclosed because hay needed air for drying. Much green hay was put in barns, for time was a great factor and haymaking a slow process when only hand labor was available. The farmer could not wait for ideal weather conditions, then expect to put up twenty acres in one day. Consequently, some hay was not well cured, so it was necessary to have ample ventilation in the mow area to prevent the hay from becoming moldy or, worse, igniting from spontaneous combustion.

First Revision. As farm production increased, so did the need for more storage and processing space. The double-pen barn provided a structurally sound unit which could be enlarged. Framed sheds were added, usually to all four sides of the original barn. Rafters were extended from the plates to the shed walls, and the roof was continued in an unbroken line (and almost always at a 12-9 pitch). Naturally the shed roofs rose only to the plate line at the gable-ends of the barn. The main barn doors either remained attached to the log pens or, more commonly, were moved to the outer shed walls. The latter change created a large central work area which often was floored at this time.

On the threshing floor, grain of a cereal crop such as wheat was separated from the stalk; for the first quarter of the nineteenth century, "flailing" by hand or "trodding" with animals were standard threshing procedures. In flailing, a hinged wooden staff was used to knock the seedpods apart. Trodding was the simple expedient of walking an animal, usually an ox, over the sheaves, thereby dislodging the grain. The sheaves were customarily placed in a large circle on the threshing floor; stories abound about the deep paths worn in earthen floors by the oxen. Certainly the wooden floor and flail were a much cleaner method, which was particularly desirable when flour was the end product of the grain. It was an extremely slow process; flailing one bushel of wheat required over two and a half hours.[18] The threshing floor was constructed of heavy plank with thinner boards underneath closing the joints. This double floor prevented any loss of grain. The open space through the center of the barn, generally called the "breezeway," allowed the wind to blow away the chaff and dust created by "winnowing" the grain, a process of alternately shaking and throwing the grain into the air while sieving. In Ohio, the main barn door usually faced west to catch the prevailing winds; a smaller door on the eastern side allowed the wind to blow through the barn. The middle bay of the three-bay barn could be considered an efficient threshing machine in which the farmer served as the prime mover.

During the 1820s and 1830s, the farmer's hand labor was reduced as horses and oxen were used to power many of the simple grain processing machines, such as the "groundhog" drum thresher and the fanning mill. The "horsepower," or sweep (capable of 200 revolutions per minute), was often built as a permanent feature of the barn, either on the main floor or in the basement of a bank barn.[19] Other simple machines, such as the corn sheller, feed grinder, and forage chopper, could be run from the horsepower, thus anticipating the convenience of the small, portable combustion engine some fifty years later. During the 1830s and 1840s, the hay press, requiring its own source of animal power, was often constructed as part of the barn framing. These presses were popular on farms along the Ohio River where there was easy transport to the southern market for the 300 pound bales.[20]

By 1840 the rudiments of today's combine, or "combined" harvesting machine for small-grain crops such as wheat, were known: the reaper, thresher, and fanning mill. Reaping and threshing remained separate operations until the twentieth century, when efficient mobile power equipment made the combine practical. However, by the Civil War, a wide variety of crop processing equipment had evolved, and the barn was gradually relieved of its symbiotic partnership with the farmer.[21]

Second Revision. With the general availability and acceptance of horse- and steam-powered implements, which were not a major influence on Ohio agriculture until at least the 1850s, barns were altered both in function and physical appearance. The most obvious alteration was the heightening of roofs to gain space for hay carriers and increase mow capacities. (Until about 1840, the middle of the Greek Revival period in Ohio, almost all roofs—barns and houses alike—were constructed with a 9 inch rise in a 12 inch run, forming an approximate 36-degree pitch from eave to ridge.)

The need for increased storage, and hay carriers, was the direct result of the mowing machine, in itself an immediate byproduct of the grain reaper of the 1840s; Obed Hussey's "improved cutting apparatus" of 1847 is still used today. Although the reaping machine had been proposed by various inventors during the first quarter of the century, it was not until the 1830s that specific machines were offered to the public, and the 1840s before reliable results could be expected.[22] Quicker harvesting meant more land could be put in production. The physical labor and time involved in scything grain or hay was enormous: reaping, binding, and shocking wheat was calculated to take two men twenty hours for one acre, in 1829–30; sixty-five years later the same amount of wheat could be reaped, threshed, and sacked in about eighteen minutes.[23] The barn had lost its function in threshing, winnowing, and straw storage, but found a new role in providing greater bin capacity for grain and the attendant milling equipment.

Another addition often made to the barns, particularly when the main doors were still attached to the log pens, was a gabled entryway. The doors, hemmed in by the sheds on either side, had to remain on hinges. However, the sliding barn door was coming into popularity by midcentury, and whenever wall space was available for the track, the sliding door was favored because it required no space in which to swing, and it worked well in wind.

Although small log farm buildings continued to be erected until the end of the nineteenth century, the large log barn had reached its peak of popularity during the first third of the century, then slowly gave way to the framed timber structure. (Of course, the framed barn was being erected concurrently with the log.) The major alterations that developed in log barns were related directly to the increase in farm productivity and the rise of mechanization, as one need influenced the other. A sawmill to cut the siding and nails were the only requisites for this type of structure.

Three types of small log outbuildings are still seen in the state, though their use has steadily declined (really four types, but springhouses are more closely related to houses than barns). These are the smokehouse, corncrib, and tobacco barn. The "Virginia smokehouse" still had its advocates late in the nineteenth century, primarily because a log structure did not retain moisture as did a brick or stone smokehouse; it allowed the heat, smoke, and moisture to escape freely through hundreds of openings in the walls and roof. Too much ventilation was thought to be better than too little.

Because an unchinked log structure allowed a free circulation of air, it was ideally suited to the storage of corn. Corn was usually cut and shocked in the field, both to allow the ears and fodder to dry and to clear as much land as possible to plant winter wheat. After the wheat was planted and the ground frozen, the corn could be husked and hauled to the crib without danger to the new crop. Where possible, these corncribs were built up off the ground to allow air to circulate underneath as well as to deter rodents. Woods described such a corncrib in 1820:

> Corn-cribs are built the same as cabins, except that they are placed on logs, so as to stand hollow for some distance from the earth; the bottom is made of cleft pieces, laid pretty close. They are built of different lengths and widths, but about six feet on the inside is deemed wide enough, as corn will dry in them better than if wider. The roof is only drawn in on one side, which two lengths of boards will cover. As they lay the top pretty flat, they most times take off the greater part, or the whole of the boards, when filling them with Indian corn ears, as they only gather the ears. When full, or the whole growth of the year is put in, the boards are put on, and the weight poles again laid on. Should a heavy shower, or even a set rain, come on whilst the corn-crib is filling, as the bottom and sides are not close, not being mudded, it will soon dry out again without damaging the corn.[24]

In other words, this corncrib was a narrow, unchinked round log structure, standing on posts, with a removable shed roof. In most respects, the configuration was exactly like the framed cribs seen today. This writer has seen several pole or "rail" corncribs, a few still in use (see fig. 104). Ear corn has all but given way to shelled corn, so apparently corncribs are as doomed as the large barns. This condition could change if fuel for grain dryers becomes too expensive. A log corncrib is pictured in Byron Halsted's *Barn Plans and Outbuildings*, a fine small book to guide the restoration of farm buildings of the latter nineteenth century.[25]

Many log tobacco barns still stand in eastern to southeastern Ohio, though most are now unused or have been converted to other purposes. Whether the tobacco was air dried or heat cured, the natural openings in the log structures provided the venting. If a building had to be tightly closed, the gaps between the logs could be covered with rough lumber or stuffed with straw or grass. These tobacco barns are usually tall in relation to their length and width (see figs. 105 and 106).

Improved processing machinery, more land in production,

improved livestock, better preservation and distribution systems each contributed to the modification of barns and outbuildings as the nineteenth century ended. Perhaps the barn was losing something of its personality, its compatability with the land and the farmer, as the machine intruded. It is interesting to speculate on the reasons for the decline of the barn in Ohio. General farms, with both crops and livestock, have become scarce; farmers now tend to specialize in just one commodity which often requires a specific structure. Aside from the Mennonite or Amish barns, few, if any, barns of the traditional general-use design are being constructed. Instead, farmers buy prefabricated structures designed for their needs, whether cattle, sheep, or hog sheds, machinery sheds, food processing and storage buildings, or cribs, bins, and silos.

Of the wide variety of farm buildings extant, the barns built during the premechanization decades are the most interesting, for, in order to survive, they have been altered by generations of owners. In their design, construction, and alterations the history of agriculture throughout Ohio can be read.

Notes

1. These structures are well defined in *The Barn; A Vanishing Landmark in North America* by Eric Arthur and Dudley Witney (Boston: New York Graphic Society, Ltd., 1972).
2. Glassie, "Barns of Appalachia." Also see Glassie's *Pattern in the Material Folk Culture of the Eastern United States* (Philadelphia: University of Pennsylvania, 1968).
3. The development of innerstate transportation, particularly the canals, and the impact on Ohio's economy during the period 1820–61, is the subject of *Ohio Canal Era*, by Harry N. Scheiber (Athens, Ohio: Ohio University Press, 1969).
4. Several good books are available on the survey of Ohio. C. W. Sherman's *Original Land Subdivisions*, done as part of the Ohio Cooperative Topographic Survey (Columbus: Ohio State University) in 1925, is a standard. A recent work is William D. Pattison's *Beginnings of the American Rectangular Land Survey System* (Columbus: Ohio Historical Society, 1970).

5. *Ohio Agricultural Statistics, 1977,* Ohio Crop Reporting Service, U.S. Department of Agriculture (Columbus: 1978), p. 6.
6. Dornbusch, *Pennsylvania German Barns.* Twenty-first yearbook of the Pennsylvania German Folklore Society.
7. Keyser and Stein, "Pennsylvania German Tri-Level Ground Barn."
8. In *The Barn,* the authors discuss the Saxon barn, with its church-nave interior and family living quarters, and its alteration to a purely farm structure in North America. Burcaw's *Saxon House,* is a look at the living quarters as they separated from the barn cum house. *Peter Kalm's Travels* describes the Dutch barn as the dominant style between Trenton and New York City—the "Dutch barn" being a direct descendant of the Saxon barn (pp. 118–19).
9. Type F or G, according to Dornbusch's summary of styles in *Pennsylvania German Barns.*
10. See Howe, *Historical Collections,* p. 108. This writer has seen photographs of a similar house in Switzerland Township, Monroe County.
11. Pain's *Carpenter's Pocket Directory* was a very influential builder's book. Rees's *Cyclopaedia;* was noted by the Englishman Henry Bradshaw Fearon when in Boston during his American tour in 1817. Fearon (*Sketches of America,* p. 105) said it was an American edition. Rees' *Cyclopaedia,* first published in England, was an important source of technological information on both sides of the Atlantic, and contained forty plates of agricultural illustrations and a lengthy text on barns.
12. Weslager, *Log Cabin in America* is the best general history of log construction in the United States.
13. Howells, *Recollections,* pp. 118–19.
14. Francis M. Thompson, *Greenfield, Mass.* (Greenfield: T. Morey and Son, 1904), Vol. II, p. 963, quoted in Bidwell and Falconer, *History of Agriculture,* p. 122.
15. Keys, quoted in Scott, *A History of the Early Settlement of Highland County,* pp. 148–49.
16. Plates 47, 48, and 49 in the *Report of the Commissioner of Patents for the Year 1856, Agriculture* (Washington, D.C.: 1857) picture the four walls of a tool house recommended for small farms. No horse-drawn harvesting implements are shown. Except in details of construction, the same tools could be dated at least 100 years earlier.
17. Kalm, *Peter Kalm's Travels* 1:118–19, entry dated 28 October 1748.
18. Commissioner of Labor, *Hand and Machine Labor,* Vol. I, Thirteenth Annual Report, 1898 (Washington, D.C.: 1899), pp. 470–73.
19. *Marvin Smith Company Catalog* (Chicago, ca. 1897), pp. 158–61.
20. Hutslar, "Hay Presses."
21. There are many books on farm tools and implements. Original company catalogs and broadsides are frequently found in libraries. Among the best contemporary sources are the exhibit catalogs from the various world expositions, beginning in the mid-nineteenth century.

22. The catalog, *Official Retrospective Exhibition of the Development of Harvesting Machinery for the Paris Exposition of 1900*, by the Deering Harvester Co. (Chicago and Paris: 1900), pictures all the models made for the exhibit of historic reaping and mowing machines, and is an excellent quick reference.
23. Commissioner of Labor, *Hand and Machine Labor*, pp. 470–73.
24. Woods, "Two Years' Residence," p. 279.
25. Halsted, *Barn Plans and Outbuildings*, p. 139. All Orange Judd publications are excellent reference sources today. Most of the material was first published in the periodical *American Agriculturist*.

IX CONSTRUCTION: TIME AND COST

Construction times and costs are moot points in the history of log architecture because of the tremendous variability of location, material, labor, size, finish, plus a myriad other details. However, time is frequently mentioned in literature in reference to speed of construction. There are many quotes in this book referring to raisings requiring only a single day; in fact, the "one-day raising" has come down to the present in oral tradition. "It was not considered a hardship at all, when several of the neighbors came with their axes, a yoke of oxen and a log chain, cross-cut saw, froe, maul, etc., and often in one day put up a log cabin and covered [roofed] it with clap boards before night. Another day or two, and the owner had put up a fireplace at one end and a door in the side."[1]

A single day is not without reason because (1) the size of most cabins or houses was moderate; (2) the trees were usually close to the building site; (3) felling and hewing were often tasks separate from the raising and finished beforehand; (4) large numbers of settlers, and work animals, were expected to assist at a raising; and (5) the single-day raising usually meant only the walls, floor joists, and rafters—perhaps the roofing—were completed. Barns could require several days because of their size; large barns were regarded as difficult tasks at best, the length and weight of the timbers being the problem. As various quotations bear out, everybody in a "community," which might include a several-mile radius, was expected to assist at a raising: "Mr. [Griffith] Foos says, that, at his raising, there were present 40 men before breakfast, and from a distance of from 7 to 10 miles; and [David] Lowry says, that at Isaac Zane's raising, there were persons from 40 miles distance."[2] Foos's house was raised in Springfield, Clark County, in the spring of 1801; Zane's house was on the site of Zanesfield, Logan County, and was raised in 1795 or shortly after.

Obviously there were many raisings in a new territory, and settlers had their own chores to do as well as help their neighbors, so time could not be wasted. This fact alone probably explains the speed of construction, for it would have been logical to prepare as much timber beforehand as possible. The finish work could then be accomplished with limited assistance. After examining many houses of varying construction—log, frame, stone, and brick—dating to Ohio statehood, this writer has sensed a certain speed of execution to the detriment of interior design. Basic shelter was needed first; refinements could be added as time and money permitted. Too many houses remain with illogical interiors to believe that the problems couldn't have been worked out, granted a short time for reflection: a window blocked by a wall or half-covered by a staircase; joists and flooring laid, then cut and headed for a stairwell; doors and windows (often crudely) cut through the exterior walls, but finished at the same time as the remainder of the interior; and so on. Log houses were less prone to these alterations because of their relatively simple construction and arrangement of interior space.

Probably the very fact a log house was being "raised" precluded any questions about fenestration, partitions, fireplace, and stairwell; the ethnic and environmental background of the community, if not the foreman or corner men, automatically set the style of the house. (This is a sound argument for the "Folk

Architecture" concept.) There is no question log houses fell into certain styles, although not elaborate of definition, in Ohio during the first fifty years of settlement. Houses with asymmetrical fenestration, gable entrances, no chimneys, and so on, which do not fit the basic patterns, must be explained. The explanations could be no more complex than speed of construction, reliance on corner men of mixed experience, or cost. The element of chance enters into the design and construction of even the simplest forms of architecture, enough so to place any typological system of identification in occasional doubt.

Aside from the time-honored one-day raising, practically any length of construction time can be found in the literature. Two days are frequently mentioned, the first for the basic structure; the second for floors, windows, doors, and fireplace/chimney. From the Revolutionary War through the War of 1812, the military built dozens of log structures in Ohio. It was not uncommon for a force on the march, as during the Indians Wars of the 1790s, to build a stockade and a few huts at every evening's bivouac. These were not elaborate feats of construction, and there were many men available, but in today's terms an amazing amount of hand labor was required. At Fort Amanda, in Auglaize County, during the War of 1812, it required a fatigue party four days to convert an "old cabbin" into a blockhouse.[3] The number in the party was not mentioned, but could have been from six to a dozen men. The logs of the cabin were cut into 13 foot lengths, on the first day (Tuesday, 23 March 1813). The following day, the blockhouse was raised. The third day, a weighted roof was constructed, and on the fourth day, "all hands busy finishing A block house & building a Shed. . . ."[4] Regardless of the number of men working on the blockhouse, it still required the time-honored one day to raise the walls.

In October 1838, one John B. Miller, of Miami County, completely rebuilt the original 1817 log house on his farm. His diary entries were brief and to the point.[5]

11th Cut and halled timber for the house.
15th Cut Wood and halled Crib logs.

16th [Jacob] Wicuff began to Wirk at house.
17th pulled down and bilt up house.
18th Shingeled house in fore[noon]. . . .
19th finished Civering house in fore[noon].
26th Toped out the Chimney. . . .
30th Chunked and Dobed house—
31st Dobbed the house.

Once again it should be noted that the actual raising took a single day, with an additional day (two half-days) to shingle the roof. The house must have been finished by the last day of October for no more entries occur. The year before, Miller had rebuilt the wattle and daub chimney on the old house; these entries are for October and November 1837:

24th halled Mud for Chimney. . . .
25th Split Stuff for Chimney. . . .
30th Took down the Old Chimley.
31st Building Chimney. . . .
1st Building Chimney. . . .
6th finished Chimney.

It is doubtful Miller spent all his time on this one job, but a stick and clay chimney must have been a slow task at best, a brick or stone chimney could have been built as quickly.

Emigrant "guides" are among the best sources for precise information on problems of settlement. Such guides, for North America, can be found as early as the mid-seventeenth century, and are still being written for Alaska and Canada. Many nineteenth-century guides included chapters on Ohio and the states and territories immediately west. Time and cost of construction were very important facts to the prospective immigrants, most of whom were from the lower economic strata of English and European society; this is why expected wages were normally included in the guides as well. Fearon, one of the famous English travelers and guide book authors, came through Ohio in 1818. His comments on the cost of necessary buildings, however, were made for Illinois where many people from his country settled. A two-room log "cabin" cost from 11 pounds, 5 shillings, to 16 pounds.[6] Fearon rated the English pound sterling at $4.44, so the cabin cost approximately 50 to 70 dollars.[7] In comparison, a "frame house" (but only 10 to 14 feet square) was estimated at 130 to 150 pounds, or from about $577 to $666. This seems an amazing discrepancy in cost, particularly when a log kitchen or stable could be built for the equivalent of $30 to $40, and a barn for about $80 to $100.[8]

In 1822 a small booklet was written for the benefit of Scotch emigrants entitled *A Brief Sketch of the State of Ohio*, by Nahum Ward of Marietta, with the written backing of Return Jonathan Meigs (ex-governor and postmaster general of the United States) and Harvey Strong (consul for Scotland). Ward owned land in Washington, Athens, Meigs, Hocking, Gallia, and Lawrence counties, and offered it for sale in tracts from 40 to 3,000 acres at 9 to 42 shillings per acre. This was at the end of the severe depression of 1818, so the shilling was probably worth 25 to 30 cents, certainly more than Fearon's estimate. "Those purchasing lands of him [Ward], can have a few acres cleared at 30s. per acre, grubbing and cutting all under 10 inches, and girdling all over, which will leave but few trees to the acre; and a house built of logs, 22 feet by 16, with small glass windows, fitted for comfortable habitation in winter, for £7."[9]

About thirty years later another emigrant guide, again dealing with Illinois and the "prairie states," presented a very detailed time and cost estimate for a log house.[10] This book, edited by Josiah T. Marshall, was composed of articles taken from various agricultural periodicals, but mainly from the *Prairie Farmer* published in Chicago. In this case, it is possible to compare some contemporary living costs and wages. The hewed log house described was 18 feet square and 10 feet high to the plate, with two finished floors and a nailed shake roof. There were two doors and two 12 light (8 by 10 inch) windows. The fireplace/chimney was constructed of wood, clay, and sticks, because bricks or stones might be difficult to procure on the prairie.[11] The construction time was estimated as follows:

Cutting, hewing, and hauling timber	4 days' work.
Raising, (mostly done by neighbors) say	1 do.
Putting on roof and gable-ends	2 do.
Cutting out doors, windows, and place for fire-place, and casing doors and windows, and making doors	4 do.
Laying floors and making a ladder to chamber	3 do.
Chinking and daubing	3 do.
Building chimney	3 do.
In all	20 days.[12]

The traditional one-day raising appears; it is interesting to note only the pen, and probably the floor joists, were included in the single-day estimate, one-twentieth of the actual construction time. The "ladder to chamber" no doubt refers to a corner, ladder-stairs. The cost of this log house was minimal:

Now, the cash out will be, for ten days' work	$5
1000 ft. of lumber for floors, etc.	10
20 lbs. of nails	1
30 lights sash and glass, (1 six light for chamber)	1 87
2 pair butts and screws, (use wooden latches)	25
400 split clapboards for the roof	2 50
Total	$20 62
But we will add for contingencies, which will make even money	$25 00[13]

Marshall follows this list with the comment that "we have allowed ten days . . . to build your house and move into it; but it would be better to have more hands, and complete it in less time."[14] Apparently he considered much of the work would be under way at the same time, which certainly would be true once the basic structure was erected.

In 1851 the Reverend R. D. Thomas, a Welshman, visited the United States to compile information for an emigrant guide (which apparently was never published).[15] Thomas was in Columbus and Newark, Ohio, in October and November, and listed various commodity prices and wages. Prices were slightly higher and wages lower in the larger city of Columbus. Averaging prices between the two cities, such food staples as wheat were fifty cents, corn twenty-five cents, and potatoes sixty-two cents a bushel; per pound, beef cost four to eight cents, pork four cents, sugar six to eight cents, tea seventy-five cents, coffee ten cents, and tobacco twelve to twenty cents. Daily wages were given, "without food." A bricklayer or stonemason could expect two dollars; a joiner, wheelwright, tailor, shoemaker, or plasterer, a dollar and a half; and a blacksmith, a dollar and a quarter. A common laborer hopefully received a dollar a day, but servants were less fortunate—from one to three dollars a week—although they usually received free board if not room. Assuming the estimated cost of a log house in Illinois would be the same for Ohio, and it was probably close, all but the servants could afford such a home. Of course, land was also required. Marshall felt a new settler could "buy land, build a house, fence and plough a farm, with $200." The "farm" was small by even nineteenth-century standards: 40 acres of cleared land and 5 acres of timber. He makes the oft-repeated comment that "all new countries are first improved by an uneasy, roving class, ever ready to 'sell out' and go to some other part of the country. . . .[16] Marshall also felt immigrants should look for such property first, because it was often sold at bargain prices. What is interesting is that the same approach was followed in Ohio fifty years earlier; and, the "roving class" is probably still roving, from city to city today.

Another guide, published in 1859 ostensibly for subjects of Queen Victoria emigrating to Canada, gives the following costs: "A comfortable log house, 16 feet by 24, with two floors, with shingled roof, £18; log barn, 24 feet by 40, £15; frame house, same dimensions, etc., £40."[17] Allowing a 5-dollar value for the mid-nineteenth-century pound sterling to simplify calculations, the log house would have cost about 90 dollars; in comparison, the frame house was about 400 dollars. The variations in cost do not seem as extreme as quoted in Fearon, when the sizes of the houses are compared. Because a log house was usually well finished, with plastered walls, woodwork, and paint, the time required to complete it was probably not too different from a framed house. However, in this instance the braced-frame barn, relative to the log barn, seems to be much higher in cost than one would expect, about 6.6 to 1 compared to 4.5 to 1 for the house.[18] This would seem to make the log barn a logical choice in the Canadian wilderness, with only slightly less speculation on the most economical house construction.

A braced-frame barn required trained craftsmen and a great quantity of sawed lumber siding. Not only was sawmill lumber expensive, but also there were areas, even in Ohio, where it was either necessary or convenient to buy the logs for log buildings. One such area was the "Black Swamp" in north-central Ohio along Lake Erie. Tarhe, "The Crane," the famous Wyandot chief, signed an agreement on 22 October 1814, to allow one Morris A. Newman to act as his agent in the sale of timber and stone on the Lower Sandusky reservation. The stone was priced at twelve and a half cents a perch, a highly variable volumetric measurement based on 16½ linear feet, ". . . and all timber on the following conditions or rates, that is, for Cabin Logs, fifteen feet square, a sufficient number to raise it one story high, three Dollars; eighteen feet, one story and half, four dollars; and twenty feet square (five dollars) one story and a half; and all timber for clabboards, punchons, and shingles and for such purposes is hereby left to said Newman's own Judgment as to their value.[19] Needless to say, the cost wasn't extreme. "Cabin Logs" presumably implies round logs; the section of a round log from Tarhe's own cabin at Upper Sandusky (see fig. 114) measures about seven inches in diameter. A one-story cabin would require between thirty-eight and forty-two logs of this diameter exclusive of the gables. Even if a settler were surrounded with trees, three dollars wasn't an unreasonable amount to pay for "precut" timber. What is implied in this agreement between Tarhe and Newman is that they obviously felt there was a demand for building logs among the settlers. It would be interesting to know how much timber was actually sold (this information might be available through federal records).

166. Clark County, Greene Township. Two story log house. (See Figures 127, 156, 170, 202, 208, 226.) Photo: 18 August 1972. Rafters and sheathing. The rafters are joined in pairs at the ridge with half-lap mortises and pegs, the standard method in Ohio. Wany-edge sheathing was also typical. Note: If the rafters are butted to a ridge board, then the roof framing was based on the balloon-frame technique which didn't reach Ohio until the mid-1830s.

167. North-central Kentucky. Date unknown. Hand-sawed roof sheathing and wood roofing pegs. A technique known to have been used in Ohio.

168. Greene County, Miami Township. Braced-frame house, dating to the early 1820s. (See Figure 216.) Photo: October, 1974. Typical example of "bald-face" or half-lap rafter mortises used throughout Ohio on all types of buildings for at least the first half of the 19th century. The use of a "ridge-pole" or board was not common in the state until balloon frame construction became known in the 1830s. The sheathing is probably original, but not the thin cedar shingles. Note the vertical sawmill kerfs.

169. Butler County, Oxford Township. Two story log house. (See Figures 68, 69, 129, 157, 160, 161, 180, 195, 201.) Photo: 1 June 1971. Northwest corner of second floor. The joists were exposed, having standing beads on their lower edges. The eave is formed by the joists extending past the wall line. A "false plate" rests on top the joists, and the rafters are pegged through both (pegs can be seen at the center where the joist is missing). This writer has seen several false plate eaves around the state, on both log and braced frame construction. The technique was frequently used on masonry buildings.

170. Clark County, Greene Township. Two story log house. (See Figures 127, 156, 166, 202, 208, 226.) Photo: 18 August 1972. False plate eave; compare to Figure 169. The ceiling joists were half-mortised in the upper wall logs. False plates (simply boards) were laid on top the joists. The overhanging eaves were then boxed-in; the result was wide, well-proportioned cornices effectively sealed against drafts. With a horizontal plate, as in Figure 165, a nailing surface was available for a soffit.

171. Ross County, City of Chillicothe. Two story log house. (See Figure 230.) Photo: 1949–53 (?). Second floor porch, north. Extended eave beams and ceiling joists. It is possible the porch was originally extended only at the gable ends, and the joists formed part of a boxed eave. The narrow, vertical window at left suggests the side light of a Palladian-style window popular during the Federal period; however, it would have been off-center in the wall.

172. Washington County, Waterford Township. Sugar Camp. Photo: *ca.* 1890. In construction, this building was similar to many rough log houses of the early 19th century. The steeple-notched logs were left round. The roofing was split shakes. The gables were sided with wide boards flushed to the edge of the end rafters.

173. Franklin County, City of Columbus, Ohio State Fair Grounds. "Log Cabin" built in August, 1974, by Charles and John Minnich. Photo: September, 1974. This round log cabin with steeple-notched corners was built as a demonstration during the state fair. The shakes for the roof were rived at the site. The roof framing is not "cabin technique" in the traditional sense, but typical of log houses with plates and rafters. Charles Minnich is an excellent hewer, and is still active.

174. Washington County, City of Marietta. Plank house, 1788–89. (See Figures 114, 151, 207.) Photo: February, 1968. First floor, southwest room of Putnam House. Ceiling joists probably date 1789. From the concave shape of the kerfs, these joists were probably hewed with a curved foot-adze. The construction crew recruited in New England to build *Campus Martius* followed traditional building practices. These joists could have been made from small diameter tree trunks, saving much time and labor.

175. Delaware County, Liberty Township. One and a half story log house. (See Figure 186.) Photo: 10 August 1967. Northwest corner, front. The sandbox for an iron stove, a detail that is rarely seen today, is probably not original to the house, but could be 19th century because of the lack of a fireplace.

176. Seneca County, City of Tiffin. Heidelberg College Campus. Two story log house. Photo: 24 October 1978. Window altered into door. The window jamb boards are visible at the sides of the door, as is the filled half-notch at the top. The second floor joists are extremely large. This is an interesting structure, with its altered fenestration. It may have been a church, school, or commercial building, for it had a gable entrance with numerous side windows.

177. Greene County, Spring Valley Township. One and a half story log house, built by or for the Elam or McKnight families about 1807. (See Figures 85, 86, 110, 111, 112.) Photo: 13 January 1973. This view of the second story floor joists shows the holes which anchored the lever used to push the floorboards tightly together for nailing. Such holes are commonly thought to be for flooring pegs. This house is now at the "Caesar's Creek Pioneer Village" in Warren County.

178. Greene County, Miami Township. One and a half story log house. (See Figures 162, 198, 204.) Photo: 12 November 1967. Though the front wall had two rows of joist mortises, this rear (north) wall had one. Perhaps the foundation sank, for the house stands on a slight rise near a spring, forcing a realignment of the floors. The 6 over 6 window sash is typical for the first half of the 19th century.

179. Greene County, Caesar Creek Township. One and a half story log house. (See Figures 61, 187, 191, 215.) Photo: May, 1971. Stairwell, southeast corner. The board and batten door had been hung with the battens towards the room. The door retained its surface-mounted spring latch, as did the door to the closet under the stairs.

180. Butler County, Oxford Township. Two story log house. (See Figures 68, 69, 129, 157, 160, 161, 169, 195, 201.) Photo: June, 1971. Northwest corner of the first floor. The west side of the first floor was divided into two small rooms (the notches for the partition wall are in the joists at the upper left) and a stairwell. The stairwell was enclosed, with its own door, and had a closet underneath. Corner stairwells usually did not extend towards the center of the house as far as this example. The first floor walls were covered with vertical, random width boards with beaded edges, as seen around the window; the darker lines of the cove mold, chair rail, and baseboard are quite apparent.

181. Franklin County, Plain Township. One and a half story log house. Back door, north. Photo: May, 1974. Though centered front and back doors were typical of Ohio log houses, examples of off-centered doors exist. This structure had doors in opposite corners of the front and back walls. The chimney/fireplace(s) were in the center of the log section, and the ladder stairs were placed to turn towards the chimney.

182. Hamilton County, Miami Township. Two story log house. (See Figures 29, 30, 31, 32, 33, 180.) Photo: 15 August 1975. This very narrow (about 5 foot wide overall) corner staircase makes a 180 degree turn to avoid the large stone chimney on the second floor.

183. Greene County, Cedarville Township. One and a half story log house. (See Figure 221.) Photo: 8 July 1967. The corner "ladder stairs," turning above the fireplace, was a standard feature in one and a half story Ohio log houses. Even when the chimney was inside the wall, the staircase would turn towards it. On the second floor, the last step was often against the side of the chimney.

184. Madison County, Somerford Township. Two story brick house built *ca.* 1818 by Valentine Wilson. Photo: 13 January 1973. Second floor stairwell, northeast corner. Corner, ladder-stairs were used in all types of Ohio houses for at least the first third of the 19th century. Stylistically, this stairwell is correct for a large log house. There are doors on the first and second floor levels as well as the attic. Note the six-panel doors with wide, central stiles, and the beaded, vertical board walls. (National Register of Historic Places.)

185. Warren County, Clear Creek Township. Two story log house. Photo: 13 August 1976. Stairwell door. The doors in this house were made of boards interlocked by tapered and dovetailed battens. This joinery technique was used for table tops in the 18th century and before. Similar doors exist in a log house near Austintown in Mahoning County.

186. Delaware County, Liberty Township. One and a half story log house. Size, 21 by 18 feet; eave, 9½ feet; ridge, 18 feet. (See Figure 175.) Photo: 10 August 1967. Original partition wall. Two vertical board walls created three rooms on the first floor. With the log walls and ceiling whitewashed, and the partitions and woodwork painted bluish-green, the interior must have been cheerful despite the small rooms and low, 6 foot 8 inch ceiling.

187. Greene County, Caesar Creek Township. One and a half story log house. (See Figures 61, 179, 191, 215.) Photo: May, 1971. Vertical board partition wall, second floor. Both this wall and the board ceiling are good examples of the type of finish found in many Ohio houses, of varied construction, during the first half of the 19th century. The elaborate molding was necessary to give strength to the door jamb as well as the depth needed to abutt the baseboard, chair rail, and peg rail. The ceiling profile is "half story." In other words, an adult can stand erect in the center of the rooms but not at the sides.

188. Madison County, Canaan Township. Two story log house, greatly remodeled. (See Figures 219, 220.) Photo: 16 November 1975. Doorway, north side. This is a good example of an exterior door of the first third of the 19th century. When this house was remodeled, the door was preserved between the clapboarding and the interior wall.

189. Franklin County, Village of Groveport. Two story log house with log addition. (See Figures 64, 125, 140, 155, 212, 225.) Photo: 11 November 1974. This six-panel door, possibly the original front or back door of the house, was stored in the attic.

190. Clark County, Bethel Township. Brick house built for John Paul, *ca.* 1820. Photo: 5 October 1973. Front door, west. This eight-panel door is a late 18th, early 19th century style popular in Ohio, and was used on log houses. The Ohio Company's "Land Office" at Marietta has a similar door, probably taken from Campus Martius and dating in the early 1790s. The six-panel door, however, was the common style until about 1840 and strong Greek Revival influence. Two and four-panel doors then become popular. Old doors are always interesting, for the marks of locks and hardware they bear.

191. Greene County, Caesar Creek Township. One and half story log house. (See Figures 61, 179, 187, 215.) Photo: May, 1971. Front door, east room. Originally a six panel door, this type of alteration—with one or more panes of glass—is frequently found. The rim-lock is typical of the 1830s and 40s; there were several makers in Cincinnati. The chair rail was carried under the window as part of the molding.

192. Columbiana County, Village of Salineville. Gristmill, divided doors. Photo: September, 1978. Door latch with wooden spring. The divided doors on the three levels of the mill had these latches. An interior stairwell door had a similar latch cased in wood. Wood-spring latches were common in vernacular architecture, but examples are rare today.

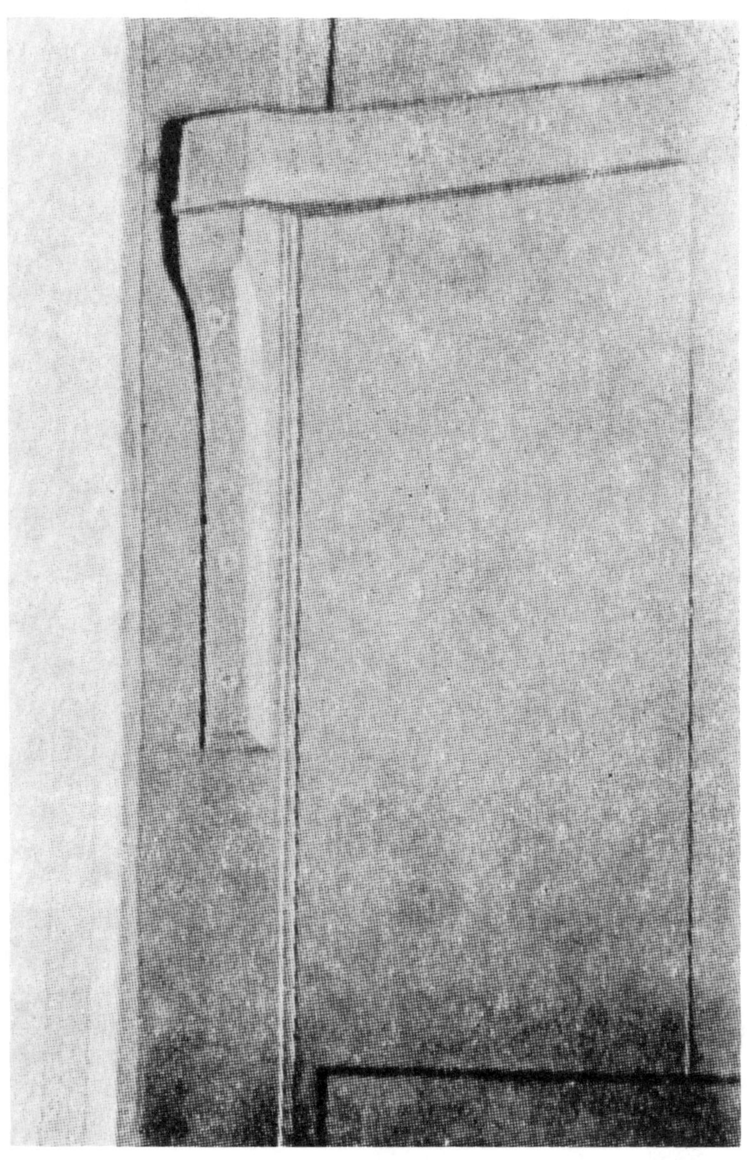

193. Belmont County, Warren Township. Two story log house built in 1807–08, by Thomas Williams. Photo: 1922, from Stanton, *Our Ancestors*, p. 223. This is an excellent example of a wooden door hinge. Apparently only two hinges were used on this board and batten door.

194. Greene County, Xenia Township. Two story log house with log addition built *ca.* 1808 by or for James Mitchell. Photo: 1930s. Back, north; chimney, west. Front porch and partitions missing. This imposing structure had a full basement kitchen. The log addition to the east was connected to the house by a breezeway. There was a fireplace on each of the three floors. The staircases were in the southeast corner. This area was settled by Ulster-Scotch Presbyterians. Several large stone houses were built about 1805. This house was nicknamed the "stone front" because of the chimney. The blind holes in the chimney were for the horizontal "putlocks" of the pole scaffolding. It was common practice to fill them in brick and stone buildings once construction was complete.

195. Butler County, Oxford Township. Two story log house built *ca.* 1805 by or for Zachariah DeWitt. Size, approximately 28 by 21 feet, 24 feet to ridge. (See Figures 68, 69, 129, 157, 160, 161, 180, 201.) Photo: July, 1973. Front of house, south, and east end. The monumental stone chimney is typical of the early 19th century. (National Register of Historic Places.)

196. Warren County, Massie Township. Saddle-bag house. (See Figures 54, 55, 56, 128, 165.) Photo: 19 February 1972. East end. The main feature of a saddle-bag house was the monumental central chimney. This was the kitchen fireplace, which was at least four and a half feet in height. The crane was still in place. A passageway, connecting the living room and kitchen, was to the left of the chimney; the area to the right was enclosed and accessible from the kitchen. About four feet above the fireplace, the chimney was shouldered for headers and floor joists; about two feet higher, there were shoulders for headers and rafters. The set-back near the roof line was to reduce the bulk of the chimney. The living room fireplace was directly back of this fireplace.

197. Clermont County, Miami Township. Two story saddle-bag house. (See Figures 52 and 53.) Photo: 15 May 1976. West, front. This space was framed-in, and doorways and a second floor landing allowed access to both pens. There could have been an outside door, but no evidence remains.

198. Greene County, Miami Township. One and a half story log house. Size, 18 feet square. (See Figures 162, 178, 204.) Photo: 12 November 1967. East (chimney) and north sides. This house has only one doorway and one window. Perhaps it was half of a double-pen structure; or, perhaps that was the intention, but the second pen was never constructed. The brick chimney, much repaired, appears original. There is evidence this house was constructed by German immigrants in 1820s. In 1976, the house was razed for logs to rebuild the tornado damaged Galloway house in Xenia; see Figure 41, *et. al.*

199. Warren County, Village of Franklin. Two story log house. (See Figures 70, 228, 229.) Photo: 15 August 1975. An early braced-frame addition was removed from this end of the house. Note the outline of a staircase on the whitewashed wall to the left of the chimney. The doors were also added. Portions of the original stone chimney may be hidden.

200. Jackson County (?). One and a half story log house with stick chimney. Photo by Prof. Wilbur Stout, Ohio State University, 1914. It seems unusual a stick and clay chimney would remain until the 20th century. It argues either for their durability or their utility. (About half the chimney is missing.)

201. Butler County, Oxford Township: Two story log house. (See Figures 68, 69, 129, 157, 160, 161, 169, 180, 195.) Photo: 1 June 1971. The original outline of the fireplace opening is just visible as an arched line of vertical stones. It appears that the firebox was twice reduced in size.

202. Clark County, Greene Township. Two story log house. (See Figures 127, 156, 166, 170, 208, 226.) Photo: 18 August 1972. Second floor, east end. This house is somewhat unusual in having four fireplaces. All were reduced in size. The bedroom walls were originally whitewashed; later they were furred, lathed, and plastered, probably when a two story frame T-extension was added to the rear of the house.

203. Noble County, Beaver Township. Two story log house. (See Figures 126, 222.) Photo: 3 May 1972. North wall. A well finished fireplace; cut-stone fireplaces are not commonly found in Ohio log houses. This house was located a short distance south of the Old National Road, so it is possible that stonemasons working on the bridges did some work on private structures. (Several stone houses are located along the old road right-of-way.) The stairwell was to the right of the fireplace, a large cupboard to the left.

204. Greene County, Miami Township. One and a half story log house. (See Figures 162, 178, 198.) Photo: 12 November 1967. The fireplace may have been repaired several times. The original mantle measures 5½ feet in height. Note how the lower sides, at the hearth level, have been charred away; most cooking was done over coals on the hearth.

205. Greene County, Beavercreek Township. One and a half story log house. (See Figure 59.) Photo: *ca.* 1903. Fireplace and mantle of the William Maxwell house, 1803. Despite the poor condition of this photograph, the design and construction of the mantle and the stone firebox are apparent, probably unchanged since the house was built. By guessing the height of the logs, this mantle stood at least 5½ feet tall.

206. Franklin County, Jefferson Township (Village of Gahanna). Braced-frame house with half-timberered kitchen built over stone springhouse. Photo: October, 1972. Kitchen fireplace mantle. This house was composed of two separate structures adjoining a central chimney. The kitchen/springhouse section appeared to be the older, perhaps dating to the 1820s. The fireplace mantle was over six feet in height, and of a style common to Ohio during the first quarter of the 19th century. The woodwork was originally painted blue.

207. Washington County, City of Marietta. Plank house with braced-frame addition, 1788–1800. (See Figures 114, 151, 174.) Photo: 26 October 1967. After the Treaty of Greene Ville in 1795, *Campus Martius* was offered for sale to the Ohio Company members residing in the "houses" or apartments within its curtain-walls. Rufus Putnam bought his section and the adjacent blockhouse. Using the material from this latter structure, in 1796 he began the remodeling of his original home and eventually doubled its size. This photograph shows the interior wall of a second floor bedroom in the addition; through the closet door can be seen the original interior plank wall. The fireplace mantel was signed "C. Mills 1800."

As a sidelight on the cost of log construction, one can turn to a famous and genuine frontier eccentric, John Chapman. Better known, of course, as "Johnny Appleseed," Chapman ranged east and west across the summit area of Ohio and into Indiana, establishing small apple and fruit tree nurseries. His life has been obscured by The Legend, as with all frontier heroes, but he was not as naive as commonly portrayed. He owned many parcels of land in Ohio and Indiana, presumably for his nurseries and for speculation. After Chapman's death in Allen County, Indiana, in 1845, his estate paid William Broom (of Wabash Township, Jay County, Indiana) forty dollars for building a log house, 18 by 21 feet, and $36 for "scoreing and hewing timber for a frame barn 30 by 40 feet, [and] 1834 feet of timber."[20] This work was done for Chapman in 1843 and 1844. Some indication of the value of the house can be gained because the estate paid $3.44 for Chapman's "laying out" and $6 for his coffin.[21] (Considering the volume of space involved, the house was the better bargain!)

While John Johnston was at the Fort Wayne Indian Agency, he had "improvements" made on his farm north of Piqua, Miami County, Ohio. Much of this work—a log house and barn and an orchard—was completed in 1808, which he dutifully noted in two small memorandum books.[22] His first house was constructed of logs, 26 by 36 feet, two stories with a double porch, and cost $300. This was the house in which the family lived until the fall of 1815 (it stood about 90 feet north of the present brick house). Johnston's large, 90- by 30-foot double-pen log barn, which is extant, cost $280. Johnston had been appointed a "Factor" in 1802, a job involving buying, selling, and bartering trade goods and furs with the Indians. His salary was $1,000 a year plus three rations of food per day, consequently he was on a par, or slightly above, the income of a skilled craftsman, and had the advantage of a guaranteed income as well as room and board. The costs of the log house and barn undoubtedly reflect Johnston's secure position; the costs are probably not out of line, considering the size of the structures. The house must have been well-finished; the barn certainly was and can still be seen with its later perimeter sheds restored (see fig. 91).

Construction times and costs were as variable in the nineteenth century as today. Perhaps the greatest differential was in the cost of materials, log houses being built from free or low-cost timber from the proprietor's own land or in the immediate vicinity. Today, suitable timber is both scarce and expensive in most counties of the state; however, then as now, the greatest expense was labor, and much of the labor went into finishing work. Marshall's $25 house was as valid a frontier dwelling as Johnston's $300 house; admitting it was only one-quarter the size, it was still adequate for a homesteader and was estimated accordingly. The selection of costs used in this chapter are meager, but such information is not easily found. Obviously, the range of costs could be extended down to zero and up to any sum commensurate with a given owner's life-style: Symmes spent $100 on his masonry fireplace when most settlers were spending that much on their entire homesteads. To understand and successfully restore any log building, one must try to learn as much about the original owner as about the extant structure.

Notes

1. Lang, *History of Seneca County*, p. 184.
2. Howe, *Historical Collections*, p. 566.
3. "Journal of Ensign William Schillinger," p. 63.
4. Ibid.
5. *John B. Miller Diary, 1836–1843*. No pagination; chronological entries. Microfilm copy, Ohio Historical Society Library. Miller farmed eighty acres in Spring Creek Township, Miami County. His farm lay just north of the farm of the present owner of the diary, Leonard U. Hill.
6. Fearon, *Sketches of America*, p. 261.
7. Ibid., p. 450.
8. Ibid., p. 261. One could assume the extra time and prepared material needed to construct a braced-frame house were responsible for the increased cost, but a 10-foot square "house" had to have been small quarters for the price. It is this writer's opinion that 130 and 150 should read 13 and 15 (pounds sterling). This would place such a small structure in

line with the other prices quoted. The alternative would be 130 to 150 *dollars*, but Fearon did not use the American monetary system.

9. Nahum Ward, *A Brief Sketch of the State of Ohio* (Glascow: n.p. 1822.).
10. Marshall, *Farmers and Emigrants Complete Guide.*
11. Ibid., pp. 26–27.
12. Ibid., p. 28.
13. Ibid.
14. Ibid.
15. Thomas, *America, or Miscellaneous Notes on the United States Useful for Emigrants.*
16. Marshall, ibid., p. 26.
17. *British American Guide-Book*, pt. 3, p. 35.
18. The danger of generalizing with too few facts is quite apparent in this chapter, even when using guide book figures, which are broad estimates in themselves. Every county in Ohio, almost year to year, would vary in the cost of construction and material; this could probably be reduced to every township during periods of boom and recession.
19. Meek, "Tarhe—The Crane," p. 70 (punctuation added).
20. Wendel Paddock, ed., *Estate* [Papers] *of John Chapman* 1935, ms. p. 17.
21. Price, *Johnny Appleseed*, p. 235. This is an excellent account of Chapman's life.
22. Available from (1) Cincinnati Historical Society, and (2) Clements Library, University of Michigan, Ann Arbor, Michigan.

X
TOOLS AND MATERIAL

Of all the hand, woodworking tools on sale at the hardware store today, most were available in similar forms two hundred years ago. Perhaps the greatest difference lies in the many variations of a single tool that are no longer obtainable. For instance, of the many types of axes once used in the United States, few were being manufactured after 1900 because felling and hewing timber had all but disappeared.

Most settlers became so familiar with the varieties and uses of wood that there were few things they could not make with hand tools. Today, it is common to hear expressions of amazement over the difficulties of erecting a log building. Difficult today, yes, but to a society reared in the use of the hand tool, and with an incredible quantity of wood on which to practice (whether they wanted to or not), such a feat became daily routine. In fact, although strenuous physically, building a log structure was probably one of the simplist of the wood crafts.

TOOLS

Felling Ax: The iron felling ax reached the Ohio Country early. About 1840 a Mr. Chidester, of Canfield, Trumbull County, cut an oak tree on his father's farm. When the tree fell, a second "stump" appeared near the center. The tree had been half cut through with an iron ax when it was 15 inches in diameter. From the scar to the outside of the tree, one hundred sixty growth rings were counted; an estimated fifteen to twenty additional rings were obscured by decay. The tree had originally been cut about the year 1660. There was a similar occurrence in Cincinnati in the year 1791. A large poplar tree was cut down; about 18 to 20 inches within the perimeter of the trunk, there was a scar left by a very wide ax blade. By counting the annular rings, an approximate date of 1680 was obtained.[1]

The felling ax was of utmost necessity in the eastern United States during colonization. By the period of Ohio settlement, it bore little resemblance to its European progenitor and had become a tool unique to the North American continent. The two significant changes in design, which evolved through trial and error, were the curved haft and the addition of counterbalancing weight to the ax head opposite the blade, which created the "polled ax." This latter development placed the haft through the eye of the ax approximately at its center of balance, lessening the tendency of the blade to deflect sideways at the moment of impact. (The phrase, "to be poll-axed," refers to a blow given with great force.) Compared to the European ax with its large radial cutting edge, the American ax blade had a shorter arc terminating at a right angle. This configuration allowed the ax to cut flush against an object, or hew closely to a line, which was of great convenience in construction.

The American felling ax became thin and flat in proportion to its width and height, not nearly as heavy in cross section as axes today. Aside from proportion, an early ax can often be distinguished by its eye. There were three basic types of eyes: (1) the "common eye," which was a cylinder with parallel sides; (2) the "adze-eye," which expanded in width towards the front of the ax head; and (3) the "reverse eye," which reduced in width towards the front edge. The adze-eye is found on most tools today. A wedge was needed to expand the end of the haft to make it fit tightly in a common eye. In the early axes which used the reverse eye, the haft (probably green wood) was driven into the eye as firmly as possible—the haft being straight, or at least not as curved as today. Ax heads were often left in water or soaked in linseed oil to keep the hafts tight.

A great deal of practical folklore built up around the ax, such as the best types of metal to use, how the edge should be sharpened, what kinds of wood made the best hafts. One of the most interesting phenomena was "weathering," in which a new ax head was allowed to remain outside, its cutting edge pointing north, for a length of time ranging up to one year. An ax thus treated was supposed to hold its sharpness. This procedure had some basis in fact, for what did happen was a vertical polarization of the ions which improved the edge-holding qualities of the metal (a blacksmith achieved the same result by striking the end of a forging; this was known as "upsetting").

Until drop forging became common, the ax, as with most cutting tools, was hand forged of soft iron with a steel insert for the cutting edge. The poll was never intended for hard pounding, as is possible with the modern steel ax. The polls were often flattened when worn-out axes were used as wedges. As the iron industry developed in the second quarter of the nineteenth century, the old style of ax gave way to a heavier, drop-forged version. Names were given to certain ax designs found in various geographic areas of the United States, and these names, including an Ohio-pattern, have continued in use to the present.

William Blane was greatly impressed by the ax work he witnessed in North America in 1822–33.

> The Western Militia are scarcely more formidable to an advancing army, from their skill in shooting than from their dexterity in the use of the axe.
>
> Every individual is brought up from his youth to the use of this tool, which is of a peculiar construction, and differs essentially from the European Broad Axe.
>
> To see the short space of time in which a Backwoodsman can cut down the largest tree, and the power he has of making it fall in whatever direction he pleases, astonishes a foreigner, who must labour for years in order to attain the same skill.[2]

(This "European Broad Axe" was the large, poll-less felling ax described earlier.) The North Americans' skill with an ax was certainly better than that of the French at Gallipolis, if the following tale can be believed:

> Their manner was to place as many men around a huge poplar or sycamore as could conveniently wield their axes, while one man watched the progress of the work, and gave notice of the first indication of its falling by a loud yell. Every one then took to his heels and fled with all speed from beneath the descending giant. In this attempt they sometimes ran in the direction of the falling tree and were killed under its branches. When fairly down they went to work in dismembering it. In the mean time another party with spades dug a deep pit along side the trunk, into which it was rolled and covered with earth, while the top and branches were . . . burnt.[3]

Apparently the Germans had their difficulties as well, as Lang noted in his *History of Seneca County*:

> Perhaps it did look awkward to see a man raise his axe over his head to chop down a tree, hacking into it all around in some fashion to get it down. But this was no laughing matter; the thing had to be learned by experience. The foreigner had no wood to chop in the land of his birth. A crooked axe-handle, and such an axe, were not in use in his country at that time [1830–40]. An American coming upon a German chopping in the wood, would often stop and show him how to *swing*, and not *raise* the axe perpendicularly. . . .[4]

The German style of chopping was no doubt governed by the European-pattern felling ax which had to be wielded very precisely because of its imbalance.

When trees were felled for clearing or building, they were cut somewhat differently than is usual today. The felling cut was generally three or four feet above the ground—even higher—depending on the reach of the axman. This was for a very good reason: to give oxen or horses sufficient leverage to break the stump free of its roots. The dirt was dug from the main roots, the roots were cut, then the hitch was applied at the top of the stump. Oxen were well suited to this type of work. A short stump meant a lot of digging and cutting before it could be raised from the ground.

Broadax: The use of the broadax to fell trees is one of the worst myths perpetrated by writers and artists. Only under emergency conditions would it have been used for that purpose. The American broadax was a direct descendant of the Germanic broad-blade ("gull wing") ax which was used like an enormous chisel for working rough timber into dimensioned lumber. A large felling ax might have a cutting edge up to five inches; the broadax could have a cutting edge of twelve inches. The cutting edge of the felling ax was sharpened to a "V," like a knife; the broadax was sharpened on only one side—beveled, like a chisel, to cut a level surface. The felling ax had a haft two to three feet in length; the broadax had a haft one to two feet long, often with an offset to allow the blade to lie flat on the work. The haft usually protruded through the eye so it could be knocked loose and reversed when the direction of the cut had to be changed.

The technique of squaring timber is relatively easy to describe, though difficult to learn without considerable practice (see appendix C). Beginning with the round log, a felling ax was used to cut a series of notches, "scores," at right angles to the axis of the log and at about one-foot intervals of the entire length. The same ax was used to split away, or "kerf," the wood between the scores. The rough-hewn surface was then smoothed with the broadax, taking short, careful strokes. This created one flat surface. Another flat surface was then hewed on the opposite side of the log in the same manner. This was all the shaping necessary. The plate and sill were usually hewed on all four sides, making it easier to mortise in the rafters, floor joists, studding, and braces. The Scandinavians and Germans built structures with full dovetail notching which required very close fitting, squared timbers. Plank walls, mortised into corner posts, also required careful hewing. However, disregarding the round-log cabin, almost all log buildings in Ohio were constructed with logs faced on two sides.

The broadax was handled in various ways, one man might cut horizontally, another vertically; cuts were made both with, and at right angles to, the grain. A vertical cut, downwards against the grain, seems to have been the standard method. In certain situations the direction of the cut might have to be altered, which accounts for the removable, crooked haft. (The bent haft also kept the user's knuckles safe.) The reversible haft was of great benefit when "scutching" flats on round log walls because the cut direction would change in the corners. The flat back of the broadax and its beveled cutting edge permitted the axman to cut a level surface on the wood. Logs hewed by a good axman show practically no evidence of the strokes; all that remains on the logs are vestiges of the scores made by the felling ax.

The broadax, and the smaller carpenter's broad- or bench-hatchet which also has a beveled edge, are still in production. Many traditional pattern tools are used in shipbuilding; however, the manufacture of such tools in the United States has all but ceased.

Auger: The hand auger, or hand screw, was a tool of great importance. Though a small hole might be chiseled, it certainly couldn't be "axed." In form, the auger bit is an open screw with a cutting edge at the tip; the chips are drawn out of the hole by the spiral action of the screw. Today, the auger is the common bit for the hand brace. A log cabin could be built without the use of nails or wooden pegs, but the better finished log house required a large number of pegged jambs and mortised rafters. The auger was the tool for that purpose. The common sizes for building were from three-quarters to one and a half inches in diameter. The larger augers had removable handles so the bit and handle could be carried in a relatively small space. The auger was a standard tool of the braced-frame carpenter. Mortises were first drilled out with the auger, then squared up with corner and framing chisels.

Saw: Perhaps the saw cannot be considered common to frontier construction, but it certainly was not rare. Most log buildings in

Ohio show liberal use of the saw, for it was the only convenient tool for cutting window and door openings and squaring up exterior corners. The saw is often thought of as a relatively modern invention, whereas it was so ancient even to the Greeks that they placed its supposed inventor(s) in their mythology. Handsaws of every size and shape and for every possible use had been devised by the nineteenth century. Making a suitable metal for saw manufacturing was a problem not solved until the advent of the rolling mill and refinements in iron smelting in the latter half of the eighteenth century. (No better tool metal has been produced than the English "cast steel," particularly for edged tools; it was a "secret" process developed by chance about 1740, in which blister steel was remelted for casting.)

Of the saws available to the settler, a type resembling the present-day carpenter's saw was the most common. It was two to three feet in length, with either an open or closed handle, and had pointed "common" or "featheredge" teeth. Of all the early hand tools, saws are the hardest to find today. They were used until broken or could no longer be sharpened, then served as a source for scrap metal.

Beetle and Frow: Shakes, shingles, and clapboards were split with a frow. The frow (or "froe") was a long metal bar with a beveled edge like a chisel and an eye for a handle at one end. It was held upright near the edge of a block of wood such as white oak, which splits easily, and was driven into the end grain with a "beetle" (a hand maul or mallet) or simply a stick of wood. The end of the frow protruded far enough to permit the pounding to continue the length of the block while the handle was rocked back and forth. This operation split off a piece of wood, a shake, and was known as "riving." The shake was from 18 to 36 inches in length, 6 to 8 inches in width, and usually tapered lengthwise from a butt of about one inch. Shakes were the common roofing material for at least the first quarter of the nineteenth century, and they continued in use in Ohio until the twentieth century in isolated areas (see fig. 102). A shingle was a better finished, smaller version of the shake. It was rived in the same manner, often from poplar or red cedar, then shaved smooth with a drawknife. A shingle-horse, "schnitzelbank," held the shingle while it was being worked. The butt end of the shingle was often rounded instead of square like the shake. The shingled roof was considered superior to other types of wooden roofing because of its closely laid surface. Certainly it required more labor to make a shingle.

A larger frow was used to rive roofing and siding clapboards. These were made in the same manner as shakes, though the initial block of wood had to be four to six feet long and was usually a quarter section of split log. All splits radiated from the center of the quarter section so that each clapboard was wedge-shaped in cross section (modern siding board is sawed or planed to the same shape). To create a water-repellent surface, the large edge of the clapboard always overlaps the small edge, as in shingling.

The deceptively simple frow was designed for a specific job, as was the broadax, and no other tool could take its place for efficiency and speed.

Adze: The long-handled adze, which was a common carpenter's tool, had a slightly curved, bevel-edged blade (with or without a hammer-poll), attached at right angles to the haft. It was used, like the broadax, as a large chisel; however, it was held and used perpendicular to a surface rather than parallel as the broadax. Both straight and curved blades were common. There were adzes for working concave surfaces as found in bowls, troughs, or barrel staves, as well as leveling flat surfaces such as joists, studs, or rafters. A good carpenter could level a floor so perfectly it appeared mechanically planed. The adze was designed for finishing a surface rather than roughing out timber. A common misrepresentation in pictorial art is the adze being used to hew a log. Working a small pole for a rafter or joist would be a more accurate rendering, for better tools, such as the ax and broadax, existed for heavy work. Time alone would tell against the adze.

The range of tools available to the Ohio settlers was almost unlimited, and what they had was dependent more on what they could transport than what they could afford—for most iron tools could be fabricated by local blacksmiths at reasonable cost. Hammers, hatchets, and chisels, even saws, files, and augers, could be made by good blacksmiths, but by 1800 most of these tools came from semi-mechanized foundries and forging shops.

In the vanguard with the settlers, or following immediately behind them, came the rough and finish carpenters, the joiners and cabinetmakers, the architect-builders, and a variety of other allied craftsmen such as stone and brick masons, each bringing their own specialized tools. In the settlements along the Ohio River and up the major river valleys, these craftsmen were plying their trades prior to 1800. While at Cincinnati in November 1790, Symmes noted that "upwards of forty framed and hewed-log two-story houses have been and are building since last spring. . . . and the great demand for labour on buildings is such as to give employment to every class from the Carpenter to the treading of Morter."[5] The following July 1791, one Reuben Read, a brickmaker of Cincinnati, paid a fine of sixteen dollars for selling "spirituous liquor, contrary to an act of the Territory of the U.S.N.W.R.O."[6] This could be the first record of a brickmaker in the state, though no doubt brickmakers were present in 1788. However, the average settlers were farmers, dependent on their own skill with tools for most of the necessities of life, still the case among many rural Ohioans and farmers throughout the country.

Since the number of sawmills in Ohio naturally increased with the expansion of settlement, most builders were never far from a source of dimensioned lumber. For example, almost all remaining log houses in Ohio have sawed floorboards and sheathing. Although some of these floors are not original, it is obvious that the majority are. The vertical sawmill was common in the settled areas of Ohio prior to the War of 1812 (as early as 1789); following the war it quickly spread to the thinly populated areas.[7] Hauling sawed scantling a few miles was easier than hewing a puncheon floor. Sawed rafters, joists, and studs are also found with enough frequency to show that convenience and time were more important than economy to most settlers.

VARIETIES OF WOOD

If the settlers complained of the lack of certain amenities of life on the frontier, they certainly did not lament a lack of timber; in fact, many hated the sight of trees and cut them for that very reason. More wood was expediently burned than was used for necessary purposes. Francis Baily was especially aware of this fact because of the diminished forests in his native England. He wrote the following comment while in southwestern Ohio in 1797:

> I have seen oak-trees, and those not uncommon, which measured near four feet diameter at the bottom, and which had a straight trunk *without a single branch* for seventy feet; and from that part to the termination of the upper branch it has measured seventy more; and these immense trees I have seen cut down for the sole purpose of making a few shingles from them to cover a house with; and even for the sake of killing a poor bear . . .; and even for less than that: I have often seen them set on fire merely to dislodge a paltry raccoon![8]

Nowlin estimated his father burned five thousand cords of wood while clearing sixty acres of land in Wayne County, Michigan.[9]

The historic period Indians maintained some forest clearings to aid both in hunting and planting corn. Such was the case in Ashland County: "These valleys at that period [Black Fork and Mohican, 1809] were nearly destitute of underbrush and small timber. It had been the custom of the Indians for a long time to burn the undergrowth in Mohican, Lake and Green townships, to facilitate the pursuit of game. Some portions of the hills below Greentown were entirely bare of timber, while in Lake and Mohican timber was scarce and much injured by fire."[10] No doubt such clearings were made by Indians in other areas of the state, and it is possible the prehistoric Indians did the same; perhaps some of the "natural" prairies described by the settlers were very old burned clearings. However, aside from these clearings and a few natural prairies, the entire Ohio Country was forested. A popular adage held that a squirrel could go from Cincinnati to Cleveland without touching the ground.

Much of the Ohio forestation was open, not the dense thickets seen today, and the light shade cast by the giant, contiguous trees allowed grasses and other vegetation to grow. This open forestation was described many times in period literature, and by pioneers reflecting on their early experiences. One area was known as the "Barrens," a belt of many thousands of acres running north and south in the Virginia Military Lands. In 1834 the Reverend Read, of the Congregational Union of Great Britain, made a stagecoach journey through Ohio from Sandusky to Columbus to Cincinnati. He was particularly impressed by the magnificent trees of the Barrens between West Jefferson and Springfield.

> *Noble Forests.*—On leaving Jefferson we plunged again into the forest, and towards evening we got on the greensward or natural road. This was mostly good and uncut, and we bowled along in serpentine lines, so as to clear the stumps with much freedom. The scenery now, even for the forest, was becoming unusually grand. It repeatedly broke away from you, so as to accumulate the objects in the picture, and to furnish all the beauties of light, shade, and perspective. The trees, too, were mostly oak, and of finest growth. Their noble stems ran up some hundred feet above you, and were beautifully feathered with verdant foliage. There, they ran off in the distance, park-like, but grander far, in admirable grouping, forming avenues, galleries and recesses, redolent with solemn loveliness; and here, they stood before you like the thousand pillars of one vast imperishable temple for the worship of the Great Invisible. Well might our stout forefathers choose the primitive forests for their sanctuaries. All that art has done in our finest Gothic structures is but a poor, poor imitation![11]

Charles Dickens described the later desolation of this region in *American Notes* (1842); he passed miles of felled trees and tree stumps while traveling from Cincinnati to Columbus by stagecoach.[12] Henry Howe quoted "early settlers" of the Springfield area, 1801–1809, to the effect that for fourteen miles north of the city a person could not have "found a sufficiency of poles to have made hoops for a meat cart. The forest consisted of large trees, with no undergrowth, and the ground was finely sodded."[13] Henry Fearon made a similar statement in 1818: "Throughout this State [Ohio] there is but little under or brush-wood, caused, I presume, by the height and spreading tops of the trees, which prevent the sun penetrating to the ground, and nourishing inferior articles of vegetation."[14] Such was the case in Symmes's Purchase. The Miami lands were thus described in an advertisement in the *Brunswick Gazette and Weekly Monitor* [New Brunswick, N.J.], 22 January 1788: "The finest timber of every kind known in the middle states, with many other sorts of more southerly production, grow in plenty here, but there is very little underwood or brush."[15] Apparently all the varieties of trees native to Ohio remain today, though the number of chestnut and American elm have been declining for many years, the chestnut almost to the point of extinction. If large enough, any variety of wood could have been used in log construction, but the popular species were oak, walnut, cherry, maple, hickory, ash, and poplar. White oak, black walnut, and the so-called yellow poplar are the most common native woods found in nineteenth-century Ohio buildings of any type of construction. In *Letters from America* (Edinburgh, 1822), James Flint gives a short, comprehensive description of woods and their uses. This excerpt was written while he was at Jeffersonville, Indiana, in August 1820:

> Several species of forest trees furnish excellent timber. The white oak is at once tough, dense, flexible, and easily split. The black locust is strong, heavy, not much subject to warping, and resists the effects of the weather for a long period of time. . . . White hickory is tough and elastic in a high degree, and is the wood in general use for handles to axes, and other tools. Black walnut grows to a great size, and is considered a mark of the excellence of the soil on which it grows. It is lighter, less curled in its texture, and probably

> weaker than that of England. The sugar-maple is curled in its fibre, and is used in making stocks for rifles. White or water maple is also curled, of a fine straw-colour, and is sometimes introduced in cabinet-work with much effect. White and blue ash trees are easily split, pliant, and readily smoothed, but less fit to bear exposure to the weather than the ash of Europe. Poplar grows to a great size, and is easily converted into boards or scantling. Red cedar is exceedingly durable as posts of rail-fences, and grows in great abundance by Kentucky River. White and yellow pines, similar to those of Canada, are brought from Allegany [*sic*] river. . . .[16]

Though certain woods might be favored for log buildings, the settlers were largely dependent on the vegetation in their own locales. Various geographic areas of Ohio did support different types of forestation. A study was conducted by the Ohio State University, under the auspices of the Ohio Biological Survey, and a map was prepared in 1966 of the "Natural Vegetation of Ohio."[17] The broad belt of hilly land from eastern to southern Ohio along the Ohio River was primarily "mixed oak forests," composed of the various oaks and hickories. The major portion of the "Barrens," between Springfield and Columbus, and between Washington Court House and Bellefontaine, also fell in this classification. Most of the land northwest of the mixed oak forests, from Cincinnati to Cleveland, was "beech forest," a mixture of beech, sugar maple, red and white oak, and white ash. In the wetter areas through this half of the state were "elm-ash swamp forests," which included white elm, black and white ash, silver and red maple, cottonwood, and sycamore. "Transitional" swamp areas produced bur oak, shellbark hickory, red oak, and basswood. Interspersed through this diagonal division of the state were "oak-sugar maple forests" of white and red oak, black walnut, black and sugar maple, white ash, red elm, basswood, bitternut, and shagbark hickory, as well as "mixed mesophytic forests" of a variety of species but no real dominants—oak, chestnut, beech, maple, tulip tree, hickory, and hemlock. Southwestern Ohio's "mixed mesophytic" forests contained a larger proportion of beech, white basswood, and tulip tree. Other variants ascertained from the survey were the "bottomland hardwood forests" in the Scioto and Miami river valleys, and the open "oak savannas" in the Maumee River valley.

In summary, some variety of oak was available in most areas of the state, as well as maple, ash, and some variety of medium to soft wood such as beech or poplar (tulip tree). Therefore, it is not surprising that oak and poplar are the most commonly found woods in extant log buildings, with beech, maple, walnut, ash, and hickory as secondary woods. Oak was the common flooring, but poplar and walnut were often used. White oak and poplar made the best shakes and shingles for they split easily and were rot resistant. However, shakes and shingles were made of any variety that would split and then did not curl after repeated wetting and drying. Pine, cypress, cedar, chestnut, ash, and hemlock were recommended by the *American Agriculturist*, and walnut shingles were found to have outlasted white oak on one Ohio barn.[18] Walnut and poplar were favorite woods for doors, walls, and interior finishing—baseboards, chair rails, peg rails, door and window frames, and mantels. It should be remembered that there were no hard and fast rules relegating a variety of wood to some aspect of log building, but preferences did exist. Strength, durability, and ease of handling were the desired characteristics.

Obviously, all cabins and most houses had to be constructed of green wood. Since wood shrinks primarily across the grain rather than lengthwise, the horizontal joints between the logs would gradually widen until the wood reached its maximum shrinkage, stabilizing at about 30 percent moisture (subject, certainly, to weather conditions and wood varieties). The shrinkage of the logs made it necessary to replace the daubing as cracks appeared. This is one of the reasons that clay was as good a daubing medium as mortar. Once the logs did stabilize, however, it was worth the trouble to insert lime mortar. That so many sound log barns remain is due to the fact that the logs are completely exposed to the air and able to dry. Most of the sound log houses remaining are ones that were sided during or soon after construction. However, if moisture got behind the siding and could not quickly evaporate, the logs are always dry-rotted. The area between the chimney and the outside wall was particularly vulnerable to dampness, because of condensation caused by heating and cooling. On extant log buildings, water damage has always been a greater problem than insect damage.

Notes

1. Cist, *Cincinnati Miscellany*, pp. 65–66.
2. Blane, *Excursion through the United States*, pp. 304–5.
3. Hildreth, "History of an Early Voyage," p. 95. This story was told Hildreth by a Doctor J. B. Reigner, who performed such labor for a short time. The story was partially refuted in the second volume of *American Pioneer*, page 187, by one Waldeurard Meulette, writing on the "Settlement of Gallipolis" (pp. 182–87). Meulette claimed only one person, a "female," was seriously injured, but not killed, by a falling tree. He did not refute the practice of burying tree trunks, however!
4. Lang, *History of Seneca County*, p. 183.
5. Jonathan Dayton, Cincinnati, 4 November 1790; Bond, *Correspondence of John Cleves Symmes*, p. 135.
6. Cist, *Cincinnati Miscellany*, p. 11. The initials stand for: "United States North West of the River Ohio."
7. Hutslar, "Ohio Waterpowered Sawmills."
8. Baily, *Journal of a Tour*, p. 214.
9. Nowlin, *Bark Covered House*, p. 133.
10. Hill, *History of Ashland County*, p. 50.
11. Howe, *Historical Collections* (1891), pp. 455–56.
12. Dickens, *American Notes*, vol. 2, chap. 6. White snakeroot was prevalent in this region, a plant peculiar to an open forest, which caused the so-called milk sickness or milk fever from which many persons died in the 1840s and 50s. When cattle ate a quantity of the snakeroot, the milk was poisoned.
13. Howe, *Historical Collections* (1847), p. 566.
14. Fearon, *Sketches of America*, p. 218.
15. Bond, *Correspondence of John Cleves Symmes*, p. 282. For similar comments concerning east-central Ohio, see Schaff, *Etna and Kirkersville*, chap. 6, pp. 83–90.
16. Flint, *Letters from America*, p. 229.
17. Ohio Biological Survey, *Natural Vegetation of Ohio* [map] (Columbus, 1966).
18. "Making Split and Shaved Shingles," *American Agriculturist*, (1879), vol. 38, p. 223; Stanton, *A Book Called Our Ancestors*, p. 233.

XI
DESIGN

Environmental factors placed certain restrictions on log architecture. The size and variety of timber available was one, the site, another. A further problem was the season of the year, or simply day-to-day weather. A major consideration was the labor supply, both men and animals. Of these, the most significant was probably the availability of suitable timber and labor.

If the timber was extremely large in diameter, handling it presented the greatest difficulty. The largest diameter logs seen in extant log buildings have always been at the lowest courses in the walls. A house wall was generally constructed of small, 12 to 15 inch diameter logs. Because a very large structure, such as a double-pen barn, had to have solid walls, most logs ran 15 to 18 inches in diameter; a smaller barn would have logs about the same size as a house. Building a tall structure would also require additional help. A one- or one-and-a-half-story house could probably be handled by four men without the use of animal power. The same four men might manage a two-story house, but would need oxen or horses (or some mechanical device) to raise the upper logs. On the other hand, it was entirely possible for one man to erect a one-story log cabin, assuming the logs had a maximum length of 12 to 15 feet and a diameter of 8 to 10 inches.

It is evident that all settlers, other than direct foreign immigrants, built very similar structures by the time Ohio was being widely settled, around 1800. Recent arrivals from countries in which log architecture was current must have continued to use their own national typologies, both in construction and design. It would be of great benefit in understanding the design of log buildings if such structures could be identified. A description of what could have been a traditional Swiss log house appears in a history of Wayne County.[1] It was constructed by one David Houmard, who was born in Canton Berne, Switzerland, in 1802. He emigrated to the United States in 1825, coming directly to Ohio. In 1826 Houmard built a log house in Paint Township, Wayne County. Assuming he had no help in designing his house, which is certainly reasonable, the following is probably as good a description of a Swiss log house as can be found for Ohio:

> The original dimensions of it were 20x30 feet, and it was constructed of logs, not hewed until after the house was erected. It was composed of two rooms, the second one on the east side being nearly square, and without being filled or mudded. Here his family, consisting of wife and child, passed the winter of 1826. The cabin was without a floor, the fire-place was in the center of the room, and, as companions of his family, the cow and calf were wintered in the same room, the cabin being house and stable both. The milk was kept in white walnut troughs, strained through old garments and clothes, and the churn was made of a hollow cherry tree, with a board nailed on at the bottom.[2]

Note that the walls were "scutched." Was this seemingly tedious process typically Swiss? It would be most interesting to know. Keeping animals within the house was certainly practiced in Switzerland, and other European countries, but all nationalities might have occasion to do so on the American frontier.

There are a few log buildings remaining in Amish and Mennonite settlements in Holmes and Wayne counties, an area largely devoted to braced-frame and half-timbered barns and houses of the 1820s and later. Among these typical Germanic structures is one style of construction which seemingly has escaped definition, probably because it is neither log or braced-frame.

The houses (only houses are known at present) are built of hewn logs, and the wall logs are spaced alternately, just as a notched-corner log structure; however, each log is mortised and pegged into vertical corner posts. The interstices are chinked and daubed, and the other finish details seem to be in line with standard hewn log construction. It is very easy to overlook these houses, because from a distance the corners are not obvious—the impression is that boards had been nailed over the notches as weatherproofing. This technique probably does not descend from notched-log construction, or from plank-wall framing; rather, it must be a modification of braced-framing in which the timbers have almost become a solid wall, perhaps visually inspired by log structures. (To actually have constructed a solid timber wall, edge to edge, would have been much more time-consuming.) The Amish and Mennonites in Ohio were from southern Germany—Bavaria, Austria—and Switzerland. This style of construction could have come from the Alpine region or perhaps braced-frame carpenters imitated, as best they could, log buildings in the United States. The latter proposition is highly doubtful, since traditionally these carpenters used both construction techniques. G. Edwin Brumbaugh described a mortised-log house in an address to the Pennsylvania German Society in 1931; the house was the only one known to him, and was located in Schaefferstown, Lebanon County.[3] To add further confusion to the origins of this aberrant construction, there are two examples in western Ohio, one of apparent German background in Celina, Mercer County, and one of supposed French origin in Wayne Township (?), Darke County.[4] However, it is possible the French immigrants to whom this house is credited, the Joseph Peron family (all emigrating to the United States between 1836 and 1850 according to the 1850 census), acquired the land from German settlers. There were a few southern Germans among the Saxons in this area of Ohio, so the circumstantial evidence remains for the origin of the mortised-log house somewhere along the Alpine mountains from Yugoslavia to Switzerland.[5]

A sharply defined, ethnic pocket exists in central western

Ohio in the area of Versailles, Darke County, and Russia, Shelby County (Range IV, Township 10). As the town names imply, French immigrants, including veterans of the Napoleonic Wars, settled in this area during the period 1835–60. There are many log houses, but only a few log barns, associated with these French Roman Catholic farmers, most seeming to date in the 1850s.[6] At least three basic forms are apparent: (1) a one- and one-half-story log pen with an L- or T-framed addition to the rear; (2) a two-story pen with a framed addition to the side; and (3) a two-story pen with a lean-to framed addition to the rear, this latter form seemingly the most consistent since the configuration is present in both frame and brick construction.

The identity of the actual builders of these structures is still open to question; in terms of woodworking technique, the log pens were well-constructed and raised by persons familiar with traditional practice. It is possible that builders were recruited from the German Roman Catholic immigrants a short distance north at the corners of Darke, Shelby, Mercer, and Auglaize counties. Perhaps their traditional, nationalistic distrust of one another was put aside during the settlement period; being of the same religious faith may also have helped. Though there is one log house attributed to a family of French brickmasons, the extant structures display such a confidence of technique that it is difficult to attribute them to immigrants who did not possess a consistent tradition of log construction. Of course, there is the possibility that the veterans of the Napoleonic campaign in Russia learned to construct log houses while in that, or an intervening, country—an intriguing, but somewhat unlikely, idea.

None of the "French" log houses seen by this writer had original fireplaces. The chimney, for a stove, is either central to the house or standing clear of an end wall to the inside of the omnipresent corner staircase; this latter arrangement agrees with some log houses reported in the German settlements in counties to the north. Fenestration follows a specific pattern in the two-story houses, with a notable feature being three or four doorways on the first floor. These give access to the two rooms within the pen and the one or two rooms of the lean-to addition.

208. Clark County, Greene Township. Two story log house. (See Figures 127, 156, 166, 170, 202, 226.) Photo: 18 August 1972. First floor, west end. Original fireplace mantle. The underside of the staircase can be seen at the upper right. The staircase was altered to turn 180 degrees to give headspace for a doorway to a kitchen addition on the west end.

209. Seneca County, Pleasant Township. One and a half story log house, built *ca.* 1846. First floor, east end. Photo: 24 October 1978. The fireplace and stairwell are original to the house. The fireplace is minimal for cooking, being about 3 feet 9 inches in height; the crane appears original, however.

210. Recreated log house interior with furniture of the late 18th, early 19th centuries.

211. Brown County, Perry Township. Two story log tavern and house. (See Figures 43, 44.) Photo: August, 1972. Wall logs and chinking, central hallway. What this writer thought were vertical saw cuts proved to be perfectly symmetrical stripes or "curls" in the maple log. This photograph shows two types of chinking, stones and carefully shaped slabs of wood, meticulously placed. Because the hallway was fully chinked and daubed, it may have been an open passage when the building served as a tavern.

212. Franklin County, Village of Groveport. Two story log house with log addition. (See Figures 64, 125, 140, 155, 189, 225.) Photo: 11 November 1974. A close inspection of the chinking will reveal one complete porch roof post and sections of at least two others. These posts were possibly from a porch attached to the two story house before it was remodeled.

213. Wayne County, Green Township. Two story log house. (See Figures 148, 149.) Photo: 6 November 1975. Southwest corner. This daubing must date after 1833 when the house was extensively remodeled and enlarged. The daubing is clay mixed with a coarse grass(?) binder; it was weatherproofed with a heavy coating of whitewash, a technique frequently mentioned in 19th century literature. A long porch was attached to this side of the house, and the logs underneath were whitewashed; these porches were typical of the 20 and 30s. When the house was again remodeled, probably in the mid-1850s, it was clapboarded, thus preserving these details.

214. Tuscarawas County. Schoenbrunn (1772–1777), Moravian Indian Mission near New Philadelphia. Photo: July, 1982. Specimens of daubing excavated in the 1920s. Buff-yellow clay, no binder. This daubing was preserved by fire, though which building and the cause of the fire are not known. The village was abandoned in April, 1777, and many buildings purposely destroyed or damaged. The daubing was smoothed by hand and with pieces of wood; the marks are very clear.

215. Greene County, Caesar Creek Township. One and a half story log house. (See Figures 61, 179, 187, 191.) Photo: May, 1971. The chair rail, baseboard, and diagonal, split plaster lath are good details. (This west room was being used as a hog house.)

216. Greene County, Miami Township. Braced-frame house. (See Figure 168.) Photo: October, 1974. Split hickory plaster lath. This type of lath is often regarded as a sure indicator of an early building, but this is not necessarily true; one has to consider the availability of sawn lath and its cost as well as builder preference.

217. Montgomery County, City of Miamisburg. Two story log tavern. (See Figure 142.) Photo: 10 May 1977. The first and second floors show traces of this unusual method of plastering. Straw of some cereal grain, probably wheat, was fastened lengthwise to the logs with split lath. This was covered with clay, which, in turn, was covered with two coats of lime plaster.

218. Adams County, Monroe Township. Braced-frame house built for Nathaniel Massie, 1797. Photo: August, 1972. North side, detail of siding. This section appears to be original, having rived clapboards, about five feet in length, fastened with hand-wrought rose-head nails; the wood has weathered away from many of the nails. The edge-beading was both decorative and functional, acting as a drip-course, and was used throughout the 19th century, but more commonly during the first third of the century. (National Register of Historic Places.)

219. Madison County, Canaan Township. Two story log house. (See Figures 188, 220.) Photo: 16 November 1975. Southwest corner. A standard siding job clearly revealed.

220. Madison County, Canaan Township. Two story log house. (See Figures 188, 219.) Photo: 16 May 1976. North side and east gable. This house was extensively remodeled. Its original entrance, probably to the south, was changed to the eastern gable, while a large "L" was added to the north. The upstairs, apparently original, was divided into three rooms by two board partition walls in a "T" configuration.

221. Greene County, Cedarville Township. One and a half story log house. (See Figure 183.) Photo: 8 July 1967. Back wall, east. The lack of windows is evidence of an original room on the back of the house. The room was probably of the "shed" type, both roofs of equal pitch, presenting a so-called New England "saltbox" configuration. The outline of the corner staircase in the north addition is obvious. The loft was illuminated by one window in the south gable.

222. Noble County, Beaver Township. Two story log house. Size, 24 by 18 feet. (See Figures 126, 203.) Photo: 3 May 1972. North end. This was a well built house. The stone fireplace/chimney was always on the interior. A springhouse to the rear was of braced-frame construction. A barn was located to the left, out of the picture.

223. Champaign County, Village of St. Paris. One and a half story house. (See Figure 224.) Photo: March, 1974. This house may have always been sided, considering the wide spaces between the logs and the absence of daubing. The opening for the fireplace is in the traditional location; part of the opening was later utilized for a doorway. The corner stairwell remains next to the fireplace opening.

224. Champaign County, Village of St. Paris. One and a half story log house, much altered and repaired. (See Figure 223.) Photo: March, 1974. In Ohio, vertical siding was not as popular as horizontal (probably because the latter imitated frame construction). This house was sided with boards and battens, applied without furring strips. This siding pattern had some popularity during the third quarter of the 19th century, and vertical siding was almost always used on braced frame barns because of the nailing surfaces presented by the framework.

225. Franklin County, Village of Groveport. Two story log house with log addition. (See Figures 64, 125, 140, 155, 189, 212.) Photo: 11 November 1974. Rear of addition, south side. This one and a half story structure was added for a kitchen. The chimney was removed, and the large fireplace opening closed.

226. Clark County, Greene Township. Two story log house, date *ca.* 1834, builder unknown. Size, 24 by 18 feet. (See Figures 127, 156, 170, 202, 208.) Photo: 18 August 1972. View of north front and east end. This house is a good example of log construction in the late Federal style. The interior chimneys are original. (National Register of Historic Places.)

227. Franklin County, Village of Gahanna. Two story log house. Size, 21 by 20 feet; eave height, about 16 feet. (See Figure 228.) Photo: 24 October 1968. This house was moved from its original location, just east of Gahanna, by the local historical society. A neatly constructed house and in good preservation, it was probably sided soon after construction. Traces of whitewash were found on the front.

228. Franklin County, Village of Gahanna. Two story log house. (See Figure 227.) Photo: 24 October 1968. This log house originally had a one and a half story, braced-frame kitchen. The joist mortises are evident, and, rising from the middle of the sides to the top center of the wall, a roof line is just visible. Two small windows overlooked the roof of the kitchen. The half-story was later raised to full height, covering the windows and requiring a doorway.

229. Warren County, Village of Franklin. Two story log house. (See Figures 70, 199, 228.) Photo: 15 August 1975. This end of the house bears evidence of three alterations: 1) A framed addition with the first floor log wall whitewashed; 2) Both walls of the first and second floors diagonally lathed and plastered; and 3) The addition removed and a large window cut through. The addition was well finished at one point in time, but had no interconnection with the log house.

230. Ross County, City of Chillicothe. Two story log house (See Figure 171.) Photo: Date unknown, probably between 1949–53. This interesting structure was located at the foot of the hill (north side) on which Thomas Worthington's home "Adena" is located. It is unfortunate a date and builder are not known, for some structural details are unlike any seen in Ohio by this writer, who knows the house only by a few photographs. It certainly could date close to 1800.

231. Tuscarawas County, Village of Zoar. Picture captioned: "M. Miller home on Third St. near Park." Photo: *ca.* 1880. The exterior detail of this log house was the same as the half-timbered houses of the Zoarites. The Germans of this famous communal settlement, 1817–1898, were from Württemberg and the Schwäbische Alb.

232. Franklin County, Washington Township (?) One and a half story log house. Photo: From Franklin County collection, *ca.* 1890, labeled "Near Wyandot Grove." (Possibly a 19th century settlement of Wyandot Indians near the Village of Dublin.) Note that the house was painted.

233. Clark County, Village of Enon. One and a half story log house with later additions. Photo: August, 1978. South, front. This small log house, which may have been moved to this site when the plat was opened in the 1840s, still bears its original exterior whitewash. Note the opening for a large cooking fireplace.

234. Ross County, Twin Township. Two story log house. Photo: 27 January 1968. North, front. The basic configuration of house and porch reflects a style that was popular in the 1820s and 30s, or just before the Greek Revival influence in southern Ohio. The lower windows were enlarged later. The 3 over 6 sashes of the upper windows are occasionally seen.

235. Franklin County, Village of Dublin. John Sells' two story log house, built 1809, with braced-frame addition. Structure torn down in 1893. Photo: *ca.* 1890. With its large stone chimney, the addition was certainly the kitchen. This arrangement was typical of the southern half of Ohio during the 1820s and 30s. The porch area had been lathed and plastered, a finish often found on houses of the late Federal style, or about 1815–35.

236. Shelby County, Loramie Township. Two story log house with a one and a half story addition, *ca.* 1835. West side, rear. Photo: 17 October 1978. This log house was enlarged lengthwise with a free-standing, braced-frame structure, a common practice in southern Ohio. It is interesting that this house design, built for a German immigrant family, was considered unusual by French immigrants a few miles away. (Oral tradition.)

237. Franklin County, Village of Franklinton (west-central Columbus). This photograph is from a stereo view entitled "Genl Harrison's Headquarters, Franklinton, War of 1812," taken *ca.* 1872 by R. F. Bowdish for the Union View Company of Columbus. This log house stood on the north side of west Broad Street, between Foos and Davis streets. It is interesting because it was remodeled in the Greek Revival style.

238. Greene County, Miami Township. Divided, or "Dutch," door in kitchen of brick house. "1828 Stacy Haines" appears in the plaster in the house. Photo: 17 February 1969. This is the only *original* Dutch-door known to the author. It is made of 3/4 inch walnut boards, beaded on the edges. The door, and the baseboard, chair rail, and peg rail, were painted red.

Of the structures that could be examined, none had window openings cut in the rear wall of the second floor. This is strong argument for the lean-to additions being original to the houses, or at least planned beforehand. The interiors were originally whitewashed, and, though no board partition walls were found, there was evidence of such walls left by lines on the whitewashed logs. Although the log pens, and often the floor joists, were hewed, the floorboards and molding came from the planing mill. The roof framing is quite distinctive, being a combination of pole rafters with the diagonal bracing and ridge boards of balloon-framed roofs, and the flat pitch of Greek Revival houses. (This writer has long been suspicious of peeled pole rafters butted to a ridge board; although the rafters look early, the ridge board should indicate a date following the introduction of balloon-framing, roughly 1840 in Ohio.) Because of the lower pitch, the rafters were not notched into the plate, but were butted and nailed. The gables were framed with studs and covered with horizontal clapboards in the usual manner.

Central log cross walls were used in the longer, 27 to 33 foot houses. There is no question the logs were notched-in to support the span and reduce the sway of the long exterior wall logs. Based on extant houses in the rest of the state, this style of construction was not common; it could reflect an ethnic preference, or it could be considered a midcentury "improvement" in technique. There is at least one house with a central log wall in Perry Township, Brown County, near the Convent of Saint Martin. Coincidence or not, this township was settled by many French Catholics.[7] There is no question the weight of the walls, and roof, was more evenly distributed to the foundation by the central wall. The plates overhang the walls slightly, and for support the upper cross logs are extended to the outer edges of the plates. This creates an odd configuration to cover with siding. It would be interesting to know if siding was originally planned for the houses; despite the whitewashed log interior walls, this was probably the intent. All the interior walls had later been covered with lath and plastered. A few ceilings showed no signs of whitewash on the joists or floorboards, so they had always been plastered. One house had clay daubing, with straw as a binder, which was protected with a thin layer of plaster.

As noted in an earlier chapter, however, the predominant nationality of the settlers along the western frontier was Scotch-Irish, immigrants who had no previous knowledge of log construction. That they quickly learned the technique of log building is unquestioned, but did they also utilize the exterior proportions and interior designs of the buildings they saw? To a limited degree, yes, but it is more likely that what they built was their own version of the rural Georgian cottages of the British Isles with which they were familiar. Such a contention is bolstered by Alan Bailey's "Housing of the Rural Poor in Nineteenth-Century Ulster," in *Ulster Folklife.*[8] The author illustrates a one-room sod house (p. 42) which, if it were log, would be at home on the American frontier. As it is, it looks much like a "soddy" house of the Great Plains. The one-room cottage was common in Ireland, Wales, northern Scotland, and isolated areas of England through the nineteenth century.[9] In very broad terms, these cottages, usually of stone, were long, low structures with a ridge equal to the width; a low eave; a chimney centered on a gable wall; and a central front door. In other words, they were very similar to the typical one- and one-half story log house in Ohio. The common denominators between the British cottages and Ohio log houses lay in the proportion of side wall to end wall to height, plus the roof pitch. From extant houses, there is circumstantial evidence to suggest that the Germans built less elongated structures and used more room partitions, even in small houses. However, a more extensive catalog of the remaining log buildings in Ohio is needed before indications of nationalistic typology can be isolated. Of all the log buildings remaining in Ohio, few have been specifically attributed to a builder—or dated, for that matter.

If any characteristics can loosely be termed "Germanic," they are a gable end or central chimney for a stove, the consequent off-center front door, and either vertical or horizontal clapboarding on the framed gables.[10] Corner notching systems were similar in Scandinavia and Germany. The shingled roof, however, was in common use in Germany, but rare in Sweden and Finland. Immigrants from the latter countries apparently did use roof shingles out of necessity before the Germans arrived, but their usual roofing was long, vertically placed split timber. Certain nationalistic traits distinguished the Swedish and Finnish structures, although both cultures used some variety in their corner notching and methods of dressing the logs. They commonly used both saddle-notched round and full-dovetailed hewed logs for walls, including log gables. The Scandinavian fireplace was usually in a corner, with the chimney often made of sticks and clay. However, by 1750 even the corner fireplace was considered old-fashioned, according to the Swedish naturalist Peter Kalm; it had given way to the large English fireplace centered on a wall. Kalm also noted that ovens were being placed outside the cottages, presumably because of the danger of fire. The oven and fireplaces were often built entirely of clay.[11] Throughout central and northern Europe, the full-dovetailed corner notch was common.[12] In Canada, the Finnish settlers occasionally hollowed the bottom edge of each log to fit over the curve of the log below. Sphagnum moss was used between the joints.[13]

The usual wall lengths of Ohio log structures are, in feet: 12, 15, 18, 24, 30, and 36. On a one- and one-half-story house, the height from the ground to the eave was commonly 10 to 12 feet, and the height of the ridge was almost always equal to the width of the house. Thus, a house 18 feet long by 15 feet wide would have a ridge height of 15 feet. Of course a two-story log house did not follow this height ratio, but had two full floors plus a loft. Today such a house has a tall, narrow appearance. All log, frame, brick, and stone houses of the early nineteenth century tended to follow the above proportions.

In determining the exterior wall proportionment, several simple mathematical and geometrical systems could have been used. Disregarding the complexities of the Grecian "Golden Mean,"[14] similar results could be obtained by making the length of the structure equal to the diagonal of the end walls squared: given an end wall length of 18 feet, the front and back walls would be a fraction over 25 feet in length. Since it was customary to lay out the building on the ground in order to place the corner foundation stones, it would have been a simple matter to obtain a diagonal measurement by squaring an end wall. Practically every "builder's book" of the seventeenth, eighteenth, and nineteenth centuries was prefaced with a section on geometry. As explained in chapter 12, a house or barn could be measured and squared with a few simple instruments; but if need be, the entire operation could be accomplished with a length of light cord and a stick.

Were log cabins and houses consciously designed? Yes. It is this writer's opinion that conscious design, perhaps proportionment would be a better word, was present in all buildings on the frontier—other than hasty, makeshift shelters. The measurements may have been learned through apprenticeship, word of mouth, through cultural tradition, or figured geometrically on-site. The wood varieties and length of timber available could affect size, as would the labor force available for the raising. Other factors might be the size of the family and the money available (probably little for the average family). The season of the year or unusual weather conditions might speed construction and thus reduce the opportunity for reflection on the design. Unfortunately, there are (apparently) no extant Ohio log cabins, or even photographs or accurate drawings of cabins, that could be measured to determine proportionment (the "cabin logs" from the Lower Sandusky Reservation were 15, 18, and 20 feet long). However, it is likely that similar ratios were used for houses, whether log, frame, brick, or stone.

An absolutely standard design, one- and one-half-story log house can be drawn with straight edge and compass (see fig. 116). The same figure could be drawn full size on the ground, with a string and a stick. In fact, halves, quarters, and eights are simply proportioned by repeatedly halving the length of a string. It is this writer's opinion that a figure similar to the illustration was scribed on the ground, perhaps outlined with pegs, so the rafters could be laid out and cut to size. After all, such a procedure was traditional to braced-frame building; barn bents were normally outlined on the barn floor so direct measurements could be taken. Figure 116 needs one given dimension, the width of the structure. A diagonal taken of the width squared gives the length. The height of the roof ridge is the house width. The standard 12/9 roof pitch (12 inches run to 9 inches rise) can also be quickly calculated by dividing the height, or the width, into eight equal parts; the eave height and the rafter lengths are equal to five-eighths of the height or width. This system is very simple. It does not produce both a length and width divisible by three, a feature surprisingly common to Ohio structures, but one can guess that these dimensions were chosen, not drawn, and if anything was geometrically proportioned, it was the gable-end of the house. A very similar, if not identical, system was in use in Williamsburg in the eighteenth century. Marcus Whiffen refers to it as the "root-two rectangle"; apparently the roof pitch was not calculated. He also mentions other possible systems of proportionment in use in Virginia, but this writer has not been able to relate them to Ohio log houses.[15] The reason geometric proportionment was important is this: Unless the builder was experienced and knew measurements by rote, he had no way of knowing at what point to place his plate logs in order to obtain a 12/9 roof pitch, and thus give an overall height equal to the width. The drawing gave these dimensions automatically, either in scale on paper or full size on the ground.

It is conceivable, though now difficult to prove, that immigrants from various European countries used various systems of measurement. Individual systems existed in practically every country in the world in the eighteenth century, and, to add to the confusion, in the large cities as well. For example, the English foot was equal to about 12 3/4 inches in Paris and 11 1/3 inches in Bremen. In Wil. Goodman's *History of Woodworking Tools*, there is an illustration of a folding rule which is graduated in four different city systems: Paris, Hamburg, Burgos (Spain), and London. Goodman cites the *Lexicon Technicum* of John Harris (London, 1714) which gives a list of European measurements converted to English feet. The variations were approximately an inch under to an inch over the English foot.[16] To end this confusion, the metric system was adopted on the Continent between about 1840 and 1875. To add to our confusion, however, measurements used for log and braced-frame buildings, particularly in Ohio with its rapid settlement by immigrants from the eastern states and directly from the British Isles and northern Europe, could be in several systems, and this may account for some of the odd feet and inches found.

Two thousand years ago, Vitruvius described an ancient argument concerning "Perfect Numbers," which were usually ten or six.[17] Perhaps some vestige of the number six remained in the eighteenth century, for Peter Nicholson's *Carpenter's New Guide* quoted common scantling sizes in units divisible by three.[18] However, a little mental arithmetic demonstrates that units of three can be quickly added, subtracted, and divided without the fractions created by the number five. Also because of the large number of surveyors throughout Ohio during settlement, it is reasonable to assume a few houses were laid out with surveyors' chains; such a chain is 66 feet (4 rods) in length, and is made of 100 links, each 7.92 inches long. Using round figures, if a house was proportioned 50 by 30 links, it would measure 33 by 19.8 feet. Some measurements could have been based on the 16½ foot rod (still used in spacing fence posts), the extra 6 inches creating a few of the odd wall lengths found today.

Joseph Moxon, in his section on "House-Carpentry" written at the turn of the eighteenth century, discusses the use of a ten-foot rod and a two-foot rule:

> We shall begin therefore to measure the *Ground-plot*, to which Carpenters use a *Ten-foot Rod* for Expedition, which is a Rod about an Inch square, and ten foot long; being divided into ten equal parts, each part containing one foot, and is divided into 24 equal parts, and their Sub-divisions.
>
> With this Rod they measure the length and breadth of the *Ground-plot* into Feet, and if there be odd inches, they measure them with the *Two-foot Rule.*[19]

In reality, there were probably as many systems of measurement and proportionment in use as one can imagine; and, if any one system was predominant, it has not made itself evident through study of extant structures.[20] In Ohio, the perimeters of log buildings are frequently divisible by three, using modern measurement devices and occasionally rounding fractions: a more positive statement cannot be made.

SOUTHERN INFLUENCE ON OHIO LOG ARCHITECTURE

There is a popular sentiment, which has been stated and reinforced by folklorists over the past thirty years or more, that log construction in Ohio—and apparently the Old Northwest—owes a typological debt to the "southern" states. It is a specious position. If any debt is owed, it is to the east-central states. A definition of "southern" is needed, for there was a decided difference between geography and cultural attitudes. During the colonial period, to a New Englander the "South" meant Virginia and North Carolina, and other scattered settlements along the seacoast. If Virginia (including western Virginia or Kentucky) is considered southern, then there was considerable "southern" influence in Ohio during the early nineteenth century; in fact, it would have existed in a major portion of the state. Today, the geographic term *South* implies states like Georgia, Alabama, South Carolina, Tennessee, Florida, Louisiana, and Mississippi, and if these are the states meant by the current use of the term, then "southern influence" on Ohio log architecture is nonsense. In fact, a good reverse argument could be made.

It is important to remember that the spread of log technology was from the Germanic settlements along the central Atlantic coast, diffused by various migration waves to the north, west, and south. The initial seventeenth-century geographic center for log construction was in southeastern Pennsylvania and New Jersey, eastern Maryland and Virginia, and Delaware. During the following three-quarters of the eighteenth century, large geographic regions utilizing log construction developed in these colonies, particularly in Pennsylvania, Maryland, and Virginia. The major immigration into Ohio came from this region during the last quarter of the century. The direct foreign immigration to Ohio that soon followed was from the Germanic states, reinforcing construction techniques already known, or from the British Isles, with no influence on log construction at all. (Immigration from the New England area is not being considered because of that region's adherence to braced-frame rather than log construction.)

Certain immigrant waves, usually bonded by ethnic and/or religious ties, such as the Scotch-Irish Presbyterians or the Quakers, that initially swept to the south into the Carolinas, Georgia, and Tennessee, then north during the latter eighteenth and early nineteenth centuries, could have introduced southern regional characteristics to Ohio, but it is doubtful they encountered anything of typological significance in that time period. Southern immigration to the north was negligible in any case, after the first quarter of the nineteenth century. No doubt there was, and is, a cultural tie to the South along the Ohio River corridor. Trade on the river from Pittsburgh to New Orleans occupied a considerable labor force for most of the century, and as in seaports around the world, the villages along the river were often more cosmopolitan than similar settlements within the state. Whether there was influence on log construction is another matter altogether, and highly unlikely.

While realizing that statistics can be misleading and misused, the following numbers are offered from the 1850 census because they show such a disparity between the northern and southern origins of Ohio residents that the error factor has to be minimal.[21] In 1850, there were 1,219,432 resident Ohioans born in the state. The second major group, 323,094, were born in the states of Pennsylvania, Maryland, and Virginia. The third largest group, 115,342, were native to Germany, which includes a small number from Switzerland, Prussia, and Austria. Next were the immigrants from New York and New Jersey, 107,511, then 88,303 from the British Isles, and 65,073 from the New England states.

The states of Alabama, Georgia, North and South Carolina, Tennessee, Arkansas, Florida, Louisiana, Mississippi, and Kentucky could muster only 31,861; without Kentucky, there would be only 18,032 "southern-born" residents in Ohio. Adding Virginia's 85,762 would bring the South's total to a par with the Germanic states (however, it has been admitted that there was a strong, early influence on Ohio from that state). In the foregoing data, it does not matter about ages or occupations or dates of immigration; what does matter is the pattern of migration, which was clearly east to west, regardless of the path followed, and not south to north.

Notes

1. Douglass. *History of Wayne County.*
2. Ibid., p. 583. Douglass noted that Houmard combined "his fine memory with his long-kept diary," so the details are probably accurate.
3. G. Edwin Brumbaugh, "Colonial Architecture of the Pennsylvania Germans," *Pennsylvania German Society Proceedings* 41(1931):26, plates 10, 11. The first floor of the Golden Plough Tavern, in York, Pennsylvania, is of mortised-log construction. It was built between 1741 and 1745 by one Martin Eichelberger.
4. This structure was moved to Indiana in 1980–81 by the Sonnenberg family.
5. A mortised-log, or plank, house is illustrated in a small engraving entitled "Interior of a Witches' House" in a book published in Geneva in 1579, *Dialogues touchant le powoir des sorcieres . . . ,* by Thomas Erastus (fig. 37, p. 64, in Givry, *Witchcraft, Magic, and Alchemy*). This type of construction was at least known in Switzerland, if not centered there. A similar construction, the *poteaux en coulisse,* was used by French-Canadians; see Richardson, "A Comparative Historical Study."
6. The author was taken on a tour of nineteen log houses in October 1978. (Mrs.) Mary Ann Brown, of the Regional Historical Preservation Office, and Jean Easton, a local resident, located most of the houses. County tax assessment records and maps placed several of the houses in the decade 1850–60.
7. The first log chapel of Saint Martin was built about 1823 by two ex-Napoleonic soldiers. French priests soon followed. A group of Ursulines immigrated from France in 1845 and founded the School of Brown County Ursulines, Convent of Saint Martin, which is still active.
8. Gailey, "Housing of the Rural Poor," pp. 34–58.

9. Mr. R. W. Brunskill of the University of Manchester believes that emigrants from rural Great Britain were quite accustomed to one-room cottages and would build similar structures in North America. The use of timber would not be unusual; for they were accustomed to utilizing any building material at hand. (Letter, 29 October 1976.)
10. There is an interesting monograph entitled *The Saxon House* by Burcaw which traces the history of this rural structure for about two thousand years. The typical floor plan combined house and barn in a long, rectangular framework, and is commonly termed the "Saxon Barn" as well as "House." As found in northern Germany, animal stalls and a threshing floor were at one end, with an open fireplace for the family at the opposite end. The very early structures had no chimney, no separation between humans and animals, and no room divisions in the living area. It is possible the late form of the house, with its many rooms and animal stalls, and its cooking room known as the "Black Kitchen," found its way to North America. This writer has so far been unable to relate the developed form of the Saxon house to any extant log structures in Ohio. For a beautifully illustrated book on the Saxon house and barn, see Josef Schepers, *Westfalen-Lippe*.
11. Kalm, *Peter Kalm's Travels*, pp. 726–28.
12. Smith, "17th Century Swedish Log Cabins." Three Swedish houses in Upper Darby Township, Delaware County, Pennsylvania, are pictured. Two have overhanging roof gables to protect centered gable chimneys; the third example has two corner fireplaces.
13. Sherwood, "Building in the North," p. 4.
14. From Pythagoras to Le Corbusier, the "golden mean" or "golden section" has been considered the ideal ratio of line to line, or, as in architecture, of length to breadth to heighth. The golden mean applies when a line is divided into two unequal parts, A and B, and A is to B, as B is to A plus B. The ratio 5:8 is the approximation commonly used.
15. Whiffen, *The Eighteenth-Century Houses of Williamsburg*, p. 59.
16. Goodman, *The History of Woodworking Tools*, sec. 6, "The Rule," pp. 188–94; specifically fig. 198 and pp. 192–93.
17. *Vitruvius, Ten Books on Architecture*, bk. 2, chap. 2, par. 5–6 (pp. 73–74).
18. Nicholson, *Carpenter's New Guide*, pp. 105–6.
19. Moxon, *Mechanick Exercises*, p. 126. The use of a measuring rod is far older than any formalized system of number notation, and such rods remain in use today. A finish-carpenter or joiner will keep all the measurements of a job inscribed full-scale on a rod, the rod serving both as a physical indicator of length and a notebook. This is an excellent system for recording measurements during restoration work, for one need not worry about fractions, even a ruler.
20. In 1684, William Penn recommended that immigrants "build then, a House of thirty feet long and eighteen broad, with a partition near the

middle, and an other to divide one end of the House into two small rooms." This was known as the "Quaker Plan," and was supposedly based on a Swedish floor plan. Quoted on p. 505, *Early American Architecture* by Hugh Sinclair Morrison (New York: Oxford University Press, 1952.) Also see Footnote 11 above.

21. DeBow, *Statistical View of the United States*, pp. 116–24 and 288–95.

XII
CONSTRUCTION PRACTICES

The purpose of this chapter is to analyze the practical problems encountered in building a log structure. The choice of site was highly important. If no roads or dominant topographic features suggested an alignment for a house, it was usually fronted to the south—or at least placed with a closed side towards the prevailing winter weather, which is from the northwest in Ohio. Naturally, level terrain did not present the problems found in building on a slope. A log house on a slope was usually placed on a partially to fully leveled site. A log barn was often purposely placed on a slope to provide good drainage of the barnyard. The site had to be cleared of brush and trees, but it was not necessary to remove the sod or dig foundation trenches. Although log houses with cellars were not common in Ohio, this was a matter of time and labor rather than lack of knowledge. Once the exterior dimensions of the house had been outlined on the ground, a cellar could be dug.[1]

Assuming no cellar was desired, the next step was to establish the dimensions of the house by working from one corner. The accurate measurement of length was no problem, for any item of any specific length could be used—an ax handle, an arm, even a stick—but, more than likely, a one- or two-foot folding rule was used to lay out a long measuring pole. The builder also had to calculate a 90 degree angle, and a true vertical and horizontal line. Today, such problems are easily solved with a builder's transit, or a carpenter's level, plumb bob, and framing square. When a sighting instrument such as a transit is not available, corners can be checked for accuracy with a homemade instrument used by builders for many centuries: a right-angle wooden triangle composed of sides of three, four, and five equal parts. Another check is to measure the two diagonals; these should be the same. Many settlers had access to surveying compasses, which were admirably suited to laying out angles, but not elevations.

There were other methods for finding true angles. Use of the drop line or plumb line to find a vertical comes first to mind, a method that undoubtedly dates to some unrecorded dawning of humankind's reasoning powers. All that was needed was a length of cord, even a thin vine might serve, and some object for weight. Although the bubble level was used on eighteenth-century scientific and surveying instruments, until well into the nineteenth century the common carpenter's level still used a small plumb-line as a vertical axis. (If a plumb bob and line were attached to the side of the large wooden triangle mentioned above, a good level could be improvised.) It was not without reason that most builder's books prior to the twentieth century devoted a chapter to geometry. Using only a length of cord with a stick tied at one end to scratch the ground—a primitive compass—a builder could lay out a right-angle corner on-site.

There were several methods of determining a true horizontal without the use of a bubble level. The large wooden right triangle, with a plumb line along its vertical edge, was one method. A simple expedient was to float a rectangular wooden bar, with sights, in a shallow container filled with water. Though tedious to use, it was possible to establish a base line because the surface of the water would be level no matter what the position of the container (this is how the drop in the bed of a canal could be measured so precisely). An obvious variant of this method would be to dig a shallow trench between cornerstones and fill it with water; the sill could then be leveled to the surface of the water.[2] Another form of level was made from a long length of small diameter copper pipe with a glass tube at each end. This device was filled with water. By sighting over the water in the tubes, or by stretching a cord in alignment with them, an extremely accurate measurement could be made. This method was widely employed in canal and road building. Today, a rubber hose is used to carry a level from one room to another when a fixed instrument cannot be placed. Though many devices and techniques were available, most probably the backwoods carpenter utilized some form of the triangle and plumb line level.

Once the outline of the house had been squared on the ground, the cornerstones were set in place. Usually these were unhewn fieldstones, of good size, and with slightly rounded upper surfaces to allow water to drain from the sills. It is often overlooked that the weight of a log structure is borne entirely at the corners, and that a massive building is dependent on a very small contact area log to log. Many log buildings seen today squat on the ground, their sills actually resting on the soil. This was not the intent of the builders. The gradual accretion of soil and subsidence of the cornerstones, because so much weight was concentrated at the corners, caused these buildings to rest flat on the ground. These builders were well aware of dry rot, and the need for ventilation.

Because the logs in adjacent walls of a building are staggered in alignment, only opposite wall logs are at the same level. The two lowest logs, the sills, normally in the front and back walls, rest on the cornerstones. These sills were often wider than the other logs in the wall, and sometimes were squared like the plate logs. The sills formed a ledge on which the joists could either be laid or mortised. If the joists were to be mortised, or simply notched into the upper surfaces of the sills, this cutting had to be done before the next wall log was in place. This is probably why many log houses have a floor system independent of the walls.

Once the sills, and possibly the floor joists, were in place, the log pen could be erected. The location of various openings had to be kept in mind as the structure went up, because the logs would be half-notched to indicate the lower and upper ends of the windows and the upper ends of the fireplace opening and doorways. These half-notches were first sawed at the sides, then the wood split away. By following such a construction plan, the building could be put under roof quickly, leaving the finishing details to the proprietor rather than the members of the raising party. To raise a house in one or two days required a man at each corner of the pen, plus any number of men and work animals to bring the hewed logs to the site and lift them into place.[3] If the timber had to be cut, then hewed while the raising was in progress, a dozen men would be too few. The usual practice was to place one man at each corner to notch the logs as they were raised to him. No corner notching was done on the ground, though the logs were half-notched for the various openings. The "corner men" were highly important, for the speed and soundness of construction depended entirely on their skill. Quoting William Lang: "In building a cabin, an accomplished 'corner man' could carry up a corner in less than one-half the time it would take an ordinary chopper. To make the notches fit the saddles neatly, required both skill and practice; and by looking at the corners of a cabin it was very easy to tell whether the corner man understood his business or not."[4] The best corner men were placed at the front of the building, certainly for aesthetic reasons. "Samuel, being a good axe-man, always had a front corner to notch down & carry up, in the building of hewed log houses & barns. . . ."[5] This attitude about the appearance of a log building is quite revealing, for it suggests that settlers seldom lost their self-conscious, social image no matter how rustic their surroundings.

With several men in the raising party, it was customary to slide the logs up strong poles ("skids") placed at an angle against the walls. Fifteen feet was about the limit that logs could be pushed into place by hand. Taller structures required animal power or some type of hoist, though with the manpower available in the military or in or near a town, very large buildings could be erected by hand. A good example of a very large log structure is the Johnston barn at Piqua, which was completed in 1808 (see fig. 91). The logs in the pen walls are just short of 30 feet in length, and rise to 18 feet. It is interesting to note that, of all the varieties of wood used, the lightest woods are found at the tops of the pens: sycamore, cottonwood, beech, poplar. Apparently the weight of the logs, and not the durability or strength of the wood, was the important consideration to the builder, one James Kigans.[6] Each white oak plate is in two sections, 60 feet and 30 feet, lapped together and pinned; in cross section they about 12 by 15 inches square. The effort required to raise a 60-foot hewed log to a height of 18 feet certainly implies mechanical leverage and/or animal power. White oak is rated at 47 pounds per cubic foot, at 12 percent moisture content. Probably these plate logs were much higher in moisture, but using the above rating, the 60-foot section would have weighed approximately 4,406 pounds. (When this plate was removed during restoration, it was estimated to weigh between 2,500 and 2,700 pounds.)

The various notching systems were used, of course, to keep the logs from sliding or twisting out of position in the walls. As noted earlier, in Ohio the common types of corner notching were the steeple and the half-dovetail. The full-dovetail must not have been preferred, or more specimens would surely remain (the tavern at Miamisburg, fig. 140, is the best example to date). The author has seen an occasional pair of logs joined in this manner to reinforce a weak corner, usually just below the plates. Because the full-dovetailed logs were fitted closely together, the technique would not have been popular for "cheap" or temporary housing. Because sawmills were quickly established in Ohio once settlement had started, the braced-frame house took the position that an elaborately constructed, closely joined log house would have assumed. It was easier to cover the logs with siding and plaster, outside and in, than to closely join and face them in full-dovetailing.

Because of the interlocking of the notches, the log pen was a very stable structural unit. One contractor told this writer that he had attempted to pull down a log barn with a bulldozer, by attaching a cable to one wall. The barn remained as a unit and tipped over on its side, and many logs had to be removed before the pen fell apart. (Since this was a barn, no doubt it had steeple notching.) During the famous "Burlington Storm," actually a tornado, in Licking County, 18 May 1825, "A house, built of large logs, in which was a family, and which a number of workmen had entered for shelter from the storm, was raised up on one side and rolled off the place on which it stood, without injuring any one."[7] However, during the Xenia tornado of 3 April 1974, the Galloway House (see fig. 41) and another log house were in the path of the storm, and neither faired any better than houses of other construction.[8]

Half- and full-lap corners are found on many small log houses built around mid-nineteenth century. There was no interlock between the logs, except weight and friction; however, corners held with nails and pegs have been reported. In this writer's opinion, all such noninterlocked structures were initially sided because there were always wide gaps between the logs to chink and daub. Whether it was felt the siding would hold the logs in position, or that an interlock was not necessary on a small structure, is open to question. Probably both views are correct, since both corner methods seem to have worked satisfactorily. The writer has not seen any of these structures razed, so it is possible the majority were nailed or pegged at the corners.[9]

Hewing the various notches was a relatively easy task for practiced woodsmen and braced-frame carpenters. The felling ax was the prime tool. Alignment of the notches also was not as difficult as it might seem. The unnotched log, when slid onto the pen, was longer than the finished wall length as governed by the notching. The protruding ends were sawed off when the house was "squared up." Aligning the notches "by eye" was possible, because the uncut log lay on the notched log it was to fit. Once the undernotch was cut on both ends, the log was rolled over and into place. Then the upper notches were cut to receive the next logs of the adjacent walls. This is why it was desirable, though not necessary, to station a man at each corner. The wood was usually green when notched, and the corners were subjected to a great deal of weight (relative to surface contact) once the building was finished. These two factors created a tighter fit than the best cornermen could have accomplished with seasoned wood, unless they worked slowly.

Many builders used templates to mark the cuts. This writer has seen the logs of one house on which the corner notches had been scribed with a pencil. The markings were too faint to photograph, but were clearly visible to the eye. The house had been located somewhere south of Urbana in Champaign County. (The modern use of a framing square and a template for fitting corner notches is described in the magazine *Foxfire.*)[10] An isosceles triangle could have served to scribe both the upper and lower cuts for the steeple notch, a right triangle for the half-dovetail. These triangles could have been made on the job. Angus T. Sherwood (1891–1967), an American who spent most of his life in the Canadian North, recorded some comments on log construction (and "Manitoba Frame") which were published in the *APT Bulletin.*[11] Three basic tools were used in laying out corners: A plumb board; an adjustable scriber; and a marking stick. The plumb board was the same width as the logs (eight inches), and was used to mark the depth of a dovetail or half-lapped corner as well as to keep the corner vertical. A plumb line was centered vertically on the board, which had an inverted-V notch at the bottom for the weight (plumb bob). The scriber, made of iron bent in a V-shape, and adjusted by a sliding keeper, was used to follow the contour of the uppermost notch, scribing it on the unnotched log. The marking stick was simply a straightedge about 2 inches wide by 18 inches long. It was used for marking the shape of the saddle on the upper log. A "try" notch was made first, then the marking stick was laid on top of each side of the saddle and its exact configuration scribed on the upper log. This is an old, probably ancient, carpenter's trick. By varying the width of the marking stick, the interstices betweeen logs could be calculated very closely.

Logs were half-notched where door, window, and fireplace openings were needed; then all four walls were raised at once without additional carpentry except corner notching. When the building was "raised to the square," (1) blocks were driven between the logs on each side of the proposed opening to support the cut ends; (2) a saw was inserted in the half-notch at the top of the opening and the logs cut through on each side; (3) planks were placed on each side of the opening (the jamb boards); (4) an auger was used to bore holes through the planks into the cut logs; (5) long wooden pegs or pins ("treenails" or "trunnels") were driven into the holes to secure the cut logs in place; and (6) the blocks between the logs were removed. This was the standard method of forming openings in log buildings. There were variants, as shown in fig. 154.

At the ceiling height, which was from 6½ to 8 feet, joists spanning the width of the building were mortised into the front and back walls. These joists were usually large, but of variable dimensions (3 by 6 inches, 2 by 8, etc.), and could be hewed or sawed. They were placed from 18 to 30 inches on-center, depending on their size. The spacing could be quite wide compared to modern practice, because the flooring was normally heavy, up to 5/4 inches thick, and did not need closely spaced joists for rigidity.

Once the eave height was reached, the front and back walls (or the walls on which the rafters would rest) were capped with the plate logs. These logs were squared, or at least hewed on three sides, because the rafter mortises had to be cut on their upper surfaces. Each rafter thrust against an open, double-step mortise (see fig. 162). Usually a wooden pin or iron spike was used to keep the rafter in place. The plates received an outward thrust from the weight of the roofing, so some method of reinforcing the corners was desirable. Although the plates could be pinned to the logs beneath, a more common method was to tie the plates together with mortised end-girts or cross beams (simply the upper logs of the end walls). Mortised end-girts were common to log barns. On some houses these end-girts were extended past the eaves ("eave beams") to support gutters. A third reinforcing method, often found in Ohio, was a mortised diagonal brace between the end-girt and plate at each corner.

Once the plates were secured, the basic log structure was complete—a solid wall log pen—with or without floors. The rafters could be set and the roof added, before any openings were cut. However, it was convenient to have a doorway in case something fell inside, and if a floor had to be laid, door and fireplace openings were needed for access. It was easier to saw off the projecting ends of the logs before the roof was constructed; the house was then "squared-up to its corners."

The simplest roof rafters were five- or six-inch diameter tree trunks ("pole rafters") hewed flat on one side. These were shaped at the smaller end for lap jointing, and notched at the butt for the plate mortises. Often the bark was not removed. This type of rafter was used with structures of frame, brick, and stone as well as log. Another type of rafter was rectangular to square in cross section, and was either hewed or sawed to a tapered profile similar to the pole rafter. These are the most common rafters found in extant log houses. A large barn roof might have squared main-bearing rafters and pole subrafters. Heavy rafters, whether hewed or sawed, were tapered lengthwise, narrowing as they approached the ridge.

The preceeding types of rafters were seated on plates and had short projections that formed the eaves of the roof. A variant framing has been found on a few log houses, notably the DeWitt House at Oxford, Butler County, and a house near Pitchin, Clark County (see figs. 167 and 168). The second floor ceiling joists were extended across the uppermost wall logs, in small open mortises, to form eaves. Thin boards were placed on top the ends of the joists; these boards were called "false plates." The rafters were butted on the false plates, and pinned or nailed through them into the joists; there was a rafter for each joist. In Marcus Whiffen's *The Eighteenth-Century Houses of Williamsburg*, the term "false plate" is traced to an emigrant's guide written by William Penn and printed in 1684.[12] The false plate was a common characteristic of Williamsburg roof framing, as was the absence of a ridgepole. The extended joists and rafters made the construction of eaves or classical cornices an easier task. The use of false plates on Ohio log houses, however, may indicate nothing more than the builder was better acquainted with brick or stone construction in which the technique was widespread. A first-generation (1830s) German half-timbered house in New Bremen, Auglaize County, also has false plates.

Regardless of framing system, each pair of rafters were fastened at the ridgeline by means of a half-lap, or "bald-faced," mortise and wooden pin. Lateral strength was given to the rafters by the sheathing. This sheathing was about one inch in thickness, one to two feet in width, and of varying lengths. Often the sheathing was as long as the house itself, because these rough boards were usually the discards, the "off-falls" (presumably from *offal*), of the logs being sawed for dimensioned lumber; this is why most sheathing is edged with bark. The sheathing boards were placed as closely together as the uneven edges permitted.

Shingle lath was also used, but did not become popular until about 1840 and the balloon frame era. Lath was usually small in width, three to four inches, though of any convenient length. It was nailed to the rafters with a spacing from six to twelve inches, depending on the length of the shingles, tile, or slate. (The latter two materials were not common to log houses in Ohio, although by 1825 the German Separatist village of Zoar, in Tuscarawas County, had a few with tile roofs.[13] There was much less chance of dry rot with lath, for air could circulate under the roofing.

Shakes and shingles were the common roofing material in Ohio, for at least three-quarters of the nineteenth century. The main difference between the two forms was the finish; shingles, often called "jointed shingles," were simply smoothed and shaped shakes. Both types were rived or sawed with a lengthwise taper, from about one inch at the butt to one-quarter inch at the tip for shakes, less thickness for shingles.

Clapboard roofing was also a popular form, though apparently not on well-finished log houses.[14] Clapboards were long shakes, and were made in two forms: Rived or sawed from blocks, but without taper; and rived or sawed from tree trunks, radially, giving a slight wedge-shaped cross section. The first type was common to log cabins and simple settlement housing, because the clapboards could be nailed or pegged directly to roof ribs or used with weight poles. Wedge-shaped clapboards, still common for house siding, were nailed horizontally to roof rafters in the same fashion as they were to wall studs. No examples of this style of roofing have been reported in Ohio, but a few remain in Virginia.[15] "Lap-shingles" were occasionally used; these were short, wedge-shaped clapboards. They were overlapped both horizontally and vertically, while standard shingles were only overlapped vertically.[16]

Whether shakes or shingles were used, the technique of applying them to the sheathing was the same. The first course was laid at the eave line, butt end down (sometimes an "undereave" or short starter course was laid first). The next course overlapped the first by about one-third to one-half, depending on roof pitch; the flatter the roof, the more overlap needed. This overlapping in courses was continued to the ridgeline. The older method of "capping" the roof was to extend the shakes on the weather side of the building a few inches above the ridge, the shakes on the opposite side butting into them. This method was replaced at some indeterminate period with a "cap course" of shakes laid parallel on the ridge. The advent of the thin, machine-made shingle, which laid much flatter than the shake, may have led to the change. Shingle and clapboard production was one of the first commercial uses of the circular saw, early in the nineteenth century.

Nails were the best fasteners for shakes and shingles, but they did not have to be made of metal. The use of wood "treenails" was noted by Gerard T. Hopkins, one of a group of Quakers traveling from Baltimore to Fort Wayne in 1804. The group crossed the Ohio River on the 10th of March; on the 12th, Hopkins made the following entry in his journal:

> "Proceeded upon our Journey travelled 31 miles [from Short Creek] & reached Randalls-Town. part of the day has been rainy and the riding very disagreeable. We have passed thro' a body [of] land heavily timber'd & very rich. There are yet but very few settlements made in this tract. The first settlers in this new country erect small log cabbins which they cover with split timber called puncheons. These they pin to the rafters with wooden pins nails are rarely to be found in any part of the house.
>
> "Their floors are hewn out of Timber and pined to the Sleepers with wooden pins. . . ."[17]

This writer has seen wooden roofing pegs from a Kentucky log house, fig. 165. These square pegs were sheared off when the old roofing was removed many years ago. Some type of tool was used to punch square holes in the hand-sawed shingle lath. It is entirely possible the tool was a small form of ax known today as a "spike-tomahawk." The spike-tomahawk has traditionally been accepted as an Indian trade item, used primarily for fighting. There was also an ice-ax of similar design.

Nails were a scarce commodity for most pioneers, but they were available if one could afford both their initial cost and the transportation charges. Although there were nail cutting and heading machines in the 1790s, production could not meet demand for many years and the ubiquitous nailrod remained in use for at least the first quarter of the nineteenth century. However, Putnam could order "cut nails" for his house in 1796, Worthington had them available for his log house in 1802, and Johnston used them for roofing in 1808. The earliest large-scale use of machine-made nails was for shingling, then house siding. The number of nails needed for the 232 frame houses counted in Cincinnati in the 1810 census would have been prodigious. These houses had to have been built at the turn of the nineteenth century, yet the majority of owners could not have been as affluent as Putnam, Worthington, or Johnston. The mass-produced nail was available wherever there was transportation. Here again is an example of the ephemeral quality of the frontier in Ohio.

If the builder had no nails or nailrod, and did not wish to

spend time making wooden pegs, then the roof had to be covered with clapboards and weight poles or some other substitute for shakes. Cyrus Bradley noted the rough cabins and houses he saw in Ohio in 1835 had "their roofs shingled or thatched."[18] Bradley was certainly a prejudiced commentator; however, John B. Miller, of Miami County, wrote the following comments in his diary in 1838: "We maid thach 310 . . ." (April 18), and "We thached Stabel . . ." (May 8.).[19] The number "310" probably refers to bundles of rye, barley, or wheat straw. A ton of wheat straw was supposedly equal to six squares, or six thousand square feet of roofing.[20] The bundles of straw were tied to a roof frame of rafters and lathes. The thatched roof must have enjoyed some popularity in the United States, for an article describing the process appeared in the *American Agriculturist* in 1879.[21] Thatch was recommended for the prairie lands of the West. The abundance of wood in the East made its use less of a necessity; however, thatched roofs were common in the New England colonies in the seventeenth century.

Bark has been mentioned several times as a roof covering; Marshall's emigrants' handbook gave the following hints:

> It may be well enough to add that *elm bark* makes a good covering for the roof, instead of shingles, In the spring of the year, when the leaves are just coming out, the bark peels off easily, and pieces as large as two men could lift can be taken off. The bark, after being stripped off, should be spread out flat to dry a little. It may then be put on the roof in strips of four or five feet in length, and as wide as the bark will allow. It should then be pinned down with hemlock or maple pins. An auger will be necessary to make the pin-holes true, so that they shall not leak.[22]

Bark eventually dried out and cracked; however, it did provide a quick, effective roof until time was available to rive shakes or clapboards.

The gable ends of the roof were framed with sawed or hewed studs, nailed or mortised into the end-girts and the end rafters. In Ohio, these gables were normally enclosed with horizontal clapboards which were either sawed or rived. One or two small windows could be framed in each gable, depending on the location of the chimney. This upper floor, or loft, which normally served as a bedchamber, was usually reached by a stairwell beside the fireplace. Sometimes the underside of the roof was whitewashed; sometimes the rafters were covered with lath and plaster; sometimes they were clapboarded. Many of the houses examined, while being well finished on the first floor, had absolutely no finish on the second.

At this stage, the house was completely "raised." The main jobs left were concerned with interior finish, beginning with the erection of the fireplace and chimney. The average dimensions of a heating fireplace in a log house were 3 to 3½ feet high, 4 feet wide, and 2 to 2½ feet deep (a cooking fireplace was about one foot larger in all dimensions). The sides of the firebox were normally at a slight angle to reflect heat into the room, but the back was usually vertical rather than slanted in at the top as recommended by Count Rumford. Assuming the fireplace opening had been cut and framed in the same fashion as the doors and windows, the first task was to lay a foundation. This was customarily of stone. Sometimes it was laid to the interior of the fireplace opening, as well as outside, to form a hearth. As a general practice, however, the foundation supported just the chimney, and a separate hearth, borne by the floor framing, was made of brick or stone. The firebox was laid on the foundation, and extended through the opening in the log wall. The log at the top of the fireplace opening could serve as a lintel. (In one log house, now destroyed, the wood lintel was faced with brick held in place with T-shaped forged nails.) In Ohio, the general practice was to use a brick or stone lintel supported by a slightly arched iron plate. The chimney was built on top of the firebox adjacent to the exterior wall surface, and extended three to four feet above the ridgeline. An interior fireplace and chimney were not common in a log house, probably because of the space they required in an already small living area. Also, although an inside chimney was advantageous in winter to convey heat to the second floor, an interior cooking fireplace created too much heat in summer. There are exceptions, but an interior fireplace/

chimney is a good sign that a house has been remodeled or was built in the 1830s and later.

In Ohio, it is unusual to find the fireplace in any position in a log house other than centered on a gable end. Most central fireplaces reported have been in standard pattern log houses with additions, placing them in the middle of the remodeled structures. A particular style of log house known as the "saddlebag" did have a central fireplace with a log pen on either side, but these houses were scarce in Ohio. Although the saddlebag house is often confused with the double-pen or "breezeway" house, they represent different concepts of interior space (see figs. 53 and 54). Log houses were also heated by stoves, which required small brick chimneys placed inside the gable ends or on the ceiling joists. Sometimes the stovepipe was run through a wall into a small exterior chimney. The opening needed was not large, perhaps just the space between two logs. Many log houses were repaired in the latter nineteenth or early twentieth centuries, with no specific purpose in mind. They were saved for sentimental reasons, or simply because they were sound buildings; in many instances, there were no reasons for reinstalling heat sources. Considering the above comments, the absence of a fireplace and/or chimney in a log house is not as mysterious as it might appear.

The cast iron heating or cooking stove has not been given just credit for its importance in the early nineteenth century. It was available in the East in the eighteenth century, but its weight and cost precluded its use in the West until frontier economics and transportation improved. By 1800 iron foundries in the upper Ohio valley were capable of casting stoves. John Johnston at Fort Wayne in 1806 listed a "4 plate" and a "6 plate" stove in his inventory of company property (the number of plates referred to the number of castings needed for the stoves). The small, boxlike Shaker stove of this period is well known today. The Zoarites made a stove similar to the Shakers' in the early 1830s; none of the original Zoar buildings had open fireplaces except the first log houses. The open fireplace had numerous disadvantages, among which were the great hazard of setting the house on fire, the difficulty of cooking on and next to hot coals, the constant draft sucked through the house, and the enormous waste of fuel.[23] Until mid-nineteenth century, most houses had open fireplaces because they were cheap and easy to construct, and there was a plentiful supply of wood.

It is assumed that the builders waited until the fireplace work was finished before laying the floor; this may not have been the case in all instances, but it does seem, from contemporary literature, that the external structure of a log building was completed before interior finishing was attempted. The presence of a floor during construction would have been of little help, and the floor could easily have been damaged by a log falling inside the pen.

As described earlier, there were several methods of placing the lower floor joists into or on the sills. (One log barn, in western Ohio, had a threshing floor built directly on the stumps of the trees felled during construction.) Since the joists normally spanned the width of the structure, front to back, the distance was usually short enough to preclude the use of a summer beam. A "summer beam" ran lengthwise through the center of a building; the floor joists were mortised into it and the sills. Summers were used in Ohio log houses, but were more common in spacious brick and stone houses and large frame buildings. The floor of a large log house with a cellar had to be structured with a central support, such as a summer and posts, or, if the distance was not too great, have joists capable of carrying substantial weight. Log joists were used in a wide variety of structures. These logs were hewed on their upper surfaces to receive the flooring. They were usually supported by "sleepers" or stone footings, when no cellar was present.

This writer has seen two puncheon floors. The first was in a log smokehouse in Greene County (fig. 111); this smokehouse is now located in the Caesar's Creek Pioneer Village in Warren County. The puncheons are of the classic description, split from the exterior radii of tree trunks and pegged to small log joists laid directly on the ground (also called "sleepers"). The size of the puncheons varies somewhat, but averages about 24 inches in length, 12 inches in width, and 4 inches in maximum thickness. All butt joints fall on the same joists, with the pegs forming two close rows down each joist. The second puncheon floor was in a large, double-pen log barn in Madison County (fig. 74), now razed. The puncheons were very large, being about 48 inches in length, 15 to 18 inches in width, and 6 to 8 inches in thickness. Because of their size and weight, these puncheons were not pegged to the log joists.

Puncheon floors in houses were probably not numerous because of the early presence of sawmills. Also, as Lang commented, "It required considerable mechanical skill to make a good puncheon floor. The puncheons were split out of straight oak logs and hewed with a broad-axe on one side, then spotted on the other to fit level on the sleepers below. All this required a knowledge of the use of the broad-axe, and some help."[24] The only puncheon house floor reported to this writer was seen in 1945 near Jackson in Jackson County. The puncheons were of walnut, at least six inches thick and about twenty inches wide; some retained their bark. They were pegged to the first floor joists.[25] To date, no puncheon floors have been reported in extant Ohio log houses. Settlers near the Ohio River, or the major navigable rivers within the state, could make use of boat planking—the ultimate (but planned) fate of countless flatboats. At Columbia, Hamilton County, which was founded 18 November 1788, the boats were used for floors, doors, and other framing material. Clapboards for roofing had been riven by the advance party when they were delayed at Maysville (Kentucky).[26] As mentioned earlier, several of Symmes's houses at North Bend were partially constructed of boat planking.

The original floors found today are generally of dimensioned lumber of standard sizes. The boards range from 3/4 to 5/4 inches in thickness, with average widths of six to eight inches. Often wider boards were used, but seldom were they narrower until the last quarter of the nineteenth century. Of the various edge joinings used, butt, tongue and groove, and shiplap were the common methods. Prior to the advent of the planing mill in Ohio, which was probably about 1830 (the earliest advertisement found was for Cincinnati in 1834), the tongue and groove edges on the boards had to be planed by hand. Consequently, this type of flooring is more apt to be found in large, well-finished houses, due to the additional labor needed to prepare the boards. (The tongue and groove of a hand-planed floor-board are almost always off-center; hand planes were usually purchased to center on a 3/4 inch board.) Most house and barn floors of the first quarter of the nineteenth century had butt edge flooring. The woods customarily used in Ohio were oak, walnut, cherry, and poplar; although a soft wood such as poplar does not seem suitable for flooring, it appears quite often.

"Pegged" floors (flat boards, not puncheons) are still found in barns; however, no pegged floors in houses have been brought to this writer's attention, though some examples may exist. Threshing floorboards, 10 to 12 inches in width, usually have two hickory or oak pegs in each end. The pegs are squared or faceted and driven into round holes. They are from four to six inches in length, and taper slightly from butt to tip. It is apparent a few houses did have pegged flooring, for the holes still exist in the joists, often with portions of the pegs still in place. In some cases, a combination of nails and pegs were used; a few pegs strategically placed in a tongue and groove floor could anchor all the flooring. A three-inch floor joist presented very little area in which to drive many pegs—none where the ends of two boards were to be butted. It should be remembered that holes in house joists were probably not for flooring pegs. An old carpenter's trick was to use a lever to press the floor-boards close together; holes were drilled into various joists for the lever. A close inspection of peg holes should always be made, with this purpose in mind.

Clay floors were not unknown in log houses, though most frequently used in cabins:

> A clay floor was made by filling up the bottom, as high as the lower log, with clay; and to make a good one the clay was mixed with water and an ox or a horse led through it for hours at a time, to tramp the clay into a paste, and when thus prepared it was pounded

> with a piece of plank and leveled up to suit. The clay floor was thus even with the lower log. . . . This kind of floor kept the wind from blowing under the cabin, added to its warmth, and was easily repaired.[27]

This type of floor was probably more common than the puncheon; clay floors have not survived simply because cabins have not survived.

The well-finished log house in Ohio customarily had double-hung sash windows glazed with glass. No doubt there were a few houses with casement and sliding windows. The movable, lower sash could not be counterbalanced, because hollow walls were necessary for the weights. The window opening could be made extra wide so the weights could be enclosed in the sides of the framing. Cylinder glass was available from Pittsburgh just before 1800, and from Zanesville by about 1815. This is the so-called wavy glass of current jargon. The "waves" were formed by the manipulation of the cylinder, which had to be slit and flattened while the glass was still flexible. The more waves, the worse the technique. Cast "plate" glass was used for special purposes such as mirrors, but it was too expensive for window glass until it was produced in quantity, by mechanical means, after the first quarter of the nineteenth century. "Crown" glass, still being produced in the nineteenth century, was also an expensive window glass. In this process, a large globe was blown, then spun and flattened into a disk. This technique left a pontil mark in the center of the disk. An iron pontil, or punty, rod was attached to the hot glass to serve as a handle during shaping. It was broken off after the glass cooled, and usually left a rough, round mark. There was great waste in cutting rectangular panes from a circle of glass. "Bull's Eye" windowpanes, so popular in artists' renderings of eighteenth-century taverns, were the centers of the crown glass disks—the cheapest glass that could be bought. Prior to the development of the Ohio valley glass industry, window glass came primarily from England and the northeastern states.

Two types of doors were common to log houses—board and

batten, and paneled. Board and batten doors are usually found as interior doors, though there are exceptions. The pegged mortise and tenon, paneled door required some skill to assemble, but was the type of work handled by the finish carpenter or joiner. The six-panel door was common to Federal period architecture, including most Ohio log housing (just as two vertical panels were common to Greek Revival, and four panels to the Victorian period). Iron box locks, a standard item of trade, were available in Ohio well before 1800. Hinges could either be made or bought. The cast iron butt hinge, also an early item of trade, was quite heavy in relation to its size. A 3 by 3 inch hinge ran from 5/32 to 3/16 of an inch in thickness. They usually bore the word "Patented" stamped or cast into them. The original patent, given in England in the late eighteenth century, covered the method of casting the hinge loops. Of course the patent meant little, and American foundries pirated the design (and continued to use the term "Patented"). A stone house in Greene County, which was occupied in 1805, still retains its original box locks, thumb latches, and "Patented" cast iron hinges.

At this point, the log house under discussion through this chapter is complete save for its chinking, daubing, and interior woodwork. "Chinking" has come to mean, incorrectly, both the filler between the logs and the mortar or clay covering it. Originally, the word meant just the pieces of wood or stone used between the logs. During construction, these spaces were held as small as possible to avoid a great deal of time-consuming finish work. The chinking was wedged, often nailed, into place because of the danger of losing it due to the shrinkage of the logs. It was then "daubed" (plastered) with lime mortar, or clay, mixed with either animal hair, grass, or straw to bind the friable materials together. Probably as much daubing was lost from the logs shrinking as from weathering. This shrinkage factor is often overlooked. In a letter dated 1832, Donald Ross of Hudson's Bay Company commented on the shrinkage of green timber: "The greatest evil . . . attending wooden buildings in this country [Canada] is the necessity of using green and unseasoned Timber, which shrinks to such a degree that the proper bearings of every part of the building very soon gets disordered however well laid at first. . . ."[28] Marshall's emigrant's guide of 1854 gives a hint on repairing loose daubing caused by wood shrinkage:

WHITEWASH YOUR COTTAGES

> Log houses pointed with lime, though apparently tight, admit much wind and water, in consequence of the logs seasoning and shrinking from the lime, or the lime becoming loose from the logs. To make them tight, apply whitewash as thick as can be laid on, which will fill the small cracks and cement the loose mortar to the logs. Salt should be put in the water before slaking the lime in it, which is said to make it hard and durable. Skim-milk or glue, is also thought to be useful.[29]

Examples of clay daubing remain today, which show that it was a reasonably durable finish. The author has seen many examples of the binders mentioned—hair, grass, and straw—used with both lime mortar and clay. Hog bristles seem to have been the most popular binder, but pork was the leading agricultural meat product in Ohio in the nineteenth century. Both sides of the chinked wall were usually daubed, though this depended to some extent on the interior wall finish. It was common to whitewash clay daubing, both to protect it from the weather and to provide aesthetic contrast to the logs.[30]

Lime for daubing, mortar, and whitewash was easily obtainable in Ohio, either from limestone or mussel shells. Limestone (calcium carbonate) heated to about 1650 degrees F., produced calcium oxide, or "quicklime." When water was added to quicklime, calcium hydrate, or "slaked" lime, was formed. This was often done in a pit in the ground; the lime paste could remain usable for years, if covered. (These pits, often used to mix plaster as well, are occasionally discovered today near nineteenth- and early twentieth-century houses, and give rise to much guesswork.) Limestone could be burned in an open fire or in a variety of earthen and stone kilns. Alternate layers of fuel (coal, wood) and limestone were placed in the kiln, which burned for about two days. Since the quicklime was removed at the bottom, a well-made kiln could be recharged from the top and kept burning for weeks. A good kiln required about one-half a cord of hard wood, or one-fourth of a ton of coal, for one ton of lime. On the frontier, mussel shells were usually burned in large bonfires; Indian shell middens were common in Ohio, and furnished much of the settlers' lime. At first, the availability of lime depended upon the ingenuity of the individual settler. Obviously, many found it easier to use clay. The professional lime-burner was not far behind the settlers, however.

Once the logs were chinked and daubed, the interior walls could be whitewashed or covered with lath and plaster. Both types of finish are found in Ohio in about equal amounts. Another method was to glue several layers of paper, usually newspapers, over the logs; this surface was then whitewashed or painted. It is a mistake to think the interior of a log house was always left unfinished—quite the contrary. Even with several windows, the unpainted interior of a log house was dull in the daytime and dark in candlelight, for the wood did not reflect light once it had darkened with aging and soot. A coat of white-wash was the simplest means of brightening the interior. "Whitewash" does not necessarily mean that the color was white (though it usually was), for various coloring agents could be added. Whitewash was a mixture of slaked lime and salt, sometimes mixed with a sizing such as animal glue; there were dozens of formulas. It was known to have sanitizing properties, and was often used to "purify" a sickroom (and is still used in barns and outbuildings for farm animals). To reproduce a whitewash finish today, it is easier to use a water-based paint. The surface appearance is almost the same, and the modern paint is less likely to crack or rub off.

The amount of interior woodwork varied according to the availability of material and the whims of the proprietor, or the proprietor's wife. Much of the trim was necessary, however, to cover cracks and joints. Baseboard trim closed the opening between the flooring and the walls. The fireplace mantel sealed the chimney opening. In most houses, trim was applied around door and window framing. The second floor was reached by a "ladder stairs" usually enclosed with a board partition and a board and batten door. Both floors frequently had one or two partition walls, made of vertical boards least one inch thick. If thinner boards had to be used, the walls were often doubled. The board and batten door was standard with such partitions. It is unusual to find boards without a beaded edge, and molding without the cyma-recta curve. These patterns lasted until at least midcentury in plainer houses. Poplar and walnut were the favorite finish woods, for both worked easily with hand tools.

Bright colors were popular for wood partition walls and all interior woodwork: Red, blue, yellow, and green, in varying shades and intensities, have been found in log houses. For early nineteenth-century houses, log and otherwise, red leads the list. Whether there was a marked aesthetic preference for red is questionable, because it was the easiest color to produce due to the abundant iron ore (ochre) in southeastern Ohio. The colors were mixed into a medium of slaked lime and skim milk which gave a translucent finish rather than an absolutely opaque surface. As a result, the colors were muted rather than intense. White lead and linseed oil were available at any time, but were more expensive than "milk" as mediums.

Were the exteriors of log houses painted? From literary sources, the answer is definitely "yes." Comte de Volney described "two rows of little white houses" at Gallipolis in 1796, and commented that the houses "though whitewashed, were nothing but huts made of trunks of trees."[31] Lang commented that hewed log houses "when whitewashed on the outside, . . . looked very cleanly and comfortable."[32] Some physical evidence also remains: The best example is a whitewashed log house in Clark County (fig. 230). A log house in Franklin County bears traces of a white paint (probably sized whitewash) under its siding; also from Franklin County is a late nineteenth-century photograph of a white log house (fig. 229). There is a log house in Wayne County with traces of a sized whitewash under the front porch area, a decorative treatment used on houses, regardless of construction, for many years. There is a ca. 1913 photograph of a "company town" consisting entirely of painted log houses; unfortunately the photograph is not identified, but the town could have been along the Ohio River (see fig. 27).

Even roofs were painted, and quite early in the nineteenth century. In the spring of 1819 the *Columbus Gazette* carried a "receipt" for making "French Cement" for shingles.[33] The cement—actually a fire-retardant paint—was made of lime, "as much as for a pail full of white-wash," 2½ pounds of brown sugar, 3 pounds of fine salt, and could be colored with yellow ochre, lamp black, or some other suitable pigment. Probably many log houses were painted between 1830 and 1850 when there was a fad for Greek Revival architecture throughout the state. The white marble temple was the symbol of classic purity, and few brick, stone, and frame buildings, old or new, remained unpainted. It would have been natural to follow the current fashion and paint a log house. Such fads for style and color came and went in the nineteenth century, as they did earlier and still do today; it is difficult to be specific about color preferences, even for a single decade. Oil paintings and colored prints of the eighteenth and nineteenth centuries are excellent for determining exterior colors. (See appendix D.)

From the number of examples remaining, the majority of log houses were enlarged one or more times. These additions took several forms and were made of various building materials, but usually not log. A framed addition to a log house, the most common technique, was easily accomplished because no complicated carpentry work was necessary to connect the addition to the log walls. Normally there were sufficient gaps between the logs for mortises to be cut. If not, the framing members of the addition could be attached to nail blocks or "scabbing." A "lean-to" addition utilized one wall of the main log structure for support. It was also quite common to move the structure, either intact or piecemeal, to a new site. There are two log houses in Franklin County which have all their logs incised with Roman numbers (see fig. 135). There is no question the houses were moved. It is logical such a system was necessary when a building was dismantled. (This writer has seen many examples known to have been moved, although the closest examination of the structures and the sites did not reveal this fact.)

Other methods of constructing additions were used. The most common was a self-supported post and beam framework scabbed to the main log structure. No doubt this type of addition was popular, because its construction did not greatly interfere with living conditions in the original house. At most, one or two windows would have to be closed with lath and plaster. The existing rear door normally served for access. A very unusual self-supported addition can be found on a house in Green Township, Wayne County. It is constructed of hewed logs mortised and tenoned into corner posts, with the whole framework abutting the original log house (see fig. 147). The vertical, mortised, and tenoned log addition on a log house in Perry Township, Franklin County, is not self-supported; there the sills and plates were mortised into the original logs. Occasionally two complete log houses were placed together, making an interior wall about 18 to 20 inches in depth. The difficulty of interlocking the logs of an addition into an older, intact log pen was undoubtedly one of the main reasons for the use of a self-supported framework.

Quite often window and door openings in a log house were changed, with or without an addition to the structure. Doors were easily converted into windows, windows into doors. Most of these alterations were done when a house was to be sided, for the siding (and interior plaster) effectively hid the necessary patching. The openings were filled with short log sections or were framed in with studding. The most common alteration made in all log houses was window enlargement. Determining the original design of a log house is not difficult for there was no way to hide alterations except under siding and plaster. However, many alterations over a long period of time do become tedious to separate unless the structure can be taken apart. What is difficult is to restore missing sections of logs without giving a patchwork appearance to the walls. The only answer is careful work in making the joints between the two areas as small as possible, and in duplicating the original worked surfaces on the patching. It is surprising how quickly new wood ages, and how soon the restored areas blend into the general tone of the old walls.

Notes

1. Cellars were apparently unusual enough in some areas of the state during settlement that they drew comment. During the fall and spring, 1806–1807, the famous merino sheep breeder Seth Adams built a large, two-story log house on his farm in Muskingum County. The house had a wide hallway, was roofed with shingles, and had a cellar. The local residents marveled at the house, in particular the cellar, which was regarded as the wonder of the neighborhood. See Plumb, "Seth Adams," p. 9. This writer has read a similar tale concerning a house in Cincinnati, yet Symmes had a two-level cellar under his house at North Bend.
2. The Romans used a level, the *chorobates*, which combined the plumb bob and water trough. See Vitruvius, *Ten Books of Architecture*, bk. 8, chap. 5 par. 1–2, p. 243.
3. Oxen were preferred. This writer's ancestral grandfather, Noah Strong, brought his oxen, Buck and Brandy, from Vermont to Greene County, Ohio, in 1807, where they were a familiar sight at raisings.
4. Lang, *History of Seneca County*, p. 186.
5. Williams, *Diary*, pt. 1, p. 61.
6. There were many "professional" log builders working in Ohio, though for the most part they remain obscure today. Another builder recorded in Piqua was Benjamin Leavell, who arrived in 1805 from Culpepper County, Virginia. He was a carpenter by trade, "and did most of the building of the log cabins of the new town" (Raynor, *First Century*, p. 16). Many of the early builders, because they bid on county contracts, could be identified from commissioners' records. Braced-frame carpenters ("barn builders") also built log buildings.
7. Howe, *Historical Collections*, p. 295.
8. Ludlum, *Early American Tornadoes*, gives many contemporary accounts of the effect of such storms on various forms of architecture. For example, the Mayfield Tornado (Cuyahoga County), 4 February 1842: "The . . . log house . . . had the appearance of having been blown up with powder. This wind . . . lifted the building *en masse* from its foundation—the logs opened—the power of the wind upon the building was broken—the logs fell back again nearly upon the foundations—a part of the timbers however being carried some distance. . . ." (p. 109) "The Great Tornado" of 20 January 1854, which commenced in Miller Township, Knox County, skipped into Tuscarawas and Carroll counties:

> The tornado passed over a field or two, tearing up fences, flinging the rails like straws for hundreds of yards, and dashed against a double log-cabin occupied by John B. Turner. Mr. Turner, hearing the noise, had just opened a door to look out, when the full force of the blast came against his house. Mrs. Turner and two children, who were standing near a huge fireplace, were literally swept into it, but fortunately escaped with a slight burning, a broken arm, and some bruises. (p. 115)

9. Like mortised-log houses, these structures fall into a typology between true notched-log and braced-frame construction. Other corner systems were tried. Burns's *Handbook of the Mechanical Arts*, "Section Eleventh," pp. 112–17, deals with a "Log Cabin or Shanty." Three corners are shown, used for walls in which the logs lay tight against one another. One method used vertical planks at each corner, pinned to the logs. Another was a staggered butt joint, the same as used in military blockhouse construction, which was most practical. This writer has seen a few small, crudely constructed houses with this corner. It was possible to anchor the corners with pins through the side of one log into the butt of the adjacent log, top to bottom of the wall, as well. Such a log house was described by Kelly's "Seventeenth-Century Connecticut Log House." The structure, pulled down in 1937, was located in Easton, Connecticut, and was known as the Bennett House. It was dated, primarily through documents, to 1671–75. Perhaps the house was an English stylistic adaptation of the Germanic log structure. It was really closer to braced-frame than log construction. On the other hand, the dating may have been wrong. By his comments, it is clear that Kelly was not familiar with log construction, though he was an authority on braced-frame structures.
10. Cook and others, "Building Your Own Log Cabin," pp. 27–29.
11. Sherwood, "Building in the North," p. 4.
12. Whiffen, *Eighteenth-Century Houses of Williamsburg*, pp. 65–66. Penn's book was entitled: *Information and Direction to Such Persons as are inclined to America, more especially Those related to the Province of Pennsylvania.*
13. "On Wednesday the 18th inst. says the Tuscarawas Chronicle of May 24, a violent storm was felt in part of this and some of the adjoining counties. In the village of Zoar where the houses are covered in the German mode with tyle, not a roof escaped destruction. . . ." Quoted in the *Columbus Gazette*, 2 June 1825. Most of the houses in Zoar were constructed of logs at this time.
14. "It is very true, that some of us who had to sleep aloft, often found our shoes, stockings, and, in fact, all our clothes, even our bedclothes, covered by a bed of snow, when we waked up in the morning; for these clap-board roofs would let the snow into the cabin with wonderful facility, especially when the wind blew with it." (Lang, *History of Seneca County*, p. 193.) No doubt Lang was referring to a weighted roof rather than a nailed clapboard roof.

15. See Upton, "Board Roofing in Tidewater Virginia."
16. There is a short but interesting chapter on "Early Shingle Roofs," by Joseph W. Doudna, in Stanton, *A Book Called Our Ancestors*, pp. 473–75.
17. Manuscript journal of Gerard T. Hopkins, Historical Society of Pennsylvania collections; courtesy of Joseph E. Walker, Millersville State College. Hopkins reached Fort Wayne on the 30th of March. Mount Pleasant (Ohio), on Short Creek, was a prominent Quaker settlement. The land and cabins mentioned by Hopkins were west of Mount Pleasant, probably near the present county lines of Harrison, Belmont, and Guernsey.
18. Bradley, "Journal" p. 229.
19. *John B. Miller Diary, 1836–43.* Miller had an 80 acre farm east of Piqua in Spring Creek Township. (See Footnote 5, Chapter 9.)
20. Richardson and Eberlein, *Smaller English House*, p. 112.
21. "Thatching Roofs with Straw."
22. Marshall, *Farmer and Emigrants Complete Guide*, p. 55. Slippery elm bark was also used in Ohio to construct bark canoes, though the common form of canoe was a dugout, usually of basswood or poplar.
23. The classic book on fireplace design is Rumford, *Essays, Political, Economical, and Philosophical*; 3 vols.; and for general history, Putnam, *Open Fire-place.*
24. Lang, *History of Seneca County*, p. 187.
25. Barsotti, from a note made Tuesday, 24 April 1945.
26. Cist, *Cincinnati Miscellany* 2:147.
27. Lang, *History of Seneca County*, p. 187.
28. Ritchie, "Plankwall Framing," p. 68.
29. Marshall, *Farmers and Emigrants Complete Guide*, p. 100.
30. A good modern formula for daubing is given in this book in Chapter 14 in the section on "Chinking and Daubing." Clay daubing could still be used, but it is perhaps best to use lime mortar today because of its better weathering properties.
31. Volney, *View of the Climate and Soil*, pp. 358–59. The Indians occasionally painted their houses as well. In 1779 the Indian town of Kendaia, on Seneca Lake, Schuyler County, New York, had over twenty log houses roofed with bark, some of the houses being "well painted." See Craft, "Historical Address," p. 364.
32. Lang, *History of Seneca County*, p. 189.
33. *Columbus Gazette* 8 no. 22; dated 29 April 1819.

XIII
FINISHING AND FURNISHINGS

The typical twentieth-century restoration of a log house almost always presents a rather gloomy interior; it is an unfortunate presumption, for an interior could be as bright and cheerful as the occupant desired. The restoration error is due, in part, to applying comments that relate to the log cabin to the log house. A good description of the making of rough furniture, as used in a frontier log cabin, can be found in Joseph Doddridge's *Notes on the Settlement and Indian Wars*. Needless to say, this information has been copied endlessly and often grossly misapplied. Chapter 12 of Nowlin's *Bark Covered House* describes the furnishings of a log cabin at a later date, combining both rustic and commercial furniture, and tells how the pieces were arranged.[2]

The Fort Wayne Indian Agency, in the first decade of the nineteenth century, was certainly a frontier settlement; however, the account books would have to be thoroughly studied to discover any amenities of eastern seaboard culture that were not available in the "wilds" of the West. Similarly, while at Columbia in Hamilton County, Francis Baily observed firsthand the quick inroads of European goods into a frontier area: "His [Mr. Smith's] warehouse was near the water-side. It consisted of but one room, where he brings down the river such articles of European manufactory as are most in demand. There are but two or three other stores of the same kind in Columbia. The profits of this trade are generally 100 per cent., and sufficiently compensate the trader for the trouble of a journey once or twice a year to Philadelphia."[3]

The Federal military establishment, strong in the Ohio Country during the 1790s, brought its own peculiar social organization to the frontier posts. Among the officers, a caste system had developed which was similar to the British and European armies; the "good life" was evident at many posts on the very edge of the frontier. Take, for example, the 1794 New Year's banquet at Fort Jefferson in Darke County (south of present Greenville) as described by Major John Buell, 2d Inf. Regt., U. S. Army, Wayne's Command. Remember, this was during the Indian Wars:

> On New Year's day I went with General Wayne and a number of other officers to Fort Jefferson and dined with General Wilkinson. Bill of fare: roast venison, roast beef, boiled and roast mutton, boiled and roast veal, boiled and roast turkey and fowls; mince, apples, tarts, etc., etc. Sweetmeats of all kinds, preserves and jellies, floating island and ice cream; plum pudding and plum cake, vegetables of every kind, plenty of the best wine. At evening we had tea and coffee in high style. Mrs. Wilkinson was present. We got back to Greenville at ten o'clock at night.[4]

No doubt such elaborate banquets were not uncommon when high-ranking officers were present at a post; the military had the necessary labor and transportation facilities. Artifact remains from Fort Jefferson are rich in English import ceramics. An elaborate meal required an elaborate service, as well as cooks and servants. Until the end of the War of 1812, foreign trade goods, particularly English, could be found throughout the Ohio Country; neither the Revolutionary War, the Indian Wars, nor the War of 1812 seem to have had much influence on commerce with the Mother Country. The Industrial Revolution developed in the United States following the War of 1812, but English goods remained highly competitive in American marketplaces until the protective tariffs of the late nineteenth century.

The first newspaper in Ohio and the Northwest Territory was the *Centinel of the North-Western Territory*, published in Cincinnati by William Maxwell during the years 1793–96. (The paper was then sold and renamed *Freeman's Journal.*) The *Centinel* was published during the tense Indian Wars period, but its advertisements were largely concerned with everyday affairs. Baily's comments about the merchants in Columbia in 1796 were not unusual, for Cincinnati had several active importers three to four years earlier. The following merchants' ads from the *Centinel*[5] publicize the variety of goods available to the settlers of the Virginia Military District and Symmes's Purchase—if they had the money:

DAVID ZEIGLER
HAS lately arrived from Philadelphia
with a valuable and choice assortment of
West Indian & dry goods, which are now
exposed for sale at the store lately occupied by
Robert Tait, deceased.
Corn will be taken equal to cash.
Cicinnati, Feb. 15, 1794.

Columbia 1st February 1794
A VERY excellent assortment of Dry
GOODS, GROCERIES, HARD WARE
and CROCKERY, just arrived and now opening
for sale on the lowest terms for cash or
country produce, at the store of GANO & Co.

WILLIAM WILSON,
HAS just arrived with a fresh and general
assortment of
DRY GOODS and GROCERIES,
which he is now opening at his store, kept by
Mr. *James Silver*, in Front Street, next door

> to where Henry Reed deceased, formerly kept
> —In the grocery line, he has Madiera, Sherry,
> Lisbon and Teneriffe wines—French and
> Peach brandies, Cherry bounse, Cyder, loaf
> and brown Sugars, Coffee, Chocolate, and
> Tea. —He means to sell on the lowest terms,
> for cash, Deer skins, Bear skins and furs.
> Cincinnati, February 22, 1794.

The term "Groceries" must have been loosely defined on the frontier! The *Centinel* has many ads by these same merchants requesting "persons indebted to the subscribers" to pay their bills. The following later ads from the *Centinel*[6] are two of this writer's favorite. Both reveal the often strange, dichotomous nature of the Ohio Country during the 1790s.

> STOLEN, or lost out of a waggon
> between Town and the Fort, on
> Tuesday or Wednesday last, a thin
> flat box containing two Paintings in
> oil, both Landscapes. One has a
> broad and richly guilt frame; the
> other, a frame of plain black ebony.
> The box they were in, was in deph
> only a few inches; in length two
> feet, or more, and about twenty inches
> wide; marked thus: *No. 16.*
>
> G. Turner
>
> Information is requested to be
> left with Doctor Strong, Fort Washington.
> The party producing the
> above will be suitably rewarded.
> Cincinnati, May 8, 1794.

> WANTED,
> IMMEDIATELY,
>
> AS an Apprentice to the Hairdressing
> business, an active Lad between 13 and 14

years of age, who can come well recommended
for his activity and manners.

PETER WELSH
Hairdresser and Perfumer

Cincinnati, April 26, 1794.

(Typographic errors were not corrected.) Cincinnati, Columbia, and North Bend were prominent rendezvous for settlers coming to the Ohio Country; Fort Washington was an important federal military post; and Cincinnati was capital of the Old Northwest Territory for several years. The business opportunities were obviously great, but no greater than offered in any of the other settlements along the Ohio River and the larger inland streams.

During the first half of the nineteenth century, good furniture woods such as poplar, walnut, maple, and cherry were in abundant supply in Ohio, and every household had need for beds, chairs, chests of drawers, blanket chests, wardrobes, and cupboards. Any log house could have been furnished with a bright ensemble of natural and painted furniture to contrast with its whitewashed walls. Patchwork quilts and woven coverlets displayed strong patterns and colors. Everyday dinnerware could have brightly colored glazes and imaginative designs. Pewter and brass utensils added their metallic luster. Inexpensive yet colorful tumblers, pitchers, bottles, and other hollow ware were being produced by glasshouses in the Upper Ohio valley.

These are just a few examples of the decorative home furnishings available soon after the Ohio Country was open to settlement. With the exception of some furniture, these items can still be seen in all their brilliance. Unfortunately, they are seldom seen grouped together in an early nineteenth-century surrounding. Today, the ordinary household wares of the eighteenth and nineteenth centuries are among the rarest cultural artifacts sought by collectors and museums: spatterware, gaudy Dutch, mocha ware, historic blue-transfer Staffordshire, midwestern free- and mold-blown glassware, pewter, decorated stoneware, and earthenware. The inexpensive, utilitarian article was not intended for preservation; that such an item exists today is due more to luck than foresight. Present scarcity does not indicate the enormous quantity of household ware that was imported to, and made in, the United States.

For several years, the staff of the History Department of the Ohio Historical Society conducted excavations at various sites prior to and during restoration work. No unusual material was found, but it was obvious that a greater variety of ceramics was available to the Ohio resident of the early nineteenth century than is commonly thought, and that there were design preferences. The sites were the springhouse and tenant house at "Adena," Thomas Worthington's estate at Chillicothe, dating prior to the War of 1812; the main house, courtyard, and springhouse at the John Johnston farm, Piqua, dating from the War of 1812; and the bakery and garden house at Zoar, dating ca. 1830. These sites bridge the main period of the log house in Ohio, and, disregarding the prestige or presumed affluence of the proprietors, the artifacts should represent the ceramics generally available in the state during the first half of the nineteenth century.

By far the most common dinnerware shards found are called "feather-edge" or "shell-edge," a plain white or off-white ware with a raised or impressed edge decoration based on the serrations of mollusk shells or bird feathers; this edge is usually tipped with either blue or green. Blue-transfer Staffordshire, particularly fragments identifiable as "American views," were frequent finds. The biggest surprise, however, was the great quantity of mocha ware shards. English mocha ware has long been a favorite of collectors, because of its bright colors and fancifuls designs, but, in Ohio at least, there had been no indication that it was a popular, utilitarian dinnerware. (Mocha ware was essentially a hollow ware, that is, pitchers, mugs, bowls, teapots, and coffeepots. Eastern Ohio yellow ware imitated some mocha patterns.) A few pieces of spatterware and Canton china were found. The number of glazed earthenware shards easily surpassed those of stoneware. However, this may not be indicative of the original quantities in use inasmuch as nonvitreous earthenware is more fragile than stoneware. Among the metallic relics found, the large curved English-pattern dinner knife, which used a round bone or stag handle, was common. There is no question the market for English dinnerware and utensils was large in Ohio; the excavated material clearly demonstrated this fact. (Remember that Francis Baily was a contemporary witness to this trade in 1796–97).[7] Household objects of wood, bone, or horn, such as plates, forks, cups, and bowls—so dear to the writer of fiction—were products of the log cabin squatters of the eighteenth century, or the more indigent settlers of the early nineteenth century.

It is interesting to note that most locally manufactured furniture, for about the first fifty years of Ohio settlement, was designed to fit into rather plain, small one- and one-half-story houses, log or otherwise. The first floor, necessarily kitchen, dining room, living room, work area, crowded into one to three rooms, had the general-purpose Windsor-type chairs, ladder-back chairs and rockers, a stretcher or drop leaf table, perhaps a hutch table, standing cupboard, chest of drawers, storage chest, candle stand, spinning wheel, as well as all the paraphernalia of the kitchen. Consider the single problem of keeping warm by the fireplace. The open fire required ample oxygen to burn; as the fire burned, it also created an updraft in the flue; combined, these two factors caused the fire to draw air from every crack in the house. It is little wonder people complained of drafts, regardless of house construction; a log house was particularly bad.[8] The fire had to receive air, and if it could not pull air from the house, it pulled it down the chimney—thus one cause of a smoking fireplace, and a common problem today because of tightly enclosed houses. The open fireplace generated specialized furniture: the wingback chair, or the settle, to protect a person's back from drafts and reflect heat from the fire; the footstool to raise the ankles from the cold drafts near the floor; the firescreen to shield the face from direct heat. Bedchambers were usually unheated in log houses, although some heat passed up the corner stairwells and through the ceiling. Furniture for the bedchamber was also highly specialized: beds normally broke down into component parts, as did many of the wardrobes, so they could be carried up the small staircases. Furniture was designed to come apart, but not to fit in covered wagons as is often claimed by latter-day writers.

Notes

1. Doddridge, *Notes, on The Settlement and Indian Wars*, chap. 15.
2. Nowlin, *Bark Covered House*, chap. 12.
3. Baily, *Journal of a Tour*, p. 201.
4. Diary of John Hutchison Buell, quoted in "Fighting the Indians of the Northwest," p. 25.
5. *Centinel of the North-Western Territory* 1, no. 17 (Saturday, 1 March 1794).
6. *Centinel* 1, no. 27 (Saturday, 17 May 1794).
7. Baily, *Journal of a Tour*, p. 201.
8. But there were advantages. In Upton's *History of the Western Reserve*, page 189, there is the comment that "This country [Trumbull County] was supposed to be a place where consumptives got well, and many did. The reason for this is easily seen. The cabins through which the wind blew, and into which the snow fell, and whose logs held not the fatal germs, were favorable places for tuberculosis patients."

XIV THE RESTORATION OF LOG STRUCTURES

At present any work perpetrated on an older building is usually referred to as "restoration," and thus the term has been applied to knocking out walls for group gatherings; to adding public restrooms; to the use of foam-plastic beams and bricks, wood veneer, ready-pegged floorboards, electric fireplaces, and similar modern exotica. This is unfortunate, because there are many organizations, and private individuals, doing restorations in the true meaning of the term: architectural restoration is a studied return to the original appearance and function (and furnishings) of a given structure. There is no question such work is costly, not only in materials and labor, but also in the time consumed by literary and on-site research. It is not surprising, therefore, that cheaper and faster alternatives are sought; however, it would be desirable if new definitions, other than "restoration," were used to describe such work.

Much work can be simply defined as "remodeling," which implies an alteration, structural or decorative, of an older building. "Rehabilitation" means repair of a building without altering any of its features, whether original or not. If a period building is newly constructed from original plans, drawings, archaeological evidence, or literary documents, it is a "reconstruction" or, sometimes, a "recreation." (Actually, an aura or atmosphere is re-created, a building is reconstructed.) "Adaptive use" means the restoration of the external features of a building while using the interior for a function other than its original purpose, that is, a warehouse into a restaurant. For the 1980s on, adaptive use may be the only affordable means to save structures other than private houses.

Each structure is an individual problem when restoration is considered, although certain basic raw materials, design concepts, and handicraft skills were common to all methods of construction. A log house of 1810 does not normally present the same complexity of construction and finish as a braced-frame house of the same period, although the need for large timber, woodworking skills, and tools could be identical. Competent restoration work demands attention to seemingly minor details. A common fault in replacing a log is to use too many hewing marks on the wood; often a replaced log looks as if it were gnawed to shape by large rodents (of course, there must have been a legion of inept pioneers and settlers).

All details of a structure should be recorded before restoration begins, then careful attention paid to evidence uncovered while work is in progress. Good photography is of first importance. Because so much information is usually discovered during the restoration process, it is very difficult to be specific in architectural drawings, and, as a consequence, in obtaining firm bids from contractors. This is the reason much restoration work is done on a cost-plus basis: cost of materials plus labor. A reliable contractor is more valuable than architectural renderings and volunteer labor, particularly on large structures. Volunteer help can be successfully utilized in preliminary cleanup and final details such as painting, landscaping, and so forth.

Preliminary Considerations. Unless a log structure is of marked historical significance and/or worthy of preservation regardless of cost, a preliminary examination should be made to establish a restoration budget. Money is the ultimate limiting factor for everybody, whether private individual or historical society, and it is best to plan on funds immediately available rather than promised.

Structurally, there are many factors that govern the feasibility of restoration. The most serious damage is the loss of an entire vertical corner of a log pen through "dry rot."[1] This condition is often found where water has penetrated behind exterior siding and the logs could not quickly dry. Each damaged log can be joined to new timber and a corner-notch cut, but the process is time-consuming and therefore expensive. Logs cut away during an alteration are less difficult to repair, as are enlarged windows or windows turned into doorways. Often a log house has had so many openings cut into it that no structurally sound logs remain, and only the siding and plaster lath are holding the walls together. A very common (almost expected) fault is the deterioration of one or both sill logs due to ground moisture; this is usually caused by a low foundation and soil accretion. Repair becomes difficult when the floor joists are mortised into the sills. Insect damage in Ohio, oddly enough, seems to be a minor problem; no doubt such damage varies geographically.[2] As part of the cost of restoration, all wooden structures should be fumigated and treated for termites. The repair of insect damage would be essentially the same as dry rot.

If the plates are found to be in poor condition due to a leaking roof, the ends of the rafters may also be lost. The plates are easier to replace than the sills, and, since the roof covering and often the sheathing have to be replaced as well, the rafters are a relatively minor job when considering the total structure.

Do not expect all interior finish to be original; its originality depends upon the care given the structure through many years and many occupants, and most log houses have been either heavily remodeled or drastically neglected—either condition demands work.

When deciding on whether to restore a log building or not,

consider the condition of the logs. Disregarding the joists and rafters, if the corners and the majority of the wall logs are sound, then the job is feasible.

Foundation. A log building is supported only at its corners; consequently, if the corner foundation stones are solid, then the building should be firm and level. Any collapse in the center of a wall cannot be blamed on the foundation, but on one or more of the structural logs. The only exception that might be noted is when the first floor joists are mortised into or rest upon the sills. In this case, the sills may be supported by additional foundation stones; this does not necessarily mean, however, that the support is continued vertically through the walls. Each log would have to be firmly blocked to the next to carry the load. This was occasionally done to support a hay mow in a barn.

Excluding the corners, the foundation served simply as a screen to prevent wind or animals from entering under the building. Of course, the foundation may extend below grade to form the walls of a cellar, although log houses with original cellars are not frequently found. If a house must be dismantled and rebuilt, there are definite advantages to be gained in placing it over a basement. The floor joists can be kept dry; burrowing animals are excluded; and modern heating, electricity, and water can be provided as daily use or emergencies dictate. Access stairs can be hidden by a trap door or in a stairwell closet. In any case, it is practical to water- and animal-proof the underfloor area if the structure does not stand on open piers; even a log barn can be protected. One method is to pour a concrete footer to a depth of two to four feet, then reset the original foundation stones on the footer so they just disappear below the grade line. Another method is to pour a thin layer of concrete on the bare earth under the first floor; three to four inches of concrete will discourage most burrowing animals Even heavy plastic sheeting placed in a crawl space will provide some protection from dampness.

Regardless of size and use, if the underfloor area is unheated it should be amply vented by grates in the foundation. These openings can be masked with plantings or objects. The dry rot found in the wood members under a structure can usually blamed on the lack of adequate ventilation.

The four corners of the foundation should be level to one another, for there are too many areas in a log structure to go awry; indeed, each log can be a problem because of its natural taper. An exception would be a building that had been gradually altered to remain level on a settling foundation. In this case it might be necessary to duplicate the uneveness if a new foundation is constructed. If an original dry-wall stone foundation is disarranged, concrete block can be used on the interior of the foundation line for support, and the old stones can be laid back in place against it. The cornerstones (sometimes known as "sleepers") were usually much larger than the fill stones in the foundation. If one or more sleepers are needed, select large field stones with a slightly convex upper surface. This curvature allows collected moisture to drain away from the sills.

The fireplace/chimney foundation was customarily a stone shelf placed on, rather than into, the earth, although it might utilize a small section of the wall foundation for support. It should be checked for firmness. A concrete pad can be laid if there is any doubt about its stability. Settlement cracks in a chimney are a guide to the condition of its foundation. *Never* consider an old chimney safe to use.

Remember that all building materials for a log structure were probably obtained within a very short distance, so select wood, stone, brick, or clay with that in mind. This certainly applies to exposed, natural surfaces. Areas that are permanently hidden from view really do not matter unless an absolutely factual restoration is intended, which is a rarity. Surfaces that are painted need only the correct textural quality.

Do not sandblast stone or brick. Both can be washed with plain water and a scrub brush. Sandblasting or acid cleaning of brick removes its thin vitreous skin; once removed, the brick is highly susceptible to water damage, though it can be partially protected by a silicone treatment, which must be renewed periodically, or paint. Usually the only brick found in a log structure will be in the fireplace and/or chimney; however, there are a few log buildings with brick foundations. Unless the stones of a foundation are soft, which is unlikely, a waterproofing treatment is not needed. Household chlorine bleach will kill mold on brick or stone.

Sills and First Floor Framing. Because a log house pen was customarily erected quickly as a unit, the first floor was often an independent structural system resting on the sills and stone footers. If the joists were to be mortised into the sills, however, this work was more conveniently done before the pen was raised. If the joists became too long for stability, such as over 15 feet, then a summer beam could be placed lengthwise through the center of the structure to halve the required joist span.

For many log houses built on a low foundation, floor framing independent of the sills or foundation was used; the joist logs, often referred to as "sleepers" (just like the corner foundation stones mentioned earlier), were laid directly on the ground or on low stone footers. These logs were usually hewn on opposite sides to prevent rolling and to provide flat surfaces for the floorboards. The floor joists normally ran at right angles to the front and back sill logs; therefore, the flooring ran parallel to the sills and at right angles to the direction of entry and exit. If extant flooring does not follow this configuration, it may be doubled or an alteration has been made either to the underframing or the entries.

Achieving a level threshold, doorsill to flooring, was not as simple a task as it might seem. If mortised, the joists had to be low enough to allow the flooring to flush with the sills. If the joists and sills were level, the flooring was higher than the threshold and a "saddle" was needed to fill the open space beneath the door(s). If the joists rested on top of the sills, then the flooring was several inches too high, and the first wall log had to be notched to form a threshold. Because the log pen was commonly raised without interior framing, there is no doubt that much juggling of the footers and joists was subsequently needed to bring the flooring close to the top of the sills; perhaps this accounts for the various thresholds found today.

The dimensions of the joists varied greatly. Log joists could range from 8 to 15 inches in diameter, while hewn or sawed joists could be 2 by 8, 3 by 6, or 6 by 4 inches, the latter a common size early in the nineteenth century. Joist size and spacing was determined by the span, the dimensions of the floorboards, the methods of attaching the flooring, and the load to be supported. As an example, a moderately sized house with 6 by 4 inch joists and nailed 1 1/4 inch flooring is commonly found with 20 to 24 inch on-center joist spacing. Hewn log joists of at least 12 inches diameter, as used for 2 to 3 inch thick puncheon floors, could range up to 48 inches on-center. A gross error, but frequently committed, is the "restoration" of a pegged floor in a structure that always had narrow joists; obviously, large strong joists were needed for pegging.

It is doubtful that many second floors were pegged. If it was absolutely impossible to obtain nails, the floorboards were left unattached. A second floor built of puncheons and log joists was simply too much dead weight for the front and back girt-logs to support. This weight could be transferred to the foundation by blocking between the wall logs, as mentioned earlier in the case of hay mows, but this writer has yet to see such an application in a house. A log pen is a very stable unit, but individual logs are susceptible to oblique outward pressure; plates and adjacent logs are often found pushed outward by the thrust and weight of the roof. Adding gross weight to the upper part of any structure that does not contain interior tie beams and support posts simply aggravates the problem.

Because the first floor framing is normally hidden from view, and must bear the greatest load, the use of modern materials and construction methods is certainly justified in all but the most critical restorations. Floors in an older structure should be carefully maintained, for a collapse while visitors are present could have serious consequences. The varieties of wood used depended on what was immediately at hand and, possibly, a guess at how long the structure might be in use. Therefore, one can expect to find any variety of wood to be in a structure, and it is perfectly reasonable to replace damaged logs, joists, and flooring with any sound local timber; however, hardwoods are preferable. The majority of remaining log structures will exhibit a variety (rather than only one) of wood.

Since even log buildings in the best condition remaining today usually have some dry rot or altered openings, there is the problem of finding large timber for repair. The first thought that most potential restorers have is to use logs from another old structure. Presumably this would be the most consistent restoration practice; however, certain points should be kept in mind. First, ideally, the structures should be close in distance to guarantee a consistency in wood varieties and reduce the expense of transportation. Second, this writer has found the asking prices for log structures to be high, particularly so when the owners admit they intend to pull down the buildings anyway. The cost of dismantling and moving the material is expensive. These costs should be balanced against using new material. Third, when a structure is obtained, the seller or donor usually expects the entire building to be removed, not just a few logs. What is to be done with a lot of useless debris, since burning is now illegal in many areas? Fourth, even though two buildings have the same corner-notching, the logs still may not interchange due to slight variances in hewing. The log source—barns are best—should have material sufficiently long to allow entirely new notches to be cut.

The preceeding text may leave the impression that old log structures should not be considered as sources for restoration material. They certainly should be considered, but from practical experience new timber is more convenient to use. It is still possible to replace any size timber, though this might vary with local conditions (and do not expect to find 30 foot logs at bargain prices). The Ohio Historical Society has conducted several restoration and reconstruction projects in recent years. As mentioned before, the longest single piece of new timber used was a 60 foot white oak plate, 12 by 15 inches perimeter (Johnston Barn, Piqua Historical Area). The largest timber by cross section were 24½ foot summer beams measuring 20 by 24 inches perimeter (Worthington Barn, "Adena," Chillicothe). Every state should have a few sawmills that can provide all the material needed for repair or new construction. Most firms can deliver to site, and the overall cost is usually very reasonable when compared to the dismantling and moving of an older building. The logs should be finished (see below) as close to the desired perimeter measurements as possible, although it is better to have them longer than necessary. Since original logs were routinely hewn to an eight-inch width, have the new logs sawed close to that size by removing several one-inch boards rather than two large slabs ("off-falls"). This will provide roof sheathing, and it certainly could provide some flooring or siding.

Practical experience has also shown that it is better to have the new logs smoothly faced than covered with fake hewing marks. Competent hewers left few marks, anyway. Logs can be drum-sanded or planed, and sheathing faced on one side, at the mill. Flooring and siding should be free of circular saw marks, at least on exposed surfaces, if the building dates prior to about 1840 in Ohio; the advent of the circular saw can vary tremendously around the state and nation. A mill band-saw imitates the marks of a vertical sash-saw quite effectively. New wood ages quickly when exposed to sun and rain and normally needs no staining to match its older surroundings. Sheltered wood surfaces, such as interior log walls, joists, board walls, sheathing, or rafters, may need artificial aging. However, because walls and ceilings in log houses were usually painted or whitewashed, a similar treatment would cover most repairs. New floors are a more difficult problem. In a way it is better to leave a new floor unfinished, though a dark walnut stain and filler looks good and ages well.

Original logs that have been cut, or damaged by dry rot or insects, can be repaired. If a log has been cut, then replacement wood of the same variety and dimension can be butt- or scarf-joined. The joints should be reinforced with metal pins or countersunk bolts and glued with a clear or tinted epoxy. If carefully done, such joints are not obvious once the new wood has darkened. It is easier to repair large logs free of a structure, but small logs can be repaired in place.

If a log is intact, but has been weakened by dry rot or insects, it often can be repaired without the addition of new wood. Large cavities can be filled with a mixture of sawdust or shavings and epoxy (unfortunately, epoxy is expensive). If it is on the interior wall of a house, this repair would probably be covered by paint and be almost invisible. On the exterior, however, it might be necessary to shape a board to cover the face of the cavity. An intact but structurally weak log can be reinforced by routing the lower side and epoxying a steel rod in the channel. Many of the planks in the Putnam House (Campus Martius Museum, Marietta) were repaired in this fashion. An entire log can be handled this way, and the repair will be invisible when the chinking and daubing are replaced. In restoration work, as much of the original structure must be saved as possible for every replacement moves the project closer to a reconstruction.

Chinking and Daubing. Wood chinking was customarily fastened in place with a few nails or pegs, for the green wall logs slowly shrank for several years. Shrinkage is still a problem if new material is used in a restoration, and minor repairs should be expected. Large timber air dries approximately an inch around its perimeter in a year, although actual shrinkage depends on the variety of wood. If large areas, or an entire structure, must be rechinked, a good substitute for wood is galvanized hardware cloth. This material can be cut into long strips, roughly folded to fit the interstices, and fastened in place with a staple gun.

Unless one wants to duplicate an original clay daubing, mortar is more practical in the long run. A mortar to imitate clay daubing is made as follows: One-fourth part cement, one part lime, four parts sand, and one-eighth part dry-color (the color is to match local clay and should be chosen accordingly). If a binder is desired, excelsior can substitute for straw or grass; a local abattoir may be able to supply hog bristle. The daubing should be recessed slightly from the log above and flushed to the outer surface of the log below, to help prevent water from entering at the top of the course. The daubing should not be spread over the logs indiscriminately, as is so often done, but used with restraint. Cracks are repairable with less visible substances. If nothing else, the daubing can be darkly tinted. The dark horizontal lines of the logs should not be broken by odd light patches of daubing.

With the general exception of log houses that were initially sided, lathed, and plastered, most walls were daubed on both sides. In fact, the absence of interior daubing hints strongly of plaster or board paneling as a wall cover. Never expect all daubing to be original to a building. If original samples are to be found, they might remain on the walls underneath the stairs or behind the chimney. Barns were seldom, and corncribs were never, chinked or daubed; smokehouses were often only chinked.

The Roof Structure. For about the first third of the nineteenth century, the standard roof pitch was 9 inches rise in 12 inches run, or about 37 degrees incline. This roof pitch was so common to all styles of buildings in Ohio that a different pitch almost always heralds an alteration or unusual, possibly ethnic, variation.

The roof framing is usually visible in a structure of a story and a half, though normally hidden by a ceiling in a two-story house. With few exceptions, the framing is visible in a barn and other outbuildings. Whether modern framing methods and materials can be used when reroofing must rest on the accuracy of the restoration or reconstruction, the intended function and public use of the building, and the interior sight-lines. Because it is not difficult to find new material of the correct period configuration, the roof is less of a problem than it may seem at first. Pole rafters, small 6 to 8 inch tree trunks hewn on one side, were common to a wide variety of structures during the first half of the nineteenth century; such rafters can still be used and are quite sound structurally.

The sectional dimensions of rafters varied according to the length of the roof span and the weight of the roof covering. Most buildings should have a few of their original rafters from which to obtain a pattern and measurements. If the rafters are obviously replaced, then check the mortises in the plate logs. Usually plates are original in any given structure; if not, then the structure is probably anything but "original," and may have been heavily altered. Pole rafters had a natural taper from butt to tip, and sawed rafters were often tapered in a similar fashion: Consequently, the plate mortises should give the largest perimeter dimensions of the rafters. At the ridge line the rafters were customarily half-lapped to one another and fastened with pegs. A ridge "pole" (usually a thin, flat board) was seldom used in Ohio until the advent of balloon-framing, ca. 1840, thus the presence of one may indicate alteration.

Waney-edge sheathing is easily procured from sawmills. It should be about one inch in thickness and as wide and long as possible. Length is important, since the sheathing ties the rafters laterally into a rigid unit. Visible circular saw marks should be removed from the sheathing and rafters, as noted earlier. Band-saw marks, or "kerfs," are acceptable, even desirable, because they are similar to the kerfs of the reciprocating sawmill.

The common method of enclosing the gables, from the rafters to the log pen, was by the use of studs and clapboards. On many log houses, these studs were blind-mortised into both the end-girt logs and the end rafters. A simpler method was to fasten the studs in half-lap mortises with pegs or nails. The clapboards were nailed horizontally to the studding; vertical clapboarding on house gables was not common in Ohio, although vertical siding was standard on barns. If opposing rafters were paired with collars, then a nailing surface for vertical gable siding was presented. This was also typical framing for barns and outbuildings.

The split shake roof is the easiest early form to duplicate. Modern "resawn" split shakes are obtainable in several lengths, 18 to 24 inches being ample for a 12/9 pitch if overlapped one-third to one-half the length. These shakes are actually split, then sawn diagonally lengthwise to make a flat surface to place against the sheathing. Although the modern shakes are usually red cedar, whereas older shakes were often white oak, they weather to a dark gray in a few months. Viewed from the interior, a shake roof seems nothing but holes and cracks, but it miraculously sheds water and seldom leaks. Shake roofs were not capped as shingle roofs are today. The shakes to the weather side (northwest to southwest in Ohio) were allowed to extend past the peak of the roof, to shield the ridge line. Board roofs, which were common in various areas of the country, can also be installed, but they are difficult to weatherproof if interior furnishings or exhibits must be protected.

If a true log cabin is being reconstructed, the entire roof system should be of the "weighted" variety: trapping (log gables) braced by ribbing, eave beams, butting poles, split clapboard roofing, weight poles, and knees. This technique disallowed the use of nails and was relegated to the rudest and/or earliest buildings; a single original example has yet to be found in Ohio and probably never will. Such roofs were replaced as soon as possible, because they did leak badly. If a new weighted roof is constructed, it definitely should be as closely joined as time and skill permit.

The eaves of a log building normally overhung the wall perimeter by at least one foot, to give some protection to the doorways, windows, and wall logs. Porches were not common until the second quarter of the nineteenth century. Wooden gutters and downspouting were used sparingly on early log houses. If gutters are desired, they can be boxed into the eaves to make them less conspicuous. If gutters are not appropriate, it is still possible to shield entries from roof drainage by attaching board deflectors to the roofing. This is an old practice and functions well, although it concentrates drainage to certain areas of the walls. Because a building open to the public quickly becomes dirty, a dry and clean entry area is important to a maintenance program. Gravel-filled trenches under the eaves and/or tiling will remove excessive amounts of water. Stone flagging and footscrapers are applicable to almost any era and style of house, save the most primitive.

Doors, Windows, and Hardware. The planks used to support the cut logs at each door and window opening often served both as the jambs and moldboards. The weather-stops, which the exterior doors closed against, were made wide enough to cover the exposed peg ends. (The pegs were usually to the inside of the window sashes and hidden by trim.) An exterior door always opened inward, and normally closed flush to the edge of the jamb and the interior wall surface. A box lock or a latch, often a dead-bolt, was mounted on the interior face of the door with the accompanying striker or keeper on the jamb. Log houses often show evidence of thumb latches on all doors, the exterior doors being locked by dead-bolts from the interior.

Both mortise and surface-mounted hinges were used, but seldom the drive-pintle type; the mortised butt hinge was standard in Ohio from the end of the eighteenth century. Drive-pintle hinges, however, were common on barns and outbuildings in the eighteenth and the nineteenth centuries. These were frequently replaced, but the telltale deep mortises can be found in the jambs. An old house door should reveal its succession of locks, latches, and hinges once it is cleaned. It is fortunate if any original hardware remains in a structure. All the hardware mentioned existed both in iron and wood, but wood locks, latches, and hinges are rarely found today.

The geographic location and probable date of a log house should be considered when choosing hardware. Although the cost might have been high, there was never a period in the history of Ohio when iron hardware, like window glass, could not be obtained. Another consideration is the economic status of the original proprietor of the house. A wealthy man might not have access to a trade center, while a poor man be settled in one; perhaps neither would have iron hardware, but for different reasons. The choice of hardware, therefore, depended on what was needed, what was available, and what could be afforded. If the literary sources exist, the original proprietor should be given a tentative personality. It is then possible, if structural evidence fails, to give an educated guess as to how the owner/builder might have handled a certain problem. Locale, date, and owner status are, however, factors bearing more heavily on finish details than basic structures when log buildings are considered.

In Ohio, windows were customarily of the double-hung sash form. The sashes were placed to the exterior of the walls to minimize the amount of water collected on the window sills. Window panes were around 8 by 10 inches, but often smaller, in size. Depending on the overall sizes of the openings, various window pane configurations were used: 9 over 9 (perhaps) for the largest, then 9 over 6, 6 over 6, 6 over 3, and so forth. Commercially available window sashes can be used today if the sizes correspond to the original openings or are close enough to allow slight alterations; appropriate molding patterns and overall designs can usually be found.

If the size is correct, old cylinder glass panes can be reused. Such glass normally does not cut well. To date, reproduction cylinder glass has been subjected to so many purposeful imperfections that it is unbelievable. The use of crown glass "Bulls-Eyes" is non sequitur with but rare exceptions. Modern single-weight window glass remains the only practical choice for the restorer, and it comes complete with its own imperfections.

The top window sash was usually fixed in position while the lower sash was movable; this lower sash was normally not counterbalanced and had to be held open with a prop. The sash was either directly fixed to the planks and logs of the opening, or it was fitted into a separate casing and installed as a unit. This latter method is frequently found, for the independent casing could be adjusted with wedges if the opening was irregular. Door casings were also handled in the same manner. However, when cased windows and doors were used, the log pen was usually sided and plastered; too many gaps were created between the logs, jambs, and casings to effectively cover with finish trim or fill with daubing.

The only window hardware needed today is a metal or wooden pin placed in a hole to the side and above the movable sash. Metal sash locks that match the period of the door hardware can be used, but early examples (even replicas) are difficult to find. A very common locking arrangement used the lower sash prop to wedge down the sash. In Ohio, it is unusual to find any indication of a sash lock on an original window in a log house, so the sash prop must have been the common method—if any were used.

Because many historic buildings now stand in isolated or neglected areas and are not visited daily, security is a problem. This is why all openings should be securely fastened. Log houses normally did not have window shutters, except in dangerous frontier conditions. Under dangerous *modern* conditions, removable, solid window covers are a possibility, though upper windows are awkward to handle. Covered ground level windows may be sufficient to prevent entry; exposed upper windows might be broken, but probably cannot be entered. Historic structures seem to suffer more from vandalism than theft.

Doors for log houses, up to about 1830 in Ohio, were of two basic styles, board and batten and six-panel. Six-panel doors were commonly used for exterior openings and first floor rooms; board/batten doors were used for closets, stairwells, and second floor rooms. Even if all interior doors were of the latter type, the exterior doors would probably still be six panel. The less finished houses, and certainly the cabins, used board/batten doors, and it is wiser to follow this course if in doubt.

Always check all door casings for altered hinges and latch keepers or striker plates; the hanging of a door, called the "hand," was often reversed. It is surprising to find how frequently doors were replaced. Older door openings were usually not as tall as modern openings, so custom-made doors may be required. Be sure a datable old door is used as a pattern, for the main stile of a six-panel door was usually much wider, the upper and lower stiles much narrower, than on a modern door.

The board/batten door is simple to construct. To be correct, the diagonal brace (if used) should begin at the lower hinge. For some reason this brace is frequently reversed in modern examples, a position rendering it almost useless. The battens should be on the interior of the door and flush with the door casing to allow the hinges to mount correctly; often a block will be required to correctly align the latch or lock.

Some door hardware must be ordered according to the "hand." To determine if a door is right- or left-hand, stand with your back against it so it cannot open; if the hinges are on the right, then it is a right-hand door. A surface-mounted latch or lock cannot be satisfactorily used on the interior side of a door which opens outward. If such a situation cannot be avoided, a mortise latch or lock will probably have to be used—but remember a board/batten door is usually too thin to be mortised.

Fireplaces and Chimneys. The chimney was usually located on the exterior of one gable end of a log house; the fireplace was centered in the first floor wall. A log house large enough for two rooms might have chimneys and fireplaces at both ends, perhaps one or two fireplaces on the second floor as well. The number of fireplaces varied greatly according to house size and climate, but a single unit was the most common. An extant log structure should still bear ample evidence of its original heating and cooking arrangements. A common alteration was to move the chimney to the inside of the wall, when the fireplace was no longer needed for daily cooking or if the house was to be sided. The opening through the wall, which had been for the front of the fireplace, was then used for the back of the firebox which was flushed to the exterior wall line. In Ohio, many chimneys of frame houses were built in a similar manner, to provide exterior ash clean-out doors.

Occasionally no evidence of a fireplace or chimney can be found in a structure. In all probability a small brick chimney, capable of negotiating the space between joists and rafters, had been in place somewhere in the house allowing an iron stove to be used for heating and/or cooking. This arrangement was common in Ohio log houses by mid-nineteenth century. A small chimney could also be seated on the first or second floor ceiling joists. If this was the case, only the rafters or sheathing, if original, might bear traces of its existence. There is no reason a midwestern log house of 1800 could not have had a stove, for stoves did find their way westward even earlier, although it was not common.

If an original fireplace and chimney are left in place and are expected to be functional, they should be closely inspected before use. It would be safer to point the chimney and reline the firebox even if they appear to be in sound condition. Regardless of its location, a chimney should extend at least three feet above the apex of the roof. If only one of two or more chimney/fireplaces is to be made functional, it is safer to choose the one on the prevailing downwind side of the house.

If an entirely new fireplace unit must be constructed, follow the dimensions indicated by structural evidence, and, if possible, use an intact old unit as a guide; never depend on a brickmason or stonemason to work unaided. Chimneys were customarily of brick or stone, depending on what raw material was available in the locale. Often a brick chimney is found on a stone firebox. From experience, one of the difficult problems encountered in restoration work is finding a stonemason who is willing to duplicate some older style of stone laying; fortunately, brick-laying techniques have not changed significantly over the years. If extensive brick or stone work is to be done, sample sections should be prepared by the mason. This is particularly important for matching new materials to an older structure.

The first major alteration made to most log houses was the construction of a frame lean-to for a kitchen, if one was not constructed concurrently with the house. The installation of a cooking fireplace in a house which, in fact, never had one is a frequent mistake. A true kitchen fireplace was large, perhaps 4 feet high by 5 feet wide by 30 inches deep, and should have left ample evidence of its existence.

The use of a clay-lined wooden firebox and a "cat and clay" chimney is really part of the earliest settlement period on the frontier, although occasionally one of these wooden units was used as late as mid-nineteenth century. It is highly doubtful if an original example exists in Ohio; however, it is certainly possible to reconstruct one from contemporary descriptions.

Ladder Stairways and Board Walls. In common use in smaller homes until about mid-nineteenth century, the corner "ladder" stairway finally gave way to the central hall stairway as the main access to a second floor; the ladder stairway was still used as a secondary access in late Victorian houses, however. The staircase was steeply pitched, hence the designation "ladder," having been designed to occupy as little space as possible. It was normally placed in a corner next to a fireplace and against the outer walls. Two or three steps led to a door, then the steps swung in a 90 degree arc to the floor above. On an average, such a staircase rose about 8 feet in about 5 feet of floor space; narrow treads and high risers were required.

The ladder staircase was used in most log houses simply because lack of space prevented the use of a central stairwell. The space beneath the steps was utilized as a closet or wood bin, and was frequently provided with a door. (This is a good area to check for original chinking and daubing.) The risers and treads were normally attached to the log walls and to the board wall screening the stairwell. Consequently, if such a staircase is missing in a log house, there should be evidence of its placement in one of the corners. One clue is joist spacing, for a wider space was often allowed between the joists where the staircase was to be constructed. Often the steps are clearly outlined in the old whitewash on the wall(s). On the second floor of a small house with an interior fireplace, the steps usually dead-ended into the chimney in an apparently illogical manner; do not be mislead into thinking such an arrangement is a bad alteration. The stairwell was seldom extended from the second floor to the attic; a trapdoor was the usual access. A ladder staircase is not difficult to reconstruct, but it must be carefully scaled. Original examples should not be too hard to find, if the restorationist feels he or she needs an example to study.

The usual method of partitioning a log house was by using vertical-board walls. The first floor of a log house only 18 feet in length was often divided into two rooms. Frequently, the room opposite the fireplace was subdivided into two smaller rooms. The best areas to examine for evidence of an original partition are the walls on either side of the front and back doors, more particularly on the sides away from a single fireplace. In other words, the doors almost always opened into the room with the fireplace. Often narrow vertical lines will be found, either as dark sooty stains or unwhitewashed strips, close to the doors and in-line with a ceiling joist. If these lines appear, check the end wall opposite the fireplace for another line indicating a second partition wall. A series of nail holes might be found on the side of a ceiling joist, for wall boards were almost always attached to these members. Original flooring often bears traces of a missing wall and the wear marks of a doorway.

Partitions were made in as standard a pattern as ladder staircases. They were composed of random width, vertical boards which were usually beaded on one edge. If the boards were about an inch or more in thickness, a single row sufficed for a wall; if less than an inch, they were often overlapped to form a doubled wall. Simple cove or quarter-round molding was used to mask the ends of the boards where they joined the floorboards. Often baseboards, chair rails, and peg rails were applied. Door openings were framed with flat trim to give sufficient depth and strength to mount hardware. Board walls were frequently painted in bright colors to contrast with the white log walls.

The second floor in a log house was normally not subdivided, unless the structure was quite large. If partitioned, the usual method was to divide the space into two rooms by a central wall paralleling the first floor partition. The difficulty of heating the second floor may have been the reason the area was customarily left open; it may also explain the practice, aside from conserving space, of placing the stairwell next to the fireplace.

Another method of partitioning the second floor, occasionally seen in two-story houses, was to create a narrow hallway along the end wall where the stairwell was located; two long narrow rooms were then formed between the hallway and opposite end wall by a lengthwise partition. The second floor in a house of one story and a half was normally open to the apex of the roof. If a better finish was desired, the underside of the rafters might be lathed and plastered, or covered with boards, and a narrow, flat ceiling formed just above head height.

Interior Finish. Log houses varied extensively in interior finish. If the interior log walls were exposed, then little finish trim was used other than a baseboard to seal the edge of the floor and molding around windows and doors to cover the log and casing joints. Board partition walls, however, might well have chair and peg rails as well as baseboards.

If extant Ohio log houses reflect general finishing practices of the first half of the nineteenth century, the use of a fireplace mantel, no matter how roughly a house might be constructed, was universal. These mantels were probably deemed more of a necessity than mere decoration in the operation of a cooking fireplace. The shelves were quite high, from 5 to 6 feet, and shallow, from 6 to 8 inches, to prevent interference with the hearth work area. The common mantel was constructed of four boards: two legs, a stile, and a shelf. The boards frequently had a beaded edge, and cyma-recta molding was often applied to the completed unit.

The use of edge-beading on finish trim, wall boards, and siding was so common in Ohio during the first third of the nineteenth century that it is surprising, and suspicious, if none is found in a structure. The cyma-recta curve was second in popularity as a pattern, and was often used in the form of applied molding on beaded trim. Less finished log houses were frequently trimmed with plain boards.

It is helpful to know if a saw and planing mill were available to the builder of any given structure. Sawmills were present in Ohio before 1800, but planing mills were rare in the mid-1830s and did not become common until the mid-1840s; even then they were located only in the larger towns. Planing mills made the use of tongue and groove flooring, paneled doors, and decorative moldings much more common than when such work was produced on the job with hand planes.

Careful attention should be paid to tool marks when attempting to date finish work. Planing mill cutters generally left an absolutely smooth surface, if correctly aligned, or slight undulations at right-angles to the grain. Hand planing normally left long striations with the grain. Elaborate molding was often executed by hand with better precision than millwork; this has led to the mistaken conclusion that what is smoothly wrought must be the product of a machine.

The interior painted surfaces of a house, if any remain, should be selectively scraped to determine original colors. Exposed log walls, joists, and ceilings were usually whitewashed, though "whitewash" could be tinted any color. It is a mistake to think that ceiling joists were always left exposed, however. If the spaces between the joists show signs of having been whitewashed, then obviously they were exposed for it was common practice to whitewash ceilings even if the walls were plastered. If the wood between the joists is bare, look for nail holes on the bottoms of the joists indicating plaster-lath was added; the plaster usually left white streaks on the joists. The ceilings and walls were rarely left unfinished.

Windows and casings were frequently painted white. Doors, mantels, wood partitions, and trim were usually painted fairly bright colors such as red, blue, green, and yellow, but in values akin to the "deep tones" produced by modern paint companies. The commonly used casein base (milk) paints were translucent in quality, that is, the wood grain showed clearly through the paint.[3] This effect is difficult to reproduce with present commercial paints. Modern translucent exterior stains, made for shingles and siding, can be used on new wood, but do not work well on old filled surfaces. A thinned oil paint can be applied, then wiped before it dries. Artificial wood-graining, sometimes highly stylized, was popular in Ohio during various periods in the nineteenth century. If applied with skill and taste, such a finish can be spectacular.

If original colors are to be matched exactly, paint charts from several companies will probably be needed. It is best to use standard color mixes, if at all possible, for the company should be able to duplicate the colors again if touch-up is needed. Several paint bases are available; a flat base seems to duplicate a whitewashed surface best, but a semigloss base should be used on finish woodwork, doors, and board walls. All colors are not available in all bases. This fact can cause a great deal of trouble, so the information provided on the paint charts should be read carefully before choosing any combinations.

If serviceable, old flooring can be cleaned, then oiled or painted; however, the wood is usually too filled with dirt to stain evenly. For the same reason, new flooring should be stained and sealed before becoming dirty. Because many original floors were walnut or cherry, it is difficult to replace them without great cost. An appropriately colored stain-sealer applied over white oak flooring will at least give the effect of a dark hardwood, and the average visitor seldom knows the difference.

Any wood that is to be painted does not necessarily have to be the correct period variety. Redwood or white cedar can be used in areas that are subject to dampness; white pine can be used for joinery work. However, poplar is still the best general finish wood whether it is stained, painted, or left natural. In Ohio, poplar and walnut are the correct varieties to duplicate most nineteenth-century interior woodwork. Unless redwood is sound heart stock, dampness will cause the grain to raise even after it is painted; redwood also splinters easily.

A great number of log houses were lathed and plastered when built. The simplest method of applying plaster lath, if the walls were sufficiently plumb, was to nail it diagonally to the logs. A better method was to nail vertical furring strips at regular intervals around the walls, using shims or kerfing logs where needed to make the surface plumb, so that horizontal plaster lath could be applied. For ceilings, the lath was usually nailed directly to the joists, though some furring might be needed to level the surface. Plaster effectively stopped the drafts with which log houses were plagued.

Because of the difficulty of obtaining a plumb plaster finish over a rough log wall, the finish trim was occasionally applied over the plaster rather than being nailed directly to the logs. For structural systems other than log, the trim was usually applied directly to the walls before plastering. This was such a consistent practice that any trim found over plaster must be considered secondary unless proven otherwise. Any well-finished nineteenth-century house might have plastered stud walls on the first floor and board walls on the second.

Exterior Finish. Log houses ran the gamut from no exterior trim, save what was also functional, to complete encasement in siding. There were strict Greek Revival log houses in Ohio, if overall proportions and trim details are considered, as no doubt there were Federal and Gothic Revival.

If the eaves of a restored house are to be open, with the rafter ends exposed, the junction between roof and plate should be as close as possible and sealed with daubing, even covered with a fascia board mortised around the rafters. The eaves were often boxed, even on plain log structures, because of the difficulty of weatherproofing the undereave area. A boxed eave can, therefore, present one exterior area to paint. Window, door, and fireplace openings were often trimmed to stop drafts and to protect the cut ends of the logs. This trim may or may not be painted; doors and window sash leave the same choice.

There is literary and physical evidence to indicate that exterior log walls were occasionally painted, white being standard during the Classic and Greek Revival periods. (Sized whitewash was quite durable as an exterior finish.) If no exterior paint is indicated on a restoration, a clear wood preservative should be used on all areas subject to prolonged dampness. If only the trim is to be painted, dark brown blends well with the general tone of a log building. It is hoped the exteriors of a few log houses will someday be painted white, with brightly colored trim, if only to show that such buildings were not always left natural.

General Information. A major problem of restoration work is to make furnishings look as new as the restored structure. It is as anachronistic to show decrepit furniture in a restored house as to show fine furniture in a ruinous house. Therefore, if the exterior of the restored log building is clean and sound, then the interior and its furnishings should be the same; it is the entire ensemble that re-creates a point in time, not just the facade or a few pieces of furniture.

Often interior colors, particularly of fabrics, are purposefully made dark as if profound gloom is the sole indicator of age. There is scant argument for subdued furnishing colors in cabins or other crude frontier dwellings, let alone soundly constructed log houses. In the log house, walls and ceilings were normally white or light-colored (even bare wood had a freshness undimmed by age or dirt); fabrics had patterns and/or bright colors; furniture was often painted; ceramics were seldom subtle in design or color; and metalware was shiny if only through use.

Log houses were probably subject to more alteration than any other style of dwelling: The walls were of ample strength to support additions, the logs were excellent insulators and worthy of retention, and the size of the original pen normally fit conveniently into a revised floor plan. The most common, and usually first, alteration was to shift the kitchen to an attached room. This removed most of the heat, noise, and odor from the main living area. The vacated space often became the dining room. The reasons for other alterations were as diverse as today, some equally as unfathomable, but are often important in interpreting the socioeconomic changes of given families.

It is always instructive to carefully scrape through layers of paint to find the original color. By counting paint layers and comparing colors, it is often possible to determine alterations to a structure. In many ways, the comparison of paint layers and colors is a better approach than the time-honored method of looking for square- and round-headed nails. There was such a great overlap in the use of nailrod, cut nails, and wire nails in the nineteenth century that it frequently is impossible to determine if each type of nail signifies a structural change or simply that a variety of nails were available.

If a log house must serve practical as well as historic ends, then an attached lean-to containing modern facilities is less objectionable than modification of the original interior. Only a basement offers completely hidden facilities without altering the main structure. Electric and telephone lines, if needed, should be buried for some distance from a restored property, if for no other reason than aesthetic. An isolated property might also require fire or burglar alarm systems, and these can be handled either through the telephone lines or through separate wires in the service trench.

The restoration of a log building is not a difficult, but rather a tedious task requiring time, labor, and, usually, money. The physical mass of timber is one problem, the myriad of finish details is another. A log building should be thoroughly examined for structural and finish detail, before any work is attempted. If there is timber damage and/or major alterations to be corrected, it is easier to strip the building to its basic structural shell than to attempt the work piecemeal (although the weather might be a factor in this decision). If there is a great deal of structural or foundation work to be done, then it is usually easier to dismantle the structure and begin rebuilding from the ground up.

Most buildings are not isolated phenomena, but have counterparts somewhere—if not in one village, township, or county, then in the next. Look for comparative examples. A log house, however humble, will in some aspects of original finish reflect both the design tastes prevalent during the period of its construction and those of the preceding generation. Only the rough log cabin seems to have remained a style unto itself from the seventeenth to the twentieth centuries. To build a mental picture of the persons and events in the locality, examine literary sources contemporary to the assumed date of the log structure. This is most helpful even if the original proprietor's history is known, for exterior finish and furnishings were often conditioned by indirect associations.

Do not expect to find much contemporary information about log architecture other than it was, in fact, used. Let the structure under restoration do the "talking." Pay attention to found artifacts, for some will be contemporary to the first-generation use of the building: A scrap of a forged hinge might set the pattern for the hardware, or a ceramic fragment give an indication of personal taste in furnishings. Record the oral history of the building and its occupants, for there is usually a pattern of truth submerged in gossip.

A good contractor can solve problems unfathomable to the layman; however, do not be mislead into thinking that an archaic building practice is unsound simply because it is no longer in use; many contractors press this argument in good faith. Know the work to be done and how the structure should appear when finished and provide the contractor with this information through sketches, illustrations, and possibly extant examples. If the job must be put out for bid, then an architect will probably be needed to formalize the specifications. Try not to hurry a job, for manuscripts or physical evidence may turn up while work is in progress that will alter the course of the restoration. Never fix an opening date until the completion of the work is clearly evident; this is a mistake often made and hard to rectify to the satisfaction of the public. Finally, if a restored structure or site complex is open to the public, decide from the outset the purpose of the restoration. If it be the re-creation of a specific historic epoch, then all functions of administration, public relations, and maintenance should remain subservient to the curatorial and interpretative program.

Notes

1. Dry rot is a misnomer, for decay fungi cannot work in dry wood. There are good U.S. Department of Agriculture publications on preserving wood. See, for example, *Wood Decay in Houses*, Home and Garden Bulletin no. 73; and, *Preserving Wood*, Forest Service Technical Bulletin no. 1334.
2. The U.S. Department of Agriculture has several bulletins dealing with insects that attack wood. See, for example, *Powder-Post Beetles in Buildings*, U.S.D.A. Leaflet no. 358; *Subterranean Termites*, Home and Garden Bulletin no. 64; and *The Old House Borer*, U.S.D.A. Leaflet no. 501. The excellent U.S.D.A. publications are available through the Government Printing Office, Washington, D.C. Most state agricultural agencies also have publications relative to their geographic areas.

3. The following excerpt on "milk" paint is from Willich, *Domestic Encyclopedia*, p. 56:

> The danger to health, and other numerous inconveniencies attending the common method of painting with white lead and oil, have induced several persons to propose various substitutes; . . . Take of skimmed milk two quarts (two Paris pints), fresh slacked lime six ounces and a half, linseed, caraway, or nut [walnut] oil, four ounces, common whiting [calcium carbonate] three pounds: put the lime into a stone-ware vessel, pour upon it a sufficient quantity of milk to make a mixture resembling thin cream. Then add the oil a little at a time, carefully stirring it to make it mix thoroughly: the remainder of the milk is then to be added; and lastly, the whiting is to be crumbled, and spread on the surface of the fluid, in which it gradually sinks; at this period it must be well stirred in, and the paint is fit for use. It is to be applied by a brush, . . . and in a few hours will become perfectly dry. . . .
>
> The quantity of paint above mentioned is sufficient for covering twenty-seven square yards with one coating.
>
> For out-door work a much greater degree of solidity is given to the paint, by increasing the proportion of lime to eight ounces and a half; of the oil to six ounces, and by adding two ounces of white Burgundy pitch [gum of the Norway spruce]. The pitch is to be melted by a gentle heat, in the oil, and then added to the smooth mixture of milk and lime.

Appendix A

Athens County Jail, 1805

Dimensions of a jail as recorded in the *Athens County Board of Commissioners' Book*, 17 April 1805. This transcription was made by the author from a photocopy of the original manuscript. No effort has been made to correct the spelling or punctuation.

3
Dimentions of a Goal

That, wheras, it appears necessary to the board of Com's that there Should be erected a Goal & Goalers house, & after mature deliberation, they have Come to the following resolve (Vis.) that the ground on which the Goal is to Stand Shall be Level & in the Solid earth. The underpining Shall be Laid two feet below the Surface of the Solid earth, the trench filled with good Stone even with the Surface, then one foot of underpining laid with Stone and morter, the outside pointed with Lime, the intermediate Space paved with Stone to The Top of the underpining, the necessarys [privy vault] excepted, which is to be ten feet deep, five feet one way & three the other, after being sufficiently walled with Stone to the Top of the pavement, and to be disposed of under that part of the goal as will be herafter directed. The Goal to be twenty four feet in length, in the Clear, & thirteen wide, to be built of Hewn timber with a double wall to be dovetail'd. The timber Shall be either oak, walnut, or poplar, Sixteen inches wide & twelve thick, Square edgd, Set up edgwise. The timber of the wall to be let down untill Space will not exceed one inch, each Stick of timber to be let down upon a Stratem of lime morter whilst raisin. The floor of the goal Shall be made of timber of a foot thick & to extend across the underpining & laid on the Short way of the building with Sufficient avenues for the Convenience of the necessary without Cuting any of the timbers in two. The prison to be divided in two appartments by a wall of hewn timber of the same dimentions of the timbers of the end of the inner wall & to be raised two feet one way from the Centre of the building. To be laid in the Same manner with lime & morter as aforesaid ———(?), the necessary to be under the middle of the building under

4

the partition So as to be Convinent to each appartment—and furnished with Sufficient Venderletters [Ventilators]. The building to be raised ten feet between the floors. The upper floor to be made Similar with the lower, the which being laid, a Stick of Timber Shall be laid over the outer wall upon the timbers of the uper floor to receive the plates—into each appartment Shall be Cut an avenue for a door. Each avenue Shall be filled with two doors, two opening into the prison & 2 outwards, the avenues to be of Such dimentions as will receive a door five feet & half high & three feet in wedth including cheeks, of ten inches in wedth & Six in thickness, to be mortised into the top timbers of the avenues. The lower end, with Sinking tennants, enterd 2 inches in a mortise of ten inches deep, the tenants made ten inches in length, Six in wedth, & one Inch & half in thickness, & to be pind to the end of each log with an inch & half pin. The inner doors of the appartment to be made of white oak plank three inches thick, doubled, & Spikd together with Spikes Seven inches long and clenchd on the oposite Sides. The doors to be hung on hooks & hinges, the hooks to be an Inch & quarter Square, to be ragd, & to extend through the Cheeks & keyd, and the hinges to be made of Axe bars & to reach across the doors well drove on with eight Spikes to each hinge, of half an inch diameter, drove through the doors & Clenchd. The gains to be Cut into the cheeks So as to receive the thickness of the doors. Each iner door Shall have a good prison Stock lock well put on with Schrews. Each inner door Shall have an avenue of Six inches, one foot & half blow the top of the door. The outer door to be doubled with plank of an inch & half thick well Spikd on & clenchd, to be hung

5

with Iron hooks & hinges. Hooks to be one inch in diameter, eight inches in length, & raggd. Hinge of half inch bars, inch & half in width, & drove on with Spikes as before mention,d and to be Securd with bars of Iron, half inch Thick an Inch & half wide, to be fastened to the cheeks on which the door hangs with a sufficient Steeple put through the end of the bar & drove into the door cheek, the other end made in form of a hasp put over a Steeple lock'd on with a double Spring'd padlock—The large room Shall be lighted with four lights of Six inches Square, the other with three of the Same Size. These lights Shall be cut between the first & Second logs below the joyce & extend through both walls in the gable end. Each avenue Shall be lind with a common Siz Iron bar Sunk its debth into the timbers of the inner wall, & in the Centre of the Same, & Sufficiently Spikd on. These lights to be of a propper distance from each other— Note: the walls Shall be begun So as to break joints—

April 18. It also appears to the board of Comm's that it is expedient for the County that there Should be built a goalers house Joining the goal, both buildings to be covered under one roof, and of the following dementions: The foundation to be laid in the front of the goal & on a level with the Sills of the Same. In length, the Same of the goal, the Short way 19 feet. The Side logs next the goal Shall be laid on So far upon the end logs of the building as to Constitute an alley of four feet—to be of an eaquel height with the goal, & the plates laid across both buildings. The distance between the joyce & Sleepers Seven feet—a sufficient number of joyce & Sleepers to be hewn to a Suitable Size & over Lain with pla(in) puncheons with a good inside Stone chimney with a fireplace, four feet between the jams at the back, with 2 iron hooks or eyes of Suitable distance to receive a Crane. April 19. There Shall be two doors, Cut two feet from the Center toward the Chimney, opposite each other, one of which opening onto the alley; two window holes, Cut & faced large enough to receive a Sash of four lites, the one Cut two feet from the front door toward the chimney, the other Seven & half feet from the Centre of the house the other way in the Same wall. To be chunk,d, & daub,d, & the outside pointed with lime. To be hewn down outside & in after it is rais,d. A partition to be between the Chambers from the wall of the goal to the roof of the Same.

[Note that the walls were to be hewn after the building was raised.]

Appendix B

Greene County Jail, 1808–09

Specifications for the third jail erected in Xenia, Greene County. The specifications were written on 6 December 1808, and amended on 16 July 1809, to include a second story. The jail was accepted on 18 October 1809. The workmanship, and/or materials, must have been poor, for the jail was inspected and declared in bad condition on 20 July 1813. It apparently burned soon after that date. The fourth jail, of stone, was completed on 16 December 1815. The following specifications are from Broadstone, *History of Greene County,* 1:143.

[*Dated 6 December 1808*]

Ordered that there be a publick Jail erected on the ground now staked out in the town of Xenia for that purpose, in the following manner and of the following material (viz.) The foundation to be dug eighteen inches deep & twenty feet square; a floor of square timber the size of the foundation to be at least one foot thick; the first logs of the building to be laid crosswise the width of the foundation. The Building to be of logs, hewed on two sides, at least one foot thick & facing at least one foot the full length; logs to be 18 feet long & the building to be raised 8 feet high, on the top of which is to be a floor of timber, one foot square, on the top of which is to be a coat of well wrought mortar at least 4 inches thick. Across the upper floor is to be a girder 10 inches thick and the face to average at least one foot, & to be pinned sufficiently with a 2 inch pin in every piece of the floor; in which (jail) there is to be a good cabin roof; the corners to be raised in half dove tailed order, and each log to be pinned at the corner with a 2 inch pin. One door in the east side to suit the shutters of the jail, which shall have 2 shutters, one hanging on the outside and one hanging on the inside. One window to suit the old grates, two of which shall be put into it. Door checks to be six inches thick and the width of the wall to be sufficiently spiked on with the old spikes; the doors to be hung with the old hangings. A suitable hole made for the stove through the upper floor.* The lower floor and at least 3 logs high to be of white oak. The doors to be secured with sufficient locks, the inside with two good pad-locks & the outside with one latch lock. The dirt to be thrown up round the outside of the wall and well beaten down.

*N.B. which is to be well plated with iron, which plate is to extend 6 inches above the floor, on which hole a small brick chimney is to be built through the roof, which is to be secured in the usual manner against sparks. On each side of the door there is to be plates of iron on the joints; between the checks & wall spiked into the checks and wall for 6 inches above and below each hinge; into the checks there is to be large nails drove within one-half inch of each other & in the same manner is to be nailed the wall for 6 inches round the door inside and outside & round; the window is to be nailed in the same manner, one foot inside and outside.

Josiah Grover, Clk. Pro Tem

[*Dated 16 June 1809*]

William Beatty, the undertaker of the jail now building in the Town of Xenia, agrees to raise another story of seven feet high in the clear, the wall to be the same sort of logs and to be raised in the same manner as the lower story; the upper floor of the lower story to be mortered as directed in a former order. There is to be five small sleepers to face even with the morter; to have a door and a window similar to them in the lower story, except the nailing around them; the upper floor of the lower story to be laid with loose plank; the upper floor of all to be laid with logs at least a foot thick, well squared and laid close to girders, and of the same kind and pinned in the same manner as was to have been on the first story; the hole for the stove pipe chimney and roof all to be done agreeably to the afore mentioned order. There is to be suitable stair steps to the upper door. Said Beatty is allowed $40 for additional work. The above undertaker is to have the benefit of all the remaining materials of the old jail and if there should not be sufficient, they are to be furnished at the expense of the county. Said undertaker agrees to compleat the whole of said work against the 15th day of August, next.

J. Grover, Clk. B. C.

Appendix C

Hewing Timber, 1867

The following excerpt on hewing is from Stanton's excellent family history, *A Book Called Our Ancestors*. The chapter entitled "The Building of Eli Stanton's Barn and House," pp. 231–42, was written by William Henry Stanton in 1921, and recalls events of 1867 on his father's farm in Belmont County. This quote may be found on pages 233–34.

The barn was to measure forty-five by fifty feet, and eighteen feet six inches from the main floor to the eaves, with the stable story eight feet six inches high. The largest posts in the stable story were twelve by fifteen inches, the main floor sills ten by twelve inches; the girder over the main floor nine by thirteen inches, and forty-five feet long. Some of the timbers were so long, they could not be sawed by the portable mill. In order to make these long timbers, the carpenters had to select a sound tree of sufficient height, and large enough and yet not too large to make a timber of the proper size. When the tree was down it was trimmed to the required length and cut off. The log was rolled, or pried up, and placed on blocks a few inches from the ground. It was then "laid off" in order to get the finished timber to the best advantage. A strong cord was immersed in Venetian Red water-paint and the surplus paint raked off on the edge of the can as the line was carefully withdrawn. At one end of the log the line was held down to the point where the side of the timber was to be formed, while at the other end the line was held tight, then raised up about a foot and snapped down, spattering a line of red paint from end to end of the log. The workman, with a common chopping-ax, stood on the log and beginning some two feet from the end chopped a series of V-shaped vertical notches about two feet apart, just into the line, then split off the long "juggles" between the cuts. This left the surface more or less rough, according to the grain of the timber. Again he chopped notches a few inches apart, until the whole surface had been carefully cut down to the line. Next came the man with the broadax. He stood on the ground at the side of the log and started at one end chipping off the high spots and leaving a fairly flat, smooth surface. With only the line to start by, he must use his eyes and plumb-bob to guide him in keeping the surface vertical. When two sides of the log had been finished, it was turned on to one finished side and two more lines made; then these sides were dressed in the same way as the first one. The weight of the log was now reduced to perhaps half. This reduction in weight was quite an item in hauling the timber to the location for the barn.

Appendix D

Paint Colors, 1852

Information on early paint colors is difficult to find. The following extract, "Outside Color," pp. 42–47 of Allen's 1852 book, *Rural Architecture*, is particularly interesting in that it substantiates the widespread use of white with green trim, and red with white trim, during the first half of the nineteenth century. This combination is still popular today around the countryside.

OUTSIDE COLOR /p. 42/

We are not among those who cast off, and on a sudden condemn, as out of all good taste, the time-honored white house with its green blinds, often so tastefully gleaming out from beneath the shade of summer trees; nor do we doggedly adhere to it, except when in keeping, by contrast or otherwise, with everything around it. For a century past white has been the chief color of our wooden houses, and often so of brick ones, in the United States. This color has been supposed to be strong and durable, being composed chiefly of white lead; and as it *reflected* the rays of the sun instead of *absorbing* them, as some of the darker colors do, it was thus considered a better preserver of the weather-boarding from the cracks which the fervid heat of the sun is apt to make upon it, than the darker colors. White, consequently, has always been considered, until within a few years past, as a fitting and *tasteful* color for dwellings, both in town and country. A new school of *taste* in colors has risen, however, within a few years past, among us; about the same time, too, that the recent gingerbread and beadwork [p. 43] style of country building was introduced. And these were both, as all *new* things are apt to be, carried to extremes. Instead of *toning* down the glare of the white into some quiet, neutral shade, as a straw color; a drab of different hues—always in agreeable and appropriate color for dwelling, particularly when the door and window casings are dressed with a deeper or lighter shade, as those shades predominate in the main body of the house; or a natural and soft *wood* color, which also may be of various shades; or even the warm russet hue of some of our rich stones—quite appropriate, too, as applied to wood, or bricks—the *fashion* must be followed without either rhyme or reason, and hundreds of our otherwise pretty and imposing country houses have been daubed over with the dirtiest, gloomiest pigment imaginable, making every habitation which it touched look more like a funeral appendage than a cheerful, life-enjoying home. We candidly say that we have no sort of affection for such sooty daubs. The fashion which dictates them is a barbarous, false, and abritrary fashion; void of all natural taste in its inception; and to one who has a cheerful, life-loving spirit about him, such colors have no more fitness on his dwelling or out-buildings, than a tomb would have in his lawn or dooryard.

Locality, amplitude of the buildings, the purpose to which they are applied—every consideration connected with them, in fact, should be consulted, as to color. Stone will give its own color; which, by the way, some prodigiously smart folks *paint*—quite as decorous or essential, as to "paint the lily." Brick [p. 44] sometimes must be painted, but it should be of a color in keeping with its character,—of substance and dignity; not a counterfeit of stone, or to cheat him who looks upon it into a belief that it may be marble, or other unfounded pretension. A *warm* russet is most appropriate for brick-work of any kind of color—the color of a russet apple, or undressed leather—shades that comport with Milton's beautiful idea of

"*Russet* lawns and fallows *gray*."

Red and yellow are both too glaring, and slate, or lead colors too somber and cold. It is, in fact, a strong argument in favor of bricks in building, where they can be had as cheap as stone or wood, that any color can be given to them which the good taste of the builder may require, in addition to their durability, which, when made of good material, and properly burned, is quite equal to stone. In a wooden structure one may play with his fancy in the way of color, minding in the operation, that he does not play the mountebank, and like the clown in the circus, make his tattooed tenement the derision of men of correct taste, as the other does his burlesque visage the ridicule of his auditors.

A *wooden* country house, together with its out-buildings, should always be of a cheerful and softly-toned color—a color giving a feeling of warmth and comfort; nothing glaring or flashy about it. And yet, such buildings should not, in their color, any more than in their architecture, appear as if *imitating* either stone or brick. Wood, of itself, is light. One cannot build [p. 45] a *heavy* house of wood, as compared with brick or stone. Therefore all imitation or device which may lead to a belief that it may be other than what it really is, is nothing less than a fraud—not criminal, we admit, but none the less a fraud upon good taste and architectural truth.

It is true that in this country we cannot afford to place in stone and brick buildings those ornate trimmings and appendages which, perhaps, if economy were not to be consulted, might be more durably constructed of stone, but at an expense too great to be borne by those of moderate means. Yet it is not essential that such appendages should be of so expensive material. The very purposes to which they are applied, as a parapet, a railing, a balustrade, a portico, piazza, or porch; all these may be of wood, even when the material of the house *proper* is of the most durable kind; and by being painted in keeping with the building itself, produce a fine effect, and do no violence to good taste or the most fastidious propriety. They may be even sanded to a color, and grained, stained, or otherwise brought to an identity, almost, with the material of the house, and be quite proper, because they simply are *appendages* of convenience, necessity, or luxury, to the building itself, and may be taken away without injuring or without defacing the main structure. They are not a *material* part of the building itself, but reared for purposes which may be dispensed with. It is a matter of taste or preference, that they were either built there, or that they remain permanently afterward, and of consequence, proper that [p. 46] they be of wood. Yet they should not *imitate* stone or brick. They should still show that they *are* of wood, but in color and outside preservation denote that they are apendages to a *stone* or *brick* house, by complying with the proper shades in color which predominate in the building itself, and become their own subordinate character.

Not being a professional painter, or compounder of colors, we shall offer no receipts or specifics for painting or washing buildings. Climate affects the composition of both paints and washes, and those who are competent in this line, are the proper persons to dictate their various compositions; and we do but common justice to the skill and intelligence of our numerous mechanics, when we recommend to those who contemplate building, to apply forthwith to such as are masters of their trade for all the information they require on the various subjects connected with it. One who sets out to be his own architect, builder, and painter, is akin to the lawyer in the proverb, who has a fool for his client, when pleading his own case, and quite as apt to have quack in them all. Hints, general outlines, and oftentimes matters of detail in interior convenience, and many other minor affairs may be given by the proprietor, when he is neither a professional architect, merchanic, or even an amateur; but in all things affecting the *substantial* and important parts of his buildings, he should consult those who are proficient and experienced in the department on which he consults them. And it may perhaps be added that none *professing* to be such, are completent, unless well [p. 47] instructed, and whose labors have met the approbation of those competent to judge.

There is one kind of color, prevailing to a great extent in many parts of our country, particularly the northern and eastern, which, in its effect upon any one having an eye to a fitness of things in country buildings, is a monstrous perversion of good taste. That is the glaring red, made up of Venetian red, ochre, or Spanish brown, with doors and windows touched off with white. The only apology we have ever heard given for such a barbarism was, that it is a good, strong, and lasting color. We shall not go into an examination as to that fact, but simply answer, that if it be so, there are other colors, not more expensive, which are equally strong and durable, and infinitely more tasteful and fitting. There can be nothing less comporting with the simplicity or rural scenery, than a glaring red color on a building. It *connects* with nothing natural about it; it neither *fades* into any surrounding shade of soil or vegetation, and must of necessity, stand out in its own bold and unshrouded impudence, a perfect Ishmaelite in color, and a perversion of every thing harmonious in the design. We eschew *red*, therefore, from every thing in rural architecture.

Appendix E

"Our Cabin," 1800

John S. Williams was born in North Carolina in 1790, a few weeks before his father's death. The remaining family came to Ohio in October 1800, finally settling in Belmont County. Williams's account of the journey and the homestead, which appeared in the *American Pioneer* in October 1843, as "Our Cabin; or, Life in the Woods," became a source of inspiration for many county historians to follow (and plagiarize). The following excerpts are from pages 442 through 449.

Chapter II

[*P.* 442] If any one has an idea of the appearance of the remnant of a town that has been nearly destroyed by fire, and the houseless inhabitants turned in upon those who were left, they can form some idea of the squatters' cabins that fall. It was a real harvest for them, however, for they received the rhino [money] for the privileges granted and work done, as well in aid of the emigrants in getting cabins up as for their improvements. This settlement is in Belmont county, on Glenn's run, about six miles north-west of Wheeling, and as much northeast of St. Clairsville.

Emigrants poured in from different parts, cabins were put up in every direction, and women, children, and goods tumbled into them. The tide of [p. 443] emigration flowed like water through a breach in a mill-dam. Every thing was bustle and confusion, and all at work that could work. In the midst of all this, the mumps, and perhaps one or two other diseases, prevailed and gave us a seasoning. Our cabin [see fig. 21] had been raised, covered, part of the cracks chinked, and part of the floor laid when we moved in, on Christmas day! There had not been a stick cut except in building the cabin. We had intended an inside chimney, for we thought the chimney ought to be in the house. We had a log put across the whole width of the cabin for a mantel, but when the floor was in we found it so low as not to answer, and removed it. Here was a great change for my mother and sister, as well as the rest, but particularly my mother. She was raised in the most delicate manner in and near London, and lived most of her time in affluence, and always comfortable. She was now in the wilderness, surrounded by wild beasts; in a cabin with about half a floor, no door, no ceiling over head, not even a tolerable sign for a fireplace, the light of day and the chilling winds of night passing between every two logs in the builing, the cabin so high from the ground that a bear, wolf, panther, or any animal less in size than a cow, could enter without even a squeeze. Such was our situation on Thursday and Thursday night, December 25th, 1800, and which was bettered but by very slow degrees. We got the rest of the floor laid in a few days, the chinking of the cracks went on slowly, but the daubing could not proceed till weather more suitable, which happened in a few days; door-ways were sawed out and steps made of the logs, and the back of the chimney was raised up to the mantel, but the funnel of sticks and clay was delayed until spring.

[*P.* 444] In building our cabin it was set to front the north and south, my brother using my father's pocket compass on the occasion. We had no idea of living in a house that did not stand square with the earth itself. This argued our ignorance of the comforts and conveniences of a pioneer life. The position of the house, end to the hill, necessarily elevated the lower end, and the determination of having both a north and south door, added much to the airyness of the domicil, particularly after the green ash puncheons had shrunk so as to have cracks in the floor and doors from from one to two inches wide. At both the doors we had high, unsteady, and sometimes icy steps, made by piling up the logs cut out of the wall. We had, as the reader will see, a window, if it could be called a *window*, when, perhaps, it was the largest spot in the top, bottom, or sides of the cabin at which the wind *could not* enter. It was made by sawing out a log, placing sticks across, and then, by pasting an old newspaper over the hole, and applying some hog's lard, we had a kind of glazing which shed a most beautiful and mellow light across the cabin when the sun shone on it. All other light entered at the doors, cracks, and chimney.

Our cabin was twenty-four by eighteen. The west end was occupied by two beds, the centre of each side by a door, and here our symmetry had to stop, for on the side opposite the window, made of clapboards, supported on pins driven into the logs, were our shelves. Upon these shelves my sister displayed, in ample order, a host of pewter plates, basins, and dishes, and spoons, scoured and bright. It was none of your new-fangled pewter made of lead, but the best of London pewter, which our father himself bought of Townsend, the manufacturer. These were the plates upon which you could hold your meat so as to cut it without slipping and without dulling your knife. But, alas! the days of pewter plates and sharp dinner knives have passed away never to return. To return to our internal arrangements. A ladder of five rounds occupied the corner near the window. By this, when we got a floor above, we could ascend. Our chimney occupied most of the east end; pots and kettles opposite the window under the shelves, a gun on hooks over the north door, four split-bottom chairs, three three-legged stools, and a small eight by ten looking-glass sloped from the wall over a large towel and combcase. These, with a clumsy shovel and a pair of tongs, made in Frederick, with one shank straight, as the best manufacture of pinches and blood blisters, completed our furniture, except a spinning-wheel and such things as were necessary to work with. It was absolutely necessary to have *three-legged* stools, as four legs of any thing could not all touch the floor at the same time.

The completion of our cabin went on slowly. The season was inclement, [p. 445] we were weak-handed and weak-pocketed, in fact laborers were not to be had. We got our chimney up breast high as soon as we could, and got our cabin daubed as high as the joists outside. It never was daubed on the inside, for my sister, who was very nice, could not consent to "live right next to the mud." My impression now is, that the window was not constructed till spring, for until the sticks and clay was put on the chimney we could possibly have no need of a window; for the flood of light which always poured into the cabin from the fireplace would have extinguished our paper window, and rendered it as useless as the moon at noonday. We got a floor laid over head as soon as possible, perhaps in a month; but when it *was* laid, the reader will readily conceive of its imperviousness to wind or weather, when we mention that it was laid of loose clapboards split from a red oak, the stump of which may be seen beyond the cabin. That tree grew in the night, and so twisting that each board laid on two diagonally opposite corners, and a cat might have shook every board on our ceiling.

It may be well to inform the unlearned reader that clapboards are such lumber as pioneers split with a frow, and resemble barrel staves before they are shaved, but are split longer, wider, and thinner; of such our roof and ceiling were composed. Puncheons were planks made by splitting logs to about two and a half or three inches in thickness, and hewing them on one or both sides with the broad-axe. Of such our floor, doors, tables, and stools were manufactured. The eave-bearers are those end logs which project over to receive the butting poles, against which the lower tier of clapboards rest in forming the roof. The trapping is the roof timbers, composing the gable end and the ribs, the ends of which appear in the drawing, being those logs upon which the clapboards lie. The trap logs are those of unequal length above the eave bearers, which form the gable ends, and upon which the ribs rest. The weight poles are those small logs laid on the roof, which weigh down the course of clapboards on which they lie, and against which the next course above is placed. The knees are pieces of heart timber placed above the butting poles, successively, to prevent the weight poles from rolling off. To many of our learned readers these explanations will appear superfluous, but the Pioneer may be read by persons much less enlightened on these subjects, and to such these explanations may be of real service.

Chapter III

[*P.* 445] It was evidently a mistake to put our chimney at the lower end of the house, for as soon as we put the funnel on in the spring, we found that the back of our breastwork settled, and was likely to topple our chimney down. This we might have remedied by a kind of frame work, had we thought of it, and had tools to make it with. So scarce were our tools that our first pair [p. 446] of bar posts were morticed by pecking them on each side with a common axe, and then blowing coals in the holes we burned them through so as to admit of the bars. But I do not think the frame-work to support the chimney was thought of. To prop it with a pole first suggested itself, at the foot of which was a large stake. These remained an incumbrance in the yard for years.

There never was any unmixed good or unmixed evil fell to the lot of man in this probationary state. So, our fireplace being at the east end, was much more like our parlor fireplace in Carolina; and besides this, while the chimney was only breast high, we should have been bacon before candlemas had the chimney been in any other position; but situated as it was, and the prevailing winds that blew inside of the house as well as outside being from west to east, most of the smoke was driven off, except occasionally an eddy which would bring smoke and flame full in our faces. Once change of wind for a few days made our cabin almost uninhabitable. Here is presented an advantage of an open house. Let the wind be which way it would, the smoke and ashes could get out without opening doors and windows, and all that sort of trouble, known at the present day, whenever a chimney seems to draw best at the wrong end; besides this, a little breeze would not, as now, give us colds.

[*P.* 448] The reader is not to suppose, from any thing that we say, that a log cabin life in the woods produces unalloyed happiness. This is not to be found in a palace, in the crowded city, log cabin, nor yet in a Fourier association. Every advantage seems to bring with it a disadvantage to give it a relish by contrast. In the ordering of a good Providence the winter was open, but windy. While the wind was of great use in driving the smoke and ashes out of our cabin, it shook terribly the timber standing almost over us. We were sometimes much and needlessly alarmed. We had never seen a dangerous looking tree near a dwelling, but here we were surrounded by the tall giants of the forest, waving their boughs and uniting their brows over us, as if in defiance of our disturbing their repose, and usurping their long and uncontested pre-emption rights. The beech on the left often shook his bushy head over us as if in absolute disapprobation of our settling there, threatening to crush us if we did not pack up and start. The walnut over the spring branch stood high and straight; no one could tell which way it inclined, but all concluded that if it had a preference, it was in favor of quartering on our cabin. We got assistance to cut it down. The axeman doubted his ability to control its direction, by reason that he must necessarily cut it almost off before it would fall. He thought by felling the tree in the direction of the reader, along near the chimney, and thus favor the little lean it seemed to have, would be the means of saving the cabin. He was successful. Part of the stump still stands. These, and all other dangerous trees, were got down without other damage than many frights and frequent desertions of the premises, by the family, while the trees were being cut. The ash beyond the house crossed the scarf and fell on the cabin, but without damage.

We visited the premises, in August, 1842, to take a sketch, and found it, as well as the country around, amazingly altered. In place of the towering [p. 449] beech on the left, stands a fine brick house, owned and occupied by Joseph Parker. Instead of a view, confined to a few rods by a dense forest, the tops of ridges and knobs may now be seen for miles, resembling a slanting view across a nest of eggs. Not one of the trees in the drawing now remain. Well do I remember the rude figure of a man which I cut on the beech to the left of, and in the distance beyond, the walnut, as well as the stormy night and the tremendous clap of thunder that shivered the ash, seen a little more to the left. The black locust, also, that is seen beyond the cabin, leaning to the left, is remembered. It was considered to be a valuable tree, and was allowed to stand after other trees were cut. Oft have I looked at its slim body, and proportionably towering height. At length fire got round it, and as is the case with every hypocrite under persecution, being rotten-hearted, it burned down. I measured its length, it was just ninety feet, and to this day, in estimating heights, I refer to the appearance of that locust, and a stump of eighty feet which was also measured. The little hickory between the house and spring, was a mere hoop pole, and we saved it. It grew very thriftily, and the last time I saw it, the finest shellbarks graced its top; but like many other things, it had but a short life after a promising youthfulness. It too is gone, as well as the white walnut which stood over the spring, and the sprout on which the spring gourd was wont to hang. But the fine, the clear, the gushing fountain of cold limestone water, is still there in the same shallow depression, and there its health-giving stream will remain and run, long after Miller, and his theory of the end of time happening this year, will both be consigned to oblivion.

Two references in the preceding excerpt are possibly obscure to the general reader:

"Fourier association," p. 448.
François Marie Charles Fourier (1772–1837), a Socialist writer of some influence in the early nineteenth century, proposed "co-operation" as an alternative to individualism and competition for the full development of human nature. Society was to be divided into *phalanges*, each consisting of 1,600 persons and based in its own build-

ing, the individuals free to vary their occupations, but all dependent upon agriculture.

"Miller and his theory," p. 449.
William Miller (1781–1849) predicted the "Second Advent" would occur with the close of 1843. This date passing, 23 March 1844, was suggested, then the 22d of October. The "Adventists" or "Millerites" were generally held in derision in Ohio, although they did attract considerable attention when they sold (!) or gave away all their possessions before the supposed end of the world. References to them are common in Ohio literature of the 1840s.

Appendix F

Log School House, 1835

This letter is one of the best commentaries found concerning the construction of a log schoolhouse. It was written about 1910 by Reuben S. Mason, who was eighty years old at the time. The school was located in Adams Township, Washington County.

"The Old Log School House"

To Hon. Daniel McAlister

Columbus, Ohio.—

My very dear old "Big Run" friend:—

You ask me, in your letter, for "a pen picture" of the school house you and I attended in 1843 & 4, and of my recollections of the place. . . .

The little building was erected in about 1835 . . . by the neighbors, voluntarily; and was afterwards maintained by contributions, as the parents thought they could afford to give; . . . The little "shanty" stood among the trees, against a hill,—close by a giant rock that had been tumbled down, in years gone by, from others up above, . . . It was located about three miles N. of Lowell, O., on a branch of old Big Run, and about a half a mile away from the main creek; was about 16 by 20 feet in dimensions; one story high, with "puncheoned" floor and "clap-board" roof. The chimney was at the back end, towards the hill, while the door was in the front, close to the W. side. The land, at this point, sloped upwardly, towards the hill—N. of the road; and, to over come the difference in grade, a larger log, than others, had been placed in front,—as a foundation,—with two shorter ones running back halfway, (on either side) and settled in the earth at the north end to gain a level.

[Page 2] These two were notched down into the first, or "foundation" log, and then another full length log placed on top of them, across the front, notched down in the same way. Then came two full length logs, along the sides,—on top of which were placed the "sleepers" that upheld the "puncheoned floor". Following these came the first full round of logs that formed the walls, and they were nine feet high. These logs were "scutched" off, on the inner side, with an Adze, to smoothen them up a little; and then the poles—the "joist"—on which the upper "puncheoned" (clapboard) floor was to be laid, were placed across,—extending over the sides of the building something like two feet—to form an "eve," outside;—the two end logs extending out, the same.

Then, across the ends of these two outer logs, and all the poles so placed to hold the upper floor, were placed two "butting poles";—so called because they held the clap-board shingles in their places, on the roof,—and were so "notched" that they could not roll off.

After this the two last wall logs, of the sides, were placed—inside of these two "butting poles"; on top of which there rested, too, the outer end of long, split, "clap-board" shingles, for the roof. . . . The "butting poles",—and the "ridge poles" [ribs] that supported the shingles all the way up,—as well as the "weight poles" that held them down, were two feet longer than the walls, and formed a kind of "cornice", projecting, at the ends,—a kind of finish, too.

Now comes the first two end logs of the eves [the trap logs]; and they, you see, are beveled off, at the outer ends—on top, to fit the pitch of roof; and notched, the same as others have been notched; and this, you see, continues till we reach the last, or center "ridge pole", at the top.

The shingles, as you see, were laid in courses, all the way across;—[page 3] the first row resting on the top log of the wall (either side) and on the second of the "ridge poles", up;—with lower end against, and partially under, the outer "butting pole", down at the foot.

Then comes what are called the "weight poles"; that which holds the clap boards in their places on the roof. These poles are smaller than the ridge poles, and are held in place by cuts of wood [knees], usually taken from the hearts of blocks from which the shingles had been split.

These cuts are placed upon the shingles;—one at either end, and in the center, one, beginning at the outer "butting pole",—the "weight pole" being placed, across, above—and thus we go on till we reach the top;—one weight pole placed to hold each row of clap boards down.

The roof being finished, men went cutting out the places for the windows, and the door; and for the fire-place. Others, still, were laying "puncheoned" floors, and clap board ceiling, on the poles across above. Then others, too, were working on the stones from which the fire-place must be made; and mixing clay, and mud, with which to plaster up the "chinks" between the logs. The chimney, as you know, was built outside;—of stone, and wood, and daubed up, thick, with mud; and broad enough for light to shine through like a window.

There were three windows in the little room, of four lights each, and glass of 8 by 10; and just below these windows—resting on some wooden pins, stuck in the walls, "a-slant", were what we called our "Writing desks";—two boards, some twenty inches wide, and twelve feet long, on which the larger pupils used to write,—their backs turned, meanwhile to the teacher and the school.

The seats,—or benches—were of "slabs", and "puncheoned" pieces, made to suit the size of those who had to use them; regulated, chiefly, by the legs they stood upon; but none of them had backs to rest against in any way. The door was fastened, only, with a latch and [page 4] string; and swung on hinges made of wood, and fastened to it with some wooden pins. The steps that led up to the door, were made of wood,—the cuttings from the fire-place, and the door—and so arranged that children could climb up and down, but, sometimes,—in the winter—climbing, there, was "tough",—so tough, in fact, that children called the place "The Crawl-down School House", on the Creek.

There was a "stair-rail", though, on either side. . . .

The spaces, all, between the logs, had been filled in with chips and stones;—the mud had been prepared, and, now, the work of plastering the chimney, and the walls, began. The wood-work of the chimney was all smeared with mud and clay, two inches thick, and plastering between the logs, bore the finger marks of workmen even to the end. The place was then cleaned out;—the puncheoned floors re-touched and leveled up, and all was ready for the teacher's work.

Yours very truly,

R. S. Mason.

"The Old Log School House," by Reuben S. Mason, is the heading of a letter found in a scrapbook, pp. 129–31, kept by Daniel McAlister. The scrapbook is entitled "Reminiscences of a Grain Dealer," and is in the collections of the Martha Kinney Cooper Ohioana Library Association, Columbus. McAlister used the Mason letter for the subject of his own letter, "A Pioneer Log School-House," written for an unknown Roman Catholic newspaper in 1910. (This clipping also appears in the above scrapbook.) McAlister, writing under the pseudonym "Grandpa," paraphrased Mason's letter as his own, giving Mason some rather backhanded credit: "I had a letter from a fellow pupil just the other day; a man now almost four score years of age; but ah, his memory is good! He spells the same as when he was a boy. He spreads his butter 'dubbel' thick, and drinks 'too kupps of Kophy every mele,' the same as he did three score years or more ago." This is poetic license with a vengeance!

The construction details of the Mason letter are occasionally confusing, but they have a ring of authenticity whether Mason was writing what he could remember or what he had been told. The phrases "you see" and "as you see" sound as if Mason was actually using a photograph or drawing, and were not mere expressions. One can only hope it wasn't the woodcut "Our Cabin" from Williams's article in the *American Pioneer*. This school had its door in the south gable, close to the west side; the chimney was centered on the north wall.

Appendix G

Log Cabin Construction, Before 1820

This excellent description of log construction appears in Antrim's *History of Champaign and Logan Counties*, pp. 12–31. The author was Judge William Patrick who died in 1891 at the age of ninety-five. The family came to Ohio from New Jersey in 1806, moving to Urbana five years later. Patrick served in the War of 1812, then worked as a cabinet maker until his retirement in 1857. Throughout his long life, he held many public offices in Urbana. Patrick was a close friend of Simon Kenton, and in later life he developed a strong interest in local history; he authored many articles on the early days of Champaign County.

CHARACTER AND HARDSHIPS OF THE PIONEERS OF OHIO.

CHAPTER I.

[*P.* 13] . . . It should be stated that there was one characteristic trait plainly prominent in that early day among the people. When it was made known that any one was in need of help, they for miles around would congregate, and if it was a cabin to be raised it was done. If assistance to roll logs was needed in a new clearing it was bestowed.

And in many instances under my own observation when any one from age, bad health or poverty was unable to open his clearing or provide shelter for himself and family, they would on a given day for miles around come together, bringing with them their own provisions at an early hour, with axes, cross-cut saws, teams [p. 14] such as they had, and such other implements as were necessary for the occasion. If the object was to open up a small clearing, a leader was appointed who gave general directions; some were assigned to cutting up the large down timber into logs, others to hauling them together, others to rolling them into heaps ready for burning, others to cut or grub out the under-growth, and either carry it to the edge of the ground and pile it in rows for a fence, or in heaps for consumption by fire, others to felling timber and splitting it into rails, and building fences where there was no brush fence, especially in front of the cabin, with a slip-gap for egress or ingress. And in some instances after the ground was cleared from debris, they would break patches and plant such vegetables as would come early and afford relief to the occupants; and indeed it was frequently the case that a dense forest in the morning, would by night-fall, present quite a little field, with the standing timber girdled, surrounded with the uncouth fences already described.

[P. 15]

CHAPTER II.

BUILDING THE LOG CABIN

If a cabin was to be built from the forest, as in the case before intimated, the leader, as aforesaid, who was always a man of experience, and dubbed Captain, would, as an initiatory step, classify the congregated masses, and assign to each their respective duties, about in this order:

1st. He would select four of the most expert axe-men as corner-men, whose duty it was to first clear off the site, square it, and place a boulder at each corner to build upon after being duly leveled, then saddle and notch down the logs in good, workman-like order.

2d. He would assign a sufficient number of suitable men to select as near the site as possible, the best large-growth, straight-grained white-oak for clap-boards, whose further duty it was to fell it, and cross-cut it into suitable lengths, split the cuts into square bolts, and with a fro rive them. Another branch of this classification was required in like manner to prepare puncheons for floors, doors, windows and chimney-corner jambs, out of such timber as was best adapted for the purposes, such as oak, chestnut or ash, as all these abounded in that part of the State, and were, when properly selected straight-grained timber, and could be made of sufficient length and width to make a good solid floor, when spotted on the under side at the ends out of wind; and to rest upon sleepers placed at proper distances apart, with dresssed, straight upper surfaces, and which, when top-dressed by a skillful adz-man, made a good substitute for plank, which at that early day could not be procured for want of saw-mills.

3d. He would then select and detail such a number as seemed necessary to cull out as near the site as possible, straight, suitably sized standing trees, and fell them and chop them off at suitable lengths for the proposed structure, with teamsters to haul them in as they were logged off, in the then usual way of dragging them on the ground hitched by a chain with a hook at one end of the log. To this force were added other teamsters, provided with rough wood sleds to haul in the clap-boards, puncheons, and such [p. 16] other materials, as would be necessary in the completion of the cabin. These preliminaries being all successfully arranged and being carried into effect, the leader would take his station and make proclamation to the balance of the forces, directing them to forthwith prepare smooth skids, the necessary number of forks with grape-vine or hickory withes around the prongs, and two or three strong cross sticks inserted through holes bored in the lower ends to give hand hold to push by; and also provide a sufficient number of hand-spikes, or tough, small, round hickory, dogwood or iron-wood, some four feet long, with ends shaved smooth to be used by the men to bear up the logs while in transit to the corner-men, or to the foot of the skids, as the case might be. Then the order would be promulgated that no one but the Captain should give any direction in the further progress of the enterprise; and as the logs would be hauled to the spot, he, with a glance of the eye would make the necessary directions; and which would be his order be conveyed to the corner-men upon hand-spikes with sturdy men at the ends walking abreast on both sides of the log, bearing it up to its destination; then the second log was borne in like manner, each being placed after being spotted flat on the under side, so as to rest level upon the corner-stones, as the end logs of the structure equi-distant apart between the ends, then the ends would be prepared by the corner-men with what was familiarly known as the *saddle*, which consisted in this: The expert corner-men would chamfer or bevel off at an angle of say forty-five degrees each side of the ends of the log, the two chamfers meeting at a point on the top-center of the log, presenting an end view of the upper half of the log. This preparation is to received the transverse logs notched at each end so as to nicely fit over the saddles. The two end logs having been placed and fitted as above described, the leader would select the two largest logs being straight for the front and rear bottom logs; being sills, these two logs when in the hands of the corner-men would be notched deeper than the other logs of the building, so as not to throw the floor too high from the ground. The corner-men at each end of the log would cut their notches so exactly at the same angle, and at the same time so as to exactly fit their respective saddles, that when put to the proper place would make a solid fit and out of wind. This dexterity in corner-men no doubt gave rise to the old aphorism, "*He cuts his notches close.*"

[*p. 17*] The four foundation logs having all been properly notched and saddled and in their places, and upon the usual tests being found square; the next thing to be done was to cut in the sills the slots, or gains to receive the sleepers, which if on the ground and prepared as already intimated by being scotched straight on upper sides, were cut to right lengths and fitted at the ends, so as to rest solidly upon said slots, and put in their places; though this was frequently done after the building was raised.

All things prepared for the superstructure, the leader still at his post, with a shrill emphatic voice selects a log, and his forces bear it to the corner-men as already intimated, resting one end of the handspikes on the top log already placed, rolling it upon the two saddled logs; it was then fitted and prepared in proper manner and placed plumb on the wall by the practiced eye, aided by the pendulous axe held loosely at tip of helve, between the thumb and forefingers of the experts. This routine being continued, until the building was too high to reach and rest the handspikes as heretofore described upon the wall; then, the skids resting on the ground at the but-ends would be reared up to the corners on the front side and one end of the building, nearest the collection of the hauled-in timber; the logs one by one selected as aforesaid, would be carried as before to the foot of the appropriate skids, and placed on them, and rolled up as far as the men could conveniently reach; and being stanchioned and held, the necessary number of forks were placed under each end of the log inside of the skids, with lower ends held firmly down to the ground, were by the order of the leader manned at the cross-handles already described at each end of the log, which was at a given word of said leader, slid up the skids by the uniform motive power thus applied, to the top, where, by the leverage of handspikes in the hands of the corner-men, it would be thrown on top of the already saddled logs, and by them rolled to the back wall; then the next log in like manner would be shoved up and received by the corner-men for the wall upon which the skids rested: these being fitted as indicated, the two logs intended as transverse would in like manner be placed on the ends of the last two logs, all being done with exact uniformity and celerity, and with dispatch and neatness fitted to their respective places in the wall. And if the contemplated cabin was intended to be more than one story, at the proper height from the top of [p. 18] the sleepers for lower floor, slots would be prepared for the joists, and if they were on the ground would be fitted in like manner with the sleepers. Then the building would in the routine already described be carried up to the square; when upon the two ends of the building would be raised the eave-bearers, projecting some twenty inches beyond the wall, and would be notched down and saddled back far enough to receive the timbers hereafter described; when the two ends in front of the building were notched at the upper tips in the form of the large capital V to rest the upper ends of the skids, then the butting pole for the back side of the cabin would be shoved up to the front corner-men, and rolled to the back eave and notched down upon the saddles projecting some fifteen inches, beyond the outside plumb of the wall; then the first rib would be sent up to corner-men in same manner, and rolled back to proper distance inside of said butting pole, and notched down, so as to give the pitch of roof from center of butting pole to top surface of said rib; then the front rib and butting pole would in like manner be sent up and placed in same order as those in the rear, then the first two gable logs would be placed in notches cut into the ribs and chamfered at the ends to suit the pitch of the roof. The other ribs and gable logs being placed, so as to preserve the intended pitch of the roof, the upper and central one being called the ridge pole is in like manner notched down in such position, as that a straight edge would from the centers of the butting poles upward, touch the upper surfaces of all the ribs and ridge pole respectively at the indicated angles. Thus the cabin is ready for the clapboards, which are laid down upon the ribs with the lower ends resting against the butting poles, with small spaces between, which are top-covered in like manner, some to break joints, and the eave courses on each side being so laid down; knees cut of the hearts of clapboard bolts, of proper lengths are prepared at each end, resting endwise against the butting poles to hold up the weight poles, which are placed upon the two eave courses of clapboards as nearly over the ribs respectively as possible; and in like manner another course of clapboards is on each side laid down abutting the weight-poles, and being kneed as described, another weight-pole is put in its place to hold down the boards, and so on until the whole cabin is roofed and weighed down as per programme.

In this connection it may be stated, that those forces that were [p. 19] detailed to prepare material in the early part of the day, would long before the cabin was raised and covered have finished their several allotments of labor, and report themselves ready for further service, and would again be subdivided and their respective duties under the direction of the leader allotted; some to cutting out the openings, such as doors, windows, and fire-places, and jambing them up with the material prepared for that purpose; others to laying down the floor as already described; others to building up the chimney, back and side jambs for outside fire-place; others to preparing "cat and clay" with which to top out the chimney and put in stone back wall and fire-place jambs; others to making door or doors as the case might be, out of long clap-boards prepared for such purpose, and hanging them with wooden hinges and fixing wooden latches; others to scotching down slightly with a broad-axe inside walls; others to chinking and daubing the cabin and filling up the hearth even with the floor and flagging it with flat stones, if such material was on hands, and putting cross sticks in windows upon which greased paper would be pasted as a substitute for glass. And indeed it may be said the whole would be completed, so that a general house-warming, as it was called—in the shape of a country dance or other innocent amusements—would be the prelude to the family occupancy the same night after the completion.

This characteristic kindness was mutual—all felt it, all manifested it toward each other. All intercourse was social; no one felt that he had a right to domineer over his poor neighbor, but the disposition was to aid and encourage.

[*P. 31*] NOTE: I have attempted to describe a log cabin raising, in its multiform delineations from the standing forest to the completed structure. And in doing so have committed myself to the criticism of many yet living, who would be more capable of the task I have assumed. I am aware that my attempt has many defects in point of accuracy of description, that will likely be pointed out as needing amendment. But my motive was not the enlightenment of the present generation, but was attempted from a desire to hand down to posterity the primitive structures up to 1820, believing that before the year 1920, this mode of building will have become obsolete, and unknown. As the new settlers of this day do not resort to the log cabin, but to the frame house or hovel, the idea of the original log cabin as already said will be unknown, hence the reason of my feeble attempt.

Bibliography

Adams, Percy G. *Travelers and Travel Liars, 1660–1800*. Berkeley and Los Angeles: University of California Press, 1962.

Aldrich, Chilson D. *The Real Log Cabin*. New York: Macmillan Company, [1928].

Allen, Lewis F. *Rural Architecture*. New York: Orange Judd & Co., 1852.

American Association for State and Local History, "Technical Leaflet" Series. Nashville, Tennessee.

Antrim, Joshua. *The History of Champaign and Logan Counties, From Their First Settlement*. Bellefontaine, Ohio: Press Printing Co., 1872.

APT Bulletin, Association for Preservation Technology. Volumes 1 through 14 (1969–82).

Athens County (Ohio). *Board of Commissioners' Book, 1805*.

Baily, Francis. *Journal of a Tour in Unsettled Parts of North America in 1796 and 1797*. London: Baily Brothers, 1856.

Baird, Henry Carey, ed. *The Painter, Gilder, and Varnisher's Companion*. Philadelphia: Henry Carey Baird & Co., 1873.

Bale, M. Powis. *Saw-Mills*. London: Crosby Lockwood & Co., 1883.

______. *Woodworking Machinery*. London: Crosby Lockwood & Co., 1880.

Barker, Joseph. *Recollections of the First Settlement of Ohio*. Edited by George J. Blazier, Notes by Rodney T. Hood. Marietta: Marietta College, 1958. (Marietta College *Bulletin* 56, no. 2.)

Barnard, Henry. *School Architecture*. Cincinnati: H. W. Derby and Co., 1854.

Barsotti, John, personal notes, 1945.

Bartlett, William Henry. "Western Clearing," an engraving. *Ladies' Repository* 15 (1855):123.

Baughman, Abraham J. *History of Richland County, Ohio*. 2 vols. Chicago: S. Jr. Clarke Publishing Co., 1908.

Bealer, Alex W., and John O. Ellis. *The Log Cabin*. Barre, Mass.: Barre Publishing, 1978.

Beckmann, John [Johann]. *A History of Inventions, Discoveries, and Origins*. 4th ed. 2 vols. London: Henry G. Bohn, 1846.

Benjamin, Asher. *The American Builder's Companion.* New York: Dover Publications, 1969. (Reprint of 6th ed., 1827.)

Berger, Rainer, ed. *Scientific Methods in Medieval Archaeology.* Berkeley: University of California Press, 1970.

Bernard, John. *Retrospections of America, 1797–1811.* New York: Benjamin Blom, 1969. (Reprint of 1887 ed.)

Bidwell, Percy Wells, and John I. Falconer. *History of Agriculture in the Northern United States, 1620–1860.* Carnegie Institution of Washington, Publication no. 358. New York: Peter Smith, 1941.

Bishop, John Leander. *A History of American Manufacturers from 1608 to 1860.* 3d ed. 3 vols. Philadelphia: Edward Young & Co., 1868.

[Blane, William Newnham]. *An Excursion through the United States and Canada During the Years 1822–23.* London: Printed for Baldwin, Cradock, and Joy, 1824.

Bognar, E. J. "The Roof Tiles of Zoar," *Magazine Antiques* 25, no. 2 (February 1934):52–54.

Bond, Beverley W., Jr., ed. *The Correspondence of John Cleves Symmes.* New York: MacMillan Company, 1926.

[Bradley, Cyrus P.] "Journal of Cyrus P. Bradley." *Ohio Archaeological and Historical Quarterly* 15 (1906):207–270.

Brickell, John. "Narrative of John Brickell's Captivity among the Delaware Indians," *American Pioneer* 1 (February 1842):43–56.

Bridges, Roger D., correspondence, 1973; Illinois State Historical Library.

Brinkerhoff, Roeliff. "The History of Richland County." *Ohio Liberal,* Mansfield, 1876 (published for the Centennial).

The British-American Guide-Book. New York: H. Bailliere, 1859.

Broadstone, Michael A. *History of Greene County, Ohio.* 2 vols. Indianapolis: E. F. Bower & Co., 1918.

Brown, R. C., and J. E. Morris, eds. *History of Portage County, Ohio.* Chicago: Werner, Beers & Co., 1885.

Brumbaugh, G. Edwin. "Colonial Architecture of the Pennsylvania Germans." *Pennsylvania German Society Proceedings* 41(1933):pt. 2. Delivered as an address before the forty-first annual meeting, 23 October 1931.

Brunskill, R. W., Senior lecturer in the School of Architecture. Correspondence, 1976; University of Manchester, England.

Buell, John Hutchison. Diary quoted in "Fighting the Indians of the Northwest." *American History Illustrated* 3, no. 9 (1969):23–26, 35.

Bullock, Orin M., Jr. *The Restoration Manual.* Norwalk, Conn.: Silvermine Publishers, 1966.

Burn, Robert Scott. *Handbook of the Mechanical Arts.* 2d ed. Edinburgh and London: William Blackwood and Sons, n.d. (Ca. 1880 reprint of 1850s material.)

Burcaw, George Ellis. *The Saxon House.* Moscow, Idaho: University of Idaho Museum, 1973.

Butterfield, Consul W. *History of Seneca County*. Sandusky, Ohio: D. Campbell & Sons, 1848.

______. *History of the Girtys*. Cincinnati: Robert Clarke & Co., 1890.

Carlisle, Ronald C. *An Architectural Study of Some Folk Structures in the Area of the Paintsville Lake Dam, Johnson and Morgan Counties, Kentucky*. U. S. Army Corps of Engineers, Huntington District. August, 1982.

Harry E. Pratt, [Caton, John Dean], ed. "John Dean Caton's Reminiscences of Chicago in 1833 and 1834." *Journal of the Illinois State Historical Society*, 28 (April 1935, to January 1936):5–25.

The Centinel of the North-Western Territory. Vol. I, no. 17 and 27 (1 March and 17 May 1794).

Childe, V. Gordon. *What Happened in History*. Harmondsworth, Middlesex: Penguin Books, 1954.

The Chronicle of the Early American Industries Association. Vols. 1 through 24 (1933–71).

The Cincinnati Directory. Cincinnati: Oliver Farnsworth, 1819.

The Cincinnati Directory for the Year 1829. Cincinnati: Robinson & Fairbank, 1829.

Cist, Charles. *The Cincinnati Miscellany; or, Antiquities of the West*. 2 vols. Cincinnati: Caleb Clark, 1845; Robinson & Jones, 1846.

Columbus Gazette. Vol. 8, nos. 19 and 22 (8 April and 29 1819).

Cook, Mike and others. "Building Your Own Log Cabin." *Foxfire*. Vol. 3 (Summer 1969), pp. 9–32, 45–69. (Reprinted in *Foxfire I*, 1972.)

Coxe, Tench. *A Statement of the Arts and Manufacturers of the United States of America, for the Year 1810*. Philadelphia: A. Cornman, Jr., 1814.

Craft, David. "Historical Address," In *Journals of the Military Expedition of Major General John Sullivan against the Six Nations of Indians in 1779 with Records of Centennial Celebrations*, edited by Frederick Cook. Auburn, N.Y.: Knapp, Peck & Thomson, 1887.

Creighton, William. "Chillicothe Court-House, Barracks, Etc.," *American Pioneer* I, no. 6 (1842):202–8.

Cresswell, Nicholas. *The Journal of Nicholas Cresswell, 1774–1777*. New York: Dial Press, 1924.

Cuming, Fortescue. *Sketches of a Tour to the Western Country, through the States of Ohio and Kentucky . . .* [1807–1809]. Pittsburgh: Cramer, Spear & Kichbaum, 1810.

Curtis, Henry B. "Pioneer Days in Central Ohio," *Ohio Archaeological and Historical Quarterly*, I (1888) pp. 240–251.

[Curtis, Walter]. *Recollections of Pioneer Life by Honorable Walter Curtis, Written by his Nephew Reverend Charles Devol Curtis*, edited by Charles Devol Curtis and Laura Curtis Preston. Manuscript, n.d., Ohio Historical Society Collections.

Cutler, Jervis. *A Topographical Description of the State of Ohio, Indiana Territory, and Louisiana*. Boston: Charles Williams, 1812.

Daily News-Advertiser (Chillicothe), 25 and 26 September 1923.

Dawes, Ephraim C. "Major John Burnham and His Company." *Ohio Archaeological and Historical Quarterly* 3(1891):40–44.

DeBow, J. D. B., ed. *Statistical View of the United States: Compendium of the Seventh Census.* J. D. B. DeBow, 1854.

Defebaugh, James Elliott. *History of the Lumber Industry of America.* 4 vols. Chicago: American Lumberman, 1906–07.

De Schweinitz, Edmund. *The Life and Times of David Zeisberger.* Philadelphia: J. B. Lippincott & Co., 1870.

Dickens, Charles. *American Notes for General Circulation.* 2 vols. London: Chapman & Hall, 1842.

———. *The Life and Adventures of Martin Chuzzlewit.* London: Chapman & Hall, 1844.

Diderot, Denis. *Encyclopedie ou Dictionnaire Raisonne des Sciences, des Arts et des Metiers.* 17 vols. (Various publishers and dates).

———. *Recueil de Planches, sur les Sciences, les Arts Liberaux, et les Arts Mechaniques, Avec Leur Explication.* 12 vols. (Various publishers and dates).

Digest of Accounts of Manufacturing Establishments in United States, and of Their Manufacturers. U.S. Census Office. Washington, D.C.: Gales & Seaton, 1823.

Doddridge, Joseph. *Notes, on the Settlement and Indian Wars, of the Western Parts of Virginia and Pennsylvania from 1763 to 1783.* Wellsburgh, Va.: Printed at the office of the [Wellsburgh] Gazette, for the author, 1824.

Dornbusch, Charles H. In *Pennsylvania German Barns* edited by John K. Heyl. Vol. 21. Pennsylvania German Folklore Society Publications. Allentown: Pennsylvania German Folklore Society, 1958.

Douglass, Benjamin. *History of Wayne County, Ohio.* Indianapolis: Robert Douglass, 1878.

Downes, Randolph C. "Ohio's Squatter Governor: William Hogland of Hoglandstown." *Ohio Archaeological and Historical Quarterly* 43 (1934): 273–82.

[Draper, Lyman C.] "Bowman's Expedition Against Chillicothe, May-June, 1779" Ohio Archaeological and Historical Quarterly, 19 (1910). 446–59.

Edmonds, Walter D. *The Musket and the Cross.* Boston: Little, Brown & Com. 1968.

Elbert, E. Duane, and Keith A. Sculle. "Log Buildings in Illinois, Their Interpretation and Preservation." *Illinois Preservation Series*, no. 3. Illinois Department of Conservation, Division of Historic Sites, 1982.

Eshleman, Henry Frank. *Lancaster County Indians . . . 1500 to 1763.* Lancaster, Pa.: 1909.

Evans, Oliver. *The Young Mill-wright and Miller's Guide.* 8th ed. Philadelphia: Carey, Lea & Blanchard, 1834.

Ewbank, Thomas. *A Descriptive and Historical Account of Hydraulic and Other Machines for Raising Water.* New York: Greeley & McElrath, 1847.

Fearon, Henry Bradshaw. *Sketches of America.* 2d ed. London: Longman, Hurst, Rees, Orme, & Brown, 1818. (Reprint by Benjamin Blom, New York, 1969.)

Ferguson, C. W. "Bristlecone Pine: Science and Esthetics." *Science* 159, no. 3817 (1968):839–46.

______. "Concepts and Techniques of Dendrochronology." In Chap. 7, pp. 183–200, *Scientific Methods in Medieval Archaeology*, edited by Rainer Burger. U.C.L.A. Center for Medieval and Renaissance Studies, Contributions: no. 4. Berkeley: University of California Press, 1970.

Field, Walker. "A Reexamination into the Invention of the Balloon Frame." *Journal of the American Society of Architectural Historians* 2, no. 4 (October 1942):3–29.

Finley, James B. *Life Among the Indians; or, Personal Reminiscences and Historical Incidents Illustrative of Indian Life and Character*, edited by D. W. Clark. Cincinnati: Cranston & Curts, n.d.

Flint, James. *Letters from America*, Edinburgh: W. & C. Tait, 1822.

Fowke, Gerard. *Archaeological History of Ohio.* Columbus: The Ohio State Archaeological and Historical Society, 1902.

Fowler, Osgood S. *A Home for All; or, The Gravel Wall and Octagon Mode of Building.* New York: Fowlers & Wells, 1854.

Fritts, Harold C. "Dendroclimatology and Dendroecology." *Quaternary Research* I, no. 4 (1971):419–49.

Gailey, Alan. "The Housing of the Rural Poor in Nineteenth-Century Ulster." *Ulster Folk Life* 22 (1976):34–58.

Galloway, William Albert. *Old Chillicothe.* Xenia, Ohio: Buckeye Press, 1934.

Givry, Grillot de. *Witchcraft, Magic, and Alchemy.* Translated by J. Courtenay Locke. New York: Dover Publications, 1971. Reprint of 1931 ed.

Glassie, Henry. "The Barns of Appalachia." *Mountain Life and Work* 40 (Summer 1965):21–30.

Goodale, Katherine. *Behind the Scenes with Edwin Booth.* New York: Benjamin Blom, 1969. (Reprint of 1931 ed.)

Goodman, W. L. *The History of Woodworking Tools.* London: G. Bell and Sons, 1964.

Graham, Albert Adams. *History of Richland County, Ohio.* Mansfield: A. A. Graham and Co., 1880.

Greene, Evarts B., and Virginia D. Harrington. *American Population before the Federal Census of 1790.* Gloucester, Mass.: Peter Smith, 1966. (Reprint of Columbia University Press 1932 ed.)

Gunderson, Robert Gray. *The Log-Cabin Campaign.* Lexington: University of Kentucky Press, 1957.

Hall, Basil. *Forty Etchings, from Sketches Made with the Camera Lucida, in North America, in 1827 and 1828.* 4th ed. Edinburgh: Cadell & Co., 1830.

———. *Travels in North America, in the Years 1827 and 1828.* 3 vols. Edinburgh: Cadell & Co.; London: Simpkin & Marshall, 1829.

Halsted, Byron D., ed. *Barn Plans and Outbuildings.* New York: Orange Judd Co., 1881.

Hamilton, Kenneth. *John Ettwein and the Moravian Church during the Revolutionary Period.* Bethlehem, Pa.: Times Publishing Co., 1940.

Harris, Thaddeus Mason. *Journal of a Tour into the Territory Northwest of the Alleghany Mountains; Made in the Spring of the Year 1803.* Boston: Manning & Loring, 1805.

Harrison, R. H., and William Engel. *New Historical Atlas of Allen Co., Ohio.* Philadelphia: R. H. Harrison, 1880.

Hasluck, Paul M., ed. *Cassell's Carpentry and Joinery.* Philadelphia: David McKay, 1912.

Hatfield, Robert G. *The American House-Carpenter.* 4th ed. New York: John Wiley, 1850.

Heckewelder, John *Narrative of the Mission of the United Brethren Among the Delaware and Mohegan Indians.* Philadelphia: M'Carty & Davis, 1820.

Hewett, Cecil Alec. *The Development of Carpentry, 1200–1700.* Newton Abbot, Devon England: David & Charles, 1969.

Hildreth, Samuel P. "History of an Early Voyage on the Ohio and Mississippi Rivers." *American Pioneer* 1, no. 3 (1842):89–105.

———. "The Old Court House and Jail of Washington County, Ohio." *American Pioneer* 1, no. 5 (1842):163–64.

Hill, George William. *History of Ashland County, Ohio.* [Cleveland]: William Brothers, 1880.

Hitchcock, Henry-Russell. *American Architectural Books.* 2d ed. Minneapolis: University of Minnesota Press, 1962.

Hopkins, Gerard T. "Journal," MS., in the collections of the Historical Society of Pennsylvania.

Howe, Henry. *Historical Collections of Ohio.* Cincinnati: Derby, Bradley & Co., 1847.

———. *Historical Collections of Ohio*, 3 vols. Columbus: Henry Howe & Son, 1891.

Howells, William Cooper. *Recollections of Life in Ohio, from 1813 to 1848.* Cincinnati: Robert Clarke Co., 1895.

"How to Build a Log-House," Orange Judd, ed. *American Agriculturist* 17, no. 7 (July 1858):200.

Hulbert, Archer Butler, and William N. Schwarze, eds. "The Moravian Records, Volume Two, The Diaries of Zeisberger Relating to the First Missions in the Ohio Basin." *Ohio Archaeological and Historical Quarterly* 21 (1912):1–125.

Hulme, Thomas, "The Journal of Thomas Hulme." In William Cobbett, *A Year's Residence, in the United States of America.* 3d ed. (London, 1828). Pt. 3.

Hutslar, Donald A. "Hay Presses Lead to Modern Equipment." *Echoes* (Ohio Historical Society), 15, no. 7 (1976):3–4.

______. *The Log Architecture of Ohio.* Columbus: Ohio Historical Society, 1977. (Reprint of monograph in *Ohio History* 80, nos. 3–4 (1971): 171–271.)

______. *Log Cabin Restoration: Guidelines for the Historical Society.* American Association of State and Local History. Technical Leaflet no. 74 (May 1974).

______. "The Ohio Farmstead: Farm Buildings as Cultural Artifacts." *Ohio History* 90, no. 3 (1981):221–37.

______. "Ohio Waterpowered Sawmills." *Ohio History* 84, nos. 1–2 (1975): 4–56.

Isham, Norman M., and Albert F. Brown. *Early Connecticut Houses.* New York: Dover Publications, [1965]. (Reprint of 1900 ed.)

Johnston, Charles. *A Narrative of the Incidents Attending the Capture, Detention, and Ransom of Charles Johnston of Virginia.* New York: J. & J. Harper, 1827. (Reprint by Burrows Brothers Co., Cleveland, 1905.)

Johnston, Frances. *The Early Architecture of North Carolina.* (A pictorial survey with an architectural history by Thomas Waterman.) Chapel Hill: University of North Carolina Press, 1941.

Johnston, John. account book and miscellaneous letters and papers pertaining to the Fort Wayne Indian Agency, 1802–1811. Ohio Historical Society microfilm collection.

Johnston, William. *Map of the Surveys in the Wyandot Cession at U. Sandusky, March 9, 1844.* (Ohio, Sheet 7.) Photocopy, Ohio Historical Society collections.

Jones, David. *A Journal of Two Visits Made to some Nations of Indians on the West Side of the River Ohio, in the Years 1772 and 1773.* New York: Reprinted for J. Sabin, 1865.

Jordan, Terry G. *Texas Log Buildings.* Austin: University of Texas Press, 1978.

[Kalm, Peter]. *Peter Kalm's Travels in North America.* Edited by Adolph B. Benson. English version of 1770. 2 vols. New York: Dover Publications, 1966. (Reprint of 1937 ed.)

Kauffman, Henry J. *American Axes.* Brattleboro, Vt.: Stephen Greene Press, 1972.

Kaups, Matti. "A Finnish Savusauna in Minnesota." *Minnesota History* 45, no. 1 (1976):11–20.

______. "Log Architecture in America: European Antecedents in a Finnish Context." *Journal of Cultural Geography* 2, no. 1 (1981):131–53.

Kelly, J. Frederick. *Early Domestic Architecture of Connecticut.* New York: Dover Publications, 1963. (Reprint of Yale University Press edition, 1924.)

______. "A Seventeenth-Century Connecticut Log House." *Old-Time New*

England, 31, no. 2 (1940):28–40. (Bulletin of the Society for the Preservation of New England Antiquities.)

Keyser, Alan G., and William P. Stein. "The Pennsylvania German Tri-Level Ground Barn." *Der Reggeboge* (Quarterly of the Pennsylvania German Society) vol. 9 (1975):1–25.

Kniffen, Fred, and Henry Glassie. "Building in Wood in the Eastern United States." *Geographical Review* 56 (1966):40–66.

Knittle, Rhea Mansfield. *Early Ohio Taverns*. Ohio Frontier Series, Booklet no. 1. Ashland, Ohio: Privately Printed, 1937.

Kreps, Elmer Harry. *Camp and Trail Methods*. Columbus: A. R. Harding, 1910. (Reprint, 1950.)

Lang, William. *History of Seneca County*. Springfield, Ohio: Transcript Printing Co., 1880.

Latham, Ronald E., trans. *The Travels of Marco Polo*. Harmondsworth, Middlesex, England: Penguin Books, 1958.

Liberty Hall (Cincinnati), 13 November 1810.

Lorant, Stefan, ed. *The New World*. New York: Duell, Sloan & Pearce, [1946].

Lossing, Benson J. *The Pictorial Field-Book of the War of 1812*. Glendale, N.Y.: Benchmark Publishing Company, 1970. (Reprint of 1869 ed.)

Ludlum, David M., ed. *Early American Tornadoes, 1586–1870*. Boston: American Meteorological Society, 1970.

[McClure, David]. *Diary of David McClure, Doctor of Divinity, 1748–1820*. Edited by Franklin B. Dexter. New York: Knickerbocker Press, 1899.

McKearin, George, and Helen McKearin. *American Glass*. New York: Crown Publishers, [1941].

Mahan, Dennis Hart. *A Complete Treatise on Field Fortification, with the General Outlines of the Principles Regulating the Arrangement, the Attack, and the Defence of Permanent Works*. New York: Greenwood Press, 1968. (Reprint of 1836 ed.)

"Making Split and Shaved Shingles." *American Agriculturist*, 38, p. 223. New York: Orange Judd Co., 1879.

Marshall, Josiah T. *The Farmers and Emigrants Complete Guide*. Cincinnati: Applegate & Co., 1854.

Martin, George A., ed. *Fences, Gates and Bridges*. New York: Orange Judd Co., 1892.

Mason, Reuben S. "The Old Log School House." In *Reminiscences of a Grain Dealer*, by Daniel McAlister. Unpublished MS. Ohioana Library collections.

Masury, John W. *A Popular Treatise on the Art of House-Painting*. New York: D. Appleton & Co., 1868.

Meehan, James. "Demonstrating the Use of Log House Building Tools at the New Windsor Cantonment." *Association for Preservation Technology Bulletin* 12, no. 4 (1980):38–44.

Meek, Basil. "Tarhe—The Crane." *Ohio Archaeological and Historical Quarterly* 20 (1911):64–73.

Mencken, Henry Louis. "A Neglected Anniversary" (pp. 4–10), "Melancholy Reflections" (pp. 10–15), and "Hymn to the Truth" (pp. 15–19), all in *The Bathtub Hoax and Other Blasts and Bravos from the Chicago Tribune.* Edited by Robert McHugh. New York: Alfred A. Knopf, 1958.

Mercer, Henry C. *Ancient Carpenters' Tools.* 4th ed. Doylestown, Pa.: Bucks County Historical Society, 1960.

______. "The Dating of Old Houses." Address given to the Bucks County Historical Society, 13 October 1923, *A Collection of Papers.* Vol. 5. (Reprinted by Bucks County Historical Society, n.d.)

______. "The Origin of Log Houses in the United States." Bucks County Historical Society, *A Collection of Papers.* Vol. 5 (Reprinted by Bucks County Historical Society, 1967.)

Meulette, Waldeurard. "Settlement of Gallipolis." *American Pioneer,* 2 (1843): 182–187. (Meulette incorrectly spelled "Mentelle" on p. 182.)

Michaux, Andre. "Travels into Kentucky, 1793–96." In Thwaites, *Early Western Travels.* Vol. 3.

Michaux, Francois. *Travels to the west of the Alleghany mountains, in the states of Ohio, Kentucky, and Tennessee, and back to Charleston, by the upper Carolinas.* London: D. N. Shury for B. Crosby and Co., 1805.

Momatiuk, Yva, and John Eastcott. "Poland's Mountain People." *National Geographic* 159, no. 1 (1981):104–129.

Montell, William L., and Michael L. Morse. *Kentucky Folk Architecture.* Lexington: The University Press of Kentucky, 1976.

Moxon, Joseph. *Mechanick Exercises; or, The Doctrine of Handy-Works.* 3d ed. London: Daniel Midwinter and Thomas Leigh, 1703. (Reprint by Praeger Publishers, New York, 1970.)

[Muskingum County]. *Biographical and Historical Memoirs of Muskingum County, Ohio.* Chicago: Goodspeed Publishing Co., 1892.

National Lumber Manufacturers Association. *Comparative Fire Test of Timber and Steel Beams.* Technical Report no. 3. Washington, D.C., 1961.

Newton, Janet Foster. "Log Cabin or Frame." *Antiques* 46 (November 1944): 270–73.

Nicholson, Peter. *The Carpenter's New Guide.* 16th ed. Edited by N. K. Davis. Philadelphia: Lippincott, Grambo & Co., 1854.

______. *Practical Carpentry, Joinery, and Cabinet-Making.* London: Thomas Kelly, 1837.

Noble, Allen G. *Studies of the American Settlement Landscape.* 4th ed. Akron: The University of Akron, 1982.

Nowlin, William. *The Bark Covered House.* Detroit: Printed for the author, 1876.

Ohio Biological Survey. *Natural Vegetation of Ohio* [Map]. Columbus: Ohio State University, 1966.

Ohio Company. *The Records of the Original Proceedings of the Ohio Company.* 2 vols. [1786–1795]. Edited by Archer Butler Hulbert. Marietta: Marietta Historical Commission, 1917.

Ohio Co-operative Topographic Survey, "Final Report . . . by C. E. Sherman." Vol. 3. *Original Ohio Land Subdivisions.* Mansfield, Ohio: The Ohio State Reformatory Press, 1925.

Ohio Cultivator. Vols. 1 through 11, 1845–1856. (Columbus).

Ohio Eagle (Lancaster). Vol. 5, no. 18, (Saturday, 22 October 1814).

Oppel, Mary Cronan. "A Guide to Rehabilitating Log Houses." *The Old-House Journal* 8, no. 8 (1980): 85, 100–3.

Orians, G. Harrison. "My Life in a Log-House." *Northwest Ohio Quarterly* 27 (1955): 145–59.

Paddock, Wendell, ed. *Estate Papers of John Chapman.* Unpublished MS., 1935. Ohio Historical Society collections.

Pain, William. *The Carpenter's Pocket Directory.* Philadelphia: J. H. Dobelbower and J. Thackara, 1797.

Patrick, James. *Architecture in Tennessee, 1768–1897.* Knoxville: University of Tennessee, 1981.

Peirce, Josephine M. *Fire on the Hearth.* Springfield, Mass.: The Pond-Ekberg Co., 1951.

Perrin, W. H., J. H. Battle, and W. A. Goodspeed. *History of Crawford County and Ohio.* Chicago: Baskin & Battey, 1881.

[Peter, Sarah Anne]. *Private Memoir of Thomas Worthington, Esq. . . . by his Daughter.* Cincinnati: Robert Clarke & Co., 1882.

Peterson, Charles E., ed. *Building Early America.* Proceedings of the Symposium Held at Philadelphia to Celebrate the two hundred fiftieth Birthday of the Carpenters' Company of the City & County of Philadelphia. Radnor, Pa.: Chilton Book Co., 1976.

______. *The Carpenters' Company of the City and County of Philadelphia 1786 Rule Book.* Princeton, N.J.: Pyne Press, 1971.

______. "The Houses of French St. Louis." In *The French in the Mississippi Valley*, edited by John F. McDermott. Urbana, Ill.: University of Illinois Press, 1965. Pp. 17–40.

______. "Pioneer Prefabs in Honolulu." *Hawaiian Journal of History* 5 (1971): 24–38.

Plumb, Charles Sumner. "Seth Adams, A Pioneer Ohio Shepherd." *Ohio Archaeological and Historical Quarterly* 43 (1934): 1–34.

[Polo, Marco]. *The Travels of Marco Polo.* Translated by Ronald Latham. Middlesex, England: Penguin Books, 1958.

Price, Robert. *Johnny Appleseed, Man and Myth.* Bloomington: University of Indiana, 1954. (Reprint by Peter Smith, 1967.)

Putnam, J. Pickering. *The Open Fire-Place.* Boston: J. R. Osgood & Co., 1881.

Ratcliffe, Donald J., ed. "The Autobiography of Benjamin Tappan." *Ohio History*, 85 (1976): 109–157.

Ravenna (Ohio) *Courier*. 21 October 1826. Quoted in Brown and Morris, *History of Portage County*. Pp. 317–18.

Rawson, Marion Nicholl. *The Old House Picture Book*. New York: E. P. Dutton & Co., 1941.

Raynor, John A. *The First Century of Piqua, Ohio*. Piqua: Magee Bros. Co., 1916 and 1967.

Rees, Abraham. *The Cyclopaedia; or, Universal Dictionary of Arts, Sciences, and Literature*. 1st American ed. 41 vols., 6 vols. plates. Philadelphia: Samuel F. Bradford, and Murray, Fairman and Co., n.d. (ca. 1818). (Fearon, *Sketches of America* [1818], mentions seeing an American edition of Rees while in Cincinnati.)

Reid, David Boswell. *Ventilation in American Dwellings*. New York: Wiley & Halsted, 1858.

Richardson, A. E., and H. Donaldson Eberlein. *The Smaller English House of the Later Renaissance, 1660–1830*. New York: William Helburn,; London: B. T. Batsford, 1925.

Richardson, A. J. H. "A Comparative Historical Study of Timber Building in Canada." *APT Bulletin* 5, no. 3, (1973): 77–102.

———. "Voyageur Construction Methods." *APT Bulletin* 5, no. 4, (1973): 85–86.

Ritchie, T. "Plankwall Framing, a Modern Wall Construction with an Ancient History," *Society of Architectural Historians Journal* 30 (March 1971): 66–70.

Roberts, Kenneth D., ed. *Tools for the Trades and Crafts*. (Pattern Book of R. Timmons & Sons, Birmingham, eighteenth and nineteenth centuries.) Fitzwilliam, N.H.: Ken Roberts Publishing Co., 1976.

Roberts, Warren E. "The Whitaker-Waggoner Log House from Morgan County, Indiana." *American Folklore*. Edited by Don Yoder. Austin: University of Texas Press, 1976.

Robinson, George F. *History of Greene County, Ohio*. Chicago: S. J. Clarke Publishing Co., 1902.

[Robinson, Solon]. *Solon Robinson, Pioneer and Agriculturist*. 2 vols. Edited by Herbert A. Kellar. Indianapolis: Indiana Historical Bureau, 1936.

Roos, Frank J., Jr. *Writings on Early American Architecture*. Columbus: Ohio State University Press, 1943.

Roosevelt, Theodore. *The Winning of the West*. Vol. 3. *The Works of Theodore Roosevelt in Fourteen Volumes*. New York: P. F. Collier & Son, 1896.

Roseboom, Eugene H., and Francis P. Weisenburger. *A History of Ohio*. Columbus: Ohio Historical Society, 1967.

Rumford, Benjamin Thompson, Count. *Essays, Political, Economical, and Philosophical*. 4th ed. London: Cadell & Davies, 1798–1802. 3 vols.

Russell and Erwin Hardware Company. *Catalog*. Vol. 1, pt. 3, 1865. Collinsville, Conn. (Reprint by Old Time Bottle Publishing Company, Salem, Oregon, as *Wishbook 1865*, edited by Lynn Blumenstein.)

St. George, R. A. *Protecting Log Cabins, Rustic Work, and Unseasoned Wood from Injurious Insects in Eastern United States.* Rev. ed. United States Department of Agriculture Farmers' Bulletin no. 2104. Washington, D.C.: GPO, 1962.

Salaman, Raphael Arthur. *Dictionary of Tools.* New York: Charles Scribner's Sons, 1973.

Sargeant, Winthrop. "An Account of Campus Martius, at the City of Marietta, Territory of the United States, North-West of the River Ohio." *Columbian Magazine,* November 1788, p. 645.

Schaff, Morris. *Etna and Kirkersville.* Cambridge, Mass.: Riverside Press, 1905.

Schepers, Josef. *Westfalen-Lippe; Haus und Hof Deutscher Bauern.* 2 vols. Münster, Westfalen: Aschendorff, 1960.

[Schoolcraft, Henry Howe]. *The Indian Tribes of the United States.* 2 vols. Edited by Francis S. Drake. Philadelphia: J. B. Lippincott & Co., 1884.

[Schillinger, William]. "Journal of Ensign William Schillinger, a soldier of the War of 1812," *Ohio Archaeological and Historical Quarterly* 41 (1932): 52–85.

Schreiber, William I. *The Pennsylvania Dutch House and Barn of Wayne County, Ohio.* Unpublished MS., n.d.

Scott, Daniel. *A History of the Early Settlement of Highland County, Ohio.* Hillsborough, Ohio: Gazette Office, 1890.

Sculle, Keith A., and E. Duane Elbert. "Log Buildings in Illinois, Their Interpretation and Preservation." *Illinois Preservation Series,* no. 3. Illinois Department of Conservation, Division of Historic Sites, 1982.

Sherwood, Angus (as told to Norman Wells). "Building in the North," *APT Bulletin* 6, no. 3, (1974): 1–5.

Shurtleff, Harold R. *The Log Cabin Myth.* Edited by Samuel E. Morison. Cambridge: Harvard University Press, 1939.

Skansen, A Short Guide for Visitors. Stockholm, 1974.

Sloane, Eric. *A Museum of Early American Tools.* New York: Wilbur Funk, 1964.

Smith, James. *An Account of the Remarkable Occurrences in the Life and Travels of Colonel James Smith, During his Captivity with the Indians in the Years 1755, '56, '57, '58, and '59.* Philadelphia: Grigg & Elliott, 1834.

Smith, Thomas. "17th Century Swedish Log Cabins Survive." *American Folklife* 3, no. 4 (1975): 1–3.

Sonn, Albert H. *Early American Wrought Iron.* 3 vols. New York: Charles Scribner's Sons, 1928.

Spencer, Oliver. *Indian Captivity.* New York: Carolton & Lanahan, 1834.

Stanton, William Henry. *A Book Called Our Ancestors—The Stantons.* Philadelphia: William Henry Stanton, 1922.

Stotz, Charles Morse. *The Early Architecture of Western Pennsylvania.* New York: Helburn, 1936.

[Symmes, John Cleves]. *The Correspondence of John Cleves Symmes*. Edited by Beverley W. Bond, Jr. New York: Published for the Historical and Philosophical Society of Ohio by the Macmillan Company, 1926.

[Tappan, Benjamin]. "Autobiography of Benjamin Tappan." In *Ohio History*, edited by Donald J. Ratcliffe. Vol. 85 (1976). Pp. 109–157.

"Thatching Roofs with Straw," *The American Agriculturist*, 38 (1879): 57. New York: Orange Judd Co., 1879.

Thomas, James C. "The Log Houses of Kentucky." *The Magazine Antiques* 105 (1974): 791–98.

Thomas, Nathan M. *Nathan M. Thomas: An Account of His Life Written by Himself*. Cassopolis, Mich.: Stanton B. Thomas, 1925.

Thomas, R. D. *America, or Miscellaneous Notes on the United States Useful for Emigrants*. 1852. MS., National Library of Wales. (Copy, Ohio Historical Society Library.)

[Thomson, Charles]. *An Enquiry into the Causes of the Alienation of the Delaware and Shawanese Indians from the British Interest*. London: Printed for J. Wilkie, 1759.

Thomson, Peter G. *A Bibliography of the State of Ohio*. Cincinnati: Published by the Author, 1880.

Thurston, Benjamin. Letter to Daniel Plumer, 15 May 1819. Ohio Historical Society Library.

Thwaites, Reuben Gold, ed. *Early Western Travels, 1748–1846*. 32 vols. Cleveland: Arthur H. Clark Co., 1904–1907.

———. *Jesuit Relations and Allied Documents . . . 1610–1791*. 73 vols. Cleveland: Burrows Brothers Co., 1896–1901.

Thwing, Leroy Livingstone. *Flickering Flames*. Rutland, Vt.: C. E. Tuttle Co., 1958.

Timmons and Sons "Pattern Book". See Roberts, *Tools for the Trades and Crafts*.

Tomlinson, Charles, ed. *Cyclopaedia of Useful Arts and Manufactures*. 2 vols. London: George Virtue & Co., 1854.

Trent, William. *Journal of Captain William Trent*. Edited by Alfred T. Goodman. Cincinnati: Robert Clarke & Co., 1871.

United States Department of Agriculture. *The Farm-Housing Survey*. Miscellaneous Publication no. 323. Washington, D.C., March 1939.

———. *The Old House Borer*. Leaflet no. 501.

———. *Powder-Post Beetles in Buildings*. Leaflet no. 358.

———. *Preserving Wood*. Forest Service Technical Bulletin No. 1334.

———. *Subterranean Termites*. Home and Garden Bulletin no. 64.

United States Forest Service. *Wood Decay in Houses: How to Prevent and Control It*. Home and Garden Bulletin no. 73. Washington, D.C., 1960.

United States Department of the Interior, National Park Service, Office of Archaeology and Historic Preservation. "Preservation Briefs," bibliographies, various publications dealing with restoration and maintenance of historic properties. (Available from Government Printing Office, Washington, D.C.)

Upton, Dell. "Board Roofing in Tidewater Virginia." *APT Bulletin* 8, no. 4, (1976): 22–43.

Upton, Harriet Taylor. *History of the Western Reserve.* Chicago: Lewis Publishing Co., 1910.

Vaux, Calvert. *Villas and Cottages.* New York: Harper & Brothers, 1857.

Verrall, Arthur F. *Preserving Wood by Brush, Dip, and Short-Soak Methods.* United States Forest Service Technical Bulletin no. 1334. Washington, D.C., 1965.

Vitruvius (Marcus Vitruvius Pollio). *The Ten Books on Architecture.* Translated by Morris Hicky Morgan. 1914 ed. New York: Dover Publications, 1960.

Volney, Constantin Francois Chasseboeuf, Comte de. *View of the Climate and Soil of the United States of America: To Which are Annexed Some Accounts of Florida, the French Colony on the Scioto, Certain Canadian Colonies, and the Savages or Natives.* London: Printed for J. Johnson, 1804.

Walker, Charles M. *History of Athens County, Ohio.* Cincinnati: Robert Clarke & Co., 1869.

Waring, George E. *The Sanitary Drainage of Houses and Towns.* Boston: Houghton, Mifflin & Co., 1887.

Weslager, Clinton Alfred. *The Log Cabin in America.* New Brunswick, N.J.: Rutgers University Press, 1969.

Western Courier and Piqua Enquirer (Piqua). 18 November 1837.

The Western Miscellany. (Dayton). Vol. I, (July 1848): 342.

Whiffen, Marcus. *American Architecture Since 1780.* Cambridge. Massachusetts Institute of Technology, 1977.

———. *The Eighteenth-Century Houses of Williamsburg.* Williamsburg: Colonial Williamsburg, 1970.

Wilhelm, Hubert G. H. *The Origin and Distribution of Settlement Groups: Ohio: 1850.* Manuscript final report for a Joint Program in Folk Art and Culture, the Ohio Arts Council and the Ohio Program for the Humanities. Department of Geography, Ohio University, Athens, 1982.

Williams, Eugene Ellis. "The Copus Battle Centennial." *Ohio Archaeological and Historical Publications* 21 (1912): 379–96.

Williams, John S., ed. "First House of Worship in Ohio." *American Pioneer* 1, no. 2, (February 1842): 41–42.

———. Our Cabin; or, Life in the Woods." *American Pioneer* 2, no. 10, (October 1843): 435–59.

Williams, Samuel. *Diary.* Unpublished MS. Ohio Historical Society collections.

Willich, Anthony Florian Madinger. *The Domestic Encyclopedia.* 3 vols. Philadelphia: Abraham Small, 1821. 2d American ed. edited by Thomas Cooper.

Willis, Stanley. "Log Houses in Southwest Virginia." *Virginia Cavalcade* (Spring 1972): 36–47.

Wilson, Eugene M. *Alabama Folk Houses.* Montgomery: Alabama Historical Commission, 1975.

Woodcock, Eldred Nathaniel. *Fifty Years a Hunter and Trapper.* Edited by A. R. Harding. Columbus: A. R. Harding, 1913.

Woods, John. "Two Years' Residence in the Settlement on the English Prairie in the Illinois Country," in *Western Travels,* Edited by Reuben Gold Thwaites. (Cleveland, 1904), 10. (Reprint of 1822 London ed.)

Yoder, Paton. *Taverns and Travelers: Inns of the Early Midwest.* Bloomington: Indiana University Press, [1969].

INDEX OF ILLUSTRATIONS

COUNTY AND STATE

ARCHITECTURE, MISCELLANEOUS

HARRISON PRESIDENTIAL CAMPAIGN

ILLUSTRATIONS, MISCELLANEOUS

GENERAL INDEX